TCP/IP Embedded Internet Applications

Edward Insam PhD, BSc

Newnes

AMSTERDAM BOSTON HEIDELBERG LONDON NEW YORK OXFORD
PARIS SAN DIEGO SAN FRANCISCO SINGAPORE SYDNEY TOKYO

Newnes
An imprint of Elsevier
Linacre House, Jordan Hill, Oxford OX2 8DP
200 Wheeler Road, Burlington MA 01803

First published 2003

British Library Cataloguing in Publication Data
A catalogue record for this book is available from the British Library

Library of Congress Cataloguing in Publication Data
A catalogue record for this book is available from the Library of Congress

ISBN 0 7506 57359

For information on all Newnes publications
visit our website at www.newnespress.com

Typeset by Newgen Imaging Systems (P) Ltd, Chennai, India
Printed and bound in Great Britain by Biddles Ltd, *www.biddles.co.uk*

Contents

Introduction

Embedded systems are now found in almost anything from toasters to hand-held notebooks to automobiles. The complexity of some of these devices can be amazing and their scope for performing intricate tasks is apparently unlimited. This does not necessarily mean that the products they inhabit are being used in a better way. For many domestic and commercial products, these potentials have only been exploited as unnecessary enhancements; an electronic sewing machine that can perform over 3000 different stitches may sound impressive, but how many of these will ever be used? A 'better gimmicks' design strategy does not necessarily result in a better product. At the same time, it is very difficult to predict the positive value these new ideas may bring to day-to-day life. Many 'must-have' products such as electronic curtains that shut automatically have been around for years, but not that many people are rushing to buy them. On the other hand, palmtops, MP3 players and cell-phones are as 'essential' nowadays as fridges and freezers.

Big changes will be expected when devices start talking to each other, and new ranges of interactive possibilities are unveiled. For years, people have talked about how every device in the world will be connected to the Internet; but many of the scenarios presented are rather far-fetched. Refrigerators that order eggs and milk may be something to talk about at conferences or show at an exhibition, but are more like an expression of the ideas of creatives and engineers rather than a reflection of real-world needs. Not that we should criticize these propositions. On the contrary, one of their functions is to catch our imagination and trigger both users and designers into developing useful technology for the future.

This book is all about enabling networking facilities into embedded systems. The timing is about right, connecting a device to the Internet at present may add unwarranted extra cost to a product; too much perhaps in relation to the perceived benefit to the customer. These costs are bound to tumble in the next few years when networking components and accessibility costs drop to a few pennies; but to justify its presence now, network connectivity has to add real cost effective value and provide guaranteed returns.

For many current applications, this value may derive from remote management. Remote management is the general term describing the controlling of resources and equipment from a remote location using existing network technology such as Ethernet or telephone lines. This can offer valuable benefits, even from today's point of view. Appliances can set off an alarm when they approach failure or operational situations such as running out of consumables. Technical equipment or plant can be remotely controlled by individuals, who may be in places far away connected to a network. Technicians can be remotely warned and make service calls only to those devices that require it. The potential savings in time and costs are obvious enough that they can be understood even in today's terms. One interesting side effect resulting from this philosophy is that the end customer (or local staff) may be left out of the loop. At present, it is usually the customer who makes the service call, and who tends to get involved, in one way or the other, in the helping or the hindering of the actual service operation. Whether this is good or bad, it is something that remains to be seen.

Fully automated remote management of specific target areas may be a nearer goal for embedded networking. Vending machines running out of stock, jukeboxes needing new tunes or remote environmental control are obvious areas. PC control of test and measurement equipment is another. Information feedback or gathering, are also new areas worth looking at. Remote devices can report on what is happening around them, collect statistics for inventory, do market research or gather customer feedback. Additionally, remotes may be selectively programmed to respond differentially based on information gathered locally and/or supplied by head office. For example, vending machines promoting one type of product in preference to others as a result of a recent local event or TV ad. The time-saving potentials of remote management and point of sale customer or staff presence must not be underestimated either. Interactivity with the customer (either directly or via message cell phones), and feedback to head office in a semi-intelligent way can open up a whole world of new possibilities.

This book introduces the technologies involved in networking for embedded systems with a particular emphasis in the use of Internet Protocol (IP) based communications. This book is not a detailed compendium on TCP/IP nor it is a discourse on how specific products or devices work. The reader should refer to the various publications and manufacturer web sites that cover these technologies for more details. The book does not cover alternative technologies such as Bluetooth or IrDA, as they are not strictly networking components, but more like point-to-point solutions, which could form part of a larger network.

Audience

This book is intended for readers with a basic knowledge of electronics, logic hardware and a certain understanding of microprocessor technology. Some basic knowledge of software including assembler and 'C' is useful but not essential. Readers should also be familiar with basic telecommunications concepts and practices.

The following constitutes the book's intended audience:

- Embedded system and circuit designers, both hardware and software, especially those wanting to add TCP/IP based networking capabilities into their products.

- Technical college and university level students in Telecommunications, Computer Science and Electronics.

- Project managers, system and circuit designers of embedded systems.

- Network software designers wanting to get a grasp of the underlying network hardware concepts.

The chapters

This book follows a chapter sequence roughly aligned with the protocol layer models commonly in used in networking and telecommunications. All software examples presented are in the form of pseudo code listings using plain language explanations. Describing a brand new topic can be more effective if presented as a sequence of events using plain language simple comments, rather than source code. Not everybody may be familiar with the intricacies of specific computer languages, and not everybody can sight read computer listings.

Where necessary, references are made to web pages, books, articles and Request for Comments (RFCs) documents. RFCs are an invaluable source of detailed information about network protocols, and the reader should download (and even better, print) any relevant documents applicable to their requirement. RFCs are written in a surprisingly clear language, and many are available in easy-to-read PDF printable formats.

The chapters are as follows:

Chapter 1 'Networking Embedded Systems' introduces the subject by showing how networking facilities could be added to microcomputer embedded systems, including some practical examples on how they are being used today. The chapter also covers issues that should be considered before embarking into the development of networking at the embedded level.

Chapter 2 'Software Design for Embedded Communications' discusses some of the specialist software techniques required for programming communications and networked embedded systems. Multitasking, scheduling, messaging, etc. are discussed, There is also some mention on how physical interfacing to the embedded system may affect parameters such as throughput and performance, including the advantages or disadvantages of using special architectures such as embedded cores and field programmable logic arrays.

Chapter 3 'Protocols and Communications Models' discusses the current protocols relevant to embedded systems, and how they relate to actual implementations. Theoretical descriptions have been kept short and with an emphasis on practical discussion and real-life applications.

Chapter 4 'Network Physical Level Technologies' describes the current techniques and hardware used in networking. This chapter is mainly a reference to low-level techniques and practices. Line driving, encoding methods, etc. The chapter will give the reader a basis for understanding how systems connect together at the lowest hardware level. It also gives underpinning information to those wanting to develop custom hardware physical layer methods. Where relevant, the relationship between the technology and the traditional system layer models is given. The chapter is divided into the two main technology areas: wired and wireless.

Chapter 5 'Local Area Network Access Technologies' discusses the current networking technologies such as Ethernet and IEEE 802. The chapter includes descriptions of current hardware devices and controllers, how they work, and how they can be used.

Chapter 6 'Data Link Management' describes the methods used by each technology to manage the link, and for establishing, maintaining and managing connections, all resulting in the transparent transfer of IP packets.

Chapter 7 'Network Layer – Building on IP' describes the IP and the layers immediately around and above, including UDP and TCP. The chapter has specific emphasis on limited resource microprocessor implementations, and discusses practical implementation techniques for reducing code size against the compromises that have to be accepted. In other words, what is possible without undermining compatibility.

Chapter 8 'Application Layer Protocols' discusses the layers above IP, and how they can be used in real applications such as e-mail connections and web servers. It includes implementation methods for TELNET, SMTP, POP3, HTTP, FTP, TFTP, BOOTP, DHCP, RTP, RTCP, NTP, SNTP and SCTP.

Chapter 9 'A Simple Implementation' describes coding examples for implementing a real-life example of a software Ethernet driver for TCP/IP. This is a guide using code examples for collating the information presented in previous chapters into a practical product.

The Author is a consultant on advanced Telecommunications systems and is available to answer serious queries on the contents on this book and on related projects. The email address is edinsam@eix.co.uk

CHAPTER 1

Networking Embedded Systems

First questions first, what is an embedded system? A common definition is a controlling mechanism, such as a microprocessor or other complex logic system, running a program inside another device or appliance. The user sees the appliance and not the controller that runs it, with the logic doing its job transparently and without making any fuzz. Few people really care about what make or model of microprocessor is running inside their washing machine, it works, and that is it. Embedded controllers are usually self contained, solidly built, with software that rarely crashes, and do not rely on software updates (compare that to your standard desktop PC!)

Nearly all embedded systems operate stand-alone. The microcontroller in a dishwasher is only connected to the push buttons, solenoids and motors it controls. Not all embedded system operate this way however. Some may communicate with others close by, or in some instances, to a remote device, which could be a large computer. The messages sent across could be used for data processing, data collection or for system maintenance.

Why Network Embedded Systems?

Networking is the common term given to the methods and techniques used for providing reliable communications between geographically remote devices. Networking requires the enforcement of common standards and the use of compatible hardware and software environments. This guarantees that communications can take place between machines that may be completely different in architecture and operating systems. It is understandable that a lot of design effort may need to be put in place to ensure that systems are compatible and can talk to each other without problems.

Figure 1-1 shows two applications where networked embedded systems may be used. Figure 1-1(a) shows a point of sale vending machine with an internal modem linked

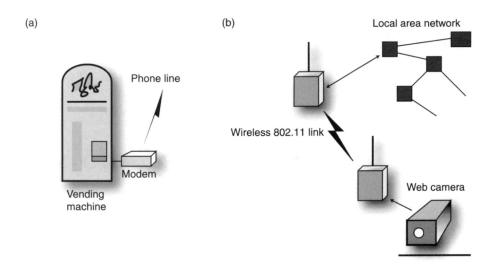

Figure 1-1: Examples of networked embedded systems

to head office via a phone line. The processor within the vending machine may be a standard microcontroller with its normal peripherals: RAM, ROM and I/O ports used for driving the various lamps, solenoids and push-button switches. The auto-dial modem is used to connect to the company's host over the normal telephone network. The central host computer may accept calls or interrogate the remote, perhaps by dialing its number at regular hourly or daily intervals. The vending machine could also originate calls by dialing head office directly; these calls could be local or long distance depending on location. There have to be enough modems working in parallel at head office to ensure incoming calls are not lost, and avoid engaged tones. With several thousand remotes in a large geographical area, this could result in major investment in plant and equipment, not including manpower, maintenance, and the cost of all the long-distance phone calls.

Fortunately, the company could make use of the Internet. Using the Internet, the remotes only need to make local rate telephone calls to an Internet Service Provider (ISP), very much in the same way a domestic user dials their local ISP to use the Internet. Head office only needs to have a direct dedicated connection to the Internet. No multiple phone lines, no modems, no long distance telephone calls. Savings are not only made in telephone system infrastructure, but also in maintenance and labour required to support in-house equipment and plant. The ISP will provide all these facilities at competitive costs.

Figure 1-1(b) shows another application where a CCTV camera uses the existing local area computer network within a building to send security images from a parking lot. Images are digitized within the camera and sent in 'network friendly' encoded form to central office, which decompresses the images, and displays them on a screen. The embedded processor within the camera needs to be fast enough to capture, process and encode the images more or less in real time. This requires very fast CPU architectures similar to those found inside PCs. Alternatively, the camera could make use of dedicated integrated circuits or custom gate arrays. The diagram shows the camera using a wireless network. These use radio waves instead of cabling, and could be of benefit in areas where it is difficult to wire cables all the way to the camera.

Both these examples are typical of embedded systems networking. By sharing the use of an existing networking infrastructure (Internet or local area network) big savings can be made.

Adding networking to an embedded system is not a trivial task. From the relatively safe confines of an appliance, networking involves sending data over a hostile medium (the world outside), and communicating with a hostile remote system, which may not really care what status our device is in, and which may be operating under different operating systems, clocks or time frames. It soon becomes obvious to the designer that serious amount of resources will have to be allocated for the proper design and implementation of good, reliable networking. This includes not just the software, but also the hardware required for providing electrical isolation, decoupling and mechanical stability. By definition, embedded systems are resource limited systems (resources in this context, are the components of a system including ROM and RAM space, I/O ports and even CPU time), and an embedded system with surplus resources is an over-engineered system. Adding networking here may mean a rethink and redesign of the same product with more components, more memory, more interfaces and more software.

What Makes an Embedded System?

The image that comes to mind is that of a tiny microchip in a small printed circuit board full of connectors, all wired to masses of switches and LED displays. These invariably cost very little, and we wonder how anybody could make them at such ridiculously low prices. We need to be more generic, and think of all the alternative forms of 'controlling' electronics that can be included in the definition of an embedded system. We could go a bit further and attempt to group them into how powerful they are or by the 'technologies' used in the manufacture of their components. The following are all examples of embedded controllers:

Special dedicated integrated circuit (e.g. LSI, ASIC)

Large scale integration (LSI) and application specific integrated circuits (ASICs) are exactly what they say they are: integrated circuits that have been specially designed and tooled to do one very specific job. In other words, miniature worlds of components emulating what otherwise would be put together using quantities of separate components on a printed circuit board. LSI chips are widely used in applications with specific processing requirements and where parameters such as speed and very low cost are important. Custom designed logic integrated circuits devices result in better performance, lower cost, and sometimes lower power consumption at given speeds. They also have some built in security protection: their operation cannot be easily copied by competitors. Applications are to be found just about everywhere: hand-held organizers, cell-phones, telecommunication equipment, musical instruments, MP3 decoders and telephony receivers. Most commercial network interface chips are nothing but LSI devices specially designed to interface between the network and a microprocessor. In a way, the 'brains' are partly in the microprocessor, partly in the LSI device connected to it.

Programmable logic devices (e.g. PLD, FPGA)

Programmable logic devices (PLDs) or programmable gate arrays (PGAs) are one of a family of IC technologies where half-completed ICs are used as a 'worktop' or basis for the design of complex logic structures. Designers complete their designs simply by programming the final cell-to-cell interconnections. GAs are ideal for small production runs and prototypes. Because of cost considerations, many designers migrate to compatible ASIC or LSI equivalents for large manufacturing runs. For this reason, GAs are not commonly seen in low-cost mass-market appliances. GAs come in many sizes, and many are powerful and flexible enough to provide complete built in 'solutions on a chip' (SOIC) implementations for communications protocols.

Dedicated CPU cores

This is a variation of the above theme. A CPU core is the 'business end' of a normal CPU built into a GA as a collection of gates and flip-flops. The CPU core emulates a standard microcomputer instruction set (but not necessarily using the same electrical circuits). CPU cores are used in very large GA designs when more program-oriented flexibility is needed. In other words, GAs can now include full off-the-peg CPU emulations built into their circuitry (*fabric*). Sizes can vary from feature limited 8-bit processors of the RISC variety, to full 32-bit Power PC compatibles. Because the CPUs are 'assembled' at the design stage, a degree of customisation is possible. For example, custom instructions can be added, or existing ones removed to save space (*real estate*) on the chip. Peripherals can be added as required, and custom communications modules can be 'wired in' from existing libraries resulting in custom CPU architectures with power and capabilities comparable, if not better, to a desktop PC. The libraries can include data conversion, encryption, compression and MPEG decoding. Applications are found in tabletop TV-Internet boxes, hand-held devices, palmtops, data cell-phones and game consoles. Specific networking components such as Ethernet are also available as software modules.

Single board computer (SBC) Processors

These are mainly based on standard Intel processor components and designs. Boards designed for embedded systems are called single board computers (SBCs) and usually include a CPU, decent amount of memory and a varying range and number of peripherals. The most common standard for interconnecting these systems is called PC-104. This standard defines mechanical connectors, board sizes, electrical bus interface levels and timings. SBCs can be very powerful, and even the smallest can easily emulate a standard PCs at the DOS or Windows CE level. The operating system is usually provided in a Flash ROM, or in a plug in Smart Card. Most manufacturers offer boards with built in 10BaseT or 100BaseT Ethernet interfaces, and include support software in the form of Winsock compatible software 'stacks'.

Small microcontrollers

These are at the lowest end of the range in terms of cost and performance. Typically of these are the 8051 cores (from various manufacturers), Microchip PIC, Zilog Z8, Hitachi, Rabbit and Atmel. These low-cost devices are very resource limited, and require the use of external network interface components such as dedicated controller chips to interface properly to a network. These micros are barely powerful enough to drive themselves, never mind the controllers, and data throughput will be at much less than ideal speeds. Computing and storage capacities are rather limited, which also restricts the range of applications. Nevertheless, small microprocessors are good enough for simple network interfaces where only short messages are required, and can find applications in data logging, data gathering and other similar low-level uses. Commercial products 'modules' based on these devices are very popular, and many are available at very low cost. These are ideal for the novice designer, and for basic development and testing purposes. Software support is available in the form of (usually free) software stacks. Within this small microprocessor range, we should also include the small GA CPU cores (such as Xilinx's Microblaze and Picoblaze or those freely available from www.opencore.org). Some of these cores are highly optimized at source and very small in terms of number of gates used. With the right set of special instructions, they can be very powerful indeed.

Common Methods of Networking

At low speeds and short distances within the same electrical enclosure, or when communicating between two or more systems in close proximity, simple communications wiring using parallel or serial data is normally used. These systems are normally described as *bus* systems, rather than network systems. Conceptually however, they serve a similar purpose. At the lower speeds, it is normal to use signal levels compatible with the common power supplies and logic levels used within the equipment, which can be 5v, 3.3v or even less. As speeds get faster, specialist schemes, using much reduced voltage swings (about 200 mV) and high frequency

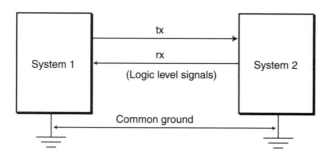

Figure 1-2: Simple interfacing between two microcomputers

terminated transmission lines are used. Figure 1-2 shows the general concept. A common ground is shared between the two sides, and data travels down single or separate connecting wires. Because of the short distances involved, it is unlikely that any spurious or noise signals will be present, and the potential difference between the two grounded ends will be minimal.

Dedicated interfaces

Many microprocessors contain built-in peripherals for interdevice communications such as serial hardware interfaces: universal asynchronous receive transmit (UART) or inter-integrated circuit (I2C) and others that provide simple one or two-way communications at various speeds. Various other simpler proprietary formats are also available: serial peripheral interface (SPI) or the various *single wire interfaces* offered by various IC device manufacturers. Software emulations of these formats are easy to implement when the microcontrollers do not include the custom hardware peripherals required. To help with design and understanding how the peripherals and interfaces work, manufacturers provide extensive examples, diagrams and application notes describing their offerings. The availability of ready made ICs makes the job much easier for the designer. It is of course; perfectly viable to develop one's own method of interfacing for communications, but it usually pays to use existing methods. These methods are ideal when working over a few meters of cable using common ground and power supplies.

Dealing with longer distances, especially where the terminals are in different sites or buildings is a completely different story. It is not practical to run large numbers of parallel cables across long distances, so serial methods using one or two cables pairs are used. Figure 1-2 shows separate connections for transmit and receive, however, some networking methods may share the same physical wire for transmit and receive (in which case, only one cable is used, and only one end can transmit at a time). It is also common in networking to 'hang' more than two devices onto the same set of wires, in order to share the one line. Methods for linking stations together and avoid their transmitters clashing must be incorporated into the design of such networks. We shall deal with this issue later.

External Influences – Interference

Mains power outlets at different geographical locations can present measurable voltage differences between their common ground (earth) points. This is of little consequence for locally connected equipment, say within the same room or office. However, the possibility of ground potential disparities increases as the separation between nodes becomes larger. Running any kind of wire or cable between far locations adds a direct electrical path between the two; see Figure 1-3. Ground currents will find an easy path down these wires making the imbalance voltage dissipate down the network cables. Induced electromagnetic pulses and spikes also aid in generating line currents. Long cables act as receiving aerials, and the noise and radiation interference can find its way into the signal by coupling effects. All these add to the signal to generate noise and distortion. The net effect is an upset of the transmitted digital signal level, and a possible increase in the risk of damage to the electronics, if the equipment is not designed to sustain unforeseen voltage surges. Commercial network cabling and rack equipment is usually designed to cope with these problems. Differential signalling, surge protective components and isolation transformers are the main building blocks used in commercial networking systems to minimize interference. ICs used at the line interface level are also specially designed to embrace minimum levels of electrical protection and immunity.

The disruptive effect of noise upsets the data voltages present in the line, resulting in errors in the received signal. These errors are represented in the simplest case by the odd 'one' data byte being misinterpreted as a 'zero' at the receiver or vice versa. In more extreme cases, errors can cause the connection to be broken or disabled for a

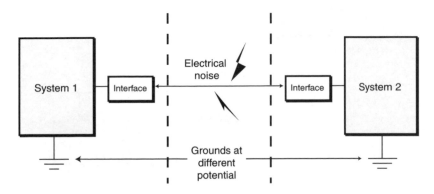

Figure 1-3: Long-distance interfacing between microcomputers

period of time. Some of the defence mechanisms already mentioned can go some way in counteracting these situations. However, further steps need to be taken in order to provide for more resilient error protection overall and to guarantee safe error-free links. This is done by schemes operating at other layers within the rest of the system under the general name of *error protection*.

Multidropping

In most networking situations, we may want more than two stations to communicate with each other. Networking technology allows the sharing of a common line (also known as the *medium*) between all its users. Electronic messages are arranged to travel on the shared medium in a way that they do not overlap or interfere with each other. When many stations share a common channel, the software at each node needs to understand what each of the messages contain, who they are addressed to, and what to do with them. Just as a highway can be full of cars passing by a destination, a network may be full of messages destined for somebody else. Incoming data at a given node will be arriving all the time, and the receiver at that node needs to ensure that only the right messages are allowed in, while still processing all the information passing through. Messages not destined for the station need to be ignored and messages destined for the station need to be acted upon as quickly as possible. This can add considerably to the overheads of any small system.

Figure 1-4 shows the general layout of a multidrop system as compared to a point-to-point system. Apart from the error management schemes introduced previously, a station addressing system needs to be implemented to ensure the right source station communicates with its intended destination. A flexible and efficient collision management system needs also to be implemented to ensure that other stations do not interfere or upset the link by transmitting together or at the wrong time.

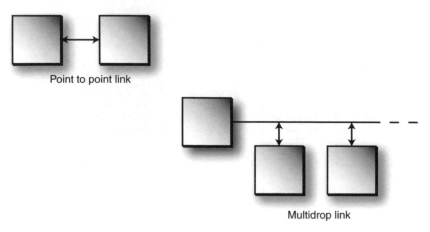

Point to point link

Multidrop link

Figure 1-4: Point-to-point versus multidrop networking

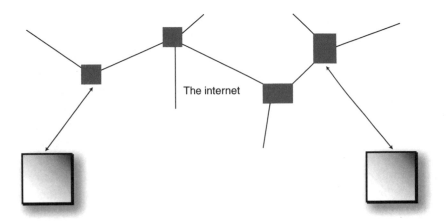

Figure 1-5: Wide area networks connect nodes using shared carriers

Local and wide area networks

One of the most exciting applications for embedded system is when they can be connected to the outside world via the Internet (Figure 1-5). At present, this can be done via phone lines and dial-up modems, or more directly via home or office local area network connections. Far-end connectivity to the Internet is provided by *carriers*. These are the third party owners of the long-distance wiring, satellite of fibre-optic networks, which provide fixed links between the customer and a remote Internet-enabled node. The carrier will guarantee speed and levels of performance between its subscribers.

Global standards

All connected systems in a network, no matter how different, must be able to 'understand' each other. The voltage levels on the line, the speeds of transmission and the methods of encoding must all be compatible, even if different hardware or software is used at each end. In order to provide commonality between all the different systems and applications, global standards for data transmission have been universally agreed. As will be shown later, standards relate to two main aspects of the communications link. The electrical or physical interface: that is, the voltages, timing sequences, and physical aspects of the connections. And the data transfer protocols, or the definitions of what the bits and bytes look like, how they are framed, what commands they perform and what they do in general.

Examples of Networked Embedded Systems

Industrial Ethernet

Industrial plant and the factory floor comprise many devices interconnected in different ways, and traditionally have used a myriad of interfaces and data formats.

13

Many of these devices are simple data collection units with little or no inbuilt intelligence. These can be temperature sensors, pressure switches, simple on–off devices, etc. One or more processing computers, commonly known in the business as *programmable logic controllers* (PLCs) are used to process this data and feed outputs to motors, actuators and back to the office for analysis. For example, several temperature readings from an oven are taken to compute a predicted time average according to the size of items placed inside. This is then used to estimate the power to be delivered to the oven in order to maintain a constant temperature, and at the same time, using a temperature control algorithm, minimize fuel costs. One of the most important requirements for industrial systems is rapid or predictable response time. This is what makes industrial networking systems different to normal office environment networks where the waiting time is not so important. Stopping a valve actuator from filling a drinks bottle requires more accurate time precision than queuing another page into the office laser printer.

Traditionally, automation systems have implemented networking in a hierarchical fashion, using a large variety of protocols and systems, usually very manufacturer dependent. Sometimes, networks from different vendors have to interoperate, that is, talk to each other. This necessitates the use of complex network translator devices. In addition to this, the need for different network hardware and maintenance techniques complicates spares holding and technician training. In order to overcome this problem, there is a growing tendency to use common and established networking techniques such as Ethernet and TCP/IP, to communicate between all levels. New application layer protocols are being designed to comply with specific factory floor requirements and to interface to existing protocols. Many current PLC industrial interfaces already use RS-232 or RS-485 ports to communicate with PCs (Figure 1-6). Initial introduction of Ethernet technology in these cases is at present achieved by the use of simple RS-232 to Ethernet converters. These convert the serial streams produced by

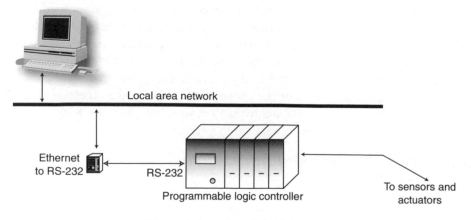

Figure 1-6: Industrial Ethernet

serial communications interfaces into Ethernet compatible frames. This allows the slow introduction of newer Ethernet type technology into older, legacy type systems. Slowly but surely, these will be replaced by rugged, more resilient, IP-based systems.

Point of sale terminals

Examples of these abound nowadays. Portable and intelligent point of sale (POS) terminals are revolutionizing retailing. Imagine you walk into a large building yard wanting to buy some pinewood. After searching through the many racks in the back yard, you cannot find what you want and ask an assistant for help. After discussing your requirements, he punches some keys on his small portable hand-held device, which also contains a small radio aerial. The small screen on this device points out which of the many racks has the item you want. After taking you to the right aisle, he then asks you to take the goods to the dispatch counter where all the bills will have been already printed and ready for payment. His hand-held device is connected to the yard's computer network by radio, and all the transactions are directly entered into the main computer system. His portable terminal is able to retrieve information on stocks, place orders, and enter customer transactions.

Environmental monitoring

Low-cost networking is an ideal backbone for local and global environmental monitoring. Distributed sensors and controllers can make use of existing local networks, including wireless networks to send their data to a central site. The Internet is an ideal medium for placing low-cost pollution and environmental measuring devices anywhere in the world, and for sharing the data among their users. With the advent of low-cost Ethernet microprocessor controlled modules, the cost of environmental monitors is very low, even at present. A school, for example, could benefit from a single weather monitor on the roof connected to the school's Ethernet system, into which all students can tap to and retrieve historical rainfall information.

Domestic applications

Domestic applications are always a soft target for any emerging technology. It is somehow always easy to conceive scenarios where sophisticated technology is always at hand to help. The doorbell rings, the washing machine repairman is at your doorstep. 'Your dishwasher just e-mailed us to say its drive belt is just about to go.' Very impressive! At another time, you may be browsing the Internet, and then decide to look at your own car's web page (We are all told that every car is going to have its own web page in the future). The screen is full of messages and prompts about your car status, its oil consumption, fuel efficiency and other things you did not even know your car had. You then notice a flashing orange blip telling you there is something that requires your attention. You look at the various gauges, and place a tick under one of the 'suggested' procedures to follow, such as buy more oil from one of the advertised brands on the page. Time saving? yes. Effective? yes. Improve quality of life? well yes, perhaps. Much has been said about the benefits or otherwise, of network enabling domestic equipment: fridges, toasters, sewing machines, etc. Although the real benefit is still to be proven, the possibilities (and ideas) are quite original, if not practical. It is not known how many people will want to receive an e-mail from a toaster, but with the current trend of product enhancement for value adding, it will not be long when these facilities will be offered as standard in many domestic products, whether we want them or not.

Computer peripherals

Traditionally, computer peripherals like printers and scanners were connected to the back of one of the workstations in a typical office network. The workstation would act as a server to all other workstations wanting to use the peripheral. Nowadays, it is becoming quite common for peripherals to connect directly to the office's local area network (Figure 1-7). That is, without the use of a workstation managing the printer driver. From the user's point of view, the printer or plotter looks just like another web site. The user accesses the printer web site using their Internet browser to control and setup its parameters (page size etc), and to send it files for printing. One very practical advantage of this method is that individual workstations do not need to have special printer device drivers installed. Any workstation with a web browser can use the peripheral immediately.

Alarm and security systems

Most alarm systems consist of door switches, cameras, infrared motion sensors and other devices spread throughout a building and wired together to a central station via

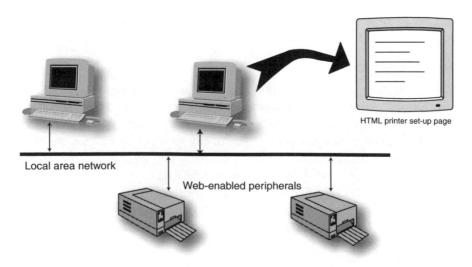

Figure 1-7: Computer peripherals sharing a local area network

a multitude of cables. The use of commonly available computer network cabling and technology makes a network based alternative attractive. There are the savings in technology costs, training, and also in stock and maintenance. The use of standard protocols such as IP also means that data gathering information can be uploaded via a router to a remote central monitoring station using the Internet. With the use of wireless networks, further savings in cabling are apparent. The major concern has always been reliability. Replacing reliable dedicated wiring with shared cabling used by various other computer systems and terminals that can cause fault conditions is always a worry. Fortunately, the reliability of network cabling is proving itself, and increasingly non-mission-critical monitoring systems are now taking advantage of network technology. Alarm monitoring is not restricted to security applications; one practical example is remote control of mains distribution units. Remote network control can be used here to sense the current taken by the outlets (including leakage currents) and also to turn the outlets on and off using predetermined sequences, either to avoid switch-on surges, or to cause reset conditions on some of the equipment plugged in, for example, PCs.

Voice over IP

A typical office has two sets of cables connecting all the desks. One set of cables is used for the phone system, the other set for computer networks. It would make sense to use a single network for both voice and data, if they could coexist at the same time. The generic name for this kind of technology is voice over IP (VOIP). A number of private telephone branch exchange manufacturers offer facilities for sharing voice and data over a single network. Applications are not just limited to the local office. Voice (and video) can be used by individuals to connect over the Internet to remote users around the globe. We can attach a telephone to one end of an Internet line; and establish a link to our friends in different part of the world with a similar phone set-up at the other end (Figure 1-8). At present, line

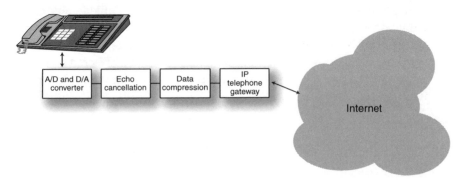

Figure 1-8: Voice over IP

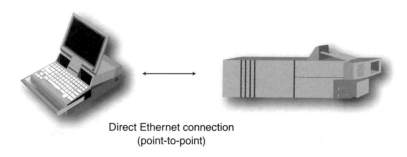

Direct Ethernet connection
(point-to-point)

Figure 1-9: Ethernet connected peripherals for the PC

costs do not make this option too attractive, but this may change as price policies shift around.

VOIP applications also include the transmission of streamed data for broadcast and multicast applications. Radio (and TV) stations can use the Internet to broadcast their programmes to listeners. Many official standards now exist for the transmission and compression of streamed data including voice and images. The standards cover not only the encoding of voice or video signal, but also the establishment and maintenance of the link. Most coding methods include some form of compression, and time-saving devices such as silence suppression.

PC interfacing

In the scientific and technical world, it is common for specialized test equipment to connect to PCs running custom programs to drive its many functions (Figure 1-9).

This has traditionally been implemented using the ubiquitous serial and parallel ports on the PC. Unfortunately, serial and parallel ports are now considered legacy technology and are being slowly phased out; new PCs just do not have them any more. Serial and parallel ports are being slowly replaced with newer standards such as USB. Unfortunately, USB (even the newer version 2) has shortcomings when used in some applications: USB is a local interface, with a limited cable length, and can only communicate with the one interface it is connected to. The use of network technology can be of interest in these cases. Scientific equipment can be shared among several uses in a network, and communications can be effected over any distance. Expect to see more scientific and test equipment with inbuilt LAN network connections as standard interfaces.

Other applications

These are some other areas where networked embedded systems are being used

- blood analysers,
- intelligent mains distribution units,

- PBX accounting systems,
- time and attendance clocks and terminals,
- badge and bar code access control,
- customer traffic analysis,
- marine equipment aboard ships,
- postal equipment and franking machines,
- CNC machines in shop floors,
- electronic signboards,
- chemical and gas chromatography instrumentation,
- ATM machines,
- warehouse inventory tracking devices,
- refrigeration and heating controls,
- swimming pool and leisure centre monitors,
- weather stations.

Points to Consider Before Networking Embedded Systems

Embedded networking development requires a combination of skills: software, hardware and the understanding of special purpose interface devices. Decisions on how to approach this challenge, where to put the effort in, and methodology for development will be dependent on cost and resources available. Adding networking capabilities to a small system can take a sizeable chunk of its resources. Software can take a big bite of program and data memory space, and hardware may need to be re-designed. The timing requirements may impose extra limitations on the processors ability to deal with its other normal routines, thus affecting other parts of the system. To add to this, specialist peripheral chips and associated circuitry can be expensive and are usually power hungry. In simple words, adding networking is not easy.

Development costs

Development investment is the total time (and cost) spent between taking the decision to design and having a working prototype on the bench. This time can be short or long depending on many factors, the most important being 'information'. A major slow-down in development is usually the time lost 'learning' how to use a resource or component. Most IC and software vendors offer application notes, assemblers, code examples and various other tools to speed development and facilitate use of their products. The offerings can vary from software in the form of stacks to peripheral interface chips that can perform some or all of the necessary networking functions under one package. To help with the initial design, many suppliers also offer development, or prototyping ready-made boards, which may include a sample device, plus all external line interfacing circuitry already built in, saving many hours of prototyping. These should be used as much as possible during development. However, under no circumstances should designers be misled by the attractive features of a 'development kit' which could divert them from the realities of costing final parts into production runs. The cheapest (or better) production parts are not always linked to the best development environments.

Learning curve

Getting used to a development environment can be hard going. Designers have to form a mental map of the various stages of development, and how the pieces are assembled together. Software manuals are not always written with the novice in mind, and component and data sheets do not always contain their information in easy to understand language. Different microprocessors and interface products require different procedures and different development tools depending on their complexity (compilers, assemblers, linkers, loaders). PLDs are at the top of this stack, involving the steepest learning curve and largest combination of stages to learn (design entry, timing analysis, synthesis, reduction, partitioning, verification, simulation, programming). Many manufacturers supply demonstration disks with step-by-step examples covering the basic design strategies, and just enough information to get started on a very basic design. However, learning the language from then on and to a competent level can take several weeks of lonely 'hands-on' type work. It is not uncommon for designers to prefer to stick to one supplier or family of devices, for no other reason than avoiding going through yet another sharp learning curve (Figure 1-10). Access to Internet and online user newsgroups or bulletin boards can be extremely invaluable at this stage. Third party courses can also

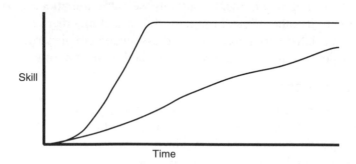

Figure 1-10: Learning curves can be steep. Choosing the wrong tools may be unproductive

be helpful. But be weary; in brand-new technologies, the trainer may only be one week ahead of their pupils.

External libraries and software

These are also known as intellectual property. As already mentioned, many suppliers offer off-the-shelf libraries or modules covering network functions, tools and utilities. Network libraries for communication protocols are also known as stacks, and are available for a multitude of devices from PC compatibles to the smallest of micros. Costs can range from free, to punitively expensive license-only agreements. If a ready-made stack is not available, developing your own from scratch can be a major unwarranted task. Developing and testing network software is not a trivial exercise and nobody should be re-inventing the wheel. On the other hand, the quality and documentation provided with some bought-in modules can leave much to be desired. Some of these stacks may not fit seamlessly with your project, or may fail to work for some unknown reason. When manufacturer's support is included in the equation (if it exists) the 'learning curve' time could be suspiciously comparable to that of designing from scratch. Do not forget that many commercial offering may have just seen the light of day, and may not have been factory tested to the full. You could end up doing many hours of adjusting and debugging before the design works to your satisfaction. The dividing line between using a provided module (where you do not know what is going on), and cooking-your-own (where you do know what is going on) can be very thin indeed. There is no substitute for knowing what is going on. Using a bought in product, and expecting that it will work perfectly as a 'black box' is a risk, especially when dealing with complex networking technology. On the other hand, knowing a little about what is going on (by reading this book!) will not only help you gain confidence, but also allow you to sort out problems much quicker.

Availability of peripheral and support devices

One thing is to find a magic IC device that can do everything you want in a cheap small package, and another is to find a month later that it has gone out of production. This should come to no surprise to microprocessor system designers who are well aware of the many problems associated with procurement. Many specialist network interface components can become obsolete rather quickly. Unlike popular IC devices, network components are not always manufactured in very large quantities. Sometimes they are designed to cater for a particular range of products, for example, a particular brand of modem, network hub interface or radio transceiver. The IC manufacturer may suddenly decide to discontinue a particular range when the end product it was aimed for becomes obsolete. Alternatively, the part may be upgraded to a more complex one (more expensive, or with different pin-outs) or require different interface technology or external set of components. A similar situation may arise with software offerings, where support and development has been discontinued, either because of lack of interest, or because the supplier is now focusing on a different product range. This situation is particularly significant with GA devices, where newer devices obsolete old ones almost on a seasonal basis.

Shortage of system resources

System resources are the various shared processing power and components such as memory available within the embedded system. Very few designers are going to over-engineer an embedded system for a mass-market application. Therefore, by definition, embedded systems are resource limited. The problem is critical with the smaller microcontrollers, which support very small amounts of ROM or RAM. Communications software requires decent amounts of RAM space to store incoming data blocks until they are processed, fast timing methods (usually interrupts) to handle incoming data requests and in some cases, variable stack space or stack facilities to hold data in recursive subroutine calls. The real problem is cost. These small systems are so highly tuned, that the inclusion of networking facilities is going to add disproportionately to their cost. A complete hardware re-design may be the only way out. The simple TCP demonstration at the end of this book takes nearly half of the resources available in a 'middle of the range' small microprocessor PIC16F877 device, for example.

Compatibility and flexibility – meeting the standards

If a design is to achieve the specific purpose of communicating between a limited number of units, and over a restricted network domain, meeting global standards is not of much concern. If your devices need to talk to others of different manufacture, share a medium used by other devices, or work over a larger third-party network, the issue of compatibility and protocols has to be addressed properly. Many protocols include many options and variables in their design. A major part of a design strategy is to decide how much of the original specifications the device will need to support (Figure 1-11). In other words, which subset of the protocols will a product need to implement. You will need to have a good understanding of the standards in order to be able to do this. If you know the standards well, you should be able to apply the right assumptions in order to simplify the design in the best possible way.

Electrical and physical implications

It may not be too obvious to some designers that integrating networking into a product also implies submitting to the various standards on electrical inter-connectivity, isolation and protection. There will be requirements to meet on suitable connectors, cabling and devices to provide correct levels of EMC and electrical isolation, special PCB layouts, track isolation on the board, etc. This quickly adds to the final cost.

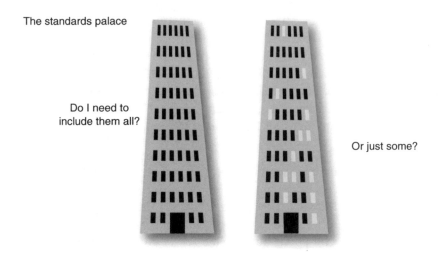

Figure 1-11: Do we need to implement everything?

Production costs

This item should really be at the top of the list, but as this is a book on technology, we shall allow this to pass. Putting development costs aside, the extra production costs arising from network-enabling a project are directly proportional to the price of the additional components used on the board, plus the cost of the mechanical and electrical interfacing components (which can add quite a lot in proportion!). One major decision at this stage is whether to use ready-made networking 'modules' for production runs. These are great for development, and for reducing 'time to market' but their cost in quantities is something that needs to be carefully considered. Some manufacturers offer large price discounts, but these are linked to purchases in the several thousands of units. At these levels, development costs will be a small proportion of the total, and designers would be wise to consider other alternatives. Stock availability, single sourcing and other related issues are also problems that must not be ignored.

Getting Started

So where do we go from here? There are three main objectives to pursue: a grasp of the underpinning core technology, a good mental map of the standards, and an overview of the devices available that can help design. With these, the designer will have a much clearer perception about networking and how it can be best implemented.

The technologies

An ideal design should not rely on a particular network technology. They should work equally well with phone connections, LAN wiring, power lines and wireless. A flexible approach allows full connectivity across different products and applications. However, each of these physical connections has widely different characteristics that can affect a device's basic functionality. Parameters such as time dependency for example, can affect the efficiency of the connection. An Internet-connected appliance may have to wait minutes, hours or days before receiving an update. Time or safety critical products should not depend on good phone lines, or lightly used local area networks to operate.

Phone lines are one of the most common methods of connecting devices. Most offices and homes have access to phone lines. Appliances using the phone lines for communications should ideally share the line without interfering with its normal use. The remote server collects information passively when the appliance calls in. However, without a special phone adaptor, the server could not call the appliance without interfering with the ring, if the same line is shared with another phone. Another problem with such systems is that the server has no way of knowing whether the appliance is down, cannot connect or has nothing to report. A more resilient system is one where the remote calls the appliance using a dedicated telephone line dedicated for incoming calls only. System faults can be more easily identified at the cost of the extra phone circuit. Even this can have its problems, for example, when the appliance has not heard from the server for a while. These limitations can be expensive and may affect the viability of the whole project. Phone systems also have their costs. To avoid making long-distance calls, low-cost 0800 numbers could be arranged, or devices could go through a local ISP or carrier. Many remotes in a local area could share a local ISP account, which could result in savings over a time. Cellular calls may cost less than landline calls in some instances, and are worth investigating. A common problem (especially with ISPs) is that they may be busy (and slow) at peak times.

Wired computer networks are more resilient. The most common direct network connection is Ethernet. The advantages of Ethernet for embedded networking are many, but the most important one is that the wires are already there. On the other hand, many existing installations provide little spare capacity, and may require the addition of extra cabling from the appliance to the hub, somewhat defeating the cost-saving purpose. Most of the time, the cost per point of an embedded Ethernet interface is much less than that of an embedded modem, including phone interface and call costs. Wireless networks (radio as well as infrared) are tempting technologies because they promise flexibility in terms of remote location and savings in wiring. However, many environmental factors are not suitable for wireless links. No-signal spots and local interference can also play havoc with the system. In system planning terms, a site survey should always be first carried out. A regularly occurring issue with these networks is security, especially if it can be accessible from the outside world.

On standards and protocols

A number of related questions may arise at this time: How much do I need to know about protocols and standards? Will they be easy to implement in my design? How can I estimate the effort required? Can I just buy a protocol off the shelf? Will it work first time, or will I need to spend a disproportionate amount of time getting it to work? Do I need to employ experts? Would it be easier to develop my own protocol from scratch?

Without going into much detail, a protocol is just a way to ensure two or more users or applications connected together can recognize and talk to each other, in other words, a protocol is a set of rules on how to communicate. These can be your own rules, or they can be drawn from existing standards. The word protocol is used in many instances when it should not. RS-232 is usually described as an asynchronous protocol, where it is in fact a specification describing the electrical characteristics of the link. The UART format is also called a 'protocol'. The format may describe how the data bits are arranged, but still does not describe what the bits mean, what the messages contain, or what the rules of engagement are. Do we need to provide error correction? Do we need to provide for means of addressing files to different destinations? Do we need to include ciphering or security information with the data? Where does a protocol fit in all this?

With a bit of hindsight, we could deduce that we may never define a single protocol to cater for all needs. More to the point, why do we need a protocol? This argument can be trivial for a simple point-to-point system where only two stations are involved and simple rules is all we need. Nevertheless, why do other systems offer fully-fledged protocol implementations? Do they really need to have them? Or are they just doing this to impress or for marketing purposes? We need to move forward from this simple model, and look at the main points that standards and protocols address. These are as follows:

Line Level Compatibility: The voltage data patterns, levels and waveforms transmitted at one end should be ideally matched for the receiver at the other end. This electrical compatibility statement may appear trivial, but it is one of the biggest headaches in network design. Without proper standards, it is almost impossible to meet.

Timing relationships: The data level transitions are determined by a clock at the source. The receiver has usually no access to this clock, so the relative timing of the signals has to be recovered or re-generated at the receiver. This includes determinations of the beginning and the end of a message. Reliable clock re-generation is the final aim.

The management of multiple users: How do we know which stations are using the line? Which ones are available for communications? Who is switched off?

How do we ensure that two or more stations cannot use the same line at the same time?

The effects of noise on the line: The communications system has to recognize errors in order to avoid misinterpreting data and provide erroneous information to the end application. It also has to implement methods for recovering the transaction in case of a drastic error situation such as a line breakage, and for continuing where it left off.

What to do with the messages: This may not sound too obvious in a low-level application, but it is a generic requirement for communications standards where applications need to communicate with each other in an abstract way. These are handled by the 'higher layers' in the communications model.

The specific techniques used by most protocols to achieve the above aims are rather similar. However, they are used rather differently in order to match the medium used and the type of network wanted. Most protocols add extra data to the transmit stream in the form of headers, checksums and some form of acknowledgement mechanism. Messages can be sent back to the transmitter to acknowledge the receipt of a section of data. Managing multiple stations introduce the concept of station addressing, user dictionaries (to know who is who). Information overlap (messages can arrive out of sequence), and sometimes the need to maintain separate communications with more than one station at the same time. Sharing a single physical medium also means that transmissions can collide (two or more transmitters trying to send at the same time). Methods for dealing with collisions are well known and many of the standards deal with this issue. For example, transmission delay rules are imposed on each station so that it can transmit only at given times to avoid multiple stations colliding. A protocol is not a simple set of linear rules, but a layered set of overlapping conditions covering different parameters of the communications process.

On designing your own protocol

Why use standard protocols? They can be over-specified and can occupy large amounts of memory consuming scarce system resources. Many 'standard' protocols include options and alternatives that can be irrelevant for many applications and a general overkill in the case of a small network system with simple requirements. Implementing a full set of standards can add heavily to development and testing costs.

Some designers will be well too aware that putting aside established standards and doing your 'own thing' for the only reason that 'standards are too difficult to understand' is a very naive approach that should be avoided at all costs. Any designer involved in network design should be aware of the basic rules of protocol definition before they even contemplate designing their own protocols or protocol variations. Nobody will disagree that many years of effort have already been spent in devising protocols to cater for just about any combination of network topography. It also makes common sense to conform to these existing standards. It is also true that many of these protocols, starting from humble beginnings, have been extended cater for eventualities and options that may never be present in your design. So why include all these extra resource consuming add-ons? As we shall see later, it is actually possible to a certain extent, to implement protocol subsets whilst maintaining overall global compatibility. It can make sense to implement a 'light' version of an existing protocol; one that does not disturb other uses, but is perfectly applicable to the application in hand. Even better, it is quite effective to build-on to existing 'bread and butter' protocols such as IP or UDP. You may have a very good reason for wanting to implement your own standard. Maybe you have a special hardware requirement at the physical layer level, such as a special purpose radio link, or an optical link with special characteristics. You may prefer to implement your protocol using techniques or components you are more familiar with. You may also be reluctant to learn new techniques. This is understandable; some networking theory can be confusing at best. Hopefully, this book will help you in understanding them better! If you want to design your own protocol, it will definitely pay to look at already existing formats, and take a leaf from their designs, there is usually a good reason why they were designed that way. It is important to understand the reasoning behind the choices. The flexibility is always there, for example, Ethernet controller chips allow for proprietary format versions at low levels, so you will still be able to use these otherwise standard components in your custom designs.

Of the many 'medium-level' protocol formats in existence, TCP/IP is now becoming a major standard for all kind of communications in local and wide area networks. TCP/IP formats and methods are being used for all kind of communications, from printer drivers and file sharing in PC networks, to industrial plant control. Central to TCP/IP is the internet protocol (IP). All the internet higher layers use IP as their backbone. This is a strong and reliable well-tested format. Anybody considering the design or implementation of higher layer protocols should seriously consider basing their designs on IP technology.

CHAPTER 2

Software Design for Embedded Communications

Many readers involved in the development of embedded systems will have reasonable knowledge of the internal workings of the devices and components they will be using. They will know how the hardware and interfaces operate, how to address memory and I/O effectively, how to handle interrupts, how to initialize and drive their peripherals such as timers, UARTs and so on. It will not be an exaggeration to suggest that a good, solid perception of these issues is an essential prerequisite of good embedded system programming. A good designer will spend time checking data sheets and application notes, absorbing all the traits of the hardware or software, until they clearly understand what they do and how they operate together. This chapter is not a guide on good programming techniques, or on information on how to deal with a particular family of devices, nor does it contain 'cookbook' code samples. The main purpose is to introduce a few programming methods and concepts relevant to networking and communications systems. Many readers may be already familiar with these, some may have heard of them in some way, perhaps well, or not well enough to use them effectively. The tools described here are basic and well known.

Setting the Stage

Many readers will be conversant with their software development environment for embedded systems. These may be a collection of programs running on a Windows or Unix workstation, and may consist of assemblers, simulators, emulators and device programmers; perhaps all linked together under a neat looking graphics Windows or Unix shell. Some readers may be doing some, if not all, of their coding in a high-level language such as C or Java.

Portability is one of the main reasons for using a high level-language. However, when it comes to specialized techniques such as interrupt handling, there are no general rules, and portability goes out of the window. The C language, for example, does not include standard facilities for concurrent programming or interrupt handling. So different manufacturers have developed their own particular implementation techniques in different ways. These are not difficult to learn, but have the side effect that similar concepts may be given different names and explanations (and vice versa). This has resulted in a lot of confusion for the uninitiated, and fuel for the many 'war-of-the-systems' discussions in online Internet newsgroups. One important things to realize is that designers should not be too concerned whether something they are working on should be called a 'thread' or a 'task', or a 'subroutine' or 'procedure', or whether they should worry that somebody at some stage may correct them on terminology. Be assured that somewhere else in the world somebody will be doing just the opposite. More important is to understand the basic concepts; terminology should always take second place.

The methods described here are described in terms of standard computer architectures: memory, stacks, function calls, etc. Many of the smaller microprocessors and microcontrollers are quite limited in this department and will not have the ability to do some of these jobs properly. For example, many single chip microcontrollers have a limited stack space, and place a bound on the number of nested subroutines that can be called at any one time. This must be kept in mind when implementing a real system. System crashes due to communications sub-systems generating stack problems are incredibly difficult to trace, and may be the simple result of unforeseen lack of user memory or stack nesting planning. Of course, this is never obvious from just looking at the listings. This is one area where some of the tools such as *profiling* may come to the rescue.

The concepts presented here are also relevant when the designs are being implemented using specialist hardware architectures such as GAs. These have the added flexibility of being able to determine the hardware 'power' at the design stage. Some embedded cores are parameter driven, their characteristics, number of registers, instruction sets, etc. can be defined at the design stage. With these devices it is not an issue of matching the software against the hardware. It is more like matching one against the other.

Some basic principles

One of the most traditional ways to describe a program is with a *flowchart*. In a flowchart, program continuity or flow is described from top to bottom as a series of paths or signal flows (Figure 2-1). Rectangular boxes describe general actions to be performed 'on the way'. These could be the loading of an I/O port or an arithmetic operation. Diamond-shaped boxes are used to represent decision points with alternative output paths or routes. The decisions are usually made on the conditions of internal flags or variables. There is normally one program start (usually placed at the top), and one or more program ends (usually at the bottom). A program that runs forever has no end point and program flow is re-directed back to a previous stage,

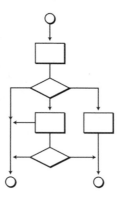

Figure 2-1: A flowchart is a simple planar view of a program

including the top, that is, back to the 'start' point. The key point about flowcharts is that a program can only be doing one thing at a time; information about timing is not visible. The flowchart can be seen as a network of roads, with the program represented by a single travelling car moving around them. The car can travel anywhere around the flow map, but can only be in one place at one time. Useful information, such as the time when the car arrives or leaves a particular point is not part of the information provided by the flowchart.

Data communications is an activity that happens in *real time*. Telecommunications data arriving at a receiver has to be handled almost immediately. If this is not the case, incoming data may get lost. The programming of communications software forces the designer to use special tools to handle this effectively. One of the most powerful tools gives a computer the ability to run one or more tasks concurrently. This is a situation where two or more operations (hardware or software) are being executed to all extents at the same time and in parallel. In order for these multiple tasks to coexist, well-defined timing relationships need to exist between the various parallel operations. For example, one operation may not be able to continue until another (running in parallel with the first) has terminated. This could be because a condition or variable being computed by the second is also required by the first. In other words, an operation may be required to wait (or block) until another terminates. Many software functions take a finite amount of time to perform. Some could take a short time, others, a very long time. Meanwhile, other operations may need to take place in the interim. In an ideal situation, short operations will be slotted in time within the longer ones to maximize processor time use in the most effective way. This kind of programming is not easily described with a standard flowchart.

Various tools and techniques are available to handle real-time programming. The writing of code for parallel operations may sound very complex, but becomes an easy task once the basic concepts have been grasped. To the uninitiated, some of the concepts may appear at first rather abstract and pointless, but the time spent in researching and understanding them is well worth taking.

One of the best ways to explain what is going on is through a practical example. We shall take the simple case of a simple microcontroller wanting to transmit an array of bytes using a standard serial interface (UART). To start with, we could just write a simple function that moves bytes one at a time, into a local register, then copy the eight data bits one at a time, to an output pin using a simple eight times 'do' loop. The 'rotate register via the carry bit' assembler instruction present in most CPU architectures will be helpful here. We may alternatively choose to take advantage of the standard hardware UART present as a peripheral in many microcontrollers. In this case, programming is much simpler. We just copy the bytes into the UART transmit register after a suitable wait until the 'transmit OK' flag has been set. In both cases, our function will only return after all the bytes have been transmitted. In the main, the serial interface will operate at a very low speed when compared to the clock of the CPU. Therefore, our function will spend a fair amount of time not doing much, just waiting in a tight closed loop for the UART to finish transmitting. Similarly, the rest of the program can do little else at this point but wait for our function to end. Functions like these are said to *hang*. That is, they will not return until some other operation (in our case transmit all the bytes) has completed. This is a very inefficient way of running a program. We would prefer the rest of the machine to carry on doing other tasks. If the data array to be transmitted is very large, the wait can be very long indeed. To make matters worse; if the transmission relies on some sort of acknowledgment from a remote, and if for some reason the hardware is disturbed or disconnected (by somebody unplugging a connector) the wait can last forever. This causes the whole machine to *crash*.

One neat way around this problem is to arrange for some means of separating the transmit function from the actual physical operation that transmits the bits. For example, the transmit subroutine could kickstart a background transmission operation and return immediately. This would allow the CPU to carry on performing other tasks as the transmit function is now 'running on its own' somewhere in the background, and will not be holding back the rest of the system. The transmit operation now becomes a background task that performs, transparently and concurrently, the actual physical transmission of the data bits without disturbing normal program flow. In practice, this is done by cunning programming and by regular software polling or by the use of interrupts. Most embedded hardware peripherals have handy facilities for sensing termination status, or for generating interrupts when their various hardware operations have finished. Software schemes only do not have the benefit of hardware parallelism and may have to rely on regular clock tick timers to provide some form of artificial interrupt signal. Like runaway cats, parallel operations will want to do their own thing, and need to be controlled. After triggering the transmit function, the main program will want to monitor the

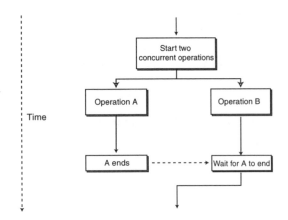

Figure 2-2: Two operations started at the same time

status of the transmission in order to know when it has terminated, or when the parallel operation has finished. Operations of this type are sometimes called *pending*, see Figure 2-2.

This simplistic view applies not only to external devices such as I/O peripherals, but also to any other form of software action that may need to take place concurrently. Many of these could be purely internal tasks, such as long computations and operations on large arrays or maths functions. In order to handle these, practical designs will need to be able to detach themselves from each operation, and consider each action as an independent task or identity. The computer will also need to support a more advanced form of *multitasking* or *multithreading*.

Concurrent Programming

A standard C program starts execution with the main function. The example in Figure 2-3 shows a simple endless loop as it may be used in a typical embedded system. The operation to be performed (in this case a simple integer increment) is performed repeatedly forever in the infinite loop. The program can be thought of as a single job that executes continuously.

An obvious way to implement concurrency is by using multiple CPUs. However, because of cost and other constraints, most practical embedded systems will have just the one CPU. Any form of concurrency can only be implemented by *time sharing* (or *time slicing*) processor time into the various activities required to run. In other words, each job is allowed to run for a given time after which, control is passed to the next job, then to the next job, and so on. The fact that each job is running broken up in time as cake slices will not matter too much to the user, who will

```
void main test ()
 { int counter;
   counter = 0;
   while (1)       // repeat forever
   { counter++;    // the task to be performed
   }
 }
```

Figure 2-3: A simple C program executing forever

```
void main robin ()
  {
    while (1)                      // repeat forever
    { if (poll_serialport())
      process_serialport();        // 1st job

      if (poll_keyboard())
      process_keyboard();          // 2nd job

      process_outputdevices();
    }
  }
```

Figure 2-4: Simple round-robin processing

perceive it (in their much slower time frame) as a continuous smooth operation. The switching will be happening so fast, that users do not notice the empty time gaps.

Figure 2-4 shows a way of implementing such a simple form of concurrency. The example shows a simple listing that reads a serial port, reads a keyboard and then outputs the data to a printer. Each function is called in turn, and is allowed to perform some, or part, of its allocated activity. This form of concurrency is known as *round robin*. An essential requirement here is that each of the functions must return quickly, otherwise the whole system will operate slowly, and the other operations will not be serviced in time. The three operations should return very fast, so that the whole cycle is repeated as fast and regularly as possible. In the example shown, this requirement is easily met for the first two functions. This is because they have been divided into two parts, one that senses or polls the input device to see if it is active, poll_keyboard(), and another that performs the actual read operation process_keyboard(). In most micros, the poll or sense operation is very fast as it only involves the reading of a single bit flag in a memory register, allowing the function to return very quickly. The read port functions should also return relatively quickly, as data will already be waiting in some register to be read. However, the last function, process_output() can present a problem. It may be difficult to ensure this function returns quickly. Sending data to a device like a printer may require an unknown wait for the acknowledge return, which can take some time to arrive. Round robin is a crude, but effective way of implementing concurrency. It has the disadvantage that entire job sections of code within the loop must be written with time constrains in mind. Operations that intrinsically take a long time or an unknown time to run cannot be used in a round-robin system.

It is possible to implement a more sophisticated, and more useful, form of concurrency by adding a real-time operating system (RTOS) to the processor. This is a separate piece of software code that sits hidden in the background, and is normally not 'seen' by the user. The RTOS relies on a central timer or clock to manage its time of operation. This regular clock rate is usually at around a few hundred times per second, and is usually derived from the main processor clock or from an interrupt source. When the microcontroller is reset, the RTOS takes over full control of the system. It then allocates time slices to each job running on the machine in a transparent manner. Unlike round robin, where each job is specifically written by the programmer to terminate quickly, the RTOS will interrupt a user job in mid-stream. When writing the code, the programmer does not have to be concerned about concurrency or job termination issues. RTOS will time slice the jobs at any point, and in its own time. It does this by allowing each job to run for a given period of time (as defined by internal job allocation tables), and cause an interrupt at pre-determined times. During the interrupt, RTOS will store all the intermediate register values and flags in protected memory, and pass control to the next job. All the register and status values, also known as context, are stored and returned in a seamless way, so that jobs can restart exactly where they left off. This time slicing operation will continue in a circular manner forever. The end result is that each job thinks it has the full processor to itself.

With RTOS, the microcontroller is able to run many jobs simultaneously, and the program code for each can be written as if they were all completely independent entities. Writing user code for an RTOS environment requires a few small changes to the way it is normally designed. The programmer will need to be aware of the existence of the RTOS, and be able to communicate with it in order to perform a few basic actions (mainly related to the use of shared resources and start-up initializations). All communications between a user program and the RTOS is via vendor-dependent interfaces, usually arranged as callable functions or as macro calls. Figure 2-5 shows some sample code generated this way using the special constructs unique to the Keil compiler.

Versions of RTOS are normally available from the vendors of software and integrated development environments (IDEs). They usually occupy a relatively small section of program space and require only a few bytes of RAM, so they can be used even with the smallest of microcontroller devices.

Threads and tasks

In the previous section, we used the word *job* to denote each of the independent sections of code. A more common name for these sections is threads (or tasks). These names are sometimes used interchangeably and may cause some confusion.

```
int counter1;
int counter2;

#run_task 1
void job1 ()
{
 while (1)
 { counter1++;   // perform 1st task
 }
}

#run_task 2
void job2 ()
{
 while (1)
 { counter2++;   // perform 2nd task
 }
{
```

Figure 2-5: Examples of real-time code

A task and a thread are essentially the same thing, although in general the word task is used when referring to embedded systems, thread is used mainly when dealing with larger machines. Tasks are the building blocks of a multitasking operating system. These are nothing more than ordinary functions that may include a number of especially allocated resources, sections of memory and set periods of time to perform a specific job. The RTOS manages the resources, and switches seamlessly between the tasks using its time slice clock. A common definition more applicable to larger systems states that a thread is one of several tasks that may be running within the context of a single *process*. A process is one of several user programs or *applications* that may be running on a system or platform. For example, a PC may have a spreadsheet program and an Internet browser open at the same time (processes). Each of these processes may have a number of tasks and threads open, perhaps to handle communications, concurrent printing or spell checking. The thread handling the printing for the spreadsheet will be conceptually different to the thread handling the printing for the browser (even though they may share the same section of program code in memory), so there may be two independent printing tasks operating at one time; one under the spreadsheet, the other under the browser. The concept of a process is more applicable to platforms and mainframes. A good operating system offers reliability by ensuring processes are protected from each other. If one process fails or crashes, all other processes can continue operating. When a process is closed, all associated threads within it are automatically closed at the same time. Processes, tasks or threads all operate within a *scope*. A scope is the range of resources accessible to each. In other words, scope is the range of resources the thread can 'see'. Resources are the various physical components of a computer system such as memory, peripherals and interfaces that may need to be shared. By the above definition, a thread cannot access resources in the scope of another thread.

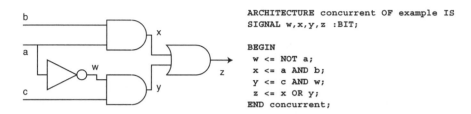

```
ARCHITECTURE concurrent OF example IS
SIGNAL w,x,y,z :BIT;

BEGIN
  w <= NOT a;
  x <= a AND b;
  y <= c AND w;
  z <= x OR y;
END concurrent;
```

Figure 2-6: Concurrent programming in logic gate arrays

The various resources of a computer system need to be shared and allocated in a logical way. This is also a job for the RTOS. These are generally called *shared resources*. For example, areas of RAM can be re-used or shared among various processes or tasks. I/O peripherals on the other hand, may be bound to one task for the duration of a program session. Peripherals can be also shared dynamically among several tasks, but measures have to be put into place for each of the tasks to request for availability of the peripheral before it can be used. A module or peripheral not available to a task is said to be *locked*. The task requesting availability of the printer will have to decide whether to wait until the peripheral becomes free, or abort the operation. For example, one task may be holding on to a parallel printer port, which will not relinquish it until all the data has been printed. All other tasks wanting to use the port will have to wait until this has completed. A good RTOS will also provide a number of internal functions that user programs can call for enumerating, requesting, allocating and relinquishing the various shared resources. Using I/O in a multitasking environment requires the programmer to be aware of these functions and be able to use these functions wisely to ensure shared resources are used effectively.

The Windows operating system screen display is a beautiful example of the management of a shared resource (the display screen) among several processes and tasks, each having its own dedicated display (the rectangular view windows) with the user prioritizing the displays by re-arranging the window panes on the screen manually.

Concurrency is the natural mode of operation for *logic gate arrays* design languages. Figure 2-6 shows a simple VHDL listing for a four-gate address decoder circuit. Although the entries in the program listing appear in order, all operations within the BEGIN END block are performed in parallel and at the same time. In other words, it does not matter in which order the entries are made in the listing. This may not be an easy concept to grasp for some software developers who are used to the sequential nature of program listings.

Multithreading and multitasking

The two terms mean effectively the same thing. However, there is a subtle difference when relating to processes, tasks and threads. As mentioned before, a process is an independent job running within a platform. Switching between processes can be rather complicated and time consuming. A process may have control over large parts of the system, for example, large blocks of RAM, which may need to be temporarily stored somewhere (like a hard disk). In other words, *rolled-out* to allow the next process to *roll-in* its own data into the same shared space, and take over. Not all RTOS support process switching. Thread switching on the other hand, implies saving just the registers and a few other localized resources, and can be done in much less time. Process switching is impractical for time critical programs, and thread switching is the preferred choice for real-time applications. Most embedded systems run one process at a time, where concurrency is handled by one or more tasks running within that process.

From a design point of view, designing a concurrent application as a collection of processes has various conceptual advantages. Each process can be considered as a separate entity, protected from each other, with full transparency when sharing resources such as RAM or interfaces. Resources will appear to multiply in size, as each process believes it has the full machine and its full set of resources to itself. On the other hand, designing a program as a single process with multiple threads forces the designer to be aware of what the other threads are doing at any time, and the use of resources has to be carefully managed via devices such as semaphores. As the program gets larger, it also gets more difficult to trace or debug. A bad pointer or overflow in one thread can cause crashes in other threads that may be very difficult to trace.

RTOS responsibilities

These are:

- pass messages between tasks,
- create and destroy threads or tasks,
- prioritize and time allocate task execution,
- coordinate multiusage of memory and I/O devices,
- guarantee a maximum time response to an event.

Scheduling is the operation by which the RTOS allocates time slots, and switches between the different jobs or tasks of execution. The user does not see the switching at all, and from its own perspective, the job appears to be running continuously. The simplest form of RTOS uses a hardware interrupt triggered at frequent time intervals. When the time comes to switch a task, RTOS interrupts the currently running task, saves its registers, status flags and other relevant time-sensitive information in a special memory area. It then replaces the same registers and status flags with register values already stored from a previous task switch. These values correspond to the registers and status flags for the next task. Lastly, it returns the interrupt. This has the effect of passing control transparently to the next task. The first task has stopped, and the next task carries on running where it left off as if nothing had happened. On the next tick clock interrupt, RTOS will pass control to the next task and so on. This operation is known as a *context switch*. The context being another word for the current status of a CPU, and its collection of volatile register values, pointers, status and carry flags etc. The block of data is known as a context record or sometimes *task control block* (TCB). The part of the RTOS performing this activity is known as a scheduler.

What needs to be saved? Context switching is an operation similar to a hardware interrupt. In a hardware interrupt, the CPU registers, the stack pointers and the status flags are saved for the duration of the interrupt. This allows the interrupt routine to use or modify the registers and flags. Common and global variables do not need to be saved. The return from interrupt instruction restores the previous context values, allowing the main program to return to exactly the same point before it was interrupted. The main difference in a context switch is that the interrupt return routine does not replace the context with the same values, but with those of the next task in the list. More advanced versions of RTOS use schedulers that allocate run times in a rather more sophisticated way by using *thread priority* schemes. This allows some tasks to get more attention than others. The time slices can be allocated on a fixed or variable time basis. Advanced RTOS systems can also detect whether a task is ready to start, or is standing idle (it may be waiting for an I/O operation to occur) and skip passing control to the task altogether on this round (as it would not be doing anything).

Switching can also be induced by the thread, rather than by the RTOS interrupts (the earlier versions of the Windows operating system worked this way). Non-pre-emptive multitasking occurs when a task relinquishes control voluntarily. Pre-emptive multitasking is the situation where the RTOS, not the task, decides when to switch.

In summary, tasks can be in a suspended state (not running), ready-to-run (not held by some I/O operation), running (normal operation) and blocking (waiting for an event). In a more dynamic environment, tasks can also be created or destroyed. That is, the total number of tasks at any one time can go up and down. Special functions in the RTOS are used to create tasks dynamically by allocating and de-allocating context memory areas using stack space.

Some common rules apply to task writing. For example, it is bad practice for one task to terminate or to destroy another. Tasks should ideally terminate themselves. Termination of a task involves the destruction of all its allocated dynamic memory space, and its entry in the RTOS service list. It is important to realize that task switching can occur in the middle of a high level statement. For example, in the C language, the simple assignment $a = c+b$ will be compiled as between 6 and 20 assembler instructions. A context switch may just happen in between any of these.

Semaphores and events

Sometimes, tasks need to pass information or communicate with each other. Tasks may also need to know the status of other tasks, for example, whether another task has started or finished an operation. Communicating between tasks can be a major headache for novice programmers. It may not be obvious to them why such complex mechanisms are required. After all, functions are only accessing the same old memory locations, so why the fuss? This can be even more annoying for designers of embedded systems, where all resources are there, plain to see, common to all, just waiting to be accessed directly. Unlike normal programs, multitasking programs have a degree of time uncertainty in respect of their behaviour and operations, and how they relate in time to one another. It is not very good practice for one task to access into the scope of another, for example, for one task to reference variables stored in another task's memory area. There is no guarantee that the second task may be in the middle of changing the variable. Worse still, the second task may have been deleted, and addressing its memory space may cause an illegal operation, causing the program to crash or abort with a fatal error.

To cater to this, RTOS provides a number of functions and tools for interthread communications. The most common ones are semaphores, critical sections and events.

Events are situations that arise from an external input, for example, a timer, or resulting from a received message from another task. The simplest event is a time-out. In Figure 2-7, the user function in Task 1 calls the RTOS function os_sleep(), which simply causes the current task to stop executing. Rather than allowing the task to hang at that point, the RTOS switches context to the next task in its list. It also makes an internal note not to return context to this first task until so many milliseconds have elapsed. This is a far more efficient way of implementing a time delay than an ordinary do-nothing delay loop. This is because the RTOS has disabled

```
#run task1
 void job1 ()
 {
  while (1)
  { counter1++;            // perform operation
    os_sleep(10);          // drop out and restart after 10mS
  }
 }

#run_task2
 void job2 ()
 {
  while (1)
  { counter2++;                // perform 2nd operation
    os_wait(lamp,50); // wait for a flag to be set by another task (not shown)
  }                     // including a time out of 50mS
 }
```

Figure 2-7: Examples of program using events

the task for the duration of the timeout, so no CPU time is lost at all. Task 2 in the figure shows another form of the *wait* event. In this case, the RTOS causes the task to stop executing as before, but will not return control until either a 50 ms time-out, or a signal flag or *semaphore* has been set. This 'global' semaphore (a single bit flag in practice) can be set by another task, thus providing a crude but safe method of inter-task communications. In other words, the function in Task 2 blocks until either of two events occurs. The event combination in this case are the timer countdown OR the semaphore 'flag' becoming true. In other words, signals can be imagined as shared bit variables, which can be safely set or tested by tasks without the risk of a clash. Signals can only be manipulated via function calls to the RTOS system. This distinguishes them from ordinary bit variables, which can be manipulated directly by the program or accessed by anybody. Needless to say, while the block operation is taking place, the RTOS will ensure very little CPU time is lost in the wait. Without events, tasks would need to wait in tight program loops sensing common bit flags until the other tasks change their values, again, a very inefficient way to write code. Events are time-efficient operations because thread switching is optimized for these activities. Together with semaphores, events are an effective way of handling multitask control and communications, consuming little or no CPU time in the process.

Semaphores and signals are mainly used to coordinate tasks and to synchronize their operation. Semaphores can also be used to control access to common resources such as peripherals. A common form of access control is *mutual exclusion*. This guarantees that only one task can access a given resource at one time. For example, if a semaphore protected function has begun execution, and a context switch takes place to another task that wants to access the same function, the second call will be blocked. When the function serving the first task returns, the blocking will be removed for the second. Critical sections are sections of code that are guaranteed to run without interruptions. A simple case common in embedded systems is when the programmer disables the global interrupt flag whilst a section of code needs to perform an action that cannot be interrupted.

Posting or messaging are alternative forms of sending messages between tasks. The messages (which could be single bits, bytes or even data arrays) are posted or placed in a first-in-first-out (FIFO) queue. The receiving task (there can be more than one receiving task, as in a broadcast) pops messages from the end of the queue, one by one, and in its own time. This form of 'blind' posting ensures there can be no clash if the receiving tasks have been deleted, are inactive, or even are taking a very long time to respond. The downside of this method is that messages can take too long to be delivered. In other words, there is no guarantee of timed delivery. Not all RTOS support messaging. A major user of messaging is Windows; this PC operating system relies heavily on various forms of posting and messaging for internal communications. Timers are used by the RTOS to provide central timing facilities. Timers usually cause interrupts that are used by the RTOS to synchronize all its other operations.

```
int sum (int a, int b)              int d;
{ int c;                            int sum (int a)
  c = a + b;                        { int c;
  return c+1;                         c= a+d;
}                                     return d+1;
                                    }
```

Re-entrant function   Non-re-entrant function

Figure 2-8: Simple examples of re-entrant and non-re-entrant code

A function or subroutine is re-entrant if it can safely be called simultaneously from multiple tasks. A function that uses no variables is the simplest example of re-entrancy as no variables are maintained during its operation. Functions that need to use local variables must allocate them in stack memory. Stack memory is dynamically allocated during program execution. Every time a function is called, memory is allocated. When the function returns, the memory is de-allocated. If a stack generating function is called within another (nested), the 'depth' of this stack increases. If this operation is done too many times, the depth may become too great, and the processor may run out of memory, causing an unpredictable, and difficult to trace crash. This push-pop methodology can be a source of major problems for small microcontrollers, which tend to have fixed, small stack areas.

In high-level languages such as C, local stack variables can be defined specifically by declaring them within the function or procedure brackets. Variables in the stack area are always private to the function that deals with them. Figure 2-8 shows obvious examples of re-entrant and non-re-entrant functions. A word of warning! Some small C compilers do not generate real re-entrant code. Stack variables are allocated in separate static areas of common memory. A function that appears re-entrant may not behave well when called recursively many times. This is not unexpected, many microcomputers do not have real stack facilities, and the overheads of simulating one in software is too much to ask.

Use in network communications software

How is concurrent programming used in networking or communications code? A typical application is in the handling of independent input and output data streams. Any serial data that arrives into a microcomputer system from the outside world is usually placed in a FIFO array or a circular memory buffer. This usually saves the receiver software from having to handle the data immediately as it arrives. Similarly, data to be sent out is placed in an output FIFO. Sections of code that handle streams, deal with buffers, and perform further processing, have to run as concurrent tasks. In the simplest case, these are implemented as simple hardware interrupt handlers. Nonetheless, they are in all respects, separate tasks. The receive and transmit tasks also need to report their status to the main program via safe mechanisms such as semaphores and events as discussed in the previous section. The semaphores link to read and write pointers, so that no data can be written as it is being read. Buffers must be designed safe from overwrite operations. The interrupt handlers could also post results to the main program, to provide a completely asynchronous transfer mechanism. Another use for concurrency is in the handling of multiple users, that is, concurrent communications ports. A good example is a web server. A web server must be able to receive requests from many users, responding to each individually. The server must keep a track of each user, their addresses, their requests, etc. The server must be able to open and close communication channels for each, create a channel (called a *socket* in TCP/IP terminology) for every new user, and terminate or destroy the port connection and the task after their call has terminated. This is an ideal application for dynamically created tasks using a stack.

State Machines

Sometimes it is convenient to think of a software program as a machine going through a number of *states*. Each state is a stable audit in time of a machine's storage values, registers and I/O conditions. In a state machine, only an external influence such as a timer or physical input will make the machine jump into another state. As the machine enters (or leaves) a state, it may perform one or more operations. Computer science people call these systems deterministic finite state automata.

The terminology is varied, but in general terms, a basic *state machine* contains three basic elements: states, events and methods. The current state is just that, that is, the present values of variables that the machine possesses at any one time when it has 'settled down'. The previous state relates to the collection of information stored by the state previous to this one. A first-order system uses registers or latches to store the information from the previous state only. These can be used during the current state to make decisions. Second- and higher-order state machines store information from states previous to the last one. These higher-order state systems are not so relevant to ordinary programs, where most applications can be implemented using simple first-order machines. Among the best-known state machines are the *Mealy* (a type of state machine in which the outputs are a function of the inputs and the current state), and the *Moore* (a state machine in which the present state depends only on its previous input and previous state, and the present output depends only on the present state).

A state can be a static point in a programming flow chart, or the current position of play in a board game such as snakes and ladders. It is usually described with a state name or number. It is usually associated with an array of data (context) that contains all the relevant variables that uniquely describe it. A machine should be able to be restarted at any point by loading its state values from stored memory and pressing the 'continue button'. In other words, a machine's current status can be stored by saving its current state values into permanent storage, which can be recalled later. Events are the external inputs that may cause a machine to make a transition from one state to another. Not all events may generate a state transition, and a state transition may even be back to itself (go to the same state, but with a different context). Typical events are: timeouts, interrupts, user commands or external I/O activities. A *global clock* is a type of event that enforces a regular synchronous operation of the state machine. The machine will only change state during a master clock transition. On the other hand, asynchronous state machines can use any event as a trigger for activating a state change. *Methods* or *actions* are the common name given to the operations performed by the machine as it enters (or leaves) a state. By performing an action, the state machine may also be instigating an operation that causes another event to be generated, maybe at some time later on. For example, a method can initiate a countdown timer, which on arrival at zero, generates a zero-count event.

The state table (also sometimes known as transition table) contains the instruction set for the machine. The example shown here shows a table for a simple machine using a push button that allows a user to run a motor for 1 min, which then switches off automatically (Table 2-1). Only three events are used in this case: (i) the push-button press; (ii) a software counter timeout; and (iii) an external input from an overheat thermostat.

The operation is very simple. Assume that after some initial reset condition, the machine starts at State 0, waiting for some event to take place. When the user presses the push button, the three actions shown in the corresponding box in the state table

Table 2-1: A state table for a simple machine

	State		
Event	**0**	**1**	**2**
Push-button press	Start time-out counter Start motor Set busy light 'on' Goto State 1		
Time out		Set busy light 'off' Stop motor Goto State 0	Warning light 'off' Goto State 0
Overheat thermostat		Warning light 'on' Start time-out counter Goto State 2	

Table 2-2: An improved version of the state table shown in Table 1-1

	State		
Event	0	1	2
Push-button press	Start time-out counter Start motor Set busy light 'on' Goto State 1	Start time-out counter	
Time out		Set busy light 'off' Stop motor Goto State 0	Warning light 'off' Goto State 0
Overheat thermostat		Warning light 'on' Start time-out counter Goto State 2	Start time-out counter

are performed, the machine then moves to State 1. While in State 1, the machine will do nothing until it receives another event, most likely a time-out. This will cause the machine to stop the motor, turn the light off and return to State 0. If for some reason during State 1, the motor overheats, the overheat thermostat event causes the machine to turn the motor off, start the time-out counter, set the warning light on and move to State 2. The machine will rest in this new state until the timer initiated during State 1 times out, causing an event that makes the machine reset back to State 0. This state transition table is quite clear and shows all the options quite clearly. At a glance, it can be seen that, at least for this simplistic application, there are a number of unfinished combinations. What would happen, for example, if the user presses the push button again when the machine is in State 1? On the existing table, nothing is programmed to happen, so nothing will happen. We can improve the table simply by adding further entries (and/or extra states) to cover all contingencies; this is shown in Table 2-2. If the user presses the push button while the motor is on during State 1, the time-out is re-started, and the motor will carry on running until the next (re-started) time-out. Also, if the motor is still overheated when in State 2, the warning lamp will stay on for an extra period of time until the motor cools down. Notice how this was done here by just adding two timer re-start methods to the table.

The above is a rather simple example, but shows the concept quite clearly. State tables are used heavily in the description and implementation of communications protocols. See, for example, RFC 796 describing the TCP connection and disconnection state transition tables (see section on RFC – Obtaining Information on Standards in Chapter 3 for information on RFC documents).

```
if (state == 0)
  { switch (event)
  { case: USER_BUTTON:
    do op...
    break;

    case: TIMEOUT:
    do op...
    break;

    case: OVERHEAT:
    do op.....
    break;
  }
}
```

Figure 2-9: Implementing a state table in software can be tedious

Implementing state tables in software

Implementing a two-dimensional (2D) object such as a state table as a 1D computer listing is not easy and makes for clumsy reading. The standard tools in the C language used for this are nested IF/THEN or SWITCH/CASE statements; Figure 2-9 shows an example. We shall need one of these for every state event combination, and the resultant listing may become very large in size and difficult to follow.

Real-life applications may have a large number of states, and SWITCH/CASE constructs may not be very practical to implement. Some C compilers are not even capable of supporting large numbers of cases within a switch. Some produce very inefficient code. Maintaining this type of verbose code by hand can also be a nightmare. One alternative is to organize the state table as a *script*. That is, as a separate 2D chart or data table, similar in format to the table shown in the state tables above. The software uses an *interpreter* to activate the commands in real time as they are read off the chart. This is, of course, a much more flexible approach as it dispenses with the hard coded switch/case table. It is usually convenient to keep the script in human-readable ASCII form for maintenance. If speed is important, entries can be stored as pointers to functions, making use of the ability of C to call a function whose address is entered as a variable. State tables can thus be stored as a structure of pointers. *Application generators* are platform-based software programs that can be used to generate scripts from plain language descriptions or from graphical inputs (e.g. flowcharts). A graphical interface is used to allow users to drag-and-drop components into the graphic canvas. The generator then produces a compiled script ready to be fed into the embedded system source listings.

State tables and logic gate arrays

State tables are a natural for hardware-based logic gate arrays. Design input methods are far more flexible than those available to ordinary software programmers. In the

```
SUBDESIGN moore
(
  clk   : INPUT;
  reset : INPUT;
  y     : INPUT;
  z     : OUTPUT;
)
VARIABLE
%    current    current %
%    state      output  %
ss: MACHINE OF BITS (z)
WITH STATES (
s0    =    0,
s1    =    1,
s2    =    1,
s3    =    0);
BEGIN
ss.clk   = clk;
ss.reset = reset;

TABLE
%  current   current      next   %
%  state     input        state  %

   ss,       y       =>   ss;

   s0,       0       =>   s0;
   s0,       1       =>   s2;
   s1,       0       =>   s0;
   s1,       1       =>   s2;
   s2,       0       =>   s2;
   s2,       1       =>   s3;
   s3,       0       =>   s3;
   s3,       1       =>   s1;
END TABLE;
END;
```

Figure 2-10: A simple AHDL listing for a Moore state machine

first instance, entries can be input in high level descriptive languages (HDLs) using standard CASE IF structure as described already. There is one crucial difference, however. In a C program, the CASE tests are tested in sequence one after the other. In HDL, all the tests are performed in parallel and at the same time. Some HDL languages include easy to use templates and built in function for entering state tables directly as 2D arrays. This can be done as text entries, or even graphically in graphical user interface (GUI) form using 'drag-and-drop' techniques to draw state boxes and the lines connecting them. Figure 2-10 shows a simple listing for a Moore machine (written in the Altera AHDL language).

High-level Languages and Resource-limited Devices

Any experienced designer who has worked in the C language with microprocessors soon learns the various pitfalls and limitations the compiled code can produce, and the various potentials for code 'tuning' or customization. Although C is meant to be portable, compilers for resource-limited devices can struggle to generate effective code without a bit of help from the programmer. Tuning the code can give some advantages in terms of speed and code space savings. Most commercial compilers will include information and hints on how to do this within their manuals; these sections are certainly worth a detailed read. Different compilers will have different applicable 'features' and the following items may apply in different ways to different products, some may be more relevant than others. Consider the list of tips shown here as a 'checklist' of things to look out for when writing code. Designers will need to deduce their own answers from experience with the particular version of compiler used. A good way to compare results is to generate a listing file after every full compilation and check the final assembly code generated.

- Eight-bit unsigned variables (bytes) are natural to the smaller microprocessor devices, and should be used in preference to 16-bit unsigned variables in arithmetic operations. This may sound obvious but one should watch out for unnecessary code creation when casting from one size to the other.

- For similar reasons, unsigned variables should be used in preference to signed variables. Best to avoid signed arithmetic altogether. Some compilers can produce excessive code when dealing with signed variables, whether 8 or 16 bits. In other words, declare all variables `unsigned char` and `unsigned int`, in preference to their signed form.

- Some processors handle bit variables (Boolean) quite efficiently. For flags and similar uses these in preference to bytes or integers as much as possible.

- Try to minimize the number of arguments passed into function calls. The particular compiler will be quite specific on how many variables it can handle easily. Above these limits, compilers will generate vastly inflated code. Using global memory as arguments increases efficiency but makes code non-re-entrant, and difficult to follow.

- Avoid sophisticated use of pointers. Avoid using them as arguments or returns from functions.

- Functions should return the least amount of information possible, preferably as a single bit or byte. Define a simple error scheme where functions return a single error bit or byte code, with zero meaning no error. Again, the compiler manual will be specific on the best format to use.

- Network protocols make big use of big-endian convention for the handling of multibyte words (where the most significant byte is stored first). Some microprocessor architectures (and compilers!) use little-endian for storage, some others use big-endian. Standard 'portable' network code is littered with conversion functions where the swaps have to be made. Quite a lot of processing time (and program code space) could be saved by hardwiring the code into the natural format used by the compiler or device, and dispensing with the conversion calls. This has the advantages of speed, but can make the code generated non-portable. Do check whether the compiler performs arithmetic in big- or little-endian mode.

- Stack size limits. Many microprocessors are limited in the number of nested calls they allow. Call nesting should be avoided as much as possible, and techniques such as linear 'popin–popout' function calls could be adopted (rather than nested). Avoid creating 'virtual' stacks, either manually, or by the compiler. They can be very inefficient.

- Avoid library functions like `printf()`, they can take a disproportionate amount of extra code.

- Some compilers allocate automatic (stack) variables as if they were static (global) variables. Some analyse the entire function call tree, and are able to overlap uses of the same memory between several automatic variables. This may provide equivalent allocation efficiency that you would get by using a real stack, but still not perfect, watch out! One way to enforce the use of automatic variables is to declare them within limited scope. For example, if there is an automatic variable that is only needed in a few lines of code, enclose the section of code in brackets and allocate the variable inside them. This makes it easier for the compiler to reallocate the memory location used for the variable for another variable in some later block in the same function. Do this in preference of declaring all your automatic variables at the beginning of a function.

- Most compilers allow the declaration of variables into specific areas of RAM space, depending on the microprocessor architecture. For example, the 8051 family has base, indexed and extended memory ranges. It can be wise spending time hand-optimizing the placement of variables and arrays into their optimum regions, depending on access frequency, resulting code size and access times.

- When developing time-critical code, try alternative coding methods, and check the code generated using the list outputs. Do expect some surprises, for example, the construct `if(var)` compiles to a single flag test assembly instruction, whereas the similar looking code `if(var&1)` results in a multiple assembler statement using a full AND of the variable and a constant.

Interfacing Issues

It is attractive to think of hardware and software development as two separate enterprises, handled by two completely different departments in a company.

A programmer in the software department may be expecting all the hardware to be working 'properly' and see it as a 'model' that could be tested locally in a PC-based simulation, whilst the real thing is being put together elsewhere. Not knowing how the real hardware 'works' may be seen as an advantage in some quarters. This follows from the argument that it is only the interface connections and not the underlying architecture that need to be properly understood. With small embedded systems on the other hand, a good knowledge of how the two sides work and interact is paramount for the making of an efficient, cost-effective system. Embedded systems are resource-limited devices, and the last thing we want to do is to impair efficiency and raise costs by the introduction of inflexible and resource-consuming task-splitting methods. Having said that, in an ideal situation we would prefer to encapsulate all 'software to hardware' interfaces into neat little modules. The interface into the hardware becomes a clean 'layer' into which software modules communicates with, neatly and seamlessly. At the very low levels of hardware interfacing, this should not be too difficult, as there are only four main operations that need to be performed. The detailed coding and implementations of these functions will depend on the hardware used, but the overall access methods and entry points should be very much compatible. This gives us the basis for defining a common 'interface' that can be used not only to provide the software designer with a set of common parameters and functions to work with, but also with means of replacing different transmit/receive hardware chipset layouts without affecting the software that drives it. The four basic operations are as follows:

- Transmit data to the remote device.

- Receive data from the remote device.

- Sense the status of the transmit/receive module, including errors.

- Set parameters, including initialization parameters, for the operation of the transmit/receive module.

As communications takes place in both directions, the functions should provide a complete bidirectional interface. From the implementation point of view, each layer drivers would do this by calling functions into each other's domain. In reality, most practical systems are designed one-sided. That is, a 'higher driver' controls the operation of the 'lower driver' by calling functions into it and by polling its various status flags. The relationship is more like a master–slave than a transparent two-way system. Information travels back by means of arguments in called routines, callback functions, message passing and interrupts.

A standard for physical layer interfaces

The Institute of Electrical and Electronics Engineers (IEEE) have been developing standards for interfacing between the various layers of the 802 communications model. One set of standards relates to *service primitives*, which define common methods for communicating between low level layers. One of the aims is to make the function's purpose obvious by just looking at their names and arguments. Service primitives are further described in ISO/IEC 8802-2 1998. The basic primitives are summarized below:

- *Request*: This primitive is passed from one layer to the layer below to request that a service be initiated. For example, a request function to initiate the transfer of a block of transmit data. Parameters may include source address, destination address, size of data to be transmitted, and most importantly, a pointer to the data block. The primitive may also contain some other service information.

- *Indication*: This primitive is passed from the layer below to the layer above to indicate an event has occurred. For example, a call to indicate the arrival of a block of data or the update of a status flag. Again, this can include parameters similar to those described above, including error notification. In practical terms, this can take the form of an interrupt, a callback, a notification via a semaphore, or a posted message. The facility can also be emulated by means of a polled system that reads a common flag at regular intervals to see if data is available for collection.

- *Response*: This primitive is passed from a higher layer to the layer below, and is used to complete a procedure previously invoked by an Indication primitive. For example, a response call to read the data from the just filled receive buffer.

- *Confirm*: This primitive is used as a reply to convey the result of one or more previous Request primitives. For example, a confirm message returning error codes from an action initiated by a previous request.

These primitives are not used only to transfer blocks of data. Other uses include equipment initialization, status reports, setting directories, etc.

Gate Arrays or Microcontrollers?

Gate arrays (GAs) brings the software designer one layer lower into the realms of pure hardware. Suddenly, new concepts such as clock timings, D flip-flops, fan-outs, race conditions and propagation delays have to be understood and brought into play. To confuse things further, all operations will be happening concurrently. Traditional sequential program flows of assembler and C are replaced by hierarchical descriptive and behavioural designs where everything is happening at the same time and controlled by external common master clock pulses.

Hardware designers new to GA designs will find confidence and quickly become conversant with the building blocks these devices work with: logic gates, flip flops, multiplexers, etc. They may be surprised to find out that many of these 'well-known' building blocks are better described as text listings written in language formats not too dissimilar from C. These listings are the various HDLs such as Verilog or VHDL. They allow the designer to describe their task or project using common language statements. There are IF and CASE statement, there are assignments, functions and procedures. Using these tools makes life simple; there is no need to break down the logic into its components, there is no need for Karnaugh maps. A designer simply enters what they want the design to do, rather than listing instructions on how to connect the logic gates together. An optimizing compiler will (with a bit of luck) do all the optimization and gate reductions as necessary for them. Another surprise for the designer is the many forms design input can take: they can input circuits graphically using 'drag-and-drop' techniques (just like drawing a circuit diagram using a CAD package). They could edit a text file using high-level language statements in Verilog or VHDL, as descriptive statements stating how the logic should work, or as behavioural statements describing what they want the module to do. If a design is better specified by a set of timed waveforms, they could open a graphical waveform editor and draw the required waveforms on a timebase scale using simple to use 'drag-and-drop' methods. The resulting synthesized module will behave exactly as intended. Some high-level tools also allow the user to enter state diagrams and transition tables using easy to use graphic editors. To help the designer even further, 'ready-made' library modules can be plugged into the designs. These are simply shown on the screen as 'black boxes' with various inputs and outputs. These black boxes can contain fully fledged operational modules such as adders, multipliers, fast Fourier transforms, communications interface modules, Ethernet interfaces (from 10 to 1000 MHz) and complete CPU cores. The latest GAs can hold four PC compatible power cores in one flat package. This give these devices plenty of raw power and flexibility.

To summarize, the benefits of using GAs are twofold, a saving in components cost as all digital functions are placed under one roof. And secondly, a flexible approach when sheer power and speed are considered. The modularity, of their design and the true concurrency offered enables plain GA designs to be far more efficient in speed terms than their microcontroller counterparts. This is not to say that GAs are a substitute for microprocessor-based systems. Many networking applications are very process heavy, in which case, the use of a program-driven microcontroller will be far more effective than using a GA. In the case of protocol manipulation, many of the computations are better done using a CPU. On the other hand, many networking designs involve the simple push through of data packets from input to output, with some streamlined processing, which can be implemented in-line and very efficiently using GA technology. A practical option is a mixed design. That is, a GA with a built in CPU core, or a GA connected to an external microprocessor as a peripheral. The fast dedicated logic performs all the time sensitive operations, whereas the CPU performs all the process intensive functions. In the GA world, the product range and terminology can be bewildering, here is a short summary of the techniques and products available:

- *PLD or programmable logic devices*: These are devices made of a number of unconnected building blocks. Each block usually consists of a D flip-flop and a number of multiple input OR and AND gates wired to the D inputs. The modules are connected to the outside world and to each other via a cross-matrix of connections controlled by fusible links. The fusible links are either field erasable or one time programmable only. By fusing different connection paths in the cross-matrix, the modules can be connected to each other in a number of standard ways, for example, shift registers, counters or logic look up tables. Devices with up to 20 flip-flops are generally known as PALs, GALs or PLDs. Devices with more than this are generally known as CPLDs (complex PLDs). CPLD software is easy to understand, and design/compile times are short. However, power consumption is relatively high, and the number of flip-flops per encapsulation is quite limited, a few hundred maximum. On-chip delays can be quite short, and it is relatively easy to predict the performance of even a complex design. With their wide fan-in, these devices implement encoded state machines nicely.

- *FPGA or field programmable GAs*: These are similar to the above but their basic building block is far more flexible. Most GAs provide for a number of different types of basic building blocks: customized for such things as counters, arithmetic, RAM memory etc. Most GAs do not use a permanent fusible link form of programming but the interconnections are stored in RAM storage. These 'programs' have to be loaded on initialization during power on, usually from a small flash PROM device attached as a peripheral. GAs cover a wide range in complexity, from 1000 to 100 000 gates, and are rapidly increasing. The devices can be reconfigured to an unlimited number of times, which offers exciting possibilities in reconfigurable logic or reconfigurable computing. Logic functions are implemented in small look-up tables, with predictable speed and time delay performances. The devices usually have about one flip-flop for every 10 or 12 gates. Power consumption is speed dependent and entirely dynamic (as opposed to PLDs where it tends to have a heavy static load). The software is more complex and takes longer to compile, and the user must pay attention to the delays in the interconnect structure. Xilinx is the pioneer and the biggest player, followed by Altera, Lattice and Atmel.

- *ASICs or application specific integrated circuits*: This describes integrated circuits that are made specifically (customized) for an application. Some ASICs require the whole chip to be designed from scratch, some manufacturers provide a road map of geographically spaced ready-made devices, such as basic gates and registers, into which the designer simply provide the final point to point wiring.

- *RISC or reduced instruction set processors*: A microprocessor with a simplified, but otherwise complete instruction set. Instructions are generally designed to be hardware efficient and usually take one clock cycle each. RISC processors can be very fast, and have the advantage that can be easily implemented as part of a gate arrays cores as a sub-module.

- *ARM*: A trade name for a specific brand of RISC processor. The ARM is essentially a 32-bit processor, but it has a set of 16-bit instructions (thumb set); 32-bit memories are more power hungry than 16-bit memories. So, designers can have a mix of 16-bit FLASH and 32-bit RAM memory in their product, and run as much as possible out of the 16-bit, using the 32-bit for timing critical sections.

3

Protocols and Communications Models

To many of us, protocols present images of thick incomprehensible documents and never-ending committees. An idea that may start in very simple form may be presented to a panel of experts for consideration. They will debate and discuss options and alternatives, no matter how obscure and improbable, and pages and pages of comments, recommendations and addenda will result. It all ends up as a thousand page plus set of manuscripts, in a language assured to baffle layman and expert alike. On the other hand, this kind of work is necessary, if only to avoid confusion and arguments. Most of the workings of a committee are there to ensure that each concept proposed is studied and analysed in detail, that they are described and specified accurately, and that any options or variations of usage are fully covered.

Not all protocols have such strict origins. The Internet protocols, one of the most popular communication protocol in existence, was not devised within the confines of a committee, but by an ad hoc collection of academics, private users and government organizations working in a loose networked fashion. Proposals and modifications to the basic schemes could be put forward by anybody who wanted to contribute, and the system grew in an organic form from the start. Some people argue that this is one of the main reasons why Internet protocols have become so resilient and effective.

What is a Protocol?

A communications protocol is a set of rules that must be obeyed by all users in a computer network. This is a very grand definition, but it is also very dry. It does not tell us very much. What do protocols exactly do? Why do we need them? Also, what is not a protocol? Some of these questions have already been discussed in general terms in previous chapters, but this may still leave many questions unanswered. Why are there so many protocols? Why are they so complicated? Does it all sounds a bit like walnuts and sledgehammers?

To gain some insight into why or how we should be using protocols, we must know a little about them, or at least gain a mental image of what they are trying to achieve. Transferring data? At what level? Just bytes? The contents of a file? Other information? A working understanding of the terminology used is also very useful. It is not essential to know exactly what each or every term means (very few people do). A common factor of all new technologies is that the terminology is never 100% understood. Different people will give different names to the same things, and many will use terms without knowing exactly what they mean. This was mentioned before when referring to programming techniques, and it still applies to network communications terms. As long as the underlying concepts are understood, this is all that matters. Having put that aside, we can start with the basics. A data communications protocol deals with the *rules* for the transmission of data between two or more points (or *nodes*, as they may also be called). Central to these rules is the concept of *layers*. Protocol layers were conceived in order to divide the duties of a protocol into manageable chunks. Think of the management structure in a company. Communication layers sit on top of each other in a hierarchical fashion. Each of the layers is independent of each other and communicates via well-defined *interfaces*. A layer does not need to know what is going on inside any of the other layers, only of its interfaces. If this does not make too much sense now, do not worry, it will be explained in more detail later on.

One of the main consequences resulting from this multiple-layer system is that software and system developers can concentrate on writing software for a specific layer. All they are given is a set of interfaces (function calls in software terms) to provide all the communications to the layers above and below. To be more specific, their job is to ensure that all arguments passed in the interface function calls are responded to in the way defined in the protocol standards. One of the drawbacks of this neat layer scheme is that software modules may end up bloated with more interface code that actual functional code. Another drawback is inflexibility, and there are always the exceptions. Take the analogy of a railway system: a train driver's job is to transport passengers using a train. He is not concerned who they are or what they do. The job of the train itself is to rotate the wheels for as long as it has fuel. It does not mind who is driving it or where it is going. In practice, things are never so simple. Passengers must be allowed to apply the emergency brake directly, bypassing the driver's 'protocol layer'. Similarly, communications protocols are not 100% perfect, and overlaps are common. This is not to say that the layer principle is not a valid one. Layering simplifies the design of communications systems, making them more resilient and predictable.

This book is mainly about networks and embedded systems. One characteristic of embedded systems is that the dividing line between hardware and software is very thin, and that most, if not all aspects of the internal operation are directly visible to the designer. Another characteristic is limited resources. It may seem pointless to devise interfaces that consume scarce resources purely for the benefit of satisfying some universal standard. On the other hand, too much interlayer optimization may result in unmanageable program code. One of the jobs of protocol design is to optimize this isolation and separation. The embedded designer must ensure that when attempting to implement a particular protocol design, they are not clogging the device with irrelevant or unnecessary protection type software. The starting point is to understand how the layers operate.

Protocol Layer Models

In the early days of computing, designers realized that adding networking capabilities to a mainframe (the only type of computer available at the time) was never easy. One thing was to write a program for a computer where every piece and component was inside the machine and 'visible' to the programmer, and another was to program software for foreign devices such as line printers, scanners, card readers and others that could be remote, switched off, under somebody else's control or otherwise 'unfriendly'. Worse still, these devices were connected using cabling that would occasionally generate data errors, be disconnected, or even plugged into the wrong machines.

Early attempts included the definition of universal communication standards. These worked mainly over low-speed half or full duplex modem connections, and were in the main, designed to handle only specific types of peripherals (card readers, line printers, tape drivers). These managed obvious problems such as error protection, addressing and identification of peripherals. They worked reasonable well and could be used on phone or leased lines over long distances. Most computer programs at the time were run in batch mode (one job at a time), so problems such as concurrency and peripheral sharing were not of much concern. As computers, peripherals and data lines became more advanced, more sophisticated methods of accessing the terminals (and other computers) became necessary.

The Standard OSI Layer Model

The International Organization for Standardization (Open Systems Interconnect or OSI) proposed in 1984 their reference model as a guide for defining a set of communications protocols without any particular implementation in mind. The OSI standards were formulated in a generic way deliberately to avoid proprietary implementations or to submit to vendor's requirements. Although direct interest in the original strict OSI model has declined, the basic concept remains. OSI is the most common yardstick or standard for describing and comparing the many protocols now in existence.

Figure 3-1 shows the basic model. The stacked blocks represent the layers. A network designer can build a protocol stack by creating, designing or purchasing

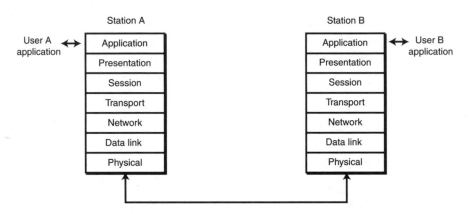

Figure 3-1: The seven-layer OSI model

individual layers and stacking them just like digital building bricks. The layering scheme allows individual layers to be changed or replaced transparently and seamlessly. For example, the physical layer could be changed from Ethernet to fibre or token ring, without the need for updates in any of the other layers.

When two users (or applications) communicate over an OSI-based network, messages wind their way through both stacks, down the first, and up the second. Application data enters at the top of the first stack, travels downwards, then across the physical medium to the other machine and back up the second stack, arriving at the destination user in the correct recovered format, just as it was originally sent. As information passes through each layer, extra information is added to the message. This is checked and removed by the corresponding layer at the other end. This extra information can contain addressing, error management, flow control, etc. The protocol thus defines a reliable transmission *pipe* between the two applications. The pipe and method of transmission are completely transparent to the underlying technology used.

Most practical networks systems do not conform in an exact one-to-one way to the OSI standards. However, they will relate indirectly to OSI standard in such as way as to maintain overall integrity, for example, some systems integrate their data link and physical link layers into one. Similarly, the data link layer may be further divided into more sub-layers. Some networks have layers that straddle two or more OSI layers. The higher layers are the more difficult to standardise. The OSI model has well-defined lower layers, and many of the standards relating to the top three to four OSI layer definitions are still to be finalised. Most of the current protocols only relate to the lower three to four layers of the OSI model, for example, the IEEE 802 series of protocols only relates to the lower two layers of the OSI model. The description of each of the layers is provided in the following sections.

Physical link layer

The physical link layer relates to the physical method used to transmit the information. Namely, the cable, fibre optics, infrared or radio system. The responsibility of the physical layer is the transmission and reception of raw bit data across the medium. That is, to send bits and to receive bits. The parameters specified in the protocol formats will include the electrical, mechanical and signal characteristics of the interface. The OSI physical layer does not, strictly speaking, describe the medium itself. In other words, the physical layer specifications describe how data are encoded into the media, the signal voltages on the line, and the characteristics of the media attachments and connections, but not the media themselves. In practice, however, the media is closely linked to the layer technology. We are all used to the fact that optical fibres tend to use infrared light, and that standard Ethernet tends to use copper wires. In general, the medium is either *wired* (as in cables), or *wireless* (as in radio or light).

Data distribution on a shared network is very simple. A sending node transmits a sequence of data (sometimes known as a *frame*) by enabling or triggering the physical network layer hardware driver to place the data onto the medium. In other words, put volts into the line. As the medium is generally shared, all other nodes connected to the same medium will receive the frame transmitted. They will read the frame into local storage, examine the destination address and pass it on to their higher layer. Dedicated hardware interfaces, such as Ethernet interface chips, exist that can perform some of these operations more or less automatically and in real time. Some other 'advanced' operations may also be performed directly and at the same time by the line driver hardware. A receiver may compare addresses and compute received checksums ignoring frames with errors. A transmitter may also delay or hold back transmission if the line is busy. The device is performing tasks that are conceptually the responsibility of the next higher layers up. This may sound confusing as one is expecting the hardware interface chip to be performing hardware layer interfacing functions only.

Data link layer

The end points that communicate over a network are called nodes, stations or devices. The data link layer is responsible for providing node-to-node communications over a single, local network. That is, to handle the control and flow of data between one node and the next. The definition of a local network is important. This is a network where all the nodes are more or less known to each other during a communication session and are within a small geographical distance from each other. Any node should know exactly how to address a message frame in order for it to reach its destination. The data link layer performs two basic functions: (i) *addressing*, where signals are only accepted by nodes or stations that have been assigned correct identifiers or addresses; and (ii) *translation*, where data size and bit format operations are performed to convert messages arriving from the upper layer echelons into formats the physical layer can understand (and vice versa). Most practical protocol implementations will send data in fixed length blocks and not continuously. A common task for the data link layer is to re-format messages into packets or frames. Frames consist of blocks of data that contain a *payload* (the user data passed down from the upper layer), plus extra data fields containing information such as addresses for both the sender and the destination, command codes to notify which protocol or parameter is being conveyed, and error checksums, which may be used by the receiver to determine whether the received frame has arrived without any errors. It is not the job of the data link layer to provide for any serious form of error management, that is, to guarantee a reliable link. This is a job for the higher layers.

In embedded systems, data link layer functions are handled by dedicated integrated circuits or modules such as Ethernet controller chips or 802 compatible radio 'black boxes'. These are the hardest facilities to implement from scratch as they involve fast logic and analog handling techniques, so it is fortunate that ready made components can just be bought in. Some additional supporting software is also required to initialise and interface to these devices, but most of the work will be done by the hardware.

Network layer

Simple networking applications (with simple needs) may implement a protocol using the physical and data link layers only. The simple addressing schemes provided by these two layers are clear and concise enough for managing the nodes and handling data in a simple dedicated local application. Once the network becomes larger, it will need to be enhanced, perhaps by sub-dividing into smaller networks or sections. A sub-divided network may consist of local networks connected together via equipment called routers, switches, gateways or bridges. The individual local networks do not need to be of the same type, and can be completely different in shape and size. One can use Ethernet, the other token ring, etc. Sub-dividing networks is common in places where the local geography makes it impractical to group all the nodes together, or where different network technologies need to coexist. One building may operate a local network using Ethernet where the building across the road will operate another local network using a different technology. The link between the two is via a single high-speed line with a router or switch at each end. The simple messaging system of the data link layer does not cater for internetwork communications, as its localised addressing system used has no global meaning. All sender and destinations are aware of each other in a non-routable way. In other words, routing information is not present.

How does node A knows whether node B is within its own local network or is at a remote location accessible only via a router? The network layer adds a further level of global addressing known as a *network address*. This is done in practice by adding further data fields to the transmitted frame. These frames now contain a sender's network address, a destination network address and few more fields of use to routers, as well as all the data fields used by the data link layer. These frames are sometimes known as packets or datagrams. The extra global network addresses will coexist with the original local data link layer addresses. This apparent duplication of addresses is not redundant, in a large network they will correspond to interim (hop) stations on the way, with the IP address ponting at the final destination. There are now two types of nodes in a network and they will be performing two different tasks: (i) *end nodes* are the standard station or device nodes as described earlier; and (ii) *routers* are nodes that have the specific task of assessing and forwarding packets received to other routers. Routers are intelligent devices that maintain tables of addresses, both local and those of remote networks, and are able to decide whether a packet arriving should be ignored (as it belongs to a local network) or routed, as it may belong to another local network. If all this sounds somewhat confusing or irrelevant, just substitute the words 'IP address' for 'network address'.

In embedded systems, network layer facilities are usually implemented in software within the microcontroller. Some services will require more support than others. This will be covered in more detail later on.

Transport layer

This layer is responsible for:

- *Fragmentation*: All physical network technologies have their own data size limits. These are usually bound by the technology used, the characteristics of the medium and various other factors, and are usually fixed. For example, Ethernet has a frame length limit of about 1500 bytes, whereas some optical devices only a few hundred bytes. Fragmentation and defragmentation are the tasks of re-assembling short length received frames into one long frame and vice versa. For example, a 64-kilobyte packet can be fragmented into about 43 1.5-kilobyte frames for transmission over an Ethernet link. In general, fragmentation converts N frames of length A into M frames of length B.

- *Frame ordering*: One side effect of fragmentation is re-ordering. Frames or packets cannot be expected to arrive in the same logical order, as they could have taken several different routes around the world to reach their destination. Frames could also be repeated. Some means are necessary to ignore repeated frames and to re-order frames arriving out of sequence. Fields within transmitted fragmented packet contain pointers to where the data block sits in reference to the full data array.

- *Access point*: A workstation PC may be running simultaneous processes when communicating with another computer. For example, transferring files, browsing the web and retrieving email, all from a single remote host or ISP.

The transport layer provides mechanisms for a process within the PC to open a channel or pipe between itself and a similar process on the remote host. This allows more than one channels to be open between computers with similar addresses. These channels are known as *service access points* (also known as *ports* in TCP/IP parlance). The technique used for separating the information arriving in parallel from many sources is called *multiplexing* and *de-multiplexing*.

- *Quality of service*: Under this heading, the transport layer can provide a number of alternative or optional services. These services come under the combinations of: (a) *Unreliable delivery* (where the payload is delivered without concern for errors). This does not mean that no error checking has been performed. Some of the lower layers may have performed some checksum filtering already. It just means that there is no guarantee that the payload arriving has no errors; (b) *Reliable delivery* (where a notification is handed up that a payload was received). This does not necessarily imply that there is a payload to be delivered without errors. It could be a simple notification to the upper layers that a payload was received, but that it had errors (the upper layers would decide what to do in this case).

The transport layer includes its extra information by adding extra fields to the data link frames. The extra fields will contain access point addresses (port addresses), fragmentation information, block ordering information, and maybe some form of local error protection and error acknowledgement fields. Typical examples are TCP and UDP. Unreliable delivery packets are usually known as datagrams.

Assuming that reliable delivery is always preferable to unreliable delivery is a common mistake. Unreliable delivery is preferable in many cases: for example, where the network is fairly reliable itself, and when messages are self-contained and self-correcting (as in the case of plain text messages for human consumption). A typical embedded system implementation will only be using one or two of the many services available in this layer. Some of these such as TCP, can make heavy demands on the system's resources.

Session layer

This layer is responsible for the establishment of a framework or *dialog* between the two nodes. This implies an organized and synchronized exchange of data is taking place between the two machines. A dialog is a formal conversation in which the two nodes agree to exchange data. In general, communications can take place in one of three ways: (i) *simplex*, where one node transmits, the other receives; (ii) *half-duplex*, where only one node can transmit at any one time; and (iii) *full-duplex*, where both nodes can transmit and receive simultaneously. A *session* is a period of time in which formal communications take place between two nodes. A full session usually has three phases:

- *Connection establishment*: Usually, one node starts by trying to establish contact with the other. It sends the other some information to which the other replies. The nodes then negotiate rules of communications (data formats, character sets) by exchanging formatted packets of data containing specific commands.

- *Data transfer*: The nodes exchange data in simplex, full-duplex or half-duplex mode, using the agreed character sets.

- *Connection release*: When the nodes no longer need to communicate, they engage in an organized disconnection sequence. Steps one and three are optional in some types of transfer.

The session layer relies on two types of connections being established by the lower layers:

- *Connectionless*: The sender node simply transmits its data assuming the receiver will get it somehow. There is no connection establishment or connection release. Data packets are just sent. This is based on the concept of a holiday postcard, you pop it in the postbox, you do not know what happens to it afterwards. UDP is an example of a protocol using a connectionless, unreliable delivery mechanism.

- *Connection-oriented*: Establishing a tied connection has some advantages. At least it guarantees that a remote node is present, and that any data transmitted will reach its destination unchanged. For this reason, connection-oriented links normally use the reliable delivery mechanisms of the transport layer. TCP is an example of a protocol using a connection-oriented, reliable delivery mechanism.

Presentation layer

The presentation layer is responsible for presenting the data to the application layer. This may include some form of format or character translation. This guarantees a common representation of the data while in transit. For example, all character sets used in the application layer could be converted to ASCII strings with escape sequences. The layer is also responsible for data encryption/decryption and for compression and decompression. Methods at each end agree before a communication on a common scheme for transmission. In many practical implementations, lower layers may implement one or more of the functions that might be associated with the presentation layer.

Application layer

This layer presents the user with access to the communications environment, which may includes data transfer, electronic mail, access to facilities such as user directories, remote job execution, remote file access and network management functions. Common software interfaces have been developed to allow programmers to access the services the network provides via function calls, for example, Berkeley Sockets and Windows Sockets. Many embedded system software vendors offer network protocol interfaces roughly comparable to those of Winsock.

The OSI Model and the Internet

The fast growth of the Internet has meant that TCP/IP based stacks have become more popular than the original OSI model. The Internet set of protocols dates back to ARPANET days and were developed before OSI standardization. For this and other reasons, they do not fit neatly with each other. The Internet model is based around four levels instead of seven. These are shown in Figure 3-2 together with their approximate correspondence with their OSI model counterparts.

Why should there be a difference in the models and what is the significance? The OSI model was created by a committee of some of the best minds in networking and took over 6 years to come to fruition. Even today, there is still argument whether the model should be seven or eight layers. Internet on the other hand, was born of necessity, and developed by a large number of people working very loosely together. In other words, the small details and slack ends of the OSI model were rearranged into a model that was tried, tested and rearranged into a workable and practical solution. This does not mean that the Internet protocols are perfect, quite the opposite, there is quite a lot of redundancy and overlap. Some of the information fields in the transmitted packets are rarely if ever used, and some others are not large enough to address current needs. The four Internet layers are described in the following sections.

Network access layer

This layer is roughly equivalent to the OSI physical and data link layers combined (described previously in this chapter). The network layer is responsible for

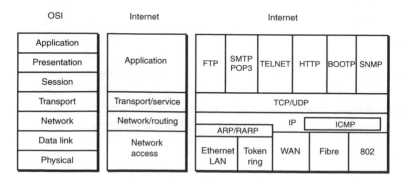

Figure 3-2: Internet layers compared with the OSI model

exchanging data between a host and the network, and for delivering data between two devices or nodes on the same network. In practice, this involves a combination of access methods defined by various other standards. These include Ethernet, IEEE 802, asynchronous transfer mode (ATM), Frame Relay, etc. The local addressing and error management methods may be different for the different technologies used. However, all components communicating within a single local network are intercompatible at their layer interface end.

Network or routing layer

This layer is also known as the *Internet layer*. The layer roughly corresponds to the OSI network layer, and is responsible for routing messages between different local networks. Devices responsible for routing messages between networks are called *gateways* or *routers* in TCP/IP terminology. The main protocol at this layer is the Internet protocol (IP). The IP frame format includes data fields for checksums and network addressing, also known as IP addresses, similar to those defined in the OSI network layer. IP addresses are crucial to the protocol. They are used throughout the Internet to identify every single node in the world connected to it. The IP protocol also includes data fields for fragmentation and block re-ordering. These roughly correspond to those defined in the OSI transport layer. It is the job of the network layer software driver to provide for means of fragmenting and re-ordering packets. However, many upper layer protocols rely on short packets only, and rarely if ever, have a need for fragmentation. Fragmentation is also inefficient in terms of transmission overheads and costs. Most system designers will prefer not to use fragmentation if they can avoid it. IP is described in RFC 791 (see final section of this chapter on how to get access to RFC documents).

Other supporting protocols are also available at this layer level. These include the address resolution protocol (ARP) and the reverse address resolution protocol (RARP). These are used by nodes to match corresponding physical addresses to their allocated IP addresses. ARP is usually related to the physical network access layer, but in practice straddles both layers, as it has to know about physical addresses and IP addresses. ARP is described in RFC 826, and RARP in RFC 903. Another protocol available in this layer is the Internet control message protocol (ICMP). This provides for some network management and maintenance functions, among these is the 'ping' function used by nodes to query the properties of other nodes in the network. ICMP is described in RFC 792.

Host-to-Host or transport or service layer

This is broadly equivalent to the transport layer in the OSI model. This layer is responsible for providing end-to-end data integrity. Two types of services are provided: a connection-oriented reliable-delivery protocol called transmission control protocol (TCP) and a connectionless, unreliable-delivery service called user datagram protocol (UDP). These service combinations are mentioned in the OSI transport and session layers. TCP is described in RFC 793, and UDP in RFC 768.

TCP provides an application with an error-free, flow-controlled and sequenced data stream between two points in the network. This is done by the opening of a virtual connection between the two stations. This connection is opened before the transaction, and closed at the end. UDP provides a connectionless environment, where packets, known as datagrams, are sent as individual blocks of information, without checking.

Application layer

This is responsible for providing the application with access to the communication environment, and therefore to other users or machines via a number of services or 'tools'. This layer spans the three upper tiers of the OSI model: session, presentation and application. The various protocols included here are: file transfer protocol (FTP), simple mail transfer protocol (SMTP), TELNET for simple terminal emulation, simple network management protocol (SNMP), network file systems (NFS) and hypertext transfer protocol (HTTP). These functions do not span a single layer of the OSI model, but cover functions and facilities in all three. FTP, for example, enables hosts to maintain a session (session layer), agree on a data representation (presentation layer) and operate a network file system (application layer). Some of these protocols will be described in more detail in Chapter 8.

The IEEE 802 Model

In February 1980, the IEEE created the 802 Networks Standards Committee to operate as a major working group in local area networks. Their remit was to create, maintain and encourage the use of generic networking standards. The series of standards developed by the committee are known as 802.X. They are also known as ISO 8802. The number 802 simply relates to the second month of year 80, the standard way of defining IEEE committees. All of the current 802 Standards are obtainable from the IEEE web site www.ieee.org, although not all standards have been finalized. The work of the 802 group is organized into sub-committees, designated as 802.X sub-committees. where the 'X' corresponds to one of many project numbers. Some of these sub-committees define standards, others serve as an advisory function.

The IEEE 802 model relates only to the two lowest layers of the OSI model, the physical and data link layers. However, it does not exactly match the OSI model. The IEEE 802 architecture defines three layers that are roughly equivalent to the OSI data link layer: These are named logical link control (LLC), the optional bridging and the medium access control (MAC) layers. Figure 3-3 shows the standard classifications and the relationship between IEEE 802 and OSI.

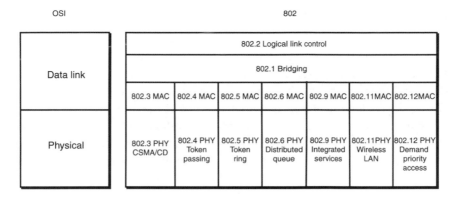

Figure 3-3: IEEE 802 compared to the OSI model

The logical link control layer (LLC-802.2)

This layer describes methods for establishing link services between a number of ports or nodes, and is common to all the physical implementations. The layer provides a number of services:

- unacknowledged connectionless service,

- acknowledged connection-oriented service,

- acknowledged connectionless service.

In a similar way to the OSI terminology, a *connectionless* service is where data is sent out without establishing a connection first. An *acknowledged* service is where reception of a transmission is acknowledged by a local feedback mechanism (usually by the transmission of another frame in the opposite direction). The need for local acknowledgment is more relevant in the case of wireless networking (radio or optical), as wired networks are reliable enough not to necessitate local forms of acknowledgment. LLC also defines the use of logical interface points, called service access points (SAP) that other computers can use to transfer information from the LLC layer to the upper OSI layers. Note that these services are also mentioned in the OSI transport and session layers. IEEE 802 provides for simple forms of acknowledgment and session control at the lower levels, but it accepts that they may be duplicated at the higher layers. The LLC layer is common to all implementations of IEEE 802, thus making it easier to replace a wired node with say a wireless node within the same local network.

Bridging layer

This is an optional layer that covers routing, bridging and internet work communications. This is an intermediate layer not always present in small implementations. This is fully described in IEEE 802.1.

The media access control layer

This roughly corresponds to the lower half of the OSI data link layer. It provides shared access for multiple devices within the physical layer. It is responsible for the generation and reception of frames, validation of data integrity via checksums, addressing and other functions that control access to the network itself. MAC is not defined in a single document, but is defined as part of the document describing the underlying physical structure. In other words, every document discussing a particular technology also discusses its own method of MAC implementation. In order to ensure compatibility between the different MAC implementation, a set of standard layer interfaces have been designed at the software function level.

The physical layer (PHY)

This describes each specific hardware implementation, its operation and its methods for managing the medium. Different media may be used within the same standard; for example, IEEE 802.11 describes wireless local area networks using radio systems at different frequencies, and using different modulation methods, and also equivalent methods using infrared optical technology.

RFC – Obtaining Information on Standards

The principal source for obtaining information on any of the protocols relating to Internet is via request for comments (RFC) documents. RFCs are published by the Internet community, with each RFC allocated a unique ascending number on acceptance. RFCs can be submitted literally by anybody who has something relevant to say about the Internet. In general, the higher the number, the later the distribution date. Reviews and updates on a given topic are common. For this reason, information on a subject may be covered by more than one RFC. There may be also be later RFCs that define better or more updated specifications for an earlier RFC. There will also be related RFCs that describe subsidiary operations or related functions. When searching information on a topic, ensure you do a thorough search of the RFC database to make sure you are using the latest information. RFCs may be obtained via e-mail or FTP from many RFC repositories. A typical address for a given RFC (say 821) is http://www.isi.edu/in-notes/rfc821.txt

The quickest way to obtain an RFC is by just entering its full number, that is, 'RFC 796' in any on-line search engine. To find out which RFC is relevant to a topic, enter RFC in the keyword field followed by any relevant keywords, for example, 'RFC CHAPS'. RFC documents are both available in plain text (.TXT files) and PDF formats. Always try to download the PDF versions as they are easier to read.

4

Network Physical Layer Technologies

The best place to start is at the beginning. And nothing better than starting with the hardware, the underlying infrastructure of all networking. Knowledge of hardware topics is relevant to all embedded designers, even to those not directly involved in hardware design, or where their work is apparently 'software only'. Understanding how the hardware ticks will give any designer a major advantage at the low-level design stages. Even if the reader is not an expert or has little knowledge of hardware issues, the information given here may be of some use to them.

This chapter covers the basic technologies involved in local networking, and how they relate to embedded systems. In other words, this is a straightforward engineering-level description of the physical components used in networking: phones, cell-phones, local area network connections and radio. Some of the sections describe the internals of hardware interface chips and components used to interface to networks. How they work and how they can be linked to microprocessors (including some hardware and software examples). It is not essential for the reader to have a basic understanding of these topics. At the same time, very detailed technical information is avoided to save clutter. More information will be found in the references indicated.

Technologies such as Bluetooth and IrDA are not covered because they are not strictly networking components by themselves but point-to-point solutions (which could form part of a larger networking system).

Introduction

We saw in Chapter 3 how the physical layer is accountable for the transmission of the raw bit data across the medium itself. The layer's job is simply to transmit and receive data. It does not matter whether this transmission occurs in digital or analog form, as long as the bits received are converted back to their original computer readable form at the receiving end. The work of designing interfaces is much simplified nowadays. Many IC manufacturers offer full network interface systems as single IC devices, which only require a few extra analogue components (such as transformer or coils) to provide isolation to the medium. Others can be directly connected to the line either electrically or via optical mechanical assemblies. Many provide the full, or a subset of the operational functional requirements of the corresponding protocol layer they were designed to implement. It will not be possible to list here all the devices currently available. Firstly, because of the large number of new devices that regularly appear on the market (which obsolete existing versions). Secondly, because many of these are rather similar in nature. Description of one generic family component will be enough to provide an indication of what the other devices can do. Readers wanting to obtain further details of a particular device or component should search the Internet looking for data sheets, application notes and implementation articles. Knowing which keywords to use in search engines is always of great help. The correct choosing of a keyword to maximize hits and minimize irrelevant returns is an art by itself. There are many facilities, such as AND–OR combinations and the negate form (the minus sign), that can be used very effectively in keyword entries to narrow a search. When searching for technical topics, for example, it is useful to include extra keywords such as 'circuit' or 'diagram' as well as the main keyword we want to filter out commercial only or summary web pages on the topic (it is assumed that the information we want will have the word 'circuit' in it somewhere!).

Networks technologies are roughly divided into *wide area* or *local area* roughly depending on the geographical distance that separates the nodes or whether third party technology is used to provide the underlying circuit that connects them. These are covered separately here.

Wide Area Networks

The term wide area network (WAN) generally refers to networks that are distributed over a wide geographical area, in other words: different building, towns, cities or countries. WANs are often constructed by linking or interconnecting individual local area networks (LANs) via bridges or routers using point-to-point public links such as phone lines, radio, optical fibre or other types of circuits. These connecting circuits and the operators that run them have the generic name of carriers. As far as individual users are concerned, there should be no distinction between a node or terminal being next door or many kilometers away. Other users and machines should be accessible in a fully transparent way, using the same interface methods, with no apparent difference between the connections. The only distinction may be perhaps, a minor delay taken for the signal to get across.

Various technologies can be involved in a WAN link. These can be analog, digital, optical, packet switching or circuit switching. The sophistication of the technologies can also range from the most modern to the most antique. A WAN technology most relevant to embedded systems is the public telephone network. In other words, ordinary telephones.

PSTN, POTS and modems

We use telephones to communicate with friends and colleagues. This very useful network is often referred to as the public switched telephone network (PSTN) or sometimes plain old telephone system (POTS). PSTN uses a combination of twisted pair lines, fibre optics and coaxial lines to connect subscribers together via central telephone exchanges. The network technology used in PSTN is known as a circuit switched network, where a connection is established between two fixed locations by the action of one station dialing the other, and where every end user station has a unique telephone number. During the time of this connection, many items of cabling and terminal plant equipment become dedicated to the connection and will not be available to other users. The connection is maintained until one or the other party terminates the call, at which point all equipment involved in the connection is released and made available to other users. The voice quality of PSTN connections varies substantially from location to location and from call to call. Voice fidelity and noise performance is affected by the age of the system, the exchange technology used, and the quality and length of the physical cabling (copper wire) used. The PSTN was originally designed to support voice-only communications where bandwidth and phase delays were rather flexible and irrelevant for voice grade connections. A guarantee of quality was only limited to the 300–3400 Hz band, with frequency dependent differential group delays of up to 1 ms common. Fortunately, the ear is rather insensitive to these imperfections, and the perceived call quality was relatively unaffected. In a typical call, a signal would pass through many mechanical switches, relays and amplifiers. All of these would generate cross-talk and interference. The quality of the call could also change by the second, with click noise and gaussian 'hiss' added to the signal in various grades.

Sending data down one of these circuits was always a hit and miss affair. A common way to improve the reliability and quality of the phone connection was to lease a dedicated line between the two end points. This usually involved the engineers at the telephone company dedicating plant equipment to the connection for the duration of the lease (which could take several months or years). Dedicated lines would be hand-tuned by the engineers to perform to a minimum guaranteed standard of service both in terms of reliability and signal quality. Different telephone companies would provide these extra services at different levels of quality (and price).

Telephone handsets are not connected directly to each other but via central telephone exchanges, also known as switches (Figure 4-1). Many businesses have many phones in the office, these are usually connected to a small unit within the premises. These small units function just like the larger telephone exchanges and are known as private branch exchanges (PBXs), or also PABX (A is for automatic). PSTN connections can

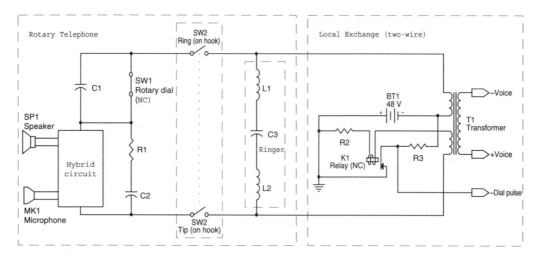

Figure 4-1: Telephone system circuit diagram

use either two- or four-wire circuits. In four-wire circuits, each pair is used to transmit the voice in one direction. In a two-wire circuit, voice is carried in both directions, and separated at each end by a balanced hybrid circuit. The purpose of the hybrid is to cancel out the analog voice signal coming from one direction and allow through the signal coming in from the other direction. Some PABXs use more than two wires to connect to a phone on an office desk. These extra wires are used to send non-standard signals to the telephone unit and switches. These can drive LEDs, sense push button switches and drive other indicators. These telephone systems are known as key and lamp units. Modern PABX use completely digital connections resulting in fewer wires between the handsets and the exchange by using time multiplexing between voice and control circuits.

Dialing is the process by which a connection is established between two parties. The dialing procedure is a simple form of a handshake. One party makes a request, and the other party acknowledges the request, either positively or negatively. When the handset is taken out of its cradle, the phone is said to be off-hook. This action closes an electrical loop on the two-wire line all the way back to the exchange, causing current (known as loop current) to flow. This change in DC current is sensed at the exchange, which transmits back to the user in response a dial-tone. This is a combination of two 350 and 440 Hz tones giving it its characteristic well-known sound. This indicates the user they can dial. The process of taking a line off-hook to ask for a dial tone is called seizing the line. This method of seizing the line is known as loop-start. An alternative method of seizing the line is known as ground-start, where seizing is effected by grounding one of the two conductors in the two wire loop to ground or common earth. Dialing can now take place. There are two fundamentally different ways of dialing a number: tone dialing and the now nearly

Table 4-1: Representation of digits by two frequencies

Code	Low Frequency	High Frequency
1	697	1209
2	697	1336
3	697	1477
4	770	1209
5	770	1336
6	770	1477
7	852	1209
8	852	1336
9	852	1477
*	941	1209
0	941	1336
#	941	1477
A	697	1633
B	770	1633
C	852	1633
D	941	1633

obsolete pulse dialing (as found in old rotary dial phones). Tone dialing uses 12 combinations of tones to represent the digits 0–9, plus the star and hash symbols. Each digit is represented by the transmission of two frequencies at the same time, and for a short period (under a quarter of a second); see Table 4-1. This universal method is known as dual tone multifrequency (DTMF) dialing. DTMF codes are also used for transmitting small amounts of digital information during a conversation (e.g. in voice-automated banking systems). It is also commonly used by alarm systems, remote monitoring and call centres.

When the exchange receives the first DTMF digit, it removes the dialing tone off the line, and starts assembling the number to be dialed in a local buffer. When enough digits are received, the exchange then proceeds to connect to the remote location. This may take the signal through one or more intermediate switches, depending on availability and how busy the network is (many of the circuits will be occupied by other calls in progress). The actual path taken by a connection may be different each time the call is made. After dialing is completed, the calling party (which could be a piece of automatic equipment making a call) will listen on the handset for a response. Call progress signals are mostly tones, which indicate the status of the connection at a particular time. Ringing tones indicate that ring voltage is being applied at the remote telephone. Busy tones indicate that the remote cannot take the call, either because it is busy, or the connection cannot be established by the exchange. In some exchanges, busy tones can vary in pitch and duration to denote whether the problem is remote or local. Various other multifrequency (MF) tones and signals are also used between the exchanges for housekeeping and other uses. These tones are not usually passed on the end parties at either end, who will not nominally hear them.

When the called party answers the phone, the loop current detection will be detected by the remote exchange and passed back to the caller's party exchange. This will now remove all tones from the line and establish a direct voice communication between the two parties. From now on, and until disconnection, all plant (cabling and switches) used for this call by the exchange will be dedicated to the connection. At the end of the conversation, the caller party will replace the phone back onto the handset (on-hook). This is detected by the exchange, which will notify the remote exchange to drop the connection and release all resources associated with the call. Many older exchanges have difficulties in detecting when the remote party replaces their phone on-hook before the caller does. There are no standard ways for the caller to reliably know when the called has gone on-hook. Some exchanges provide a small change in loop current level. Others may provide a short tone. Most terminal equipment has to rely on the resulting silence on the line.

Receiving a call works in a similar way. When the phone is on-hook (i.e. on the cradle), the loop circuit is diverted to the bell via a capacitor (a modern phone will emulate this using digital logic). The phone looks like a high DC resistance to the exchange, so it can know whether it is on-hook or not. When the call arrives at the exchange, it places a large AC ringing voltage on the called party line; this will make the bell ring (Figure 4-2). When the user answers the phone, the circuit is closed

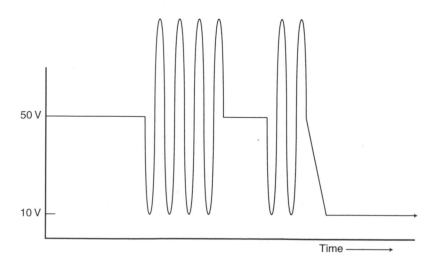

Figure 4-2: Voltage on a telephone line

(or looped). The exchange detects this, removes the ringing voltage and then connects the called to the caller via the speech analog circuit.

Computer interfacing to phones

Direct interfacing to the telephone system is not easy. In fact, it is not legal in many countries. The main reason for this is safety. Connecting 'not approved' equipment to the telephone network could cause electrical power loops that may damage the equipment, cause signal overloads and in the worst case, cause electric shocks to engineers working on the system at the exchange. All equipment connected to the PSTN must meet strict standards in terms of safety and electrical operability. Some manufactures supply encapsulated direct access (DAA) modules. These potted units are based on transformers or opto-isolators and will have been designed to provide the right electrical isolation from the phone network. Using these modules does not assume that the equipment designed is free from approval requirements. Designs still need approval and common sense and care in the design of tracking for PCB layouts and connectors. Using such a module, an embedded system could easily connect to the telephone network. This would allow a microprocessor to dial out, answer calls and provide for simple communication with remote systems using simple DTMF tones (or even synthesized speech). Even the smaller of modern microprocessors are sophisticated enough to generate DTMF tones purely in software (perhaps with the aid of a pulse width modulation counter). DTMF software detection is possible but it is more reliable in practice to use external DTMF detector chips. Examples of these are the Holtek HT-9170, and the MITEL or CLARE M-8870. These are quite cheap, and only require a low-cost TV type 3.58 MHz crystal to operate.

Next in the evolutionary ladder are modems. These include all the facilities of a DAA access, but also have the facility for encoding and transmitting data down the line at much faster rates. Modems are devices that convert a digital stream of data into tones and signalling pulses that can be carried over the PSTN. This signal encoding method is called modulation. Most modems also include facilities for dialing out and answering calls. They connect directly to the phone circuit, and replace a normal telephone. Early modems used two separate tones or frequencies to denote '1' and '0' digital states. The tones were designed to fit neatly within the available 300–3400 Hz voice bandwidth. These modems were very slow by modern standards, but very resilient to the noise, amplitude and phase variations that were encountered during a typical connect session. Later on, modems started to include fixed or dynamically adjustable programmable delay filters. These filters were used to automatically compensate for propagation characteristics. Some modems required the filters to be hand tuned before a session. Others included built-in microcomputers that performed real-time algorithms that modified the filter taps continuously during a session.

As networks became more reliable and predictable, mutlilevel multiphase modulation methods started to be used. These novel modulation methods increased throughput

Table 4-2: Currently available modem speeds

Standard	Speed (bps)	Year Introduced
V22	2400	1984
V32	9600	1984
V32b	14 400	1991
V32c	19 200	1993
VFC	28 800	1994
V34	28 800	1994
V42	57 600	1995

speed manifold. The International Telecommunications Union (ITU) has been defining standards known as the V series to define modem speeds. In general, speeds have been slowly increasing over the years, to the extent that the theoretical data carrying capacity of a standard PSTN connection has more or less been reached by now. Table 4-2 shows the speeds currently available.

Modern modems also incorporate some form of data compression in their transmission to achieve higher speeds. One of the most common compression standards used is Microcom's MNP class 5 compression. When both modems use MNP5, data transmission speed can effectively double on the average. The V42b format uses hardware data compression as standard.

The extra facilities used for establishing a connection (through standard dialing) and for terminating a connection can be remotely controlled by a computer attached to the modem via a RS-232 standard serial connection. Modems are sometimes described as Hayes compatible. This relates to the modem originally developed by the Hayes Company in the 1980s which used commands sent via the same serial port used for data communications. Special code sequences were used to separate them from normal data and to control modem operations. As modems have become so standard, it is now common to assume the physical layer as not just the PSTN connection, but also the modem, which includes the now common AT command set. The interface to the physical layer becomes a serial cable terminated in an RS-232 or equivalent connection. Miniature modems are available in encapsulated form only a few centimetres across. These can be easily incorporated within an embedded system's PCB footprint. Their interface to the outside world is via a serial interface operating at logic levels obeying AT style commands.

Digital voice networks

The integrated services digital network (ISDN) was developed in the 1980s to replace the analog telephone system. Although deployment has not been as widespread as expected ISDN has found niche areas in specific business areas such as printing and publishing. The basic ISDN specification defines a 64 kbps digital link that can be used for data or voice. This is about two to four times the speed offered by modern analog PSTN modems, which is not an overwhelming improvement. The future of ISDN will depend on its cost compatibility with PSTN and with newer technologies such as ADSL. Interfacing to ISDN requires a special unit containing a line driver, serial to parallel converters and 8-bit A/D and D/A converters. Voice is usually transmitted as 8-bit digital data at 8000 samples per second. This is obtained from the original analog signal by a simple logarithmic level compression known as u-Law (in the United States), or A-Law (in Europe) this is also known as G711. A typical ISDN line will run at 144 or 192 kbps, and contain two bearer (B) voice/data channels at 64 kbps each, plus a data (D) control channel used for dialing and other control information. Various higher speed, multiplexed combinations of 64 kbps lines are available. These include T1 (1.544 Mbps, 23 + 1 channels) or E1 (30 + 2) channels. A T3 line is made up of 28 T1 lines (672 channels) and supports a data rate of 44.736 Mbps.

Cell-phones

The cell-phone network comprises a collection of individual networks all linked together. Public or private companies also known as carriers operate the transmitters, switches and connection to the PSTN and other networks. Many hand-held cell-phones have built-in serial interfaces, and are able to be used like standard data modem. The interfaces use the common Hayes AT command set. This is enhanced by the addition of specific commands for cell-phone communications, such as sending short message system (SMS) messages. All enhanced messages start with the character string 'AT + C'. A number of these commands have recently been adopted by the mobile phone industry as 'standard' and are defined in GSM07.07 and GSM07.05 of the GSM specifications (control of mobile phones over a serial interface). The physical interface nominally uses RS-232 signal levels, but may also accept TTL levels (some cell-phones can also use infrared links). There are about 55 extra AT type commands in all. Extra facilities include access to some of the phone's internal facilities, phone books, fast call, SMS messaging, changing ring tones and speaker volume. A cell-phone with a RS-232 link effectively allows the remote terminal or PC take over control of the phone for all data aspects, no need to use the phone's keypad. In addition to the standard AT commands, some manufactures have defined extra commands. The Siemens 35 serials, for example, uses the prefix 'AT^S' to precede their vendor-specific set of commands.

DCE–DTE – wiring up a modem interface

The standards used for connecting a terminal to a modem are popularly called the 'RS-232 interface'. There is a lot of ad hoc terminology associated with RS-232, which when used out of context, tends to confuse people. The standards were originally designed many years ago to interface a terminal or visual display unit (VDU) to a modem, which in turn communicates with a remote modem connected perhaps to a mainframe. The data itself is transmitted as a serial stream of bytes, with one wire used for transmission, another for reception. A number of extra control and status wires were also defined in order to aid the connection. The purpose of these is mainly to check whether the modem and terminals at either end are present and ready to operate. Nowadays most systems operate with only three lines (data plus ground), however, many still require some of the control lines to be set, or connected to, specific levels or control connections at the other end.

A flying knowledge of the traditional interface specifications will help in unravelling the intricacies of a pin out specification that has to be met, or when designing an RS-232 interface to other equipment. The traditional description goes as follows: The local user terminal is known as the data terminal equipment (DTE). The modem is known as the data circuit equipment (DCE), as shown in Figure 4-3. The remote modem is the remote DCE, and the remote mainframe is the remote DTE. Even though the original standard defines a 25-wire connection, only eight lines are commonly used, hence the relatively recent use of 9-pin DIN connectors. Nominally, a male connector is used at the DTE end, and a female connector at the DCE end. A PC is considered a 'terminal' and therefore a DTE. Hence, the serial port D type

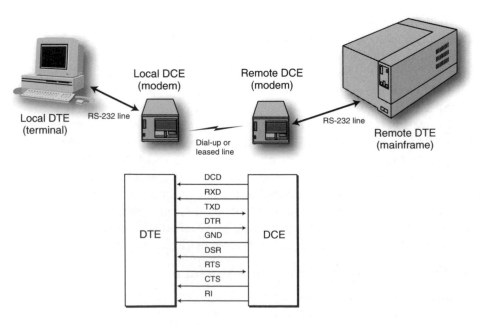

Figure 4-3: DCE–DTE interface

connector on the back of a PC is always a male connector. The defined signals and their descriptions are as follows (pin descriptions are for a 9-way/25-way D-type):

DTR (data terminal ready) (DTE to DCE) pin 4/20: The DTR line is generally ON when the terminal is ready to establish a connection. A terminal will turn DTE ON before it wants to use the modem, and OFF when it has finished using the modem, say after terminating a call. A terminal may also leave DTR ON when not using the modem in order to allow the modem to receive calls. In other words, the DTE line is used as an 'enable' line for the modem.

DCD (data carrier detect) (DCE to DTE) pin 1/8: When this line is OFF locally, the modem indicates to the terminal that the remote modem has not taken control of the line. That is, the remote has not placed a carrier (tone) on the line. When the remote modem places a carrier on the line, the local modem will set its DCD line ON. In other words, the DCD line tells the terminal that there is a carrier on the line generated by the remote modem.

RXD (receive data) (DCE to DTE) pin 2/3: Received serial data appears on this line. As the DTE is the receiver, the definition of 'receiving' is always assumed to take place from DCE to DTE.

TXD (transmit data) (DTE to DCE) pin 3/2: The DTE sends serial data to the modem using this line. The DTE is the transmitter, so the definition of 'transmitting' is always assumed to take place from DTE to DCE.

DSR (data set ready) (DCE to DTE) pin 6/6: A modem will switch its DSR line ON when it is ready to receive commands and data. A terminal must wait for DSR to be set before setting any control lines or sending data to the modem.

RTS (request to send) (DTE to DCE) 7/4: When a terminal is ready to transmit data, it switches the RTS line ON. This indicates to the local modem that it is ready to transmit data. The RTS line is sometimes used to control the direction of data transmission in a half-duplex connection. The modem uses the RTS line as an indicator of when to place a carrier on the line. In most full-duplex modems, this line is usually left ON all the time.

CTS (clear to send) (DCE to DTE) 8/5: When CTS is ON, the local modem is ready to receive data from its DTE and the local modem has control over the telephone lines for data transmission.

RI (ring indicator) (DCE to DTE) 9/22: When the modem receives a telephone call, the RI line switches ON. This line may switch alternatively in an ON/OFF pattern corresponding with the received ringing cadences. This informs the terminal that a telephone call is coming in.

GND (ground) pin 5/7: This is the local signal ground. Do not confuse this with the protective ground (pin 1 on the 25-way connector, no equivalent on the 9-pin connector). Protective ground is connected to the metal cabinet and should not be used for signal purposes.

The general sequence of events is described in the specifications as follows:

- The local DTE switches DTR ON. The user, either manually or via AT compatible sequences, sets up the modem and dials up the phone number of the remote station.

- If DTR at the remote location is ON, the remote modem's RI turns ON, indicating to the remote DTE that a call is being received.

- The remote modem answers the call, and sends line tones to the local modem via the phone line. Upon detection of these tones, the local modem accepts there is a modem at the other end. The two modems will start a negotiation sequence to define parameters such as speed, etc. When a connection has been agreed, both modems will set their DSR line ON.

- On receipt of the DSR signal, the local DTE switches its RTS ON. This indicates that it is ready to send data. This signal is passed on to the remote modem's DCD circuit.

- The local modem switches CTS ON, indicating to the local DTE that it can transmit data.

- The local DTE sends data through its TXD line.

- The remote modem receives data through its RXD line.

- When data transmission is finished, the local DTE drops RTS, which causes DCD to drop at the remote modem, and eventually CTS at the local modem. Transmission of data can now start in the other direction in a half-duplex system, or transmission of data can be discontinued by hanging up the phone line, by the DTE dropping its DTR line, or by disconnecting the physical circuit between the two modems.

- All lines will now go to the OFF state. The system is ready to start communications all over again.

Modern modems do not always generate the control signals in the same format or order as described above. This is because the standards were developed mainly for modems with separate dialing, or for leased line, half-duplex operation. Modern modems do not really need a full set of control lines and can happily operate with AT command style signalling on the data lines only. At most, a modem may expect the terminal to supply an ON condition on the RTS and DTR lines for the duration of a session. The terminal can also ignored the feedback supplied by the DCD/CTS/DSR circuits, which can be used otherwise for line status information. All control is normally carried out via serial command codes over the RXD and TXD lines. The full nine-wire connection (also known as a 9WT cable) is not always required with a modem. Most modems can operate with a three-wire link (TXD, RXD and GND, also known as 3WT), with or without the control lines hardwired back to outputs to provide steady state conditions.

A modem to terminal (DCE to DTE) cable is usually wired as a one to one (i.e. pin 1 to pin 1, pin 2 to pin 2 and so on for the nine pins in the nine-way D-type connector). To connect two DTEs together, you will need to use a cable where the pins have been swapped around. This is known as a NULL modem cable. The connections are shown in Table 4-3.

The electrical standards for RS-232 define a logic '1' (or ON condition) to be represented by a positive voltage somewhere between $+3$ and $+25$ V, and a logic '0' (or OFF condition) by a negative voltage somewhere between -3 and -25 V (see Section title 'Line drivers and receivers – transmission standards). The RS-232 standard is popular for simple transmission of data with microcontrollers and embedded systems. One of the disadvantages is the difficulty of generation of these levels from single rail power supplies. Many IC devices are available off-the-shelf that can perform this task (e.g. MAXIMs MAX232 family), but their cost and other may tempt the designer to cut corners and use simpler methods. Most UART devices in microcontrollers use logic 1 to denote the OFF condition and logic 0 to denote the ON condition. Converting from RS-232 to TTL or CMOS logic levels require not only a voltage level shift, but also an inversion of the signal. A simple CMOS inverter could be used to drive a RS-232 input at short distances. Most RS-232 commercial interface receivers do not require a negative input, and can accept quite happily a zero voltage as an OFF condition (a series $100\ \Omega$ resistor should be added for safety). A similar argument applies when going the other way. Figure 4-4 shows a very simple interface circuit.

Full modems are also available as encapsulated modules, in which case the computer interface is directly at TTL levels. Some of these can include a lot of extra

Table 4-3: Connections via a NULL modem cable

9-way	25-way	Cable	25-way	9-way
3	2	TXD	3	2
2	3	RXD	2	3
7	4	RTS	5	8
8	5	CTS	4	7
6	6 + 8	DSR	20	4
5	7	GND	7	5
4	20	DTR	6 + 8	6

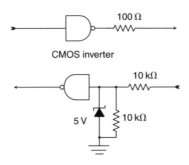

Figure 4-4: Simple RS-232 local interface

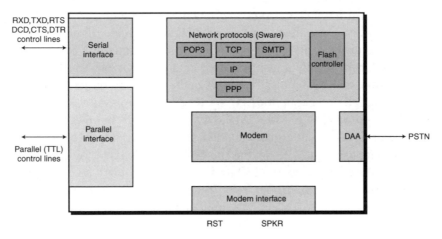

Figure 4-5: Cermetek module incorporating modem, micro interface plus TCP/IP stack

functionality. Figure 4-5 shows the Cermetek 'iNET' series module, which incorporates not only a modem, but also a microcontroller plus complete TCP/IP stack. The module can be controlled by means of high-level commands from another microcontroller, or directly via I/O pins. For example, the grounding of one pin can instigate the module to send an e-mail to another user via the connected dial-up line. For more information, see www.cermetek.com.

The AT command set

The AT command set allows a modem to be fully controlled from the serial line. Most modems have an autospeed sense facility. This allows the terminal to communicate with the modem at any speed, without having to set any parameters or jumpers on the software or within the modem. Autospeed works by the modem sensing the first few serial characters sent, and measuring the average width of incoming data zero crossings. The modem operates in two basic configurations: *control* (where AT

Table 4-4: Common AT commands

AT command	Description
ATDT123456	Seize the line and tone dial the given number
ATH0	Hang up the phone (go on-hook)
ATH1	Lift the handset (go off-hook)
ATVn	Display results as digits ($n = 0$) or as text ($n = 1$)
ATSnm	Set register n to value m
ATS$n = $?	Query contents of register n
ATIn	Report modem information, e.g. $n = 7$ model and make
ATZ	Reset the modem to default settings

commands cause the modem to perform special functions) and *data* (where all data sent to the modem is transmitted transparently to the line). Special command sequences are used to jump from one mode to the other. A particular difficult sequence is the one to move from transparent data mode to control mode (the *escape sequence*). This is because the sequence has to be one that is not used in normal data transmission. In practice, the default used is a combination of a 1 s time delay followed by three plus symbols ($+++$) followed by another 1 s delay is used. All AT commands are sent as text characters terminated in a carriage return. The modem will usually reply to each command with an error number or with a verbose message. For more information on AT codes, enter the keyword 'AT command set' in any Internet search engine. The most common AT commands are given in Table 4-4.

Local Area Network Technologies

A local area network (LAN) is defined as a simple set of connected stations using similar technology and geographically close to each other. A LAN may or may not have a connection to the outside world or to another LAN. Some LAN technologies were developed as far back as the 1960s, purely from the necessity of connecting mainframes to each other and to their peripherals. There have been many LAN technologies developed since then. The most commonly used today are Ethernet, token ring and their 802 variants, with wireless technologies also becoming popular.

Some basic networking concepts

Networking is a subject rich in specialist terminology. Most communications in a network follow a *client–server model*. A device, whether a computer or peripheral (e.g. a video terminal) is a client when it accesses resources provided by another computer, which is then known as the server. Depending on application, computers can be both clients and servers. Peripherals, such as printers or plotter are usually client only. However, a dedicated embedded system providing data logging functions, for example, can be acting as a server. In some environments, such as small offices or the home, computers can act both as clients or servers without real distinction, for example, when sharing files or documents between various users in an office. This type of network is sometimes known as an ad hoc or peer-to-peer network.

The cable, wiring or fibre used to connect the computers together is generally referred to as the *network medium*. To access a network, all computers must contain a network interface card (NIC) also known as a *network adapter*. This translates the serial voltages on the line to the parallel digital bytes and words understood by the computer or peripheral. In order to identify each user or computer, each station needs to have assigned a unique address known as a hardware or MAC address. A low-level unique address is usually hardwired by the manufacturer into each NIC in existence.

The physical medium is shared, therefore each device must obey a certain set of rules to know when to take control of the line, and how to respond to signals received. These collections of rules are known as protocols as discussed in previous chapters. A wired network is where all stations are physically connected together, either directly or via central units known as hubs. A wireless network is one where there is no proprietary physical connection between the stations. This can be either via radio, infrared or even some third party provided medium such as power lines.

Wired technologies

Wired connections are by far the most common. The main media in use are coaxial cable, twisted pairs and fibre optics. For each of these, specific network technologies or specifications have been designed. The medium must have properties that will ensure a reasonable error performance for a guaranteed distance and rate of date delivery (i.e. speed). It must also support two-way or multiway communications.

Fibre optics systems use mainly infrared light for data transmission. At each end, fast opto-couplers and diodes are used to translate the signal to electrical levels. Most fibre-based systems can only transmit one way, so a pair of fibres are required to implement a two way system. Hubs are also required at each junction as fibre systems can only operate point-to-point. Fibres are used mainly in areas where high speed, security and/or electrical isolation are important.

Coaxial cable systems were very popular in the early days of networking, mainly because it made use of cheap and commonly available 75 or 50 Ω coaxial cable, nominally used for video and radio frequency applications. In a coaxial system, nodes are connected together via a single backbone, that is, the cable is laid out as a single line, passing through all stations, this is also known as *bus topology*. A resistive 75 (or 50) Ω terminator R is placed at each end of the cable to absorb all reflections. The nodes act on receive as high impedance signal pickoffs, and on transmission, as current drives into the (resistive) line. To all extents, this line looks to all the devices connected just like a purely resistive load of $R/2$ Ω; such a known load resistance allows the transmitters to use simple current generators to inject a fixed amount of current into the line. The voltage generated on the line is of the order of half a volt for a typical Ethernet network, this allows receivers to use dynamically adjustable thresholds sensors to determine zero crossings, and also to detect voltage overloads caused when two or more station transmitters are attempting to drive the line together. This provides a simple form of collision detection. To avoid ground loops, the coaxial cable shield connection is grounded at only one point; network adapters must therefore incorporate isolation hardware to float all the power supplies and other circuits directly connected to the cable, adding somewhat to their cost.

Twisted pair (TP) systems are more recent. The most basic for TP cable consists of one or more pairs of insulated strands of copper wire twisted around one another. The twisting is necessary to minimize electromagnetic radiation and resist external interference. It also helps to limit interference with other adjacent twisted pairs (cross-talk). In theory, the more twists per metre a cable has, the better the isolation. However, this increases the capacitance per meter, which can result in increased load requirement and an increase in high frequency attenuation. There are two main types of twisted pair cables, unshielded twisted pair (UTP), and shielded twisted pair (STP), which contains each pair of wires within an aluminium foil shield for further isolation. The impedance of a typical twisted pair is of the order of 100–150 Ω. Lines are fed in voltage differential mode; a positive signal level is fed to one wire, and a corresponding negative, or inverted signal to the other. This makes the total radiation field around the pair cancel to zero. TPs can be used in bus topologies, as described before, or star topologies, where each computer or terminal is connected by a single cable to a central hub. The signal sent from one station is received by the hub and redirected to all the other stations on the star network.

Driving the wire

A major parameter in line characteristics is its impedance. Impedance is a function of the cable's *inductance per unit length* and its *capacitance per unit length*. These in turn, are a function of the cables physical characteristics and dimensions such as diameter and separation between the conductors. The general formula for impedance is

$$Z = \sqrt{L_0/C_0}$$

where L_0 and C_0 are the distributed inductance and capacitance per unit length. A typical cable may have a distributed inductance of 0.2 μH/ft and distributed capacitance of 20 pf/ft, resulting in a line impedance of about 100 Ω. Line impedance can be calculated directly from the physical shape and dimensions of the cable. This is a function of the logarithm of the ratio of distance between pairs to the diameter of the conductors. Because the ratio is logarithmic, small discrepancies in the physical characteristics of the line will have little impact on the impedance. Another major line parameter is transmission or propagation delay. Signals in transmission lines do not travel at the speed of light, but somewhat slower. The time delay for a line section of length L is given by

$$T = M \sqrt{L_0 \cdot C_0}$$

where M is the length of the cable in feet, and L_0 and C_0 are the inductance and capacitance per unit length as previously defined. A typical twisted pair may present a delay of 1.5 ns/ft, which roughly corresponds to 60% of the speed of light. A special case occurs in a multi drop system where many receivers are hanging off one transmission line at regular intervals. The high resistance of the receivers may not contribute much to the line impedance, but their input capacitances will. If we assume for simplicity that the extra capacitors are evenly distributed along the line, the extra capacitance (per unit length) has the aggregate effect of reducing the nominal line impedance by 10–20%. It is common practice in multidrop systems to use lower than normal terminating resistors to compensate. The extra added capacitance also has the effect of increasing propagation delay.

The behaviour of transmission lines when fed from discrete data sources may require some clarification. A line driver will 'see' the transmission line at low frequencies (or at DC) simply as a piece of wire. If we take low-frequency measurements with test equipment, we shall see the capacitance of the cable, the DC resistance of the wire, and the load resistance connected at the remote end. The line will just look like a capacitor and a resistor in parallel. At high frequencies, however, the behaviour changes drastically. A line driver feeding fast rise time pulses into the line will 'see' it as a pure resistance of $Z \, \Omega$ (the line impedance). The distributed capacitance is magically cancelled by the distributed inductance, and the line appears purely resistive. A single, short pulse, generated by a data transmitter device will travel, more or less unchanged in shape down the line, at a speed related to the transmission delay of the line. At even higher frequencies, cable losses come into effect, and the signal begins to be lost in radiation rather than propagated to the far end. As digital signals are composed of square edged pulses, which contain multiple frequency components, the net result is that the remote end will receive a low pass filtered version of the signal generated at the source. *Pre-emphasis* is a technique where the high-frequency components of the signal are amplified more than the lower frequency ones just before transmission. This compensates for length-dependent cable losses and results in a sharper signal being received at the detector. Pre-emphasis can also be applied at the receiver end by adding passive filters before the detector.

When a pulse arrives at the far end of a transmission line, one of a number of things can happen. If the line is terminated with a resistor of value Z (the same as the impedance of the line), the pulse will be dissipated in the resistor, and the voltage on the line will drop to zero after the pulse has ended. If the terminating resistor has a different value than Z, the pulse will be reflected and travel back to the source. If the line end is open circuit, the pulse will be reflected back with the same amplitude and polarity. If the line is short circuited, the pulse will be reflected back with the same amplitude but inverted polarity. If the signal generated by the source is a continuous data stream (a normal sequence of ones and zeros), the voltage at any point on the line will be the sum of the stream going in one direction and the delayed stream reflected back. Any receiver detectors on the line may be confused by this aggregation and fail to detect data properly. This is why it is so important to ensure lines are properly terminated.

A number of termination 'options' are commonly used in practical implementations of data networks. External load resistors are said to 'match' the transmitters and receivers to the line. 'Match' is a technically incorrect description as the purpose of the resistors is not necessarily to match the impedance of the line, but to maximize the signal to noise ratio and therefore the performance of the system. This can be achieved by minimizing the effects of reflection at the receiver end only. Most line driver ICs have output resistances (impedances) of nearly 0 Ω, and (relatively) very large input impedances. In Figure 4-6(a), the line is directly driven from a zero impedance source. The load resistor at the receiver will ensure there are no reflections going back to the transmitter so there is no need to include a load resistor at the transmitter end. Figure 4-6(b) shows a multidrop system where load resistors are placed at either end of the cable. The low-impedance transmitter will send waves in both directions, neither of which will be reflected back. So again, there is no need to add a load resistance at each of the transmitters.

Network cabling hardware is now standardized into a small number of options. The popularlty of LANs has meant that manpower experience for cable laying is strong, which lowers installation and running costs. In other words, it makes sense for embedded networks to make use of existing cabling techniques and know-how. The most popular methods of cabling at present is CAT cable, with the most common known as CAT-5 (Table 4-5).

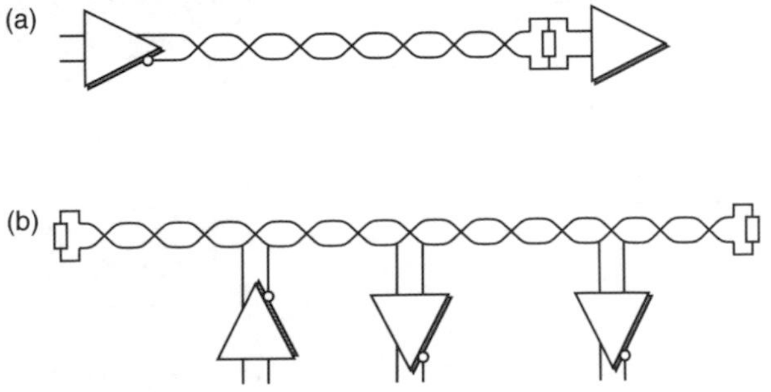

Figure 4-6: Multidrop termination methods

Table 4-5: Typical characteristics of unshielded CAT-5 cable

Wire type	Four pairs – 24 AWG solid or stranded
Line impedance	100 Ω ± 10%
DC resistance	9.4 Ω per 100 m
Capacitance	5.6 nF per 100 m
Propagation delay	5.7 ns/m
Propagation speed	66% of light speed
Attenuation at 20 MHz	9.3 dB per 100 m

Line drivers and receivers – transmission standards

The most common point-to point standard is RS-232, also sometimes referred to as EIA-232. RS-232 is the format used by the communications port on Windows PCs and the TTY port on UNIX systems. Even though most newer PCs do not have RS-232 ports (they are being replaced by USB ports). The standard will still be around for a while. RS-232 is an unbalanced point-to-point unidirectional interface, Figure 4-7 shows the electrical equivalent. This is a resilient standard that relies on its use of relatively high voltage levels to define logic ones and zeros, plus a dead voltage transition band in between the two. The standard also defines rise time and load drive performances to guarantee a performance of up to 20 kbps at up to 50 ft of distance. A logic '1' is represented as a voltage between +3 and +25 V; and A logic '0' between −3 and −25 V. The dead band ensures a certain level of noise immunity.

RS-423 (also known as EIA-423) is similar to RS-232, but features a reduced output voltage swing. This enables it to support higher data rates (up to 100 kbps) and longer distances (up to 4000 ft). The standard specifies an unbalanced driver, and a balanced receiver. RS-423 supports unidirectional, multidrop (up to ten receivers) service. Advantages over RS-232 include multiple receiver operation, faster data rates, and lower power supplies (usually ±5 V). Figure 4-8 shows the electrical equivalent circuit.

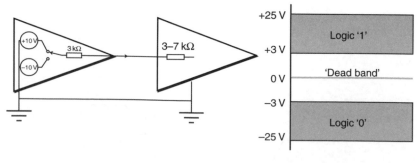

RS-232 receiver thresholds

Figure 4-7: RS-232 equivalent circuit

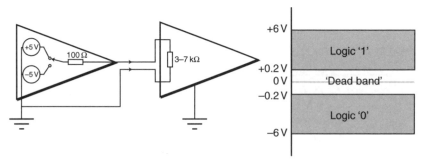

RS-423 receiver thresholds

Figure 4-8: RS-423 equivalent circuit

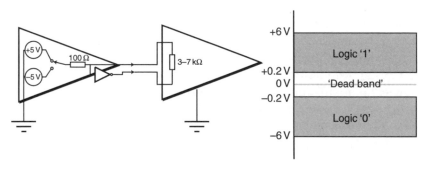

RS-422 receiver thresholds

Figure 4-9: RS-422 equivalent circuit

RS-422 (also known as EIA-422) is a full differential wire version of RS-423. The receiver design is identical to that of RS-423, but the transmitter now generates a full differential signal. The maximum data rate is 10 Mbps, and the maximum distance is 4000 ft. The standard defines a unidirectional, single driver, multiple receiver (up to 10 receivers). Unlike the previous standards, RS-422 requires the lines to be resistor terminated to minimize reflections. In a differential scheme, one wire carries a positive version of the data, whereas the other wire carries a signal of the opposite polarity, this differential arrangement minimizes radiation and interference from external noise interference. Differential links offer a degree of common-mode protection, and they are more insensitive to differences in ground voltages at either end. Figure 4-9 shows the electrical equivalent.

RS-485 (also known as EIA-485) adds the ability to use a single line in both directions. RS-485 provides all the advantages of RS-422 along with supporting multiple driver operation (up to 23 stations). This fact allows for multipoint (party

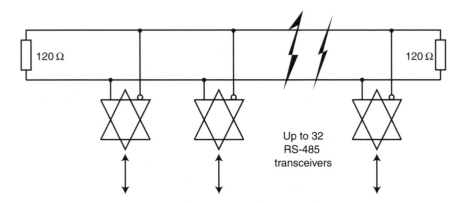

Figure 4-10: RS-485 – typical configuration

line) communications. The maximum rate is 10 Mbps, and the maximum distance is 4000 ft. The signal levels on the line are relatively small (about 200 mV) and offset from ground, so RS-485 IC devices can operate off a single 3.3 or 5 V power rail. To allow line sharing, RS-485 interface transmitters have 'transmit enable' and 'receive enable' signals to turn the transmitter tri-state (i.e. disconnected from the line) when not in use. RS-485 networks, and its variations are commonly used in factory floor networks because of the noise immunity, and ability to connect multiple devices. It is also used as the basis for many advanced standards such as Ethernet, 802, etc. Figure 4-10 shows a typical configuration.

RS-485 is a specific instance of what is generically known as a low voltage differential signalling (LVDS) system. These are characterized by low voltage swings, high throughput, balanced line, multipoint systems. LVDS systems are popular in backplane high-speed bus systems. EIA-644 is one such standard offering speeds of up to 655 Mbps. RS-485 also offers a fail-safe feature. For RS-485 receivers, signal inputs between −200 and +200 mV are undefined. That is, if the differential voltage on the RS-485 line is 0 V, no receivers will be able to determine whether this should be a logic '1' or '0'. This situation usually happens when no transmitters are using the line, and is therefore 'floating'. To ensure a defined output under these conditions, most of today's RS-485 transceivers require failsafe bias resistors. This is implemented by adding a reasonably high value pullup on one line and a corresponding pulldown resistor on the other line. Common values are in the order of 500 Ω to 2.2 kΩ. The trade-off is noise immunity versus current drawn.

Figure 4-11 shows a summary of the current line driver technologies.

Wireless technologies

Wireless systems refer mainly to infrared and radio technologies. However, wireless system may include others where the transmission medium already exists or is shared

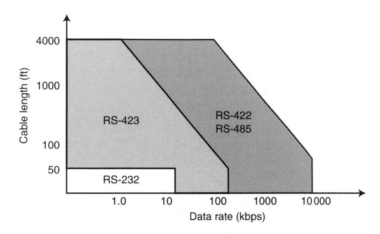

Figure 4-11: Summary of current line driver technologies

with other services such as power lines (mains). Most of the current specifications for wireless networking are covered by the IEEE 802 standards, and more specifically, by the 802.11 wireless LAN standards. A wireless IEEE 802 network consists of one or more fixed stations (or base stations). These will service multiple mobile stations. An important aspect of IEEE 802 is that mobiles can move freely between different fixed station radio ranges, and still be able to maintain a seamless connection. A wireless transceiver cannot listen to the network for other transmissions while it is transmitting. This is because its own transmitter will drown out any other remote signal that may be present. All traffic is therefore half-duplex in nature. Stations avoid collisions by listening before transmission and by using random back-off delays to delay transmission when the network is busy (if some other station is transmitting). This collision avoidance method is known as carrier sense multiple access with collision avoidance (**CSMA/CA**). A two-way handshaking sequence is used between communicating stations (ready and acknowledge packets) to help maintain reliable delivery of messages over the air. This 'local' error management system helps reduce the delays that would be caused if all error were to be handled by the upper protocol layers. There are two primary types of wireless LANs: RF-based and IR-based.

Radio

Allocation of the radio spectrum has been traditionally in the hands of government and other regulatory bodies. The use of radio systems implied obtaining special licences, usually with restrictive specifications on their use, at a price. In exchange, the user is allocated a set of radio channels locally free from interference from other users. Other users would be allocated different frequencies in the same band. During the last few years, many governments around the world decided to allocate sections of the radio spectrum for free unlicensed use. These are for low power systems, with no guarantee or conditions regarding the way they may be used on how they may interfere with each other. In most practical cases, this is not a problem. A local transmitter may operate within the confines of a building, office or home. There is usually enough isolation, in terms of distance, walls, building materials and space to provide enough radio isolation with other users, for example, in the other house down the road. Frequency allocation for RF-based LANs are relatively similar around the world, with some countries allowing more or less of the same band spectrum to be available. In general, the existing industrial, scientific, medical (ISM) band is used for transmission at the following frequency bands:

- 902–928 MHz,
- 2.40–2.4835 GHz,
- 5.725–5.850 GHz.

Data is transmitted using various techniques including spread spectrum technologies called frequency hopping and direct sequence. In frequency hopping, the transmitter hops from frequency to frequency, in a pseudorandom manner every few milliseconds. The direct sequence method involves exclusive-ORing, a pseudorandom bitstream with the data before transmission. The most popular radio networking technology on these bands is IEEE 802.11. The frequencies are shared with other radio-based non-compatible services such as Bluetooth.

Infrared

Nearly all of the optical methods used for networking use infrared (IR) light. Two types of IR-based wireless network methods are used: diffused IR and point-to-point IR. Diffused IR bounces signals off walls, ceiling and floors. The data rate is limited by the multipath effect, whereby multiple signals radiate from a single transmission, each taking a different path to the receiving stations. Point-to-point IR uses line-of-sight IR LEDs or lasers and provides a faster data rate than diffused IR. It can also work over longer distances (up to 1 mile). Devices communicate by shining modulated beams of IR light at each other. This implies that they must be within visual range of each other (a pretty obvious argument). To ensure a level of compatibility between different products, most standards specify minimum and maximum power levels, beam widths, and mechanical arrangements for the optical components to ensure devices have a 'predictable' working range, this is in the order of 1 m or so. A number of IR standards 'methods of communications' exist. They should not be confused with each other, as they can be quite different (and incompatible). Most infrared systems uses 'near'-IR light of wavelengths between 850 and 900 nm. This is the same wavelength range used by TV remote controls, car door openers, remote earphones and night illuminations for CCTV security cameras. The reason for this is simple; light sources and detectors for these wavelengths are cheap and readily available.

IrDA is normally confused with networking. IrDA stands for infrared data association (www.irda.org). This is a standard mainly used for communicating peripherals, PCs and laptops with each other. It is strictly not a networking protocol. IrDA publishes reference documents covering various aspects ranging from the physical aspects of the IR beam, wavelength, power, beam angle, etc. to definitions of the layered protocol structure required to perform its software functions. IrDA is now used in computers, printers, keyboards, digital cameras, security modules, toys and even ATM machines.

Neither of the above has anything to do with the infrared systems used in TV or video recorder remote controls now in common use. The systems are completely incompatible.

Low-level Encoding

Driving a radio transmitter or a differential twisted pair with a digital signal is only part of the story. Data has to be detected and reconstituted at the other end. The receiver has to know quite a bit about the data: where the data transitions are, the clock rate, the amplitude levels, etc. A receiver rarely gets a perfect version of the signal transmitted. Most transmission media have the nasty property of distorting the transmitted signals: by smoothing the edges of sharp pulses and by delaying some parts of the transmitted signal more than others. Figure 4-12(b) shows a typical received data pattern compared with its transmitted counterpart at Figure 4-12(a). The effect is more evident when seen as an eye diagram in Figure 4-12(c). This is nothing more than a multitude of received data patterns superimposed over each other many times. An eye pattern is very useful for visually estimating the amount of distortion and dynamic range of a received data signal. The ratio between the total signal and the extent of the internal eye is used as a measure of the quality of the signal.

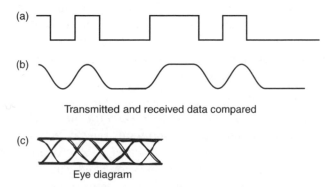

(a)

(b)

Transmitted and received data compared

(c)

Eye diagram

Figure 4-12: Signal degradation at the receiver

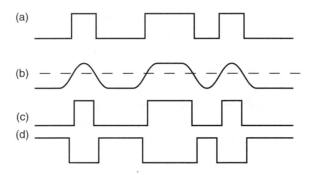

Figure 4-13: Unbalanced thresholding causes uneven pulse widths

Most line receivers use a simple threshold mechanism to slice the incoming analog data around its average or zero DC level and produce an equivalent digital stream. The differential nature of the input signal will ensure that slicing will be independent of common signal interference and common mode noise that may have been added to the signal on its way. No matter how well designed, threshold mechanisms may not always guarantee that the edge resulting from a one to zero transition will time match with the edge from a zero to one transition. This may cause a certain amount of timing distortion, where the resulting data stream 'ones' are wider than the 'zeros', see Figure 4-13, where original waveform (a) has been distorted into a narrow (c) and a wider (d) version by uneven thresholding (b).

Having recovered a digital stream, the receiver's job is now to derive the reference or clock signal. A clock signal is a regular pulse, synchronized to the input data rate that can be used by the receiver to clock the incoming data into its shift registers. A receiver can derive clocking information from a data stream by sensing for regularly occurring events, such as a data edges, measuring the times between signal transitions, and comparing them against a locally generated clock. This situation may not be helped if the transmitted data does not contain too many time level transitions (a condition not uncommon when transmitting highly correlated data such as long bit strings of the same level, as in ASCII characters). Such uneven data streams may cause the average DC level of the received data to shift, resulting in distorted recovered data, and a bad clock recovery signal.

A good, effective transmitted code should have many properties: a DC average or zero, or near zero, to ensure clean thresholding. Data transitions should be frequent, in other words, the maximum number of contiguous ones or zeros should be limited to a small number, say no more than 5 or 6. Another good property, comma-free, ensures that overall frame (or word) synchronization can be achieved quickly and reliably. This is obtained by ensuring sequential bit patterns obey certain rules that only occur at specific times. The best known example of a code with the comma free

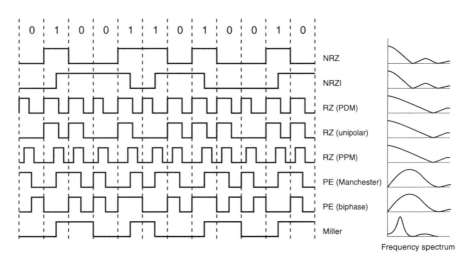

Figure 4-14: Some data encoding methods compared

property is data patterns generated by UART devices. Here, the first bit preceding the transmitted data byte is always a zero. A receiver that loses frame synchronization can always scan the incoming stream and re-lock to this position predictable 'start bit'. Polarity independence is another useful property. Codes with this property produce the same data output even when their signal polarity voltage levels are reversed, that is, when a differential pair is connected the wrong way round. Self-clocking codes are those that contain enough extra information to ensure a form of quick clock recovery. Data Encoding is the process of converting these correlated signals into other signals with the more desirable properties. This process may result in a data stream having more transmitted bits than the original. This data efficiency loss is the tradeoff that has to be paid in order to gain more flexibility at the receiver end. Figure 4-14 shows a number of data encoding methods.

Non-return to zero (NRZ)

NRZ is just the original data unchanged in format, but where the actual voltage levels used for transmission are specified (in volts). In NRZ signalling, one logic state is represented by one voltage value, and the other logic state by another voltage. The range can be zero to positive volts, or negative to positive volts, or even positive to negative. These correspond in a one-to-one fashion to the input logic ones or zeros in the original data stream. For analysis purposes, it does not matter whether a one is mapped to a high voltage or a low voltage, this is only relevant when the code is used in a practical arrangement. The power spectrum of a NRZ bit stream is also shown in Figure 4-14. This is the typical spectrum of a single pulse or random stream at a rate of $1/T$ bits per second (T is the width of the pulse). There is a zero at exactly $1/T$, and most of the power is concentrated in the area between DC and $1/2T$.

Differential return to zero (NRZI)

This is obtained by 'differentiating' the original data stream. The encoding works by generating an output data transition if the original data was a logic one and no transition if the original data was a logic '0'. The information is carried by the presence of a transition irrespectively of whether it was a one to zero change or a zero to one change. A long sequence of ones results in a square wave at the bit rate. A long sequence of zeros results in a static level. Some people may define this code as producing a transition on a zero input rather than a one input, this is just an equivalent statement. The receiver only looks for transitions (in whichever direction) to generate a one, otherwise it generates a zero. This code is polarity independent. That is, swapping the twisted pair connections will not result in an inverted decoded signal. The power spectrum is the same as NRZ. This coding is usually applied to improve the DC balance of a data stream.

Return to zero (RZ)

In RZ codes, the signals are made to return to the zero level between bit transmissions. Other names for RZ codes are pulse position modulation (PPM) and pulse width modulation (PWM). In one version of the RZ code, the normal bit time is sub-divided into two time slots. The code differences between ones and zeros by the position of the transmitted half bit in the two slot sequence. If the bit is at the first position, it is a logic '1'. If the bit is at the second position, it is a logic '0'. A second variation uses three time slots. Short pulses (occupying the first slot only) denote a one, longer pulses (occupying the first two slots) a one. The third slot is always empty. RZ codes require more bandwidth than NRZ codes, but have the advantage that they can be self-clocking, as there is always a recognizable data transition at the beginning of every bit time.

Phase encoding (PE)

This describes a collection of 'equivalent' codes. Relevant names include Manchester, split phase or phase shift keying. These codes use signal transitions rather than signal levels to denote the presence of ones or zeros. A bit time is sub-divided into two equal time slots and all codes provide at least one transition per bit interval. This results in a waveform with twice the number of zero crossings as the original. These guarantee reliable clock recovery at the expense of twice the bandwidth. PE codes are generated by XOR combinations of the original NRZ data with its generating square wave clock. In Manchester coding, transitions in the middle of the bit interval specify whether the original data is a zero or one. For continuity of the waveform, there may be no transition in the boundary between two bit intervals. The standard definition states that a positive transition in the middle of a bit interval denotes a logic '1', whereas a negative transition denotes a logic '0' (an alternative definition of the code specifies opposite polarities). Manchester coding is the method used in Ethernet. Another variation is known as differential Manchester encoding. A one bit is indicated by making the first half of the output equal to the last half of the previous bit's signal, that is, no transition at the start of the bit-time. A one bit is indicated by making the first half of the signal opposite to the last half of the previous bit's signal, that is, a zero bit is indicated by a transition at the beginning of the bit time. In the middle of the bit time, there is always a transition, whether from high to low, or low to high. Each bit transmitted means a voltage change always occurs in the middle of the bit time to ensure clock synchronization. This method is used in token Ring, and it has the advantage that a preamble is not required as clock recovery can be immediate. Another variation of this format shifts the bit transitions to the middle of the bit time. A zero is transmitted as a full cycle of a square wave, and a one as a half cycle. This results in a form of square wave version of FSK, a long sequence of zeros will result in a square wave at the bit rate, a long sequence of ones will result in a square wave of half the bit rate. PE codes have no DC component, and are self-clocking, hence their popularity in transmission systems. Their main disadvantage is that they require twice the bandwidth as their NRZ counterparts.

Miller codes

These are also called delay modulation (DM) codes. These codes are interesting because they require less bandwidth than their equivalent NRZ source counterparts. In a DM code, input logic '1' is represented as a mid-bit interval signal level change, and an input logic '0' is represented by a signal level change at the end of the bit interval if this logic '0' is followed by another logic '0'. If the input logic '0' is immediately followed by a logic '1', no signal level transition at the end of the first bit interval is applied. This rather complex description hides a code that uses less spectrum than its NRZ equivalent. It is also DC free, self-clocking and to a certain extent, error detecting. Because DM relies on data history, a slip on data reception may carry through many bits, resulting in synchronism loss over many bits. DM codes have a certain amount of ambiguity and require proper sequence initialization. For example, the DM sequence 1010101010 can either denote an all ones or an all zeros input sequence.

Bit stuffing

Bit stuffing refers to the method where extra bits are added (stuffed) into a transmitted sequence. Bit stuffing causes the transmitted sequence to be longer than the original data; this is usually compensated for by an increase of the overall transmission rate. Bit stuffing can be regular, where N bits are added to an M bit packet on a regular basis. Or irregular (or untimed), where bits are added to the sequence only as required based on some rule or principle. Bit stuffing is used in practice to ensure a transmitted sequence does not contain too many consecutive logic 1 s or 0 s, a common method is to stuff a zero every time the number of consecutive transmitted 1 s reaches eight. This ensures there is at least one data transition after no more than eight consecutive 1 s. Bit stuffing is also used to include unique 'escape' framing sequences in an otherwise 'data only' stream.

Block translation codes

These codes have names such as 4b5b and 8b10b. In a 4b5b code, every incoming consecutive sequence of 4 bits is replaced with an output sequence of 5 bits (in 8b10b codes, 8 bits are replaced with 10). The 4-to-5 bit mapping increases the transmission rate of the channel in a 5-to-4 ratio, the advantage of this form of encoding is that it can improve DC balance, aid in clock recovery, and provide for some form of error detection. The 4-to-5 conversion table is designed in such a way as to scramble the data and minimize transition times (Table 4-6). The resulting DC balance is not perfect for short sequences however. In many cases, 4b5b encoding is followed by NRZI encoding, resulting in a polarity insensitive data pattern. When followed by a NRZI encoder, the code is guaranteed to contain no more than four 1s or 0s in a row. A secondary advantage of using this code is that 'invalid' 5 bit pattern sequences can be used as frame markers or for carrying other information. More information on 4b5b codes can be found in the IEEE 802.3 documentation. 4b5b encoding is used in 100Base Ethernet where a 100 Mbps signal is carried using a 125 Mbps stream. An equivalent Manchester coding format would have required 200 Mbps.

5b6b codes are similar to 4b5b codes but improve on them by offering full DC balance (3 zero bits and 3 one bits in each group of 6). 5b6b encodes incoming 5 bit

Table 4-6: 4 bit to 5 bit conversion table

4 bit Code	5 bit Code	After NRZI
0000	11110	10100
0001	01001	01110
0010	10100	11000
0011	10101	11001
0100	01010	01100
0101	01011	01101
0110	01110	01011
0111	01111	01010
1000	10010	11100
1001	10011	11101
1010	10110	11011
1011	10111	11010
1100	11010	10011
1101	11011	10010
1110	11100	10111
1111	11101	10110

data patterns into pre-determined 6 bit symbols, chosen from a balanced data pattern table, which always contains equal numbers of zeros and ones. This provides guaranteed clock transitions synchronization for receiver circuitry, as well as an even power value on the line. The block encoding method also provides an added error-checking capability; invalid symbols and invalid data patterns, such as those with more than three zeros or three ones in a row, are easily detected. The 5b6b format is used in 100VG-AnyLAN, where the clock rate on each of four pair is 30 MHz. The total data rate is therefore 120 Mbps. Since each 6 bit of data on the line represents 5 bit of real data due to the 5b6b encoding, the rate of real data being transmitted is 100 Mbps. In 8b10b codes, each 8 bit byte is assigned a 10 bit code. For encoding, the data byte is split up into a three most significant bits nibble and a five least significant bits nibble. This is then represented as two decimal numbers with the least significant bits first. For example, the byte 101 00110 is represented as the decimal pair 6.5. The 10 bit code groups must either contain five ones and five zeros, or four ones and six zeros, or six ones and four zeros. This ensures that not too many consecutive ones or zeros occurs between code groups thereby maintaining clock synchronization. Two comma sequences are used in the standard definition of the code to aid in bit synchronization. In order to maintain a DC balance, a calculation called the running disparity calculation is used to try to keep the number of zeros transmitted the same as the number of ones transmitted.

Multilevel codes

These codes use more than two voltage levels for transmission. For example, MLT-3 uses the three relative levels: 0, +1 and −1 V. The transmitted signal is only allowed to change in the fixed order 0 +1 0 −1 0 +1, thus emulating a pseudo sine wave with no 'out of level' discontinuities (Figure 4-15). This ensures the transmitted spectrum is band limited to about half that of the original NRZ data stream. Encoding is relatively simple: a one to zeros or zeros to one transition in the original source data is represented as a change to the next 'state' in the transmitted wave. No transition in the input results in no change. MLT-3 uses considerably less bandwidth

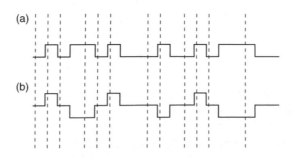

Figure 4-15: The three level MLT-3 code

than the equivalent binary code, and is used extensively in high-speed 100 Mbps and higher LAN systems.

8b6t is another three-level code that replaces each 8 bit byte with a code of 6 three state symbols. To represent 256 different bytes, 729 three state symbols are possible. Unlike MLT-3, no switching from '+1' to '0' to '−1' is required. 8b6t allows an arbitrary use of these three states, 256 symbols have been chosen as a one-to-one re-mapping of every possible byte, in a way similar to 4b5b. The re-mapping table is listed in IEEE 802.3, Annex 23A, with nine special symbols used for starting and ending delimiters and control characters, these are also listed in IEEE 802.3, Section 23.2.4.1. To reduce bandwidth rate even further, the transmitted bits are fanned-out into three cable pairs instead of a single pair, this is called T4 multiplexing. The maximum speed waveform required for this 100 Mbps Ethernet system is now only 12.5 MHz, slow enough for low quality Category 3 twisted pairs. When bytes in 100BASE-T4 are transmitted, three pairs are used in transmission. Of the four pairs in Category 3 cabling, three pairs are used to send data while the remaining pair listens for collisions. The same pairs used in 10BASE-T are always transmitting on one pair while always listening on the other. The two pairs not used in any other type of Ethernet are available for either direction to borrow, carrying information in the same direction as the data flow. Three pairs are always used to send data in a single direction across a 100BASE-T4 cable. 100BASE-T4 uses a slight modification of the physical sub layers from 100BASE-TX. A frequency of 31.25 MHz is slow enough to travel well over CAT-5, but still too fast for CAT-3, which is only certified for 16 MHz. For fast Ethernet on Category 3 UTP, 100BASE-T4 has been developed. Using the techniques of 100BASE-TX as a starting point, 100BASE-T4 combines and improves 4b5b and MLT-3 into 8b6t (Table 4.7).

The combination of 4b5b and either NRZI or MLT-3 provides an adequate signal for 100BASE-FX and 100BASE-TX. The signal is slow enough to be transmitted across fibre or CAT-5, but dense enough to encode 100 Mbps. 100BASE-FX uses 4b5b encoding to increase the speed from 100 to 125 Mbps, then cuts it in half with NRZI to a maximum of 62.5 MHz. 100BASE-TX cuts that figure in half again with MLT-3, down to a maximum of 31.25 MHz. If the resulting 100BASE-TX signal does not meet FCC emissions requirements, a 'stream cipher' has been defined to allow 'scrambling' of the signal after 4b5b encoding and NRZI encoding, but before MLT-3 encoding. The idea behind the 'stream cipher' is to randomize the signal to reduce the generated EMI emissions. From a security perspective, the cipher itself is useless.

Another commonly used multilevel code is PAM-5. This code also employs multilevel amplitude signalling. A five-level signal (−2, −1, 0, 1 and 2 V) called pulse amplitude modulation 5 is used, which works in a similar manner to MLT-3. Actually only four levels are used for data, the fifth level (0 V) is used for the four-dimensional 8-state Trellis forward error correction used to recover the transmitted signal from the high

Table 4-7: 8b6t encoding table

Hex Value	6T Pattern					
00	+	−	0	0	+	−
01	0	+	−	+	−	0
02	+	−	0	+	−	0
03	−	0	+	+	−	0
04	−	0	+	0	+	−
05	0	+	−	−	0	+
06	+	−	0	−	0	+
07	−	0	+	−	0	+
08	−	+	−	−	+	−
10	+	0	+	−	−	0
3F	+	0	−	+	0	−
5E	−	−	+	+	+	0
7E	0	0	+	−	−	+
80	+	−	+	0	0	−
C0	+	−	+	0	+	−
FF	+	0	−	+	0	0

noise. Two bits are represented per symbol and the symbol rate is 125 Mbps in each direction on a pair because the clock rate is set at 125 MHz. This gives 250 Mbps data per pair and therefore 1000 Mbps for the whole four-pair cable set.

Checksums and Error Protection

Checksums are extra bits added to a normal data stream. Their purpose is to add integrity to the block to ensure any errors can be recognized by the receiver. The position of the checksum bits in the stream carries no information and is in general immaterial, as their relative position with respect to the data block does not carry any relevant information. Checksum bits can be interleaved with the data, placed at the front or at the back. It is common practice to append checksums at the end of a data block, mainly to allow serial computing logic to have access to the data bits before performing the checksum calculations on the fly. Most checksums are calculated by performing linear mathematical operations on the original data block. These may not be immediately recognized as normal day-to-day arithmetic operations, but operate under similar principles, only under a different number field. Other names for checksums are cyclic redundancy, or parity check calculations.

Errors and noise

How good are checksums at detecting and correcting errors? Protocols documents usually specify given CRC sequences (or polynomials) to be used with a particular code. Are some magic CRC combinations 'better' than others? What is an error anyway? Historically, error protection schemes were based on the assumption that errors strike data streams randomly and with a predictable probability hit rate. For random additive noise, the shape of this probability curve is known as a Gaussian bell. This concept of the binary symmetrical channel (BSC) stated that 'bit errors' were statistically likely to happen in proportion to the overlap between the Gaussian bell and the data threshold or slice level of the receiver, which in turn, was related to the signal to noise ratio for the transmission system. Figure 4-16(a) shows the two original data levels as they would appear at the transmitter, and in Figure 4-16(b) at the receiver after additive Gaussian noise has been added. Note how the amplitude of the resulting voltage levels is now a statistical function based around the original voltage levels. The width of this bell-shaped curve is a function of the rms value of the added noise. Note also, how at the zeros threshold voltage level the two curves overlap, implying that there is a non-zeros chance of a transmitted logic '1' to be erroneously received as logic '0' (and vice versa).

A simple receiver will use such a zero volt threshold circuit to recover the binary signal. As can be seen from Figure 4-16(c), there will be some probability that bits will be interpreted wrongly because of the added noise. This probability is proportional to the area of the bell curve under the threshold. In other words, the areas of overlap at the zero threshold line statistically determine what proportion of bits will be read as errors.

Errors will affect a data block at random, and bits in any position in a data stream can be hit with equal chance. We need a method for relating this to error protection

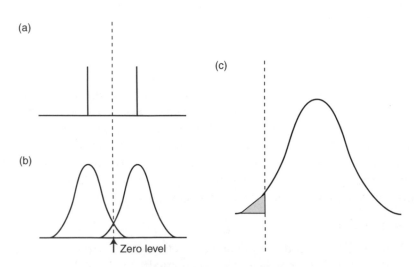

Figure 4-16: Gaussian noise added to a binary signal results in an error probability

methods, and a measure of how good, or how bad a particular protection method can be. Central to this is the concept of the Hamming distance between two data blocks (literally the number of different data bits between them, irrespectively of their positions). Devising encoding methods that maximize Hamming distance between transmitted codewords enable developers to place a computable bound on the number of bits in error that a codeword can accept before being interpreted as another codeword. This is the essence of traditional error protection theory. In practice, the BSC model is only valid in data communication systems, like deep space probes, where the only source of added interference is wideband Gaussian noise. In reality, bit errors can happen with relatively equal statistical probability whether singly, in bursts, or in correlated patterns. The definition of a channel has also been widened to include storage devices such as magnetic disk drives and RAM memory. The traditional mathematical techniques for generating wide Hamming distance codewords still apply today, but the behaviour in respect to error performance is more difficult to compute or generalize. Codes that detect all combinations of multiple errors are not easy to create. A typical claim for a code may be statistical more than predictive, for example, 'correct all one and two error bit patterns, and detect most of three bit pattern errors'.

Parity

The most effective protection method by far is the single parity bit check. This will detect any one bit error combination in a block of data of any length (to be technically correct, a single bit parity check will detect any odd number of errors, but no even number of errors). The only overhead for this protection is the addition of only one extra bit to a data block, which can be of any length. An 'even' parity code bit is computed by the XOR addition of all the 'one' bits in the block. So if the total number of ones in the original block is odd, a 'one' parity bit is added. If the total number of ones is even, a 'zero' parity bit is added. This has the net effect of ensuring all transmitted codewords have an even number of 'one' bits (for an even parity code). Decoding is very simple, if the received codeword has an odd number of ones, it is considered in error. Unfortunately, if the received block had two, four or any even number of errors, the decoder will miss the error, and accept the block as valid. It may be intuitive to assume that the situation could be resolved by just adding more parity bits. This is true. However, adding more parity bits in any old way does not go to improve error protection in a cumulative fashion. The parity bits need to be computed in a systematic way, otherwise they will be nothing more than trivial permutations of one another.

We can look at error protection encoding in another way. A data block of N bits can have 2^N possible bit combinations, that is, a four bit data code has 16 possible combinations. These can be visualized as points in a two-valued N-dimensional space. Every valid codeword occupies one point or space in this universe, and the code is said to be full, that is, all points in the universe are occupied by valid codewords. Assume we now add K parity bits to our data block. The resulting transmitted codewords will now have M bits (where $M = N + K$), these will now live in a two valued M-dimensional space with 2^M points, of which only 2^N will be occupied by 'valid' codes. The other 2^{M-N} places will be unoccupied. Any occupied points here will be considered as 'invalid' codewords. After transmission, the received codewords must all live in the 'valid' points, and any received codewords in the 'invalid' positions will be considered as errors. This is because the error bits will have changed one or more of the dimensions (assuming of course, that the dimension change is to an 'invalid' point in our space). Remembering that Hamming distance was defined as the 'hop' distance between two points in this universe, that is, the number of dimension changes, it would make sense to ensure that valid codewords are 'geographically' distanced as far from each other as possible, and all the gaps in between filled with 'invalid' codewords. In geometric terms, we ideally want to design our codewords to maximally occupy this space, more or less in the same way gas molecules spread out to evenly fill an enclosed volume. We do not want the codewords to be bunched into one corner of this universe, as the average Hamming distance between them will be one in the main, and errors would not be detected, making the coding method useless. We can visualize one simple example. That of the simple one parity bit as mentioned previously. One bit parity encoding converts a 2^N space into a 2^{N+1} space. Here, half the codewords are 'valid' and the other half are 'invalid'. It so happens that this simple encoding operation results in a very symmetrical geometrical lattice where the minimum hamming distance between any two codewords is two (the layout looks like a multi dimensional chessboard pattern). Codes that are so well geometrically spaced are called good and efficient.

However, it does not automatically follow that the addition of extra parity bits provides a dimensional expansion formula where Hamming distance increases in proportion. The mathematics of ensuring this happens for a given code are non-trivial. Only special cases can be guaranteed to have these properties. These have been given various names such as Hamming, BCH, Reed–Solomon, etc. It is very difficult to develop non-trivial codes that have optimal properties for every codeword in this universe. However, it is somewhat easier to develop coding schemes where the property applies to not all, but a high proportion of the codewords. The performance of these codes is measured against minimum and maximum bounds on performance, and on a statistical basis. Some of these bounds are (yet) unattainable, others give a rough measure of what can be achieved. The most basic theorem states that in order to correct P errors in a block of 2^N bits, we need at least $P * N$ of those bits to be 'parity' bits. The proof is rather simple; we need to know where the errors are, and the code should at least provide position indices to them. An N bit pattern can index a single error position in a 2^N bit array, P of these patterns could point to P error positions, hence at least $P * N$ bits are needed. Note the word 'could'; the theorem is only a bound, and it does not tell us how to generate or compute the parity bits. It does not even tell us whether codes with such properties exist. (The standard Hamming code is a specific case for $P = 1$.) Another reassuring well-known theorem states that a 'randomly chosen' subset of 2^N codewords in a set of 2^M messages will give us a code that is statistically as good, in terms of error protection, as any code obtainable using any other (more complex) means. In other words, pick any set of codewords at random, and they will be as good, on the average, as any others. The first problem here is, of course, that systematic codes can be decoded using systematic maths operations. Randomly chosen codes can only be decoded using massive look-up tables. The second problem is more mundane, and more to do with bad luck than anything else. The chances of selecting a code that turns out to be bad are about the same as the chances of toast falling buttered side down from the breakfast table.

Polynomials

One of the many techniques used to represent data bit patterns in a code is as elements in a polynomial finite field. This is akin to modulo arithmetic, where numbers are represented as polynomials with bit positions represented as the power of a root element X. For example: $1 + X + X^2 + X^4$ represents the binary bit pattern 11101. It is not the purpose of this book to cover finite field theory. However, the main concepts are worth looking at. In a finite field, all members can be derived from a primitive element (read number) such that all the elements in the set can be obtained from the powers of this element. For example, element A can, together with its powers, form the set $1, A, A^2, A^3, A^4, A^5, A^7, \ldots$ Because this is a finite field, the set will wrap to itself, so that for some value of P: $A^P = 1$. In other words, the set has P members, including the unity member $A^P = A^0$. The primitive element A can itself be a polynomial (i.e. a bit pattern) such as '$1 + X + X^2$' or simply 'X'.

The elements in a set obey the simple rules of arithmetic including addition and multiplication, although these operations are not performed in the way we might expect with ordinary integers. Addition is performed by modulo two additions of the coefficients, and multiplication by two as a one bit rotation of the pattern (with fold back). An important concept in field theory is the field generator polynomial. This can be visualized as the equivalent of a prime number. This is a polynomial that has no factors, and from which all other elements can be derived by power multiplication. We can visualize this with ordinary modulo number analogy. Although not exactly equivalent, it can give us a perception of what it is happening here. In normal modulo 7 arithmetic, where the set members are 0,1,2,3,4,5,6. The element 2 is a 'primitive'. The elements generated by a regular operation (i.e. shifting by 2) are: 2, 4, 6, 1, 3, 5, 7. All the members in the set can be created by this operation. In modulo 6 arithmetic, on the other hand, where the members are 0,1,2,3,4,5, element 2 is not a 'primitive'. The set of numbers created by the same operation are only 2 and 4. In other words, the operation generates a non-maximal 'sub-field'.

Codes are constructed by multiplying (or dividing) a binary message data block by one (or more) primitive polynomials. A polynomial division results in a divisor and a remainder. By transmitting the product (or the remainder) of such operation by appending the generated bits to the message, the receiver can work out if errors have occurred in a transmission. An error free transmission will result in a locally calculated remainder to be zero. A non-zero remainder will indicate that an error has occurred. The more advanced forms of error correction use the remainder polynomial to compute an error location polynomial, which identifies the position of the error in the received data stream. This conversion is no trivial task.

CRC polynomials are simply known 'good' field generator polynomials, or sometimes products of two or more such polynomials. In general, other polynomials could be used to the same effect. Including a specific CRC polynomial in a protocol specification just ensures that both the transmitter and receiver are using the same number.

Managing the Medium – Handling Collisions

A shared transmission medium, whether wired or wireless, is a common resource. It is also a medium shared by many users. When one node or station is active on the medium, other users should not interfere and should 'listen' only. That is, they should not attempt to use the line at the same time. When two or more transmitters are active on the line at the same time, receivers will only pick a garbled version of the data. This condition is known as a *collision*. Collisions are a normal part of many networks. They cannot be avoided, but their effect can be reduced by the intelligent use of avoidance mechanisms. Collisions result in wasted time and bandwidth, as data will have to be re-transmitted when collisions occur.

There are a number of ways collisions may be kept to a minimum. One way is to separate the medium into physically separate sections. For example, use different wavebands for radio systems, or use different wiring runs, loops or pairs for cabled systems. This is not always practical, as the advantages of a shared medium would be lost. Such splitting would defeat the purpose of sharing a common medium. In many cases, no alternatives are available. Another way to avoid collisions is to split the *time* of the transmissions. Instead of physically separating the media, we separate the times at which stations are allowed to transmit. Stations could synchronize their clocks to a regular heart beat pacer signal. This allocates each station a unique time slot, in which they are allowed to transmit. Overlaps should never occur in theory. The main disadvantage of this method is that unused time cannot be re-allocated to other stations, and the medium will become very much underused.

A more practical system allows stations to transmit when they wish, but they must follow a strict set of rules to minimize collisions. For example, they could listen to line voltages before they transmit. This by itself is not enough; two transmitters could for example, start transmission at exactly the same time missing each other completely. Stations could also be out of radio or optical range of each other, and not be able to 'read' each other. In these cases, more sophisticated methods of collision control have to be used.

Wired networks

In wired systems such as Ethernet, all stations are in range of each other. Collisions are detected by the simple expedient of sensing for signals on the line before transmission. Ethernet systems are called carrier sense multiple access with carrier detect (CSMA/CD). It is carrier sense, because it all stations must listen on the wire for other data before placing their own. It in multiple access because each station has equal access to the wire providing no other station in using it. Carrier detect means just that, the transmitter is able to detect other carriers on the line from all other stations at all times. In case of collision detection, Ethernet goes into a re-transmission phase based on an exponential random back-off algorithm. In other words, it waits longer and longer every time there is a clash. This ensures that at some stage, the line will be hopefully free.

Wireless networks

Radio systems, as described in IEEE 802.11, have to work differently. The normal CSMA/CD collision detection mechanism would require radios to work in full-duplex and be capable of transmitting and receiving at once, an approach that would increase bandwidth and cost significantly. In a radio environment, it is not always possible to ensure that all stations can hear each other all the time (a basic requirement for collision detection). A transmitter sensing the medium and finding it free does not necessarily mean the medium is free near the remote receiver, which may be in range of another transmitter also wanting to use the medium. In order to overcome these problems, 802.11 uses a carrier sense multiple access with collision avoidance (CSMA/CA). A station wanting to transmit first senses the medium. If the medium is busy then it waits for some time before trying again. If the medium is free, it sends a sense packet. The receiving station, on reception of the packet, radios back an acknowledgment (ACK) to the transmitter. Receipt of the acknowledgment tells the transmitter that no collision at the receiver occurred. If the transmitter does not receive the first acknowledgment then it retransmits the sense packet until it receives an acknowledgment. This relatively complex method reduces the probability of a collision on the receiver by a station that is hidden from the transmitter. A duration information flag is used to set a 'reserve time' variable in all stations. The duration information also protects the transmitter area from collisions from stations that are out of range of the acknowledging station. Because the sense packets are short in duration, the overhead of any collisions happening is also reduced, since these are recognized faster than if the whole packet was to be transmitted. This procedure will be described in more detail in a later chapter.

CHAPTER 5

LAN Access Technologies

When people talk about LANs, they usually mean Ethernet. There is no doubt that Ethernet is one of the most common protocols for this type of networking. The majority of PC networks, and many industrial systems, use Ethernet as their low-level carrier. Other systems, such as token ring are used in many places, but are not as popular and ever present as Ethernet, especially in new installations.

This chapter discusses current networking technologies of interest to embedded systems, such as Ethernet and IEEE 802. It also includes descriptions of current hardware interface devices and controllers and how they work.

Ethernet and IEEE 802

Many people confuse the terms Ethernet and IEEE 802. The two are very similar, but there are some notable differences. The reasons are mainly historical, Ethernet was developed by Xerox in the 1970s, who were soon joined by Intel and Digital to form the DIX development group, their first version of Ethernet was introduced around 1980. At about the same time, the American Institute of Electrical and Electronic Engineers (IEEE) was looking at standardizing various recently developed network technologies (other people were also working in the area). They chose to start with the already existing specifications from the DIX group. This resulted in the basis for various draft specifications. One of which, 802.3, was based on the current DIX version of Ethernet at the time. However, in 1982 the DIX consortium released version 2 of their own Ethernet specifications, which differed from their original and from the already specified IEEE 802 standards. Since then, both parties have made further changes, and the standards have digressed even further. The correct naming for the non-IEEE standard is now Ethernet II, or Ethernet (RFC-894), as it is described in document RFC 894. The IEEE went on to develop further compatible standards for similar LAN technologies. For example, IEEE 802.5 for token ring and 802.11 for wireless LANs. These use different methods for line management and collision avoidance, but converge at the top layers into a single common protocol.

How Ethernet Works

Before delving into the technology, a few technical terms must be defined. The original IEEE specifications were targeted at a specific 10 Mbps data transfer system using base band signalling and low-loss 50 Ω coaxial cable with a maximum cable run of about 500 m. This type of topology was known as a bus where up to 100 stations could connect together in a backbone or chain. This technology is still used and commonly known as 10Base5 or thick Ethernet. Stations were connected to the network via devices known as transceivers or attachment units. These made onsite installation very simple as the boxes pierced the coaxial cable to obtain a connection, avoiding the use of crimp tools and difficult-to-solder coaxial connectors.

In 1988, 10Base2 was introduced. This is now standardized as IEEE 802.3b and defines a similar bus topology to 10Base5, but using cheaper 50-Ω RG58U coaxial cable. This system was also referred to as thin Ethernet. Standard RF coaxial cable using standard coaxial BNC connectors and terminators are used. In 1990, 10BaseT was introduced. This is specified in IEEE 802.3i. 10BaseT is also a 10 Mbps system, but uses twisted pair cabling instead of coaxial. The system uses a differential low voltage scheme to transmit data on the line to minimise radiation. The basic topology is point-to-point star, with stations connected to each other via central hubs. As a special case, two stations can be connected together without a hub, but a special crossover cable must be used (this special null cable simply swaps the transmit and receive pairs). Some time later, a higher-speed version was also developed. This was called 100BaseT, and to all extents was a higher-speed version of the 10BaseT format. This new format is also called fast Ethernet. To avoid placing high-frequency signals in cables (which can cause radiation), the various IEEE committees devised a variety of alternative bandwidth saving transmission formats. For example, 100BASE-TX uses two pairs of high-grade cable. 100BASE-T4 operates on four pairs of standard grade cable, and 100BASE-FX requires optical fibre.

The data bit stream

In all forms of Ethernet, data is transmitted in packet form (called frames), even if the data supplied to the driver arrives continuously. The 10 Mbps Ethernet systems use Manchester encoding with a 10 MHz basic rate clock. When no data is transmitted, the line is quiet, that is, there is no signalling on the line, and the line floats at around 0 V. In 10Base2 coaxial systems, this allows transmitters to transmit data by simply injecting current into the constant impedance of the shared cable. Transmitted frames are usually preceded by preambles, which consist of long sequences of ones and zeros. Preambles are required to initialise the receiver's automatic gain and clock recovery circuits. In some networks, the idle time is also used to broadcast system type negotiation information. The 100 Mbps systems use a variety of schemes to reduce line bandwidth and electromagnetic radiation. These limits were imposed by government FCC requirements, which restrict cable radiation above 30 MHz. 100Base-TX uses a scrambled 4b5b modulation scheme followed by a three-level MLT-3 encoding. The 4b5b encoding increases the data rate from 100 to 125 Mbps, but the MLT-3 encoding reduces the effective bandwidth to 32.5 MHz (this is slightly above, but just acceptable by FCC standards). 100Base-T4 also uses a multiple level encoding, but by sharing transmission over four pairs, overall bandwidth is reduced. Because of this, it also allows the use of lower specification (i.e. cheaper) twisted pair cables. The 100 Mbps systems also use hubs and can interwork with 10 Mbps on the same network.

Data framing

Ethernet transmission packets are known as frames. The basic clock bit time is either 100 or 10 ns, depending on whether 10 or 100 Mbps is being used. Apart from this, there is no nominal difference between the contents of frames generated by 10 or 100 Mbps systems. The minimum frame size is 64 bytes (bytes are also referred to as octets), and the maximum size is 1518 bytes. There is a good reason for setting these limits; signals take a finite time to travel down a cable (they travel at about two-thirds of the speed of light). Therefore, for a given maximum and minimum length of network cable, there will be some well defined wait times a node requires to ensure other nodes have not placed their own data on the cable (the travel time has to be included in the calculations). The maximum and minimum frame sizes are therefore a function of the combination of maximum cable lengths and required collision wait times.

Frame structure

Ethernet II and 802.3 frames are structured slightly differently. Figure 5-1(a) shows the structure for an Ethernet II frame; and Figure 5-1(b) for an IEEE 802.3 frame. Ethernet 802.3 frames begin with a 7 byte preamble. This is a straight sequence of alternate ones and zeros (not shown in the diagram) used to re-synchronize the receiver clock recovery circuits. The preamble is followed by a frame delimiter byte (SFD), this tells the receiver the preamble has ended and what follows from now on is data. The nominal value for the SFD byte is ABhex, this is immediately followed by 6 bytes of the destination address, and 6 bytes of the source address. Destination and source addresses are also known in network technology as MAC addresses, NIC addresses or even Ethernet addresses. The address fields are then followed by a 2 byte frame length word, which specifies the number of bytes contained in the data payload that follows. The payload can have between 46 and 1500 bytes (the frame headers and checksum have taken 18 bytes from the top limits of 64 and 1518). Following the payload is a 4 byte frame check sequence (FCS), which is a simple cyclic redundancy check word the receiver can use to check whether data has arrived intact.

Ethernet II frames differ slightly from 802.3 frames (Figure 5-1a). The preamble is similar, although the SFD field is described in the specifications as forming part of the now 8 byte preamble. In practice, both Ethernet II and 802.3 have the same 8 byte preamble bit patterns. This distinction is made only to correspond with other

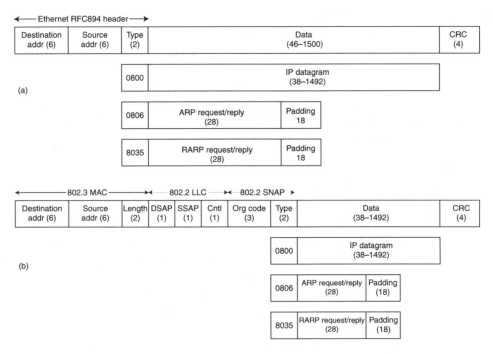

Figure 5-1: Ethernet II and Ethernet 802 frame types

network standards that may have different pre-amble formats. The two following destination and source address fields follow the same pattern. The next field is not a frame length field, but a type field. The type field is used to identify which kind of higher layer protocol the user payload carries. IEEE 802.3 frames also contain a similar type field but it is placed a few bytes later in the header (see below). Type field codes are always greater than 0600 hex, allowing Ethernet II frames to be easily differentiated from IEEE 802.3 ones simply by checking the different values on this field (frame lengths can only be less than 1500 bytes, which translates as 05DChex). Most TCP/IP networks in PCs and embedded systems use Ethernet II as the transmission format; the simplicity of just using one type field makes Ethernet II the simpler of the two options.

Data payload

The main job of the Ethernet receiver is to strip out the headers, and pass the payload to the rest of the system. Before it can do this, the receiver needs to use the information in the destination address to resolve the frame and ignore it if the address field does not correspond to the one it is expecting. The receiver will also perform a frame error check based on the FCS and dump the frame if errors were detected. In 802.3 frames, further headers are included; these are known as logical link control (LLC) and sub-network address protocol (SNAP) headers (SNAP is described in RFC 1042). The purpose and placement of these fields is mainly to conform to other requirements of the IEEE 802 standards, including IEEE 802.2 on LLC.

Ethernet is a simple wired protocol and most of these features are not implemented. The LLC and SNAP fields are included purely for compatibility and, except for the payload type field, are filled with constant values. The LLC header will contain the fixed values DSAP = AAhex, SSAP = AAhex, CNTL = 03hex. The SNAP header will contain a 00hex organizational code, followed by the 2 byte type field containing the protocol as already described. Ethernet frames with full LLC/SNAP fields are said to be Ethernet 802.2 compliant. These frames are in complete compliance with the IEEE 802.2 standard, and can fully interoperate with frames resulting from or destined from other network sources based on other compatible IEEE 802 standards. Of interest to TCP/IP networks is the protocol-type field in the SNAP header. This field is the same as the type field in Ethernet II frames and as discussed above, denotes the network protocol used in the data payload portion of the frame. The most common type fields are 0800hex for IP, 0806hex for ARP and 8035hex for RARP.

In all modes of Ethernet, field values longer than 8 bits, that is, 16 or 32 bits, are always transmitted big-endian fashion, that is, with the most significant byte transmitted first. For example, 0806hex will be transmitted as the sequence 08hex first followed by 06hex. Similarly, the 32 bit word 12345678hex is transmitted as the 4 byte sequence 12hex, 34hex, 56hex, 78hex. This is important, as many microprocessors perform internal arithmetic little-endian fashion (least significant byte first) and the incoming stream bytes will need to be swapped around before performing any operations on them.

Ethernet addresses

Ethernet source and destination addresses are 6 byte patterns uniquely allocated to each hardware node or workstation. This is an important number as it is the only way hardware connected to a network can recognise other devices. Ideally, every single Ethernet interface in the world will have a unique, differently allocated address number. Do not confuse Ethernet addresses with IP addresses. Ethernet addresses are allocated to the hardware, or network card used in a machine. IP addresses are allocated to the high-level application or user that may be operating the computer.

In a typical Ethernet card, the address is stored in a flash EPROM set alongside the controller chip. On power on, or board reset, the Ethernet controller will automatically download the contents of the flash EPROM to its own registers. Ethernet addresses are allocated to hardware manufacturers in blocks, who then proceed to initialize each and every network card sold with a different number. These unique numbers are sometimes known as organizational unique identifiers (OUI). Anybody can apply for a OUI number: to obtain an official

MAC/Ethernet/OUI address, download the OUI application form and cover letter from: http://standards.ieee.org/regauth/oui/forms/index.html. Alternatively, contact the IEEE Registration Authority by e-mail or by phone on +1-732-562-3813 or fax +1-732-562-1571. The cost for an OUI allocation at the time of going to press is US$ 1650.00.

For development purposes, or when used within a close private LAN, any non-conflicting set of MAC address could be chosen. However, if the network is connected to the outside world, there is the possibility of a clash with a remote address of a similar number. Fortunately, the standards allow for non-OUI generic addresses to be used (see below). Many routers are programmed to ignore these type of addresses, and therefore provide some isolation from the outside world.

Figure 5-2 shows the 6 byte address format. The significance of the special bits in the sequence is as follows.

The first bit of the address (bit 47 in the MSB first sequence) is the individual/group (IG) bit. If the IG value is zero, the address designates an individual address. If the IG value is one, the address designates a group address, generally known as a multicast. A MAC address of all ones (FFFFFFhex) designates a broadcast address; frames containing this destination address are sent to all stations on the network. The next bit is the universal/local administration bit (UL). When UL is zero, the next 22 bits correspond to the unique vendor code allocated by the IEEE to each manufacturer. For example, 00AA00hex is Intel, and 08005Ahex is IBM. The last 24 bits are the numbers each vendor allocates locally to each adapter. If the UL bit is one, the full 46 bit address is locally administered, often by the software running on the networked device. It implies that the MAC address was not allocated by the IEEE. The routing bit in source addresses indicates whether MAC-level routing information is present. This is mainly relevant for other technologies such as token ring. The bit is usually zero.

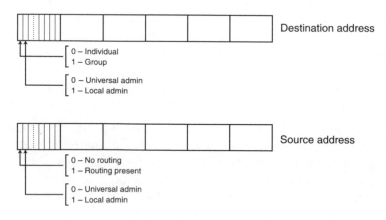

Figure 5-2: Special bits in Ethernet address fields

Error handling

A first-level check on the quality of the received frame is performed at the receiver by calculating the Ethernet FCS checksum. Any frames in error are generally dropped, and a general message is passed to the rest of the system noting that a frame has been received in error. Error handling by these lower layers is nothing more than simple checks on quality. Most of the real error management will be performed at the higher layers. This is the most efficient way to do this for this technology. During the development of a protocol, deciding how much error protection should be performed at a particular layer is a real art. Doing too little, forces the higher layers to do all the work, and many 'bad' packets will be passed up, resulting in wasted bandwidth. Doing too much, means that there may be lots of delay and congestion at the low levels, especially if error management is handled repeatedly by more than one layer. The method of error management will also depend on the physical medium, and how predictable and reliable it is. A highly reliable wired LAN network will require less error protection than a radio-based system.

Interface Devices for Ethernet

Luckily for the embedded designer, there are many products in the market dedicated to Ethernet interfacing and networking. Most of these were developed specifically for building into PC network cards using either the ISA or the PCI bus. Their generic name is Ethernet controller chips. Some of these are divided into two separate chip devices: a bus-interface device, and a line-interface device, roughly separating the digital from the analog functions. Many others have both facilities built into a single integrated circuit.

Controllers developed for the ISA bus are of special interest to embedded designers as they are very easy to interface to. Controllers developed for the PCI bus are much more difficult to interface to and require more support logic and software. In many cases, the same device family is supplied by manufactures in both forms, ISA and PCI. Table 5-1 shows a list of ISA bus devices commonly available at the time of going to press. Many have been available for some time, and although now obsolete

Table 5-1: Commonly available ISA bus devices

Device	Manufacturer	Description (Mbps)	Contact
RTL8019S	Realtek	10	www.realtek.com.tw
CS8900	Cirrus	10	www.cirrus.com
LAN91C96	SMS	10	www.smsc.com
LAN91C9111	SMS	10/100	www.smsc.com
DP83840A	National	10/100	www.national.com
DP8390	National	10	www.national.com
Am79C874	AMD	10/100	www.amd.com
AX88796	Asix Electronics	10/100	www.asix.com.tw

for building into PC network card designs, they are popular for embedded system design, and still manufactured in quantities. It is unlikely that they will disappear from the market in the near future.

Rather than describe the workings of a specific device, all information supplied here will be generic. For detailed information on particular devices, the reader should consult the data sheets and application notes which can be downloaded from the web. Most of the devices work in a very similar fashion, and the descriptions provided here will be, more or less, relevant to all.

What the chips do

In essence, they are nothing but sophisticated UARTs. Received data from the line is filtered, decoded, converted to parallel 8 (or 16) bit words, and placed into a local buffer. The hardware will strip out unwanted headers and perform simple error detection. The microprocessor can read the clean 'payload' data by recalling it off internal RAM memory within the controller (also named direct memory access, or DMA). Similarly, during transmission, the microprocessor places a transmit block of data into the controller's buffer, and triggers the device to send the frame. The controller will perform all the necessary operations such as data framing, collision detection etc. This makes the overall design of an embedded Ethernet controller interface very easy.

The controller will need to be initialized once, usually at the beginning of the program, by writing constant data into its various control registers. After initialisation, the controller is ready to transmit and receive data from the line. To transmit a block, the RAM buffer is loaded, and a number of registers are set to trigger the transaction. To receive data, a bit in a status register is sensed regularly. If set, data has been received and is ready for collection from the RAM. Alternatively, these actions can be made to automatically generate interrupts. Timing constrains must also be met in order to avoid overflowing the (finite) internal RAM buffers with too much received data. The limiting factor in performance will be the associated microprocessor, and how fast it can handle data transfer operations.

Bus interfacing

The interface to the bus, that is, between the Ethernet controller and the microprocessor, can be either via memory or I/O mapping. The controller will include all necessary signal pins to support both schemes. Access to the chip is via 8 bit wide paged registers. This allows a small external address range to span a larger number of internal registers. This was a traditional decision made on the PC ISA bus arrangement, which only had a small number of allocated ports for each peripheral. In practice, an Ethernet controller may have 64 internal registers, organized as four pages of 16 registers each. Only four address lines to the outside world will be required. Data transfers to and from the DMA is via reads and writes to a single register. This is mapped internally to the internal data transmit and receive buffers within the controller. The interface includes an auto increment pointer, so repeated reads or writes to the same register results in sequential accesses to the DMA buffer. Internal DMA storage varies between zero to 16 kbytes depending on device. Designers familiar with the programming of UART peripherals chips such as the 8251, will find interfacing to Ethernet controller chips an easy task, only that there will be more internal registers to initialize. It is important for the designer to choose the right method of data transfer access, that is, 8, 16 or 32 bits, as this affects performance greatly.

The line interface side

Most chips connect to the outside world via two differential transmit/receive pairs. The chips will already generate the right voltage levels and wave shapes, so no external buffering or wave shaping will be necessary. However, some external components, such as isolation transformers (also known as magnetics) and filter capacitors are still required to provide electrical isolation for the line. On the board side, the connection is terminated in a standard eight-way RJ45 socket to provide for 10BaseT connectivity. To provide for 10Base2 or 10Base5 coaxial interfacing, more complex external devices (including a floating power supply) will need to be added. Figure 5-3 shows a typical 10BaseT interface circuit. The transformers are standard 1:1 pulse transformers, and are available from several manufacturers who specialize in miniature transformers for Ethernet applications.

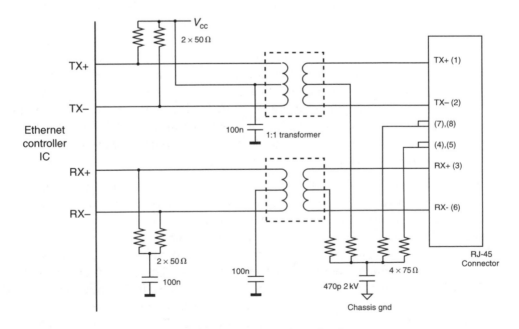

Figure 5-3: Line interface circuit

The transmitter

Before transmission to line, the controller chip needs to convert the supplied block of data into a valid Ethernet frame. A preamble is added to the front of the packet and a 4 byte checksum added at the end. Frames smaller than 64 bytes are padded with zeros to guarantee the minimum frame size rule. Note that most transmitters require a full Ethernet frame to be supplied by the external microcomputer. This frame must include not only the payload (e.g. an IP datagram), but also the Ethernet source and address information, plus type field. Only the preamble and the checksum are added locally. Once the correct frame has been assembled, and once the collision detection mechanism has given it the go-ahead, the bytes are sent sequentially from the RAM buffer, one at a time in serial form, to the transmit modulator.

On 10 MHz systems, the serial data is encoded using Manchester coding before being outputted after shape filtering in voltage differential analog form. Some devices offer programmable control of slew rate and amplitude of the outgoing waveform. The Manchester encoding process combines clock and NRZ data such that the first half of the data bit contains the complement of the data, and the second half of the data bit contains the true data. This guarantees that a transition always occurs in the middle of the bit time. The Manchester encoding process is only done on actual frame data. The idle period between packets contains no data, and can be used for other purposes such as auto-negotiation pulses. The shape of the transmit pulse is not square, but rounded to limit the transmit bandwidth spectrum; an internal waveform generator ROM is used to look up the shape of the rounded pulse. The waveform generator consists of a ROM, DAC, clock generator and final low-pass filter. The DAC output goes through the low pass filter in order to 'smooth' the steps and remove any high-frequency components, the DAC values are determined from the ROM outputs, which are chosen to shape the pulse to the desired template and are clocked into the DAC by the chip rate clock generator. In this way, the waveform generator re-shapes the output waveform to be transmitted onto the twisted pair cable to meet the pulse shape template requirements outlined in IEEE 802.3, Clause 14. Finally, a current line driver converts the shaped and smoothed waveform to a current output that can drive the external cable $100\,\Omega$ load.

On 100 MHz systems (100Base-TX), the serial data to be transmitted is first put through a 4b5b converter. The encoder also substitutes the first 8 bits of the preamble with the SSD delimiters and adds an ESD delimiter to the end of every packet as defined in IEEE 802.3. The 4b5b encoder also fills the period between packets, called the idle period, with a continuous stream of idle symbols. The 5b data is put through a serial 'scrambler' done by XORing the data stream with a pseudorandom binary sequence as defined in 802.3; this is required because the original 5b encoded data may have repetitive patterns that can result in peaks in the RF spectrum large enough to keep the system from meeting FCC standards. The peaks in the radiated

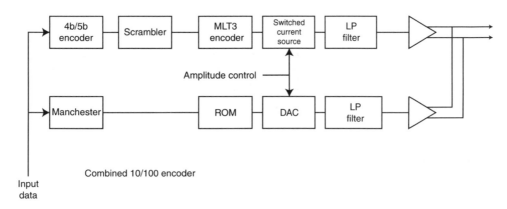

Figure 5-4: Combined 10/100 transmitter section

signal are reduced significantly by scrambling the transmitted signal. The resulting data is then encoded into a three-amplitude level MLT-3 form before being put through a final filter and outputted as differential analog signals. Some devices provide for user programmed facilities to control amplitude and slew rate of the output signal, these take the MLT-3 three-level encoded waveform and uses an array of switched current sources to control the rise/fall time and level of the signal at the output. The output of the switched current sources then goes through a final low pass filter in order to 'smooth' the current output and remove any high-frequency components. In this way, the waveform generator re-shapes the output waveform transmitted onto the twisted pair cable to meet the pulse template requirements required by the FCC and outlined in IEEE 802.3. The waveform generator eliminates the need for any external filters on the transmit output. Figure 5-4 shows a typical combined 10Baset/100Basetx transmitter section.

The receiver

On 100 Mbps systems, the twisted pair is fed directly to the receiver input circuitry. The receiver first removes any high frequency noise, equalizes the input signal to compensate for the effects of the cable, and qualifies the data with an amplitude check and squelch algorithm. The signal is then fed to the MLT-3 decoder, which converts it back to two-level NRZ format binary digits. The incoming signal also goes to a clock and data recovery block, which recovers a constant running clock in sync with the incoming data. The recovered clock is used to latch the valid data into the device, and recover the timing edges required for converting the three level data back to NRZ format. The binary data is then unscrambled and decoded by a 5b4b converter. Once the basic frame has been recovered, it is fed to the checksum filter, and finally stored in FIFO RAM within the controller.

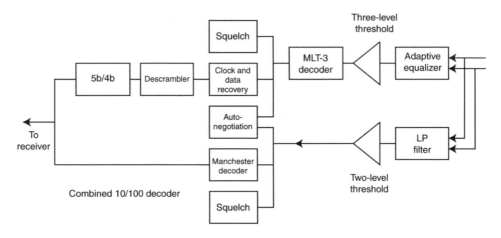

Figure 5-5: Combined 10/100 receiver

The 10 Mbps operation is similar to the 100 Mbps operation, except that there is no scrambler/descrambler, and the decoding method uses is Manchester instead of 4b5b. On 10 Mbps systems, the output of the receive filter goes to two different types of comparators, squelch and zero crossing. The squelch comparator determines whether the signal is valid, and the zero crossing comparator is used to sense the actual data transitions once the signal is determined to be valid. The output of the squelch comparator goes to the squelch circuit, and also used for link pulse detection and reverse polarity detection. The output of the zero crossing comparator is used for clock and data recovery in the Manchester decoder.

In both 10 and 100 Mbps systems, the frame processor computes the received checksum and compares it with a locally generated value. If the two are the same, the received frame is stored in the next available internal FIFO RAM buffer. Different devices have different methods for allocating receive memory. Some use a circular FIFO wrap-around buffer, others use list of pointers, each pointing at a different segment in RAM. Once the user program reads a buffer, it is its responsibility to make that buffer available for further input. The user program must also peel off the data fast enough to avoid buffer overflows. Figure 5-5 shows the block diagram of a combined 10/100 receiver.

Squelch

The squelch function determines if the data input contains valid data. In 100 Mbps systems, squelch is one of the criteria used to determine link integrity. The squelch comparators compare the signal inputs against fixed positive and negative thresholds, called squelch levels. The output from the squelch comparator goes to a digital squelch circuit which determines if the receive input data on that channel is valid.

If the data is invalid, the receiver is in the squelched state and data is ignored. If the input voltage exceeds the squelch levels at least four times with alternating polarity within a 10 μs interval, the data is considered to be valid by the squelch circuit and the receiver enters the unsquelch state. In the unsquelch state, the receive threshold level is reduced by approximately 30% for noise immunity reasons, and the input signal is deemed to be valid. The device stays in the unsquelch state until loss of data is detected. Loss of data is detected if no alternating polarity unsquelch transitions are detected during any 10 μs interval. When the loss of data is detected, the receive squelch is turned on again.

The squelch algorithm for 10 Mbps mode is identical to the 100 Mbps mode except that the 10 Mbps squelch algorithm is not used for link integrity but to sense the beginning of a packet. Also, the receiver goes into the unsquelch state if the input voltage exceeds the squelch levels for three bit times with alternating polarity within a 50–250 ns interval. The receiver will also go into the squelch state when idle is detected. Squelch requirements are defined in IEEE 802.3, Clause 14.

Collision detection

On 100 Mbps systems, collisions occur whenever transmit and receive occur simultaneously while the device is in half-duplex. Collisions are sensed whenever there is simultaneous transmission and reception (non-idle symbols detected on the input). When collisions are detected, the MAC terminates the transmission. The collision function is disabled if the device is operating in full duplex mode. Collision in 10 Mbps mode is identical to the 100 Mbps mode except that reception is determined by the 10 Mbps squelch criteria. In Ethernet, the collision handling algorithms use the CSMA/CD method described in 802.3. When a collision is detected, the transmitter will wait for a random time, and tries again. The back-off algorithm is fully described in 802.3.

Auto-negotiation

Auto-negotiation algorithms are required for two purposes: To automatically configure devices for either 10/100 Mbps or half/full-duplex modes, and for establishing an active link to and from a remote device. The auto-negotiation algorithm is defined in IEEE 802.3, Clause 28. Auto-negotiation uses a burst of link pulses, called fast link pulses (FLP), between 55 and 140 μs (in order to difference them from real data) to pass up to 16 bits of signalling data back and forth between the controller and the remote device (which could be a hub). Once a negotiation has been initiated, the controller first determines if the remote device has auto-negotiation capability. If the remote device is not auto-negotiation capable and is just transmitting either a 10BASE-T or 100BASE-TX signal, the local controller will sense that and place itself in the correct mode. If the controller detects FLP signals from the remote device, then the remote device is determined to have auto-negotiation capability and the device then uses the contents of its registers to advertise its capabilities to a remote device. The remote device does the same, and the capabilities read back from the remote device are stored in its local registers. The controller negotiation algorithm then matches its capabilities to the remote device's capabilities and determines what mode the device should be configured to according to the priority resolution algorithm defined in IEEE 802.3, Clause 28. Once the negotiation process is completed, the controller then configures itself for either 10 or 100 Mbps mode and either full- or half-duplex modes (depending on the outcome of the negotiation process), and it switches to either the 100BASE-TX or 10BASE-T link integrity algorithms (depending on which mode was enabled by auto-negotiation).

Jabber

A jabber condition occurs when the transmit packet exceeds a predetermined length. When jabber is detected, the transmit outputs are forced to the idle state, collision flags are asserted, and register bits in the status registers are set to notify the user. Many devices allow jabber to be disabled by the setting of a corresponding register bit. The jabber function is usually disabled in the 100 Mbps mode.

Interframe gap

There is an obligatory 9.6 μs interval between the last transmitted frame and the next (corresponding to a 96 bit time delay at 10 Mbps). This allows other stations wishing to transmit to take over the line during this time.

Diagnostic loopback

Loopback modes are used mainly for test purposes. During loopback, the transmit data is fed back to the receiver without being transmitted to line. Loopback can be arranged at the digital level (i.e. out of the encoder back into the decoder), or at the output line level, that is, the transmit differential signals are looped back to the receiver amplifier. Most Ethernet controllers provide comprehensive loopback and diagnostic facilities.

Machine-independent interface

The machine-independent interface (MII) is a nibble wide packet interface defined in IEEE 802.3. Its main purpose is to interface controller devices that are split between bus- and line-side operations. The controllers described in Table 5-1 do not make use of MII because both bus- and line-side functions are performed within the chip. Some controllers provide MII access lines for external connection to a separate PHY interface component (e.g. a fibre optics driver).

Reset

The controller chip performs an internal system reset when either the external RESET pin is asserted high for at least a few milliseconds, or when writing a bit to a given control register. When reset is initiated (and the flash EPROM is present) the controller will load the EPROM data to obtain the configuration data for the registers, I/O base addresses, and MAC addresses. If a flash EPROM is not present, the external software program will need to write the right addresses into the registers directly.

DMA buffers

Arriving frames from line are placed in internal RAM buffers within the controllers after receive processing. Different controllers have different methods of allocating RAM to receive and transmit frames. Some allocate memory sections dynamically with pointers; others place the incoming data in a FIFO or circular buffer. The user interface is presented with a pointer to the start of the received block. It is nominally the responsibility of the user program to retrieve the data as quickly as possible, and then release the memory allocation or advance the pointer to the next buffer available. Although the DMA area is commonly accessible both to the controller and to the user interface, some simple Ethernet devices do not offer full asynchronous dual port access facilities. In order to avoid memory clashes (where both the internal hardware and the user need to access the same section of memory), the user interface must provide for some sort of arbitration logic. This can be implemented by the user program sensing a wait or ready line such as IOCHRDY while writing or reading to the data registers. This tells the user that memory is available or that a DMA transaction has taken place.

DMA memory is usually arranged internally as 16 or 32 bit wide words. The most efficient way to read DMA data is by using full 16 bit (or even 32 bit) wide access. In order to conform to legacy ISA specifications, most controllers allow for limited '8 bit only' access. In which case, the program must access both upper and lower bytes as two separate operations. Many controllers cannot use their internal memory effectively while in 8 bit mode, and only a proportion of this memory may be available to the user. For example, the RTL8019AS has a total of 16 kbytes or RAM, but only 8 kbytes are available in 8 bit mode.

Control registers

Most controllers use four (or five) external address lines to access up to 64 internal register locations. These registers are paged, which means that the device internally may have more than 16 registers but only 16 are accessible at any one time as input/output. Switching between pages is effected by writing a page number to one of the registers, the next read or write operation will then access the register in the now selected page. On power reset, the device will usually default to page zero. Tables 5-2 and 5-3 show register maps for two common devices, the RTL8019AS and the LAN91C9111, respectively. In the RTL8019AS, location zero (register CR) contains the common page number. On the 91C9111, this is at address 0Ehex. Note how all the pages mirror the same register used to select the page. This means that the page register is accessible at the same address number from all pages.

Table 5-2: Register map for RTL8019AS

Nr (Hex)	Page 0 [R]	Page 0 [W]	Page 1 [R/W]	Page 2 [R]	Page 3 [R]	Page 3 [W]
00	CR	CR	CR	CR	CR	CR
01	CLDA0	PSTART	PAR0	PSTART	9346CR	9346CR
02	CLDA1	PSTOP	PAR1	PSTOP	BPAGE	BPAGE
03	BNRY	BNRY	PAR2	–	CONFIG0	–
04	TSR	TPSR	PAR3	TPSR	CONFIG1	CONFIG1
05	NCR	TBCR0	PAR4	–	CONFIG2	CONFIG2
06	FIFO	TBCR1	PAR5	–	CONFIG3	CONFIG3
07	ISR	ISR	CURR	–	–	TEST
08	CRDA0	RSAR0	MAR0	–	CSNSAV	–
09	CRDA1	RSAR1	MAR1	–	–	HLTCLK
0A	8019ID0	RBCR0	MAR2	–	–	–
0B	8019ID1	RBCR1	MAR3	–	INTR	–
0C	RSR	RCR	MAR4	RCR	–	FMWP
0D	CNTR0	TCR	MAR5	TCR	CONFIG4	–
0E	CNTR1	DCR	MAR6	DCR	–	–
0F	CNTR2	IMR	MAR7	IMR	–	–
10–17			Remote DMA port			
18–1F			Reset port			

Table 5-3: Register map for LAN91C9111

Nr (Hex)	Page 0	Page 1	Page 2	Page 3
0	TCR	CONFIG	0 MMU COMMAND	MT0-1
2	EPH	STATUS	BASE PNR	MT2-3
4	RCR	IA0-1	FIFO PORTS	MT4-5
6	COUNTER	IA2-3	POINTER	MT6-7
8	MIR	IA4-5	DATA	MGMT
A	RPCR	GENERAL	DATA	REVISION
C	RESERVED	CONTROL	INTERRUPT	ERCV
E	BANK	BANK	BANK	BANK

Interrupts

Most controllers provide one (or more) interrupt pin outputs. Interrupts are required when the controller needs to notify the main program quickly about an event. For example, on reception of a valid frame, the receiver will set a flag in one of the registers, and generate an interrupt (if the interrupt enable flag is set). This interrupt signal is brought out as an external device pin, which is connected to one of the interrupt inputs of an external micro controller. Depending on device design, receiver interrupts can be generated once for every frame received, or when the receive queue (FIFO of packets) reaches a certain value. This allows the interrupt service routine to process more than one receive frame in one operation. Interrupts can also be generated during transmit after the completion of a successful transmission, or when the transmit FIFO is empty. Interrupts can also be generated during error conditions, that is, when receiving an illegal or erroneous frame.

Base addressing

Ethernet controllers designed for the PC ISA bus normally present the full 20 bit address pins to the outside world. As only four to five address lines are used by the chip, the rest are hardwired to an internal address enable decoder. This allows the controller chip to perform full address decoding directly off the ISA bus without the need for external components. Internally, the upper 16 lines are compared with a constant stored in a look-up table. This look-up table can be internally programmed depending on the state of some of the external pins, or by the chip reading initial status from an externally connected EEPROM during hardware reset. This allows external systems such as 'plug-and-play' to re-configure base address and interrupt locations for the device. The default base address when no programming has taken place is 300 hex. This is the standard 'legacy' address range allocated for network I/O cards in PC systems.

User bus interface

Bus interfacing is very simple and straightforward and can be easily implemented in software (by bit banging) or in hardware (using direct mapping and hardware read/write lines). Detailed bus timing will depend on the microprocessor used; see Figure 5-6.

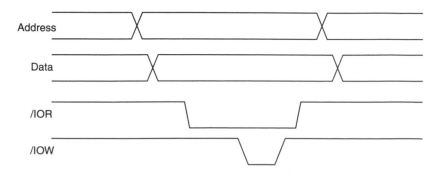

Figure 5-6: Bus interfacing to and from an Ethernet controller chip

For a register read operation, the microprocessor places the wanted address on the bus (bringing the address select line AEN low at the same time). After a short setup time (about 50 ns), it asserts the /IOR line (by bringing it low). The controller will attempt to access the register data and place it on the bus. Because of DMA restrictions, some chips may take longer to read some registers. This will be indicated by the IOCHRDY line driven by the controller going low for a time, inserting wait states. The microprocessor should wait for this signal to become active, and then read the data port after IOCHRDY goes high. Lastly, the microprocessor should de-assert its /IOR line (by setting it high). A write operation is just as simple. The microprocessor places the address, AEN low and data on the bus. After a short setup time, assert the /IOW line by bringing it low. The controller will lower the IOCHRDY signal until it is ready to accept the data. The micro waits for the IOCHRDY line to go high (meaning the controller has read the data) and then de-assert /IOW to end the cycle. The IOCHRDY signal going low acts as a 'busy' indicator, as the controller may not always be ready to receive external commands. This is usually of the order of a few microseconds, and most slow micro controllers can do without using this line.

To conform to ISA standards, many Ethernet interface chips such as the Realtek 8019 can be configured for 8 or 16 bit data transfers. The mode of operation is selected by linking one or more of the device pins to ground (IOCS16B in the Realtek 8019), and also by initializing some of the internal registers (both must be done). The 8 bit transfer mode can simplify the bus logic and software, especially for 8 bit microprocessors. However, this doubles the access rate and in some cases reduces the amount of internal memory available for transfers. Some 10/100 Mbps devices also allow for 32 bit transfers.

Figures 5-7 and 5-8 show examples of memory and I/O mapping between a microprocessor and an Ethernet controller. Some microprocessors, such as the 8051 series, use an octal latch clocked by the ALE line to generate the high end addresses. As the Ethernet controller only requires four lines, this is not always necessary. Note how the address inputs pins to the controller have been hardwired to generate the base address of 300hex. With memory mapping, a single 8051 mov@dptr, instruction can be used to move data from the accumulator to any of the registers in the current page. In I/O mapping, bit blatting needs to be used to generate the /IOR and /IOW pulses. Do not always assume that I/O mapping is slower than memory mapping. Many operations require the movement of data from a single register to a pointed memory location. In 8051 cores with a single pointer, this may require the pointer to be swapped between the two pointers. I/O mapping could be faster in this case.

Fast access

For very fast throughput, as may be required for voice or video streaming, a small microprocessor will not be fast enough. This is because microprocessors require

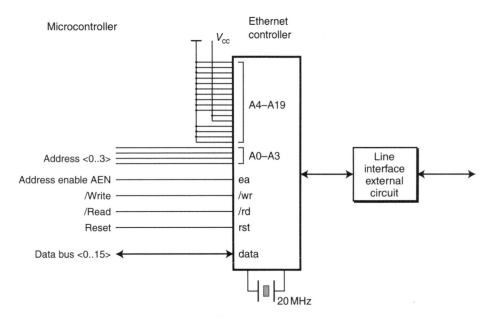

Figure 5-7: Generic Ethernet controller interfacing

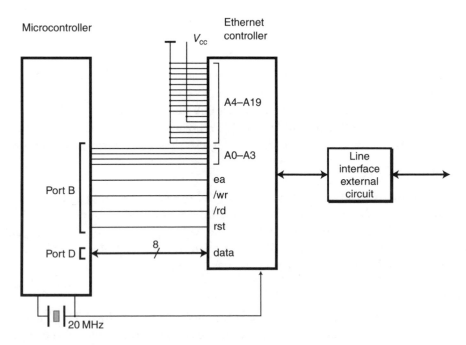

Figure 5-8: I/O mapping between a microprocessor and Ethernet controller

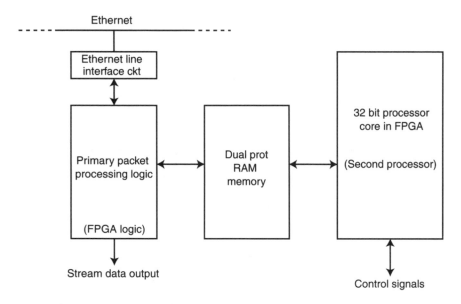

Figure 5-9: Dual processor fast Ethernet

many instructions to transfer data from one location to another. Figure 5-9 shows a design concept using a FPGA with an internal CPU core (an embedded processor). Arriving frames are pre-processed by the FPGA hardwired logic (first processor), and stored in dual port RAM for further processing by the program based embedded PC core. Pipelined functions such as checksums, header address comparisons etc are handled by the first processor in real time. Operations such as management of state tables, connection establishment and other higher-layer software intensive functions are handled by the second processor. Designs like these can be fast enough for real-time 100 Mbps and even 1000 Mbps systems. Most GA families provide, as add-in modules, full Ethernet 10/100/1000 Mbps MAC and PHY layer interfaces. These devices can connect via MII hardware interfaces to separate physical layer analog connections.

Pin connectivity

Table 5-4 shows pin-out conventions for three of the most common Ethernet controller devices. Note how similar they are (apart from their names). The SMS series can handle more data pins when used in 100 Mbps mode and for 32 bit data transfers. As an example, Figure 5-10 shows a full circuit diagram connection between a Realtek 8019AS and a microprocessor bus.

Initialization

Low-level firmware is required for initializing and driving the chips. There are three basic tasks to be performed: (i) initialization (usually performed once at the beginning of the program); (ii) transmit frame; and (iii) receive frame. Helper functions are also

Table 5-4: Pin-out conventions for three common Ethernet controller devices

Realtek RTL8019	Cirrus 8900	SMS 91C111	Notes
SD0–SD15	SD0–SD15	D0–D31	Data bus. The 8019 and 8900 support 8 and 16 bit accesses (8 bits by connecting only to the lower 8 pins). The 91C111 can supports 8, 16 and 32 bit accesses. Lines nBE0, nBE1, nBE2 and nBE3 are used to select which nibble to access
SA5–SA19	SA3–SA19	SA3–SA19	Address bus. Usually hardwired to a fixed value such as 300 hex to correspond to the default base address
SA0–SA4	SA0–SA3	SA0–SA3	Address bus. Used to select one of the registers at the currently selected page. The 91C111 uses lines nBE0 and nBE1 to address the lowest bytes
AEN	AEN	AEN	Denotes address line is valid
IORB	nIOR	nRD	I/O read strobe. Used for asynchronous read of a register value
IOWB	nIOW	nWR	I/O write strobe. Used for asynchronous write of a register
	nELCS	nADS	Address strobe for systems using address latching, similar to ALE in microprocessor systems
IOCHRDY	IOCHRDY	ARDY	I/O access control. This signal is negated on a leading nRD or nWR. It is then asserted when the read or write has taken place. Nominally used as a wait signal
RSTDRV	RESET	RESET	A high value held for a few milliseconds will cause a system reset
INT[0.7]	INTRQ[0.2]	INTRO	Interrupt output
IOCS16B	nIOCS16B	nLDEV	Used to select between 8 and 16 bit accesses Note that internal register values will also need to be set in order to select between 8 and 16 bit access modes
SMEMRB	nMEMR	None	Used for memory mapped access
SMEMWB	nMEMW	None	Used for memory mapped access

needed to poll or sense the controller to see if data has been transmitted, or if there is data available for reception or there has been an error condition. Interrupts can be used instead of polls. These are the generic steps required in order to initialize a typical controller. For more information, refer to the individual data sheets.

- Perform a global device reset, either by raising the hardware reset line, or by setting the reset bit in one of the control registers.

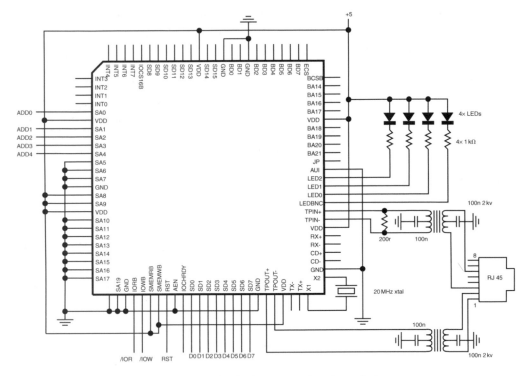

Figure 5-10: Realtek 8019AS bus interfacing

- Remove the transmitter from the line: This is required in order to ensure any setting up will not place unwanted data on the network.

- Initialize DMA areas and relevant pointers. Allocate RAM areas for transmit and for receive frames. It is also possible with some devices to allocate areas dynamically (on the fly, during a session), but in most cases; it is easier to set then once. Most controllers have user accessible red and write settable pointers to the DMA areas.

- Store the MAC address in the controller's registers. This is required to perform address comparisons on incoming frames. Most controllers are able to automatically download a MAC address from a connected flash EEPROM device. If no EEPROM is used, the values must be written to the registers during initialization.

- Initialize internal operation of the controller. Set such things as speed, number of bit transfers, mode of operation etc. by writing the corresponding data to the paged registers.

- Enable interrupts (if used).

- Restore the transmitter connection to the line, and set the TX/RX enable bits. This places the controller on line and enables it for reception and transmission.

The listings in Chapter 9 show a typical initialization sequence for the Realtek 8019. Sequences for other devices will be found in their respective data sheets and application notes.

Transmitting a frame

The general sequence for transmitting a data frame is as follows. It is assumed that the microprocessor has already prepared a valid frame for transmission, including addresses and protocol type fields (but not checksum, as it is computed during transmission).

- Allocate transmit buffer space. Some controllers may have a fixed area allocated for transmission, some other need to have this are allocated just before transmission.

- Wait for successful allocation. Test the condition to ensure the controller was able to allocate a transmit buffer and that data can be transmitted to line.

- Place the transmit data in the DMA buffer. The frame will include address, type and payload. The controller will later add preamble and checksum.

- Issue a transmit command, by setting a flag into one of the registers. The transmission is now placed in the output queue, and the controller will now attempt to transmit the frame now if the line is clear, or wait until later.

- Wait for transmission completion, either by polling a flag or waiting for a transmit completed interrupt. Check the error status and handle any possible errors if relevant.

- Release the memory allocated for the transmit frame if necessary.

See Chapter 9 for code examples for the Realtek 8019AS.

Receiving a frame

The general sequence of operation for receiving a frame is as follows. Two methods are possible, using interrupts, or by regular polling; the program flow following this, is the same in both cases.

- Sense the frame received flag either by polling or by interrupt. The controller notifies the program that a frame has been received that either matches the address, or has a broadcast address. The controller will have allocated an area of internal DMA RAM and copied the receive frame into it.

- Process the frame by retrieving the pointer to the DMA receive area, size of frame, and reading the DMA buffer into the microprocessor byte or word at a time.

- Release receive resources by deallocating the memory allocated for the frame so that it can be used again.

See Chapter 9 for code examples for the Realtek 8019AS.

Using ready-made modules

Why make if one can buy? Over the last few years, many ready-made network-enabled modules have appeared in the market. In general, they consist of a microprocessor, 10BaseT Ethernet interface chip, plus associated magnetics, all in a small printed circuit board, usually smaller than a credit card. Network software is supplied in the form of ready-to-use software stacks, usually containing a number of higher level application interfaces such as web servers and email handlers. Development modules are also offered in the form of printed circuit cards, complete with power supplies, LEDs, RS232 interfaces and sometimes with solder tab side panel where custom hardware can be wired on. These PCB modules are ideal for getting used to networking and as an easy introduction to embedded networking.

One easily overlooked problem is the physical handling of the chips. These come in tiny flat pack packages with lead pitches of half a millimetre in some cases. Soldering these miniature devices onto printed circuit boards by hand can be a very difficult task indeed. By buying a ready made module, these problems do not arise. The learning value of these self contained devices for prototyping is unquestionable. A harder question will arise when considering final production. Should one use a ready module as a 'plug-in' into your circuit? or should one obtain the separate components and wire directly onto your PCB? This can be a hard decision, and some comments have already been made in section on Points to Consider Before Networking Embedded Systems in chapter 1. In some cases, the decision is made for you. The supplied software may come under license, and the supplier will only allow you to use it under certain conditions. Many developers new to networking will want to avoid getting buried in the complexity that surrounds prototyping and ready made solutions are the easy route to market. When development and production costs are added together, modular solutions can be just as attractive as budget low-cost approaches using in house designs, especially for low production runs. It is not possible to list here all the modules available at one time, as there are far too many on offer. New ones appear very regularly, and others become obsolete or out of production just as fast. A list of some existing modules is given in Table 5-5, this is by no means exhaustive, as so many manufacturers are involved in the production of embedded modules. A good source for the latest information are web sites dedicated to embedded systems such as www.embedded.com, alternatively enter keywords such as 'embedded TCP/IP' or 'free TCP/IP stack' on any online search engine.

Complete IC devices with built combined controller and microprocessor are also available. For example, The Dallas DS80C400 network microcontroller

Table 5-5: List of some existing modules

Ceibo TCP/IP-51	8051 based	www.ceibo.com
Picdem.net	PIC based	www.microchip.com
Rabbit	Custom	www.rabbitsemiconductor.com
Netburner	Coldfire MCF5272	www.netburner.com
i2Chip.inc	Iready/Seiko 7660	www.i2chip.com
Siteplayer	8051	www.siteplayer.com
Technologic	PC-104 Intel 586	www.embeddedx86.com
JK Microsystems	Intel 386	www.jkmicro.com
Sumbox	Intel 386	www.sumbox.com
Beck	Intel 186	www.bcl.de
WinSystems	PC/104 Pentium	www.winsystems.com

offers an 8051 core, 10/100 Ethernet MAC, three serial ports, a CAN 2.0B controller and 64 I/O pins all in one package. A full TCP IPv4/6 network stack and OS are also provided in ROM. The network stack supports up to 32 simultaneous TCP connections and can transfer up to 5 Mbps through the Ethernet MAC. Its maximum system-clock frequency of 75 MHz results in a minimum instruction cycle time of 54 ns. Access to large program or data memory areas is simplified with a 24-bit addressing scheme that supports up to 16 MB of contiguous memory.

Wireless Technologies 802.11

Wireless does not necessarily mean there are no wires involved. The technology also refers to networks where existing cabling may be used for other purposes. For example, the mains power grid. Wireless media is drastically different to standard Ethernet (a wired media system). This is a reason why the Ethernet specifications were not simply enhanced to operate in a wireless environment. The main differences are:

- *Unpredictable media*: the medium has neither absolute nor observable boundaries. Parts of the media (in geographical terms) can be shared with other similar wireless networks operating in different domains, perhaps in somebody else's network.

- *Lack of full connectivity*: stations may not be able to hear each other and therefore LAN-based carrier sense mechanisms may not work properly.

- *Time-varying propagation properties*: signal levels may change drastically during a session.

- *Unpredictable effect of mobile stations*: stations can wander in and out of domains while communicating.

Standard Ethernet practices are not applicable to wireless technologies because:

- Destination address does not necessarily mean destination location. In wired LANs an address is always related to a physical location. In wireless LANs, an address can be a message destination, not necessarily a fixed location.

- Collision detection is impractical because this would require a full duplex radio set (cost implications).

- The medium error rate is minimal (in comparison to wireless systems). A typical radio link may need to tolerate regular error rates in the range of ten per million. Wireless systems must include some form of low level error correction capabilities to compensate.

At present, there are several contending LAN technologies for wireless systems. Among these, IEEE 802.11 is the most supported by hardware manufacturers, and fast becoming the preferred standard for wireless LAN applications.

IEEE 802.11 architecture

The original IEEE 802.11 specifications date back to 1997, and refer to a 1 and a 2 Mbps standard operating in the ISM 2.4 GHz radio band. The initial 802.11 standards defined two basic forms of spread spectrum modulation: frequency hopping (FHSS) and direct sequence modulation (DSSS). In 1999, the IEEE published an enhancement to the specifications called 802.11b. This improved on the original standards by providing a DSSS-based system offering up to 11 Mbps. More recently, the IEEE 802.11a standard was presented. This defines operation at up to 54 Mbps using orthogonal frequency division multiplexing (OFDM) in the 5 GHz frequency band. The IEEE 802.11a standard offers a number of high-speed data rates available, 6,9,12,18,24,36,48 and 54 Mbps, and promises to be popular with high-speed peripherals.

All systems are upper-layer compatible with the existing IEEE 802.3 Ethernet type systems. Most wireless LANs implemented today comply with the 802.11b version of the standard. Because of their direct compatibility with other IEEE 802.x networks, they can be incorporated into an existing LAN with little effort. The 802.11b components are small, making them attractive with hand-held and point of sale mobile terminals for communicating within an office or warehouse, alarm systems and environmental monitoring devices. Falling prices and increasing performance are making wireless LANs very attractive for many products where ordinarily a wired connection would have been established. The biggest problem is interference. This is not because of the standards, but because of the frequency allocation. IEEE 802.11 allocations are shared with other users. These include BlueTooth, domestic video senders, microwave ovens and other LAN systems. Security is also a concern. Wireless LANs cannot be controlled in extent or coverage, and can spread outside the confines of the office, making eavesdropping a real problem.

Overall network topologies

Wireless networks topologies are different to wired LANs. In a wired network, the system manager knows who and where all the nodes are. In a wireless network, nodes can be out of range, disconnected, or roaming (traveling across nodes). Signal strength can vary considerably from one second to the next, and offices and buildings can be full of 'dead spots' where radiation cannot reach. Network topology must be flexible enough to allow multiple domains to coexist, and for stations to be easily identified and accepted when they join a new network. IEEE 802.11 defines two basic topologies: BSS and ESS. A simple wireless LAN may be formed by one or more roaming cells or stations without a central unit. This is called a basic service set (BSS), also known as an ad hoc network; see Figure 5-11.

Another format uses many cells with a single access point. The access point is a fixed unit connected to the wired LAN in the building. This is called an extended service set (ESS). The access points are connected through some kind of backbone (called distribution system or DS). This backbone is typically Ethernet and, in some cases, may be another form of wireless itself. The whole interconnected wireless LAN, including the cells, their respective access points and the distribution system, is seen as a single 802 network to the upper layers of the OSI model. The IEEE 802 standard also defines the concept of a portal. A portal is a device that interconnects between an 802.11 and another 802 LAN. This concept is an abstract description of part of the functionality of a 'translation bridge'.

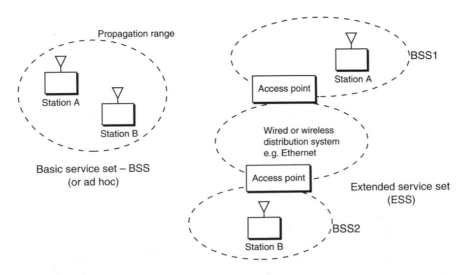

Figure 5-11: IEEE 802.11 network topologies

Table 5-6: Global spectrum allocation
2.4 GHz band

US	2.400.0	2.483.5
Europe	2.400.0	2.483.5
Japan	2.471.0	2.497.0
France	2.446.5	2.483.5
Spain	2.445.0	2.475.0

The basic bit data format

As with other IEEE 802.x protocols, 802.11 contains a MAC layer and a physical layer. The current IEEE standards define a single MAC, which interacts with three PHY layers. These are: direct sequence spread spectrum (DSSS), frequency hopped spread spectrum (FHSS), and infrared (IR). The DSSS and FHSS PHY options were originally designed to conform to FCC regulations 15.247 for operation in the unlicensed 2.4 GHz ISM band. This radio band is particularly attractive because it enjoys worldwide allocations for general use, as summarized in Table 5-6. The FCC established the operating rules specifically to facilitate shared use of the band for the transmission of data and voice by multiple users in this unmanaged, unlicensed environment. It stipulated the use of spread spectrum techniques (either DSSS or FHSS) when radiating in excess of 1 mW.

The DSSS encoding method used in 802.11b is not new. Similar technology is being used in GPS satellite navigation systems and in CDMA cellular telephones. In the basic 1 Mbps DSSS system, the data stream is combined via an exclusive or (XOR) function with a high-speed pseudorandom numerical sequence (PRN) as shown in Figure 5-12. The PRN specified by 802.11b is an 11 chip Barker code. This

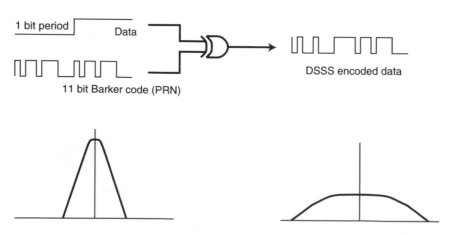

Figure 5-12: DSSS encoding using an 11 bit pseudorandom chip stream

particular sequence has well-known autocorrelation and comma-free properties that makes it suitable for this application. The term chip is normally used to denote bit positions in a PRN to denote the fact that the Barker code does not carry any binary information by itself. The result of the XOR operation is an 11 Mbps digital stream, which is then modulated onto the 2.4 GHz carrier frequency using differential binary phase shift keying (DBPSK). The effect of the pseudorandom modulation (or scrambling) is to spread the transmitted bandwidth of the resulting signal by a ratio of 11:1 (hence the term 'spread spectrum'). The total bandwidth required is of the order of 20 MHz; the peak power of the signal is also reduced by a similar ratio. The total power spectrum of the signal however, is unchanged, it is only spread over a wider bandwidth. Upon reception, the signal is recovered using a correlation process with a locally generated version of the same pseudorandom chip sequence. The correlation process has a significant benefit; it reduces the level of narrow band interference, which falls in band by the same 11:1 ratio. This effect is known as processing gain.

In the 2 Mbps DSSS option, the modulation system used is differential quadrature phase shift keying (DQPSK), which effectively doubles the bit rate without increasing the radio bandwidth. The penalty to pay is a slightly lower dynamic range and signal to noise ratio. This is not too important for systems that are in close proximity. Although there are 11 channels identified for DSSS systems in the United States and Europe, there is a lot of channel overlap. When multiple devices are located in close proximity, it is recommended to use frequency separations of at least 25 MHz. Therefore, the ISM band will accommodate three non-overlapping DSSS based 802.11b channels.

FHSS relies on a completely different approach. In this method, the carrier frequency hops from channel to channel in a pre-arranged pseudorandom manner. The receivers are programmed to follow-hop in the exact sequence as the transmitter. If one channel is jammed, the section of data lost data is simply retransmitted when the system hops to a clear channel. Information is modulated using either two-level frequency shift keying (2FSK) at 1 Mbps, or four levels FSK (4FSK) at 2 Mbps. The occupied single channel width of a FHSS band is restricted to 1 MHz. IEEE 802.11b specifies 79 channels (United States and Europe) over which the FHSS radios hop in a pre-determined manner. There are 78 different hop sequences; so several nodes can be located in close proximity to each other with a fairly low probability of collision on any given channel. IEEE 802.11b does not specify a hop rate, that parameter is left up to local regulations. In the United States, FCC regulations stipulate a rate of 2.5 hops/s, or a channel dwell period of 400 s; see Figure 5-13.

Complementary code keying modulation

The faster 5.5 and 11 Mbps DSSS systems use complementary code keying (CCK) to further compress the 1 Mbps data stream, while still maintaining the same overall

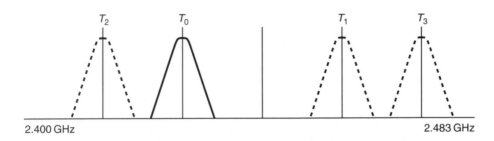

T_2 T_0 T_1 T_3

2.400 GHz   2.483 GHz

Figure 5-13: FHSS frequency hopping modulation

bandwidth. CCK is a multilevel, dual-phase coding scheme. Input data is XORed with spreading chip sequences much in the same way as in the 1 Mbps system. However, the spread sequences have eight chips each (as opposed to 11 chips with the Barker sequences). Each data input symbol is modulated with one of 256 chip sequence combinations.

The chip codes are based on complementary codes, which are in turn related to Hadamard and Walsh functions. The codewords have unique autocorrelation functions that allows them to be detected independently of each other. CCCK uses a DQPSK encoding method to transmit codewords as 0° and 90° phased signals (the 5.5 Mbps uses only one phase). Before modulation, the transmitter partitions the input data into nibbles (4 bits) or bytes (8 bits). At 5.5 Mbps, it uses two of the bits to select one of four complex spread sequences from the 256 table of CCK sequences. It then QPSK modulates that symbol with the remaining 2 bits. Thus, there are four possible spread sequences to send at four possible carrier phases, but only one is sent. This sequence is then modulated on the 0° and 90° outputs. The initial phase reference for the data portion of the packet is the phase of the last bit of the header. At 11 Mbps, 1 byte is used as above where 6 bits are used to select one of 64 spread sequences for a symbol and the other two used to QPSK modulate that symbol. Thus, the total possible number of combinations of sequence and carrier phases is 256. Of these, only one is sent. Figure 5-14 shows a summary of all the modulation schemes.

The 802.11b radio

Many manufacturers have developed complete radios as chip sets, or as printed circuit board layouts. These incorporate all the PHY functionality into a small piece of ready-made hardware. The modules may or may not also include some of the MAC level functionality as well.

Receiver

Figure 5-15 shows a typical radio front end. The RF section of the circuit is relatively straightforward. The input RF at 2.4 GHz from the shared transmit/receive aerial is fed to a band pass filter and then to an RF variable gain amplifier. The integrated

DSSS BPSK 1 Mbps	DSSS QPSK 2 Mbps	BMBOK 5.5 Mbps	QMBOK 11 Mbps

Data in:

1 bit encoded to one of two codewords (Barker code) true/inverted

2 bits encoded to one of four codewords (Barker code) in two 90 degree phases

4 bits encoded to one of 16 modified Walsh function sequences

8 bits encoded to one of 256 modified Walsh function sequences in two 90 degree phases

Output:

Normal:

Quadrature:

11 chip Barker sequence (1 Mss)

2 × 11 chip Barker sequences (1 Mss)

8 chip sequence (1.375 Mss)

2 × 8 chip sequences (1.375 Mss)

Figure 5-14: Summary of encoding methods used in 802.11 radio systems

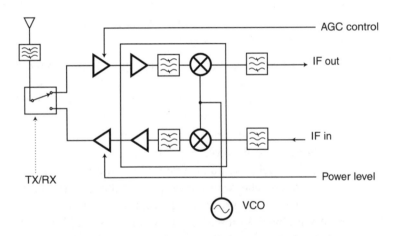

Figure 5-15: Typical 802.11b radio receiver front end

receivers have limited intrinsic dynamic range, and their gain needs to be critically adjusted by the control microprocessor in order to ensure the radio outputs levels are relatively constant in amplitude. In practice, both RF and IF amplifiers are fed from an AGC signal derived from a D/A converter to provide this compensation. The 2.4 GHz RF stage is followed by a mixer or converter stage. The input signal is mixed with a locally generated VCO signal to result in an IF signal of about 280 MHz. This is fed to an IF SAW band pass filters with a bandwidth of about 17 MHz, which is just wide enough to pass the 11 Mbps chip data. The VCO is an integrated PLL IC serially controlled by the microprocessor. The 14 allocated RF channels in the band

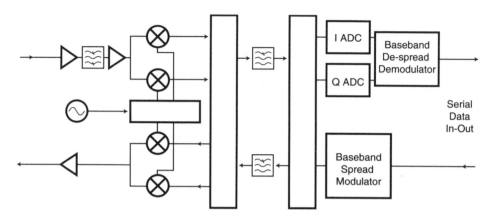

Figure 5-16: IF stages and quadrature demodulator

are selected by choosing one of 14 PLL LO derived frequencies. The oscillator ranges between 2132 and 2204 MHz, that is, twice the IF frequency below the assigned channels. The use of a lower frequency IF makes filtering much easier, although the latest generation of radio sets can now do the processing directly at the 2.4 GHz rate without the need for a mixer stage.

Figure 5-16 shows the IF processing stages. The IF signal goes through two limiting amplifiers and further 280 MHz SAW band pass filtering. The purpose of the limiters is to fix the amplitude of the signal to a relatively fixed value (around 200 mV) under all input signal conditions. This leveling is in addition to the AGC provided by the variable gain RF and IF stages. The signal is then demodulated to base band using two quadrature multipliers at the IF frequency. The reference used is a locally generated phase-locked 560 MHz oscillator, from which the two quadrature 90° out of phase signals are generated. The resulting outputs of the quadrature mixers are low pass filtered and fed to a base band processor. Here, the quadrature signals are analog to digital converted in wideband 3 bit converters at a rate of 22 Mbps, which results in two samples per chip. At this point, the signals are base band spread spectrum and of a constant vector amplitude. In other words, each quadrature I and Q input may vary in amplitude, but their combined vector sum will be constant in amplitude. The baseband processor then correlates the signal with a locally generated PN spreading to remove it and to uncover the differential BPSK (or QPSK) data. The processor initially uses differential detection to identify and lock onto the signal. It then makes measurements of the carrier and symbol timing phase and frequency and uses these to initialize tracking loops for fast acquisition. Once demodulating and tracking, the processor uses coherent demodulation for best performance. At this point the data packets, which now resemble MAC packets, are fed to the MAC processor (not shown) All packet signals have a preamble followed by a header containing a standard IEEE 802 frame including a start frame delimiter (SFD), headers and a cyclic redundancy check (CRC). The MAC processes the header data to locate the SFD, determine the mode and length of the incoming message and check the CRC. The MAC then processes the packet data and sends it on through the bus interface to the host computer. The MAC checks the CRC to determine the data purity. If corrupted data is received, a retransmission is requested locally by the MAC, which handles the physical layer link protocols.

Transmitter

Data from the host computer is sent to the MAC processor via the high speed bus interface. Before any communications however, the MAC sends a request to send (RTS) packet to the other end of the link and receives a clear to send (CTS) packet to ensure the line is clear. The MAC then formats the payload data packet (MPDU) by appending it to a preamble and header and sends it on to the baseband processor. The baseband processor scrambles the packet and differentially encodes it before applying the spread spectrum modulation. The data can be either DBPSK or DQPSK modulated and is a baseband quadrature signal with I and Q components. The BPSK spreading is a PRN chip sequence that is modulated with the I and Q data components. Transmit quadrature single-bit digital inputs are low passed and applied to the quadrature IF modulator/demodulator from the baseband processor. The IF signal is bandpass filtered and applied to the up mixer. A variable gain RF amplifier feed the transmit aerial with a controlled signal. This is to ensure no more RF signal than necessary is transmitted.

MAC processor

The MAC processor converts the serial data signals from the demodulator to bus compatible parallel buffered data. It also generates all the serial control and PLL programming signals under register control. Internal firmware implements the full IEEE 802.11b wireless LAN MAC protocol. The MAC will locally supports BSS and IBSS operation under the optional point coordination function (PCF). Low-level protocol functions such as RTS/CTS generation and acknowledgement, fragmentation and de-fragmentation and automatic beacon monitoring are also handed locally without host intervention. Active scanning is performed autonomously once initiated by host command. Host interface command and status handshakes allow concurrent operations from multithreaded I/O drivers. Additional firmware functions specific to access point applications are also available. In summary, the operations for the MAC engine are:

- internal encryption engine executes IEEE802.11 WEP,

- implementation of the MAC protocol specified in IEEE 802.11-1999 and 802.11b,

- host interface supports 16-bit interfacing to PC ISA or PCMCIA bus,

- carrier sense multiple access with collision avoidance (CSMA/CA) with random backoff,

- WEP security,

- short/long preamble with multirate,

- RTS/CTS handshake and NAV management,

- MAC level acknowledgments (media access control),

- re-transmission of unacknowledged frames,

- duplicate detection and rejection,

- broadcast and multicast frames,

- fragmentation and re-assembly,

- distributed coordination function (DCF),

- point coordination function (PCF),

- beacon generation in an ad hoc network,

- probe response generation in an ad hoc network.

Practical radio interfacing

To save the designer from having to lay RF-critical printed circuit boards, many
WLAN chip makers have products available that can be obtained in the form of
ready-made modules. These include stand-alone cards as well as PCMCIA
compatible plug-in cards. Two types of user interface are practical, at the system
level, where the user has to generate all the control SDI signals and data is presented
as baseband serial rate at 2 Mbps, or via the built in MAC manager. Two typical
MAC managers are the AMD79C930 and the Intersil HSP3841. These provide bus
interface at the ISA or PCMCIA levels. The 16 bit PCMCIA interface is similar in
concept to ISA in terms of timings, but requires a few extra register management
operations to handle the full PCMCIA protocol.

Primitive level interfacing

This allows direct control of the radio, bypassing the MAC controller. The
advantages of using this method are that raw radio facilities can be accessed directly
and used for custom design, or for special protocols (e.g. audio). The disadvantages
are that IEEE 802 MAC facilities are not present, and they must be implemented
separately in software if the IEEE standards are to be met. Access is via two serial
SDI interface modules consisting of separate clock, data and chip select signals,
which can be easily implemented in bit-bang software or FPGA firmware. The
modem management interface (MMI) is used to read and write internal registers in
the baseband processor, set the PLL division ratios and access per-packet
information. The modem data interface (MDI) provides the receive and transmit data

paths which transfer the actual data. The MMI interface uses individual chip selects and shared clock and data lines. In the Intersil PRISM chipset there are four signals: SD (serial data), SCLK (serial clock), R/W (read/write) and CS_BAR (active-low chip select). It provides the following basic functions:

- initialization settings for the radio,
- method of coding,
- PLL synthesizer (set operating channel frequency),
- RF stage gains, transmit and receive,
- T/R switching.

The MDI operates on the data being transferred to and from the baseband on a word-by-word basis. There are no FIFOs, and the user software must be able to control the protocol in real time. The MDI performs the following functions:

- serial to parallel conversion of received data from the baseband,
- generation of CRCs (HEC and FCS) from the received data stream to verify correct reception,
- decryption of the received data when WEP is enabled,
- parallel to serial conversion of transmit data, with the serial timing synchronized with the TX clock,
- insertion of the CRCs (HEC and FCS) at the appropriate point during transmission,
- encryption of the transmitted data when WEP is enabled.

Interfacing at the PHY level is best done with a dedicated high-speed device such as a PGA. Some FPGA manufacturers provide detailed application notes on how to do this.

PCMCIA bus interfacing

Many MAC host interface chips are fully compatible to the PC Card 95 Standard (PCMCIA v2.1), which is in turn similar to the standard PC ISA bus. The MAC interface connects directly to the correspondingly named pins on the PCMCIA interface connector with no external components required (other than resistors). The controller operates as an I/O card using less than 64 I/O address locations. Reads and writes to internal registers and buffer memory are performed by standard I/O accesses. Attribute memory (256 bytes) is provided for the CIS table, which is located in external memory. Common memory is not used. The logical view of the MAC controller from the host is a block of I/O mapped registers. These appear in I/O space starting at the base address determined by the PCMCIA socket controller.

CHAPTER 6

Data Link Management

This chapter describes the support provided by the data link layer. This layer is responsible for providing node-to-node communications within a single local network. In other words, the layer manages control and flow of data between each of the nodes of a network. The two relevant operations here are *addressing*, where each node or station is assigned a unique address so that they can recognize each other, and *translation*, where messages arriving from one layer (upper or lower) are converted to messages the opposite layer can understand.

What is the Job of the Data Link Layer?

The previous chapter covered a few of the basic networking technologies available and the methods used for transferring data between nodes and for maintaining a connection, namely the physical PHY layer. Some of the functions described there, such as addressing and collision handling, were more the remit of the data link layer in the model, but because of their close interlinking with the hardware components, had to be included as part of that section.

Figure 6-1 shows where the data link layer fits in relation to the various conceptual models. The functions the layer manages are as follows:

> *Basic level error management*: The layer provides the simplest form of error handling consistent with the quality of the channel. Little provision for error management may be required for example, in reliable channels such as wired Ethernet. More sophisticated error management methods will be needed for less predictable channels such as wireless networks. From the diagram above, we can see how the IEEE has developed parallel data link layer MAC strategies depending on the physical method used. This allows the provision of the right kind of error management for each physical media characteristics.

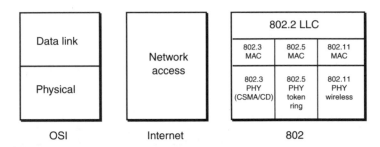

Figure 6-1: Data link layer model correspondence

Channel contention: The layer is responsible for ensuring the shared medium is used effectively. Various carrier sense techniques are used to guarantee only one station makes use of the medium at a time. Again, the techniques will depend according to the physical characteristics of the medium.

Addressing: Each station connected to the network must have a unique physical address. The layer must include facilities for stations to know of the existence of others in the network, and to access facilities for accessing or recognizing the address of other station in the network, even using centrally provided facilities for allocating and managing these addresses.

Data flow: The layer is responsible for ensuring that data transferred from the upper layers is queued and transmitted onto the medium, and that data received is separated from its preambles, and clock information, and after simple quality checking, that is, checksum calculation, passed on to the next layer up.

Data packaging: The layer is also responsible for packaging the data into acceptable blocks or frames of sizes ideally suited for the physical medium. This may include breaking the data into smaller grouped segments, and reassembling them on reception. Some applications may send data continuously (streamed), others blocked into large or small chunks. One job for the data link layer is to break these down into manageable sized packets or frames. Frames consist of blocks of data containing a payload (the data to be sent) plus a header that containing data and control fields such as addresses, commands and checksums. The receiver uses these to determine what to do with the frame and whether it has arrived without any errors.

Within the data link layer, the MAC layer provides for

- *Individual methods for channel contention*: by the use of various carrier sense techniques, such as hidden node detection, and ACK methods for local error management and re-transmission requests.

- *Management of overlapped multiple networks*: these are networks that may be present in the same medium space. This is mainly relevant in the case of wireless technologies.

- *Privacy and access control*: by the use of passwords and encryption.

- *Dynamic addressing*: including facilities for seamless moving between and across overlapping nearby networks.

The LLC layer provides for a variety of data flow channel services including unacknowledged connectionless, connection oriented and acknowledged connectionless services. As their names imply, different qualities of services can be provided by this layer. There is some overlap in the way these services may be used by the layers above. For example, a local network user database manager may use a connection oriented channel, whereas IP services may use an unacknowledged connectionless channel (do not confuse these services with similarly named ones offered by higher-layer protocols). LLC also provides for encapsulation, which is another word for data packaging. The LLC is responsible for presenting clean payloads to the layer above, and to perform all conversions required to transform a data payload into one suitable for transmission down the medium.

In the Internet model, the network access layer encompasses both the OSI data link layer and the physical layer. The network access layer is a combination of access methods defined by various standards. These include old and new access technologies from Local Area Networks (LANs) and Wide Area Networks (WANs). In the IEEE 802.x model, the data link layer covers the logical link control (LLC defined in IEEE 802.2) and the media access control (MAC). Because the operation of the MAC is intertwined with the physical method of transmission, the MACs are defined individually for each of the physical formats used. For example, 802.3 describes CSMA/CD (Ethernet), 802.5 token ring, and 802.11 wireless technologies.

To explore link control further, we must relate it to the general technologies it applies to, in WANs and LANs. These are discussed in the next sections.

Wide Area Networks – SLIP/PPP

A WAN is described as one connecting two local networks together via a third party carrier service. A subset of the definition also includes a point-to-point link between two nodes using a full time wired connection. The connection can be an optical link, a microwave link, or in many practical cases, an RS232 link via dedicated or dial-up modems. Whichever method is used, there is a constant connection link between the two points, and there are no procedures for 'connection establishment' or 'connection termination' as such. This is because dedicated lines are always assumed to be on. If the link is to be established, it is considered as a separate manual operation. Even in the case of dial up modems, the connection establishment is left to the operator (who may perform this by hand). To all extents, the physical connection during the session will be considered as a dedicated point-to-point link.

In a WAN, the carrier is a shared medium, collections of data from several sources need to be multiplexed on transmission and de-multiplexed at the other end.

Furthermore, the carrier may also be supporting other forms of signalling, so data has to be encapsulated. Encapsulation is a method in which blocks of data are framed by special control characters. Special patterns (which may be interpreted by the channel as various forms of signalling) are avoided by the use of data conversion techniques and the use of escape sequences.

The most relevant WAN link layer technologies for embedded systems are SLIP and PPP, although they have found their way into other applications that require managed point-to-point connections, including wireless systems such as Bluetooth. The facilities provided by these technologies are as follows:

- *Separate control and data transmission (data delimitation)*: It is useful to be able to separate the actual data from control or signaling information. Control information is used in carriers for many purposes, debug and management of the link, setting up parameters, other facilities or users also using the carrier using different protocols etc. This is implemented in both SLIP and PPP by the use of unique separator characters.

- *Separate protocols*: This is needed in order to allow the transmission of different protocols down the shared line. SLIP is purely a point-to-point transparent link, and does not provide any such facilities; PPP on the other hand, includes facilities for separating data sections according to the protocol being carried.

- *Limit the data pattern set (data translation)*: Some carriers are sensitive to certain data sequences. For example, special codes may be used for flow control over a slow serial link. If these characters appear in a normal data stream, they may interfere with its operation. In other words, the link may not like certain byte patterns and they should not be sent as data. In order to avoid this, SLIP and PPP make use of escape sequence that convert otherwise illegal characters into valid multiple byte sequences.

- *Integrity checks (error protection)*: Serial lines are prone to errors, which can mean both noise and erratic line disconnections. PPP includes a checksum calculation for every packet sent.

SLIP

SLIP stands for serial line Internet protocol. It is nothing more than a simple method for encapsulating IP datagrams (or any other type of serial data) for transmission over ordinary serial lines such as modem connections. SLIP provides nothing in terms of addressing, security, compression, or error detection. It provides however, for data delimitation and for limited data translation. SLIP was popular in the early days of the Internet for connecting home computers to ISPs via dial up lines. SLIP is fully described in RFC 1055.

SLIP uses one special character (The END character, or C0hex) to accomplish encapsulation. The END character is transmitted immediately after the last byte of every datagram sent on the link. This END separator provides a detectable separation between messages, which the receiver can use to identify and separate the received datagrams. Most SLIP implementations use the END character as a start delimiter as well as an end delimiter. In other words, datagrams may have an END character at the beginning and at the end of their packets. Spurious characters that may have been received in the dead time between a terminating END and the starting END of another datagram are simply ignored. It may also happen that normal data may contain a C0hex byte, in which case, SLIP replaces it with the two byte sequence DB-DChex. The byte DBhex is known as the 'escape' character. The receiver performs the opposite operation, by converting every DB-DChex byte pair into the single byte C0hex, thus restoring the original data. Similarly, to avoid confusion with any escape characters appearing in the original stream, these are replaced with the two byte sequence DB-DDhex. When the receiver sees any of these two pairs, it replaces them with the relevant single byte. In summary the rules for SLIP are as follows:

- All messages are terminated with an END character. Optionally, these can also appear at the beginning of the message. END characters can only occur at the beginning and at the end of the SLIP frame. More than one END characters can follow one another, these are just ignored.

- SLIP escapes any END character (C0hex) appearing within the original data with the two byte sequence DB-DChex. This sequence must be translated back by the receiver handler to the original C0hex.

- SLIP escapes any ESC character (DBhex) appearing within the original data with the 2 byte sequence DB-DDhex. This sequence must be translated back to DBhex by the receiver handler. For example, if the original data contains the sequence DB-DChex, the transmitter will send DB-DD-DChex.

Figure 6-2 shows an example of a SLIP sequence, before and after encoding. There is no size limit for SLIP packets, although most implementations use an agreed limit of 1006 bytes (not including delimiters). This is based on the original Berkeley UNIX implementation. SLIP does not support any form of negotiation, therefore the translation format is fixed for all transactions. SLIP also supports a form of header compression known as C-SLIP, this is described in RFC 1144. SLIP is of dubious value for transmitting data other than IP datagrams between different systems and its standardization may have been over-rated. For those occasions where private data needs to be transmitted over a custom serial link, it may be more cost effective to develop a proprietary escape-based protocol. This may still be based on the SLIP concepts of encapsulation and translation, but using a wider range of control codes to improve on the start–stop limitations and to provide for translation for other forbidden code sequences including 8–7 bit conversions.

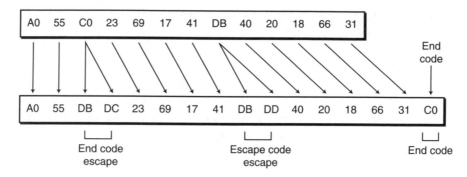

Figure 6-2: Example of SLIP escape sequences

PPP

PPP stands for point-to-point protocol. It was developed as a major improvement over SLIP. Among the improvements, PPP provides extra flag fields for identifying which protocol is being carried, to test the link itself, and to negotiate a variety of channel 'options'. In this way, PPP offers data link control mechanisms comparable to those of a LAN. PPP is used in both synchronous and asynchronous data links. In asynchronous data links, the standard format is start-top code with eight bits and no parity. PPP is fully discussed in RFC 1661, 1662 and 1663, it covers the following basic services:

- *Encapsulation*: Data link encapsulation method that supports different escape convention standards, by means of a 'negotiated' look-up table.

- *Link control protocol (LCP)*: Capable of negotiating data link characteristics, and configuring and testing the link in a number of ways. LCP is described in RFC 1548 and 1662.

- *A family of network control protocols (NCPs)*: These can be used to configure the link for the various network layer protocols that will use it. This can include addressing, number allocation, compression and other issues. NCPs are described in RFC 1332 and RFC 1877.

- *Multilink protocol*: An extension to PPP that allows to bundle links from different sources and destination, that is, perform multiplexing. Multiple physical connections (i.e. multiple modems operating in parallel) can also be made to appear as one logical link, to increase overall speed, for example.

The various control protocols are designed to make PPP as versatile as possible by automatically negotiating and agreeing on each parameter in turn. A transmitter or receiver can agree or disagree on requests made by the other end, or suggest alternatives. PPP is mainly used over full-duplex serial WAN interfaces, although it can also operate in half-duplex mode under certain circumstances. At the lowest

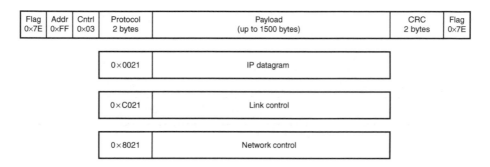

Figure 6-3: PPP encapsulation

level, PPP requires different formats for encapsulation and translation. For ordinary point-to-point serial links (such as modems), PPP encapsulation follows a scheme similar to SLIP.

PPP header

Top of Figure 6-3 shows the basic PPP frame. The flag byte (7Ehex) is used as a delimiter. Each frame begins and ends with a flag byte. This is followed by an address byte, which is always FFhex in single point-to-point. This is followed by a control byte, which is fixed as 03hex for simple links. Next comes the protocol field. This is similar in context to the Ethernet field already discussed in the last chapter, although the actual values are different: 0021hex means the payload contains an IP datagram, C021hex means the payload is a link control data, and 8021hex means the payload contains network control data. This is followed by the payload, and ended with a 2-byte error control CRC field.

PPP escape sequences

Since the byte 7Ehex is the flag character, any occurrences of this byte anywhere else in the frame must be escaped. In data synchronous data links, this is done by bit stuffing, that is by adding extra bits to the transmitted data, which must be stripped off at reception. In start–stop (UART) asynchronous data links, this is done by pairing character sequences, just like SLIP. The rules are:

- Any occurrence of the byte 7Ehex in the original data is transmitted as the 2 byte sequence 7D-5Ehex.

- Any occurrence of the byte 7Dhex in the original data is transmitted as the 2 byte sequence 7D-5Dhex.

- PPP also allows other byte sequences to be escaped. This facility is negotiated between the two sides, usually at the beginning of a session. A programmable look-up table called the async-control-character-map (ACCM) is maintained

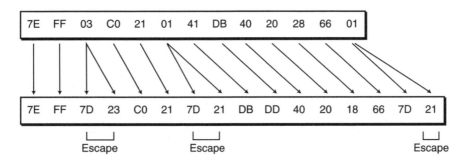

Figure 6-4: PPP escape sequences

at both ends to define the characters to be escaped. For example, it is usual to set transmitted characters less than 20hex to be escaped using the 7Dhex byte. For example, 01hex is transmitted as 7D-21hex. The general escape procedure is to complement the sixth bit of the next character after the 7Dhex escape byte. The default ACCM sets all characters below 20hex to be escaped.

It is important to note that escaping must be added just before transmission, and escaping removed just after reception. All control bytes, including header bytes and checksums go through the escape mechanism. All internal processing however is done in the un-escaped form. See Figure 6-4 for an example.

PPP header compression

In a serial point-to-point link, most PPP frames will contain the same 3 byte header <7E-FF-03>. Some implementations transmit these headers in compressed form. A receiver must be able to detect normal and compressed headers equally. In compressed form, either the address and/or the control bytes FFhex and 03Hex can be omitted (it is common to omit both). For example, the normal sequence <7E-FF-03-C0-21-...> can be received as <7E-C0-21-...>, <7E-FF-C0-21-...>, or even <7E-03-C0-21-...> One clue for detecting the right format is that the protocol field is always even (bit 0 is always a zero). A simple header decoding algorithm would ignore any odd bytes following the flag character. For completeness, the receiver should also cater for situations where unconventional escaping has modified the header. For example, the receiver should be able to recognize all the following as valid headers

- <7E><FF><03>

- <7E><FF><7D><23>

- <7E><7D><DF><03>

- <7E><7D><DF><7D><23>

PPP CRC field

The CRC or FCS field contains 2 bytes (although a 4 byte option can be negotiated). The FCS is calculated over all bits of the address, control, protocol, payload and padding fields (e.g. everything except the flag bytes and the FCS itself). The FCS is calculated before escape conversion. The FCS generator polynomial is $1 + X^5 + X^{12} + X^{16}$. A demonstration procedure that accumulates a checksum given a data byte is shown in Figure 6-5.

PPP protocol field

At the framing level, the protocol and payload contain the fields shown in Table 6-1.

Each PPP packet is preceded by a protocol identifier, a list of common protocols relevant to embedded applications is shown in Table 6-2. Certain rules exist for protocol type numbering. All first bytes must be even, and all second bytes must be

```
WORD  CheckAccrue(byte data, WORD cksum)
{  WORD cs; int i;
   cs= ( data ^ chksum ) & 0xFF;
   for (i=0; i<8; i++)
   { cs = cs/2;
     if (cs&1) cs = cs ^ 0x8408;
     cs = cs ^ (cksum/256);
   }
   return  cs;
}
```

Figure 6-5: PPP checksum program

Table 6-1: Protocol and payload fields

Protocol ID (16 bits)	Information or payload (Variable length)	Padding (Variable length)

Table 6-2: Common protocols relevant to embedded applications

Protocol ID	Description
0021	Internet protocol (IP)
002D	VJ compressed IP
002F	VJ uncompressed IP
C021	Link control protocol (LCP)
C023	Password authentication protocol (PAP)
C025	Link quality report
C223	Challenge handshake authentication (CHAP)

odd. That is, the least significant bit of the least significant byte must be one, and the least significant bit of the most significant byte must be a zero.

Protocol field values in the 0000–3FFF range are used to identify the network layer protocol in use, for example, 0021 for IP. Protocols in the range 8000–BFFF identify the network control protocol, and protocols in the range C000–FFFF are link control protocols. The payload field carries the actual data to be passed on. The minimum length is zero. The maximum length in bytes (including padding, but excluding the protocol field) is defined by the variable maximum receive unit (MRU). This variable is negotiated during link setup, and the default value is 1500. This makes PPP more or less size 'compatible' with Ethernet frames. The padding field may carry any number of bytes up to the MRU value (usually zeros), these bytes will be ignored at the receiving end. Padding is normally used to run up a sequence to a give number of bytes.

The PPP connection

The PPP connection can be broken into several phases. The starting point is a carrier detect condition between the two links that triggers one end (the client) to try establishing a connection with the remote (the server). For example, a home user (client) establishes a connection with an ISP (server) by dialing up. This first phase uses link control protocol (LCP) to detect and negotiate the options with the remote. Having negotiated the basic options, the authentication phase follows. During this phase, the server verifies the client ID and password using the password authentication protocol (PAP). Compression protocols can also be negotiated here. Finally, the server finishes by allocating an IP network address number to the client for the session, and then go into data transparent mode. The format for the negotiating protocols are very similar. Either side starts by requesting a facility, to which the other end replies with an acceptance or denial, together with a list of services it itself can offer. The negotiation converges into an accepted set of facilities for both parties. PPP uses a state table to determine the sequence of operations. This is shown in Figure 6-6. This is a simple diagram and does not show all possibilities such as time-outs or user change of state requests.

OFF state. This is the state of the link before and after a session. No communication is taking place between the nodes. All system values are set to their defaults. An external event (such as a carrier detect signal from a modem) triggers the transition to the establish state,

Establish state. During this state the LCP is used to negotiate configuration by the exchange of configure frames. The exchange is completed when the Configure-Ack is both received and sent. The table will then move to the next state. Any non-LCP frames are silently discarded during this state.

Authenticate state. Authentication is not mandatory. If present, it is used to ensure the client is an authorized one. When the client has been authenticated, the state table

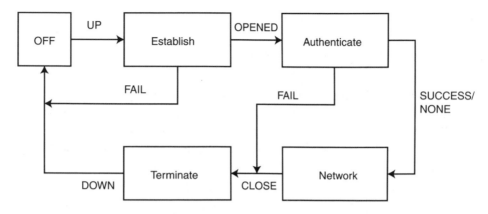

Figure 6-6: PPP state table

Table 6-3: Typical format of LCP Packet

C021hex	Code (1 byte)	ID (1 byte)	Length (2 bytes)	Options (var length)

will move to the next state. During this state, only LCP, PAP and LQR frames are accepted, others are silently discarded. If a LCP Configure-Request packet is received, control will pass back to the establish state (this is not shown in the diagram for clarity).

Network layer state. During this state (and only during this state) IP packets are freely exchanged between the two sides. Other link traffic may include LCP and NCP packets. If a LCP Configure-Request packet is received, control will pass back to the establish state (this is not shown in the diagram for clarity).

Termination state. The link is closed through an exchange of LCP packets. The link can also be closed by an abnormal timeout or other drastic causes. After the exchange of termination packets, it is the responsibility of the controller to physically terminate the link (e.g. put the phone down). During this phase, only LCP packets will be accepted.

Option negotiation

All protocols, LCP, NCP, etc. use similar methods for option negotiations. This is summarized as follows (refer to RFC 1661 for the full description).

LCP packet format. All LCP packets are identified by type field C021hex. The typical format is given in Table 6-3.

The code field is the command carried by the packet. The ID field is a single byte (which can be randomly generated) used to pair up requests and replies. A station making a request with a given ID field, will receive a reply from the remote using the same ID number. The length field is the total size of the message including code, ID, length, and options field. The options field carries the packet payload and can be of zero length. The more relevant code options are as follows (please refer to RFC 1661 for more details):

01hex Configure-Request: This is transmitted to force the link into the establish state. The options field is filled with requests to change link defaults. Upon receipt of a Configure-Request, the other end must reply with a Configure-Ack or a Configure-Nak reply depending on whether it can accept the suggested changes.

02hex Configure-Ack: This is echoed by the remote when ALL the options in the Configure-Req transmitted have been accepted. The ID field must match that of the request, and the options field must be a repeat (echo) of the options accepted. In other words, the options field is returned back to the sender.

03hex Configure-Nak: This is echoed by the remote when one or more of the options in the Configure-Req transmitted are recognizable, but cannot be accepted. The ID returned is the same as sent, and the options field is filled ONLY with the options that were not accepted (but in the same order as sent). This allows the sender to reconfigure a new set of options and send further Configure-Req packets with the changes until all options are finally negotiated.

04hex Configure-Reject: This is echoed by the remote when one or more of the options in the Configure-Req transmitted are invalid or are not recognizable. The ID returned is the same as sent, and the options field is filled ONLY with the unacceptable options from the request.

05hex Terminate-Request: This is sent by one end when it wants to terminate the connection. These should be repeated at regular intervals until a Terminate-Ack is received from the remote.

06hex Terminate-Ack: This is sent in response to a Terminate-Request.

07hex Code-Reject: This is sent when an LCP packet was received with an unknown code.

08hex Protocol-Reject: This is sent when an LCP packet was received with an unknown protocol code.

The options field is made up of groups of *configuration option fields*. Each of these consist of the three fields shown in Table 6-4.

Table 6-4: Configuration option fields

Type (1 byte)	Length (1 byte)	Data (var length)

One or more of these groups are placed together into the options field of the LCP protocol packet. The type field indicates the configuration option that is requested for change. The length field is the total number of bytes including the type, length and data bytes. The data field depends on the request: The type field can be one of the following:

1 – Maximum receive unit: Used to inform the remote that the sender can take larger (or smaller) packets than the default of 1500. The data field is sent as an unsigned two byte word.

3 – Authentication protocol: Provides a method for negotiating a protocol to be used. This is an optional configuration, as authentication is optional. The data field can be either C023hex denoting simple password authentication, or C223hex denoting CHAPS authentication.

4 – Quality protocol: Provides a method to negotiate the use of a specific protocol for link quality monitoring. The default is disabled.

5 – Magic number: Used to negotiate a 'magic number' to be used for link quality control, and for test purposes.

7 – Protocol field compression: Used to negotiate the compression of the PPP protocol field.

8 – Address and control field compression: Used to negotiate compression of the Data Link Layer address and control fields.

PAP packet format

PAP stands for password authentication protocol. PAP packets are identified by type field C023hex. PAP provides a simple method for establishing their identities using a two-way handshake. This is done only during initial link establishment. PAP is not a secure system, passwords are sent in the clear. And there is little protection from snooping or attacks. A more powerful secure protocol (CHAPS) can be used instead in more secure links. All PAP packets are identified by type field C023hex. The typical format is given in Table 6-5 (for more details see RFC 1334).

The code field is the command carried by the packet. The ID field is a single byte (which can be randomly generated) used to pair up requests and replies. A station making a request with a given ID field, will receive a reply from the remote using the same ID number. The length field is the total size of the message including Code, ID,

Table 6-5: Typical format of PAP Packet

C023hex	Code (1 byte)	ID (1 byte)	Length (2 bytes)	Options (var length)

length and options field. The options field carries the packet payload and can be of zero length. The more relevant code options are as follows:

01hex Authenticate-Request: Used to begin the authentication handshake. This is repeated until a valid Authenticate-Reply is received.

02hex Authenticate-Ack: A positive reply to the request.

03hex Authenticate-Nak: A negative reply to the request.

CHAP packet format

CHAP stands for challenge handshake authentication protocol. CHAP packets are identified by type field C223hex. CHAP provides a more advanced method for stations to prove their identities. CHAP is a far more secure method than PAP as no information is sent in the 'clear'. CHAP is described in RFC 1994.

IPCP packet format

IPCP stands for IP control protocol. Its purpose is to help in configuring and enabling an IP transaction between two nodes. The main application of IPCP is the assignment of IP network address to the client by the server. IPCP is described in RFC 1332.

Table 6-6 gives the steps in a typical PPP transaction.

Table 6-6: A typical PPP transaction

Server	Client	Comments
Establishing connection phase		
LCP Req 2,3,5,7		The server starts LCP negotiations by requesting three options (only the negotiation option codes are shown, each of the data fields will contain the actual data to be negotiated). The options in this example are: 2 = ACCM. A list of characters to be escaped (the list is in the data field). 3 = Authentication protocol to use (again in the data field: C023 for PAP, C223 for CHAP). 5 = Magic number to be negotiated. 7 = Whether to enable protocol compression
	LCP REJ 2,5,7	The client accepts option 3 (assume PAP for this example), but rejects options 2,5 and 7. Possibly because the client cannot handle complex escape sequences, and cannot implement compression
LCP Req 3		The server sends an updated request. It has given up requesting options 2,5 and 7, and is now only requesting option 3. Requests must be repeated, even if accepted previously, until all options are accepted

	LCP Ack 3	The client accepts this latest updated version
	LCP Req 2	The client can also make its own requests from the server!
LCP Ack 2		The server accepts the request!

The above negotiations carry on until both parties have agreed on all options. In case of disagreement, one of the other party will terminate the connection by sending an LCP terminate

Authenticating user phase

	PAP-Req	Client triggers the server into authentication mode. The
	'name, pw'	data fields contain the username and password
PAP-Ack		Server acknowledges request

After authentication, the state table moves to the IP initialization phase. During authentication however, the receiver can still accept LCP requests

IP Initialization phase
IPCP-Req

	IPCP-Ack	
	IPCP-Req 4	Client triggers server to provide a dynamic IP
	'0.0.0.0'	address, by sending an invalid one
IPCP-		Server Nacks the request, and offers an IP
Nak, 'IPaddr'		address to be accepted by the client.
	IPCP-Req 5	Client replies by asking for this IP address to be
	'Ipaddr'	allocated to it
IPCP-Ack 4		Server acknowledges the proposed IP address
'IPaddr'		

Standard IP transfers can now begin

Local Area Networks

Wired networks collision management

The mechanism for detecting collisions was briefly described in previous chapters. This is usually handled automatically by the hardware dealing with the physical interface, but sometimes may require some software intervention. Collision handling in Ethernet uses the CSMA/CD backoff algorithm method described in IEEE 802.3. In summary, when a collision is detected, the transmitter will wait for a random time, and try again. When a collision occurs, the station sends a jam signal lasting 48 bits, then ceases all transmissions. After the first collision, each station waits either 0 or 1 slot time before trying again. If two stations collide again because they pick the same delay backoff random number, then each station randomly selects 0, 1, 2 or 3 slot times, these are known as delay windows (after k collisions, a delay of 2^k slots is chosen). Finally after the tenth attempt (back-off limit) the window is limited to 1023 slot times. The attempt can continue up to 16 more times (attempt limit) with the same delay limit. If a collision occurs again, the MAC layer discards the frame and reports a failure. The exponential time growth ensures a long delay when only a few stations collide, but also ensures that the collision is resolved in a reasonable time when many stations collide. The user interface is notified when the frame has been finally transmitted either via interrupts, or by the setting of a flag register. It is always wise to check the status of this register before placing new bytes in the DMA area of the controller as many do not support transmit queueing.

Wireless network collision management

The basic access mechanism is called the distributed coordination function. This is a carrier sense multiple access with collision avoidance (CSMA/CA). The methods used are somewhat different to wired LAN for good reasons:

- Implementing a collision detection mechanism would require the implementation of a full duplex radio capable of transmitting and receiving at once, an approach that would increase the price significantly.

- In a wireless environment, we cannot assume that all stations hear each other (which is the basic assumption of the collision detection scheme). The fact that a station wants to transmit and senses the medium as free does not necessarily mean that the medium is free around the receiver area.

The collision avoidance (CA) mechanism was designed to overcome these problems. It uses a positive acknowledge scheme, and it works as follows:

- A station wanting to transmit senses the medium. If the medium is busy then it defers. If the medium is free for a specified time called distributed interframe space (DIFS), then the station is allowed to transmit.

- The receiving station checks the CRC of the transmitted packet and returns an acknowledgement packet (ACK). Receipt of the acknowledgement by the transmitter indicates that no collision occurred and that both ends can hear each other. If the sender does not receive the acknowledgement within a short time, it retransmits the fragment until it receives acknowledgement. The procedure is abandoned after a time-out has expired after a number of re-transmissions.

In order to reduce the probability of two stations colliding because they cannot hear each other, IEEE 802.11 defines a virtual carrier sense (VCS) mechanism: A station wanting to transmit a packet first transmits a short control packet called request to send (RTS). This packet includes the source, destination, and the duration of the following transaction (in this case the length of the expected reply to be sent back). If the medium is free, and the receiver has read the transmission, it will respond with a response control packet called clear to send (CTS), which includes the same time duration information. All other stations on the network receiving either the RTS and/or the CTS, set their VCS time indicator (called NAV, for network allocation vector), for the given duration, and use this information together with the physical carrier sense when sensing the medium. This mechanism reduces the probability of a collision around the receiver area by a station that is 'hidden' from the remote transmitter for the short duration of the RTS transmission. This is because the station hears the CTS and 'reserves' the medium as busy until the end of the transaction. The duration information on the RTS also protects the transmitter area from collisions during the ACK (from stations that are out of range of the acknowledging station). RTS and CTS are short frames, this mechanism reduces the overhead of collisions, and since these are recognized faster than if the whole packet was to be transmitted. This is true if the packet is significantly bigger than the RTS, so the standard allows short packets to be transmitted without the RTS/CTS transaction. This is controlled per station by a parameter called RTS threshold.

Exponential back-off algorithm

Back-off is a standard method used to resolve contention between different stations wanting to access the medium. The method requires each station to choose a random number (n) between 0 and a given top value, and wait for this number of slots before accessing the medium. At the same time checking if a different station has accessed the medium before. The slot time is defined in such a way that a station will always be capable of determining if another station has accessed the medium at the beginning of the previous slot. This reduces collision probability by half. Exponential back-off means that each time the station chooses a slot and happens to collide, it will increase the maximum number for the random selection exponentially. The IEEE 802.11 algorithm must be executed in the following cases:

- when the station senses the medium before the first transmission of a packet, and the medium is busy,
- after each re-transmission,
- after a successful transmission.

Wireless network operation

IEEE 802.11 defines two basic topologies BSS and ESS. These were also briefly described in previous chapters.

Basic service sets (BSS)

The BSS is the basic building block of an IEEE 802.11 LAN. Each BSS area roughly corresponds to the coverage of a number of stations. A central concept of a BSS is that all stations must 'hear' each other, that is, be within radio or optical range. The association between stations is dynamic, stations can come in and out or range or be switched off. To become a member of a BSS, each station must become associated to the network. These associations are dynamic and are managed and maintained by the use of a distribution system service (DSS). IEEE 802.11 architectures are integrated with others using portals. These are the points at which a non IEEE LAN connects to an IEEE 802.11 distribution system.

IBSS networks. An IBSS is a BSS that has no backbone infrastructure and consists of at least two wireless stations. This type of network is often referred to as an ad hoc network, because it can be constructed quickly and without much planning. The ad hoc wireless network will satisfy most needs of users occupying a small area such as a single room, office or home. This may include file transfer between two notebook users, a coworkers meeting outside the office, etc. The IEEE 802.11 standard addresses this need by the definition of an 'ad hoc' mode of operation. In this case, there is no access point, and part of its functionality is performed by the end-user stations (beacon generation, synchronization, etc.). Other access point functions, such as frame-relaying between two stations not in range, or power saving, are not supported.

Extended service set (ESS) networks

In an extended network, central access points are used to monitor and manage the network on a local basis. Stations are allowed to move from the coverage of one access point to the next (roaming). The IEEE 802.11 standards include facilities for passing-on users seamlessly from one LAN to the next. The coverage of two or more access points can also overlap. IEEE 802,11 also includes procedures for sorting out what happens in these situations and to which access point the user should log to first. When a station wants to access an existing BSS (either after power-up, sleep mode, or just entering the BSS area), the station needs to get synchronization information from the access point (or from the other stations when in ad hoc mode). The station can get this information by one of two means:

- *Passive scanning*: In this case, the station just waits to receive a beacon frame from the access point (the beacon frame is a frame sent out periodically containing synchronization information).

- *Active scanning*: In this case, the station tries to locate an access point by transmitting probe request frames, and waits for probe response from the access point. Both methods are valid. A method is chosen according to the power consumption/performance trade-off.

The authentication process. Once the station has located an access point, and decides to join its BSS, it goes through the authentication process. This is the interchange of information between the access point and the station, where each side proves the knowledge of a given password.

The association process. Once the station is authenticated, it then starts the association process. This is the exchange of information about the stations and BSS capabilities, and which allows the DSS (the set of access points) to know about the current position of the station. A station is capable of transmitting and receiving data frames only after the association process is completed.

Roaming. Roaming is the process of moving from one cell (or BSS) to another without losing a connection. This function is similar to the cellular phones' handover, with two main differences: on a packet-based LAN system, the transition from cell to cell may be performed between packet transmissions, as opposed to telephony where the transition may occur during a phone conversation. This makes the LAN roaming a little easier. On a voice system, a temporary disconnection may not affect the conversation, while in a packet-based environment it significantly reduces performance because re-transmission is then required. The IEEE 802.11 standard does not define how roaming should be performed, but defines the basic tools. These include active/passive scanning, and a re-association process, where a station which is roaming from one access point to another becomes associated with the new one.

Keeping synchronization. Stations need to keep synchronization, which is necessary for keeping hopping synchronized, and other functions like power saving. On an infrastructure BSS, this is achieved by all the stations updating their clocks according to the access point's clock, using periodically transmitted beacon frames. These frames contain the value of the access point's clock at the moment of transmission (note that this is the moment when transmission actually occurs, and not when it is put in the queue for transmission). Since the beacon frame is transmitted using CSMA rules, transmission may be delayed significantly. The receiving stations check the value of their clocks at the moment the signal is received, and correct it to keep in synchronization with the access point's clock. This prevents clock drifting which could cause loss of synch after a few hours of operation.

Fragmentation and re-assembly. Typical LAN protocols use packets several hundred bytes long (the longest Ethernet packet could be up to 1518 bytes long). There are several reasons why it is preferable to use smaller packets in a wireless LAN environment:

- Due to the higher bit error rate of a radio link, the probability of a packet getting corrupted increases with the packet size.

- In case of packet corruption (either due to collision or noise), the smaller the packet, and the less overhead it causes to re-transmit it.

- On a frequency hopping system, the medium is interrupted periodically for hopping (e.g. every 20 ms), so, the smaller the packet, the smaller the chance that the transmission will be postponed after dwell time.

It does not make sense to introduce a new LAN protocol that cannot deal with standard 1518 byte packets as used on Ethernet, so the IEEE decided to solve the problem by adding a simple fragmentation/re-assembly mechanism within the MAC layer. The mechanism is a simple send-and-wait process, where the transmitting station is not allowed to transmit a new fragment until one of the following happens:

- an ACK is received for the fragment, or

- the receiver decides that the fragment was retransmitted too many times and drops the whole frame.

It should be noted that the IEEE 802.11 standards do allow the station to transmit to a different address between retransmissions of a given fragment. This is particularly useful when an access point has several outstanding packets to different destinations and one of them does not respond. The standard defines four types of interframe spaces, which are use to provide different priorities:

SIFS – short interframe space: This is used to separate transmissions belonging to a single dialogue (e.g. Fragment-Ack), and is the minimum interframe space. There is always at most one single station to transmit at any given time, therefore giving it priority over all other stations. This value is a fixed value per PHY and is calculated in such a way that the transmitting station will be able to switch back to receive mode and be capable of decoding the incoming packet. On the IEEE 802.11 FH PHY this value is set to 28 μs.

PIFS – point coordination IFS: This is used by the access point (or point coordinator, as called in this case), to gain access to the medium before any other station. This value is SIFS plus a slot time (defined in the following paragraph), that is, 78 μs.

DIFS – distributed IFS: This is the interframe space used for a station willing to start a new transmission, which is calculated as PIFS plus one slot time, that is, 128 μs.

EIFS – extended IFS: This is a longer IFS used by a station that has received a packet that it could not understand. This is needed to prevent the station (which could not understand the duration information for the VCS) from colliding with a future packet belonging to the current dialogue.

Frame types in IEEE 802.11

The IEEE 802.11 standard specifies an overall frame format as shown in Figure 6-7. This structure is found in all frames that stations transmit, regardless of frame type. The MAC forms the frame and passes control to the physical layer convergence protocol (PLCP) in the form of MAC service data units (MSDU).

Frame control. This field carries control information being sent from station to station. The *protocol version* field is nominally zero. The two bits in the *type* field describe the frame type.

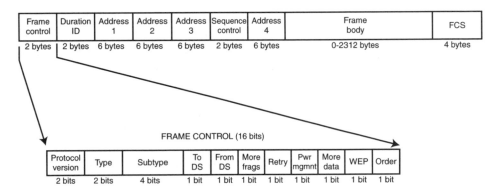

Figure 6-7: MAC frame format

Table 6-7: Two bits describing the
frame type

Bits	Frame type
0,0	Management frame
0,1	Control frame
1,0	Data frame
1,1	Reserved

The sub-type field defines the function of the frame, and will depend on the frame type. The *to DS* field indicates the frame is destined for the distribution system. It is zero for all other transmissions. The *from DS* field is set for any frames leaving the distribution system. Both the to DS and from DS fields are set to one if the frame is being sent from one access point through the distribution system to another access point. The *more frag* field is set to one if another fragment of the same MSDU follows in a subsequent frame. The *retry* field means the frame is a retransmission of an earlier frame. The *power* field indicates the power management mode the sending station will be in after sending the frame. A one means a sleep, or power save mode. The *more data* field will be set if the station has additional MSDUs to send. This field alerts the receiver to be ready for additional frames. The *WEP* field tells the receiver that the frame has been processed by the WEP algorithm, that is, the bits have been encrypted using a secret key. The *order* field tells the receiver that received frames must be processed in strict order.

Duration/ID. In most frames, this field carries a time duration value. Each frame contains information that identifies the duration of the next frame transmission.

Addresses 1, 2, 3 and 4. These contain different types of addresses, depending on the type of frame being sent. These may include the basic service set identification (BSSID), source address, destination address, transmitting station address, and receiving station address. IEEE 802-1990 defines the structure of the addresses, which are all 6 bytes in length. These addresses are in the same format as all other IEEE 802.x protocols, and correspond to the hardware or MAC addresses in Ethernet.

Sequence control. Four bits of this filed consist of a fragment number sub-field. This indicates the fragment number of a particular frame sent (MSDU). The next 12 bits are the sequence number sub-field, starting at zero, and incrementing by one for every subsequent MSDU transmission. Each fragment of a specific MSDU will have the same sequence number.

Frame body. This is the variable length payload, which can be of zero length. In the case of a data frame, the field may contain a LLC data unit (also called a MSDU). Management and control frames may include specific parameters in this frame body that are relevant to the particular service the frame is implementing.

FCS. A 32-bit checksum sequence using a CRC.

MAC frame types

The MAC layer uses a variety of frame types to carry out delivery of MSDUs between LLCs. Management frames are used to establish initial communications, and provide services such as association and authentication. Control frames are used to provide functionality during the transmission of data frames. They are used to provide flow control in the form of RTS, CTS and ACK packets. Data frames carry the actual payload, but can also contain supervisory frames or unnumbered frames from the LLC layer.

Logical Link Control – LLC

The LLC layer is the highest layer of the 802 reference model. It provides functions similar to the traditional data link control protocol high-level data link control (HDLC). The purpose of the LLC is to exchange data across end users using any LAN in an 802-based MAC environment. LLC is independent of the 802 topology, transmission medium and medium access control technique used.

802.2 Logical Link Control

802.3	802.4	802.5	802.11
CSMA/CD	Token bus	Token ring	Wireless

Higher layers can expect to pass data down to the LLC layer expecting a decent error free transmission. The LLC appends a control header to the passed packet creating a LLC protocol data unit (PDU). The LLC uses the control information in the added headers to provide its services. The LLC PDU is passed down to the MAC layer,

Table 6-8: LLC and SNAP headers

LLC Header			SNAP Header	
DSAP(8)	SSAP(8)	Ctrl(8)	Org Code(24)	Type(16)

which in turns appends its own header, forming the MAC frame, which is lastly passed on to the physical layer (Table 6-8).

In Chapter 4, we discussed the extra LLC/SNAP fields in IEEE 802 frames. The DSAP is the destination service access point, which specifies the unique identifier within the station through which a remote station can access. The SSAP has the same meaning, but for a source station. These numbers are globally assigned by the IEEE (see RFC 1700 or RFC 1340). The control part in the LLC header can have either 1 or 2 bytes, depending on the LLC protocol used, but it is generally set to 03hex (this is defined as unnumbered information). The SNAP extension is denoted by the field code AAhex in both DSAP and SSAP fields. The organization code is assigned by the IEEE, and is usually zero. The protocol type is a 2 byte value denoting the protocol used in the payload. The values are the same as those used for Ethernet II.

The LLC layer is responsible for:

- link initialization and disconnection,
- framing data unit,
- synchronization,
- addressing the correct SAP point,
- message acknowledgement,
- error protection,
- flow control.

The LLC layer also provides for three basic types of data flow services:

- unacknowledged connectionless,
- connection oriented,
- acknowledge connectionless.

These services apply only to the communication between peer LLC layers, and must not be confused with similar sounding services provided by upper-layer protocols such as TCP.

Address Resolution Protocol

The address resolution protocol (ARP) is a simple protocol used in wired LANs to provide information about other connected nodes. As mentioned in Chapter 5, ARP is one of the protocol payloads an Ethernet frame can carry (others are IP, and RARP, the reverse address resolution protocol). ARP is a simple query–response packet protocol used to match workstations hardware addresses to IP addresses. In other words, ARP is the protocol used to identify nodes in a LAN. ARP is described in RFC 826.

In a typical LAN, computers need to spend part of their time probing each other. That is, sending short packets too see who else is around the locality. Each computer builds up a table of neighbour active nodes, which is maintained dynamically as nodes are connected or switched off. The table contains mappings of IP versus hardware MAC addresses, this is necessary because a message arriving for transmission from a higher layer may only contain a destination IP address, which must be mapped to a physical hardware destination. Before sending a message to another station in a local network, a computer will consult its own table. If there is no MAC address entry for the wanted IP address, an ARP query broadcast message is sent out, and a wait for a reply will be initiated. The table is dynamically maintained, flushed and refreshed every few minutes.

ARP makes use of the special MAC 'broadcast' destination address (FFFFFFFFFFFFhex), which is accepted by all Ethernet stations on the network. The broadcast message says, 'Hey out there, anybody with IP address 190.168.0.15?' The one and only node having this IP address allocated will reply with a frame containing its own hardware MAC address.

You can see this in action if you have a Windows PC computer. Open an MS-DOS box from the desktop, and enter 'C:>arp -a'. This will display the current IP/MAC address directory pairs for all the local machines in your network. You may see nothing, especially if there was no recent network activity (remember the tables are dynamic and flushed every few minutes). Next, enter 'C:>ping 192.168.0.15' (or the address of any other known station in your network), and wait to see any replies. Then try 'C:>arp -a' again. Assuming you had a ping reply from another node, the screen will show the mappings. Any embedded Ethernet controller must include some form of ARP reply processing in order to respond to ARP 'who are you?' requests from other nodes on the network. The controller will also need to be able to query other nodes in the network for their MAC addresses (ARP requests).

Figure 6-8 shows the basic format of an ARP packet, and how it relates to the Ethernet received frame. The type field is always 0806hex, which denotes ARP (in IEEE 802 frames, the type field is a few bytes further into the data payload). The hardware type and protocol type fields indicate what types of address the ARP packet

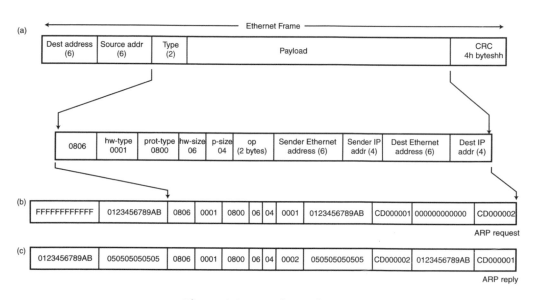

Figure 6-8: ARP frame format

is carrying. `0001hex` and `0800hex`, respectively indicate that the pairing is between a hardware MAC address and an IP address. In a normal Ethernet network, these fields will be always set fixed at these values. The hw size field indicates the size in bytes of the MAC address (always 6 bytes), and the protocol size field indicates the size in bytes of the IP address (always 4 bytes). The op field indicates whether the ARP packet is a request (01hex), or a reply 02hex). The next four fields that follow are the sender's hardware and IP addresses, and the target hardware and IP addresses. Notice there is some duplication of information. The sender's hardware address is supplied both in the Ethernet frame header, and in the ARP request packet. Figure 6-8(b) shows a filled ARP request frame. For this example we assume our MAC address is `0123456789ABhex` and our IP address is `CD000001hex`. The IP address of the remote we want to contact is `CD000002hex` and its MAC address, which we do not know at the outset, is `050505050505hex`. Note how the Ethernet destination frame address in the request frame is `FFFFFFFFFFFFhex` (the broadcast address) as the frame is being sent to all nodes on the network. Note also, how the ARP request destination address is filled with zeros. This field will be ignored anyway. Figure 6-8(c) shows the reply from the remote. Note how the addresses have been swapped around, as the destination and source addresses now correspond in different fields. Note also, how the remote has included its MAC address within the ARP response frame. This address is also echoed in the frame header.

CHAPTER 7

Network Layer – Building on IP

The purpose of the network layer is to help route messages between different local networks. Central to this layer is the concept of exclusive network addresses, where every terminal connected to the network has its own uniquely assigned address. One of the most common protocols in this layer is the Internet protocol (IP), used worldwide throughout the Internet. Every node connected to the Internet must have a different IP address, which can be allocated on a permanent basis, or on a per-session basis, that is, for the duration of a telephone call to an ISP. This chapter is not a treatise on IP, it only covers those aspects most relevant to embedded systems designs and applications. More information can be found in the relevant literature, and more specifically in RFC 791, which is the main document describing IP in full detail.

Internet Protocol

The IP protocol is so adaptable that it has become a common denominator in many communication environments. Physical layer interfaces pass their messages to upper layers that end up generating IP formatted packets. Application layers above use the IP protocol as their basic underpinning building block. By making IP the common standard, systems can work transparently with each other, and afford a clean degree of interoperability (Figure 7-1).

On its own, IP is a simple, effective, and well-tested protocol for carrying blocks of data. It is perfectly feasible for systems designers to develop simple communication systems based purely on IP. Custom designed IP packets will travel around LANs, WANs and the Internet just like any other message. By itself, the IP protocol provides a connectionless datagram delivery system. Within this basic definition, there are no connections, no circuits, no logical paths, just open-ended transmissions. To use the correct terminology, IP provides a connection between services rather than nodes. Services are the general term used to denote the facilities provided by the next layer above the network layer, whereas nodes are the terms used to denote physical

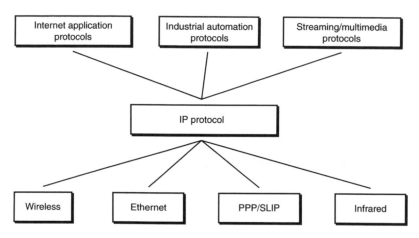

Figure 7-1: IP as the common standard

units. IP blocks of data are usually referred to as packets when talked about in general terms, or as datagrams, when mentioned in the context of connectionless unacknowledged data, the two terms are interchangeable. The basic IP format provides an unreliable service, as there are no built-in guarantees that datagrams sent will arrive at their destination. Routers along the line may decide to forward datagrams along different paths and routes, not necessarily the same for each consecutive datagram. Some may be lost, some may arrive out of sequence, and some may even be duplicated during their travel. It is a job for the higher layers to handle these mishaps, and provide the reliable service to the end application by providing error management. Designers wanting to use IP packets 'raw' must ensure they include their own supporting mechanisms for identifying, sorting and checking every packet received. Fortunately, IP headers carry all the necessary information fields for ensuring this.

The basic IP packet format consists of a header followed by a payload. The header can be between 20 and 60 bytes in length, and is always a multiple of 4. It contains various data fields relevant to the protocol being transported, its operation and management. The payload that follows the header is the user data, which is passed intact to the next layer up; this will usually contain a message in the higher layer protocol format. An IP protocol handler will look only at the IP header, modify or strip it, and pass the payload only to the next layer in the chain. Each IP packet contains a full 32 bit network destination and source addresses. The format of these addresses is recognized to all other users as a network IP address. IP addresses are usually written for human consumption in four decimal digit form, for example, '192.168.0.1', also known as dotted decimal notation. Each of the decimal numbers represent one byte in the 4 byte IP address. For example, the number above corresponds to the 32-bit word C0A80001hex.

Addressing. IP addresses are allocated centrally by the Internet Network Information Centre, and are grouped into address classes. Ranges of addresses are allocated to organizations depending on their size and requirements. These addresses must be uniquely different from each other. Address ranges can also be allocated in a shared or free-for-all basis. These work on the assumption that they will be restricted to nodes in a LAN and that they will not be visible outside it. If the LAN is connected to the rest of the world, the router will isolate these from the outside world.

Fragmentation. This is a very useful function provided by IP. The IP protocol allows for datagrams to be sent singly, containing a single block of data, or to be sent as a collection of smaller sized datagrams, each containing a part or section of the original data block. The process of converting a long datagram into two or more shorter datagrams is called fragmentation. The reverse process is called de-fragmentation. The IP header contains all the fields required for the software handler at each end to perform the break-up or glue-together conversions. In the OSI model, 'fragmentation' is also mentioned as one of the tasks of the higher transport layer. Transport layer fragmentation may be performed independently of IP fragmentation, which is mainly used for dealing with physical layer frame size limitations. In other words, IP fragmentation is a local feature mainly used to break down packets so that they can be transmitted by the size constrained physical layer components.

Figure 7-2 shows an IP datagram and how it relates to an Ethernet II frame. Figure 7-3 shows how it relates to an IEEE 802.3 frame. In both cases, the Ethernet type field for the IP protocol is `0800hex`.

The IP header

The IP packet contains quite a few field elements. Not all of them are used all the time, and many are only relevant in certain applications. The rest can be set to default values (usually zero). This enables simple software implementations to ignore these most of the time. The size of the header section is always a multiple of 4 and can be from 20 to 60 bytes, depending on whether an options field is attached at the end

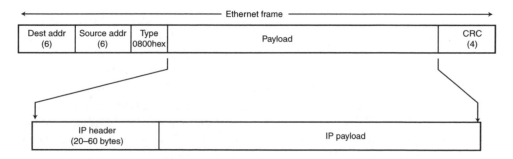

Figure 7-2: IP datagram and its relationship to an Ethernet II frame

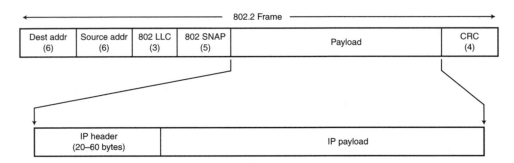

Figure 7-3: IP datagram and its relationship to a IEEE 802 frame

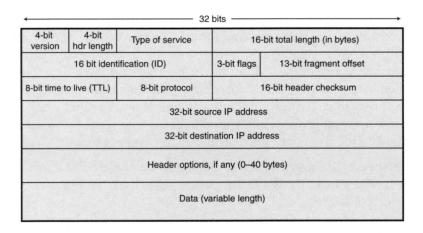

Figure 7-4: IP header format

(Figure 7-4). Multibyte (16 or 32 bit words) are stored most significant byte first (big-endian fashion).

The description of the fields is as follows:

Version/header (1 byte): The first byte of the IP header is divided into two nibbles of 4 bits each. The first nibble denotes the version number of the IP environment. The current version for IP is 4, so this nibble will always be set to 4. The second nibble denotes the number of 32 bit words present in the header, in other words, the header size in bytes divided by 4. A standard IP header with no additional options field will contain 20 bytes (four 32 bit words). The field in this case will be the byte 45hex, denoting a version 4 IP datagram, with a 5 × 4 = 20 byte header. Headers containing more than 20 bytes, are followed by an options field. This options field can contain between 0 and 40 bytes, and is used to carry supplementary information. Many IP headers will have no options field, in which case the first byte will be 45hex.

Type of service (TOS, 1 byte): This may be used to specify a particular quality of service required. Many systems ignore this byte. This is not generally required for small systems and can be left as zero. See RFC 1349 for more details.

Datagram size (2 bytes): The total size of the datagram in bytes. This number includes the size of the header, the size of the options field (if any) plus the total size of the payload. Note that, because of the 2-byte field size, the maximum datagram size is limited to 65 535 bytes. This places a limit on the size of the payload to 65 515 bytes, which is computed from the maximum datagram size minus the size of the header (including options field).

ID (2 bytes): A 16-bit word field indicating an identification number for the packet. This field value is effectively a 'number plate' identification and is usually automatically incremented for every consecutive packet sent by a node (except for grouped fragmented packets where all packets have the same ID). There are no fast rules for defining which ID numbers should be used. At the beginning of a session, the ID is usually set to some random value, and incremented on each subsequent IP transmission. The number will wrap around to zero when it reaches 65 535. ID fields are used to identify possible repeated packets, and as a simple form of recognizing packets out of sequence.

Fragmentation (2 bytes): The field is divided into two parts. The lower 13 bits indicate the offset, or position of the first byte of the payload relative to a larger virtual 'unfragmented' 65 535-byte buffer. The upper 3 bits contain flags related to the state of the current fragmentation. Fragmentation is mainly relevant for transmitting stream data from a sound or video source, usually associated with the UDP protocol. Other protocols such as TCP, have other size limitations, and are unlikely to generate segments large enough to necessitate fragmentation. Systems that do not use fragmentation can set the field to the default zero value. Implementing fragmentation can be an expensive task for a small computer system. The receiver needs to allocate time-out counters and a 64 kbyte buffer for each recognized source to ensure that all received datagrams are aligned correctly in their respective storage space slots.

Time to live (TTL, 1 byte): This flag is used to ensure the datagram does not travel forever in a network. Each time an IP datagram passes through a bridge or a router, its TTL field is decremented by one. If an IP datagram arrives at a node with a TTL value of zero, it is dropped or discarded. In other words, the TTL flag is a self-destruct counter. There is a definite purpose for this field; sending a datagram to an unrecognised IP address may cause the various routers along the way to bounce the packet around like a hot potato. If the TTL field were not available, this packet forwarding would carry on forever. Setting TTL to a too-high value can result in network congestion; a reasonable value is 80 or less. Most datagrams never go through so many interim nodes to reach a destination anyway.

Table 7-1: Most common values of protocols

Code	Description
0 × 01	ICMP
0 × 06	TCP
0 × 11	UDP

Protocol (1 byte): This indicates the type of data carried by the user payload. The most common values are given in Table 7-1. This field can be used in custom IP protocols to isolate the special IP packets and differentiate them from normal protocol carrying packets. The list above is not complete and designers must check with the various RFC documents for any possible clashes.

Checksum (2 bytes): The checksum field is carried out over the header, the optional header, but not including the payload data (which usually contain their own independent checksums). See next section on checksums for information on how they are computed.

Source and destination addresses (4 bytes each): These fields contain the 32 bit IP address of the source. i.e. the originator of the message, and the destination. The addresses are stored as 32 bit words, most significant byte first. For example, the IP address '192.168.0.15' is stored as C0A8000Fhex.

Optional header data (0–40 bytes): Options fields contain extra header data. Option fields are sometimes appended 'on the fly' by routers and gateways. Option fields must contain a multiple of 32 bits, and have no more than 40 bytes in length. Zero padding is usually employed to fill any unused fields to an even value. Option fields are used in system debugging, maintenance, monitoring and error reporting, for example:

- security and handling restrictions,
- record route (each router record its IP address),
- time-stamp (each router records its IP address and time),
- Strict and loose source routing (list of IP addresses that the IP datagram must pass through).

The IP checksum

It has been said that the IP checksum calculation could be by far, the most often performed piece of software or firmware subroutine function in the whole world. There may be a grain of truth in this, every time an IP packet passes through a router or arrives at a destination, its checksum is looked at, recomputed and possibly changed. The same checksum method is used not only in IP but also in higher protocols such as ICMP, UDP and TCP.

IP checksum calculations are performed in 16 bit unsigned word mode. A checksum value is a 16 bit word representing the addition (called the checksum) of a given array of byte data. In this context, bytes are arranged for the purposes of the calculation, in pairs to form 16 bit words. In the case of an array with an odd number of bytes, the odd (last) byte is virtually 'padded' with a zero byte to form a 16 bit word. This does not mean that the extra byte is actually added to the array, only that the extra byte is virtually added to the computation. For calculating the checksum, it does not matter if byte to word pairings are done most significant byte first or least significant byte first in the arithmetic. However, for storage or transmission, specifications state that the 16 bit checksums should be aligned most significant byte first (big-endian fashion).

The checksum is calculated over the supplied array by performing a simple 1's complement addition of all its 16 bit words. The array may be, for example, a complete IP header or an ICMP message. The checksum field itself may be part of this array, in which case it must be first set to zero before performing the computation. The checksum field in an IP datagram is strictly defined as the bit inverse of the checksum addition of the other fields. Therefore, once the checksum is calculated, it has to be bit inverted before placing it back in the checksum field. In other words, the checksum calculation of all the 16 bit words in an array, including the checksum field itself, must add up to FFFFhex.

Most computers do not have special instructions to perform 1's complement addition. Fortunately, a 1's complement addition can be implemented with a normal 2's complement adder using a technique known as end-around-carry. Using this technique, a standard computer addition is performed, with any resulting carry simply added back to the result (Figure 7-5).

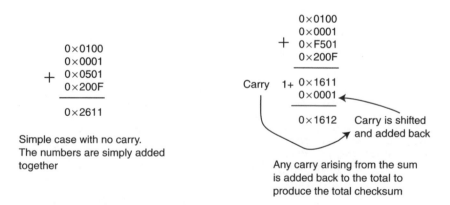

Figure 7-5: Calculating Internet checksums

There have been many arguments whether a more sophisticated CRC-type checksum would have been preferable as an IP checksum (RFC 1145, 1146). In practice, this simple method has performed well and efficiently. The simplicity of the format has found many friends with software developers when debugging programs and checking printouts with only the help of a small hand-held calculator with hex functions.

IP checksums are fully described in RFC 1071 and 1624, which also includes some pseudocode samples. The method of using plain addition for calculating checksums has many interesting properties that allow simplifications and short cuts during calculations (e.g. when making only a few changes to the data array). Some of these techniques are described in RFC 1071, 1624 and 1141. The shortcuts allow checksum calculations to be performed on the fly and in real time without resorting to a full arithmetic loop re-calculation over the whole of the array.

The pseudocode in Figure 7-6 shows a checksum calculation over an array of 'nb' bytes pointed at by a pointer 'p'. It works by first creating a local 32 bit zero initialized variable which accumulates the word pairings in the array one at a time. If the array has an odd number of bytes, the last byte (shifted) is added as a special case. The last line performs the end-around-carry by adding the high 16 bit words to the low 16 bit word. A multiple operation has to be used here because the addition itself may generate a further carry (which will need to be fold-back added again). This multiple operation can be done with a while loop (as demonstrated in RFC 1071), or by performing the fold-back operation as two single operations (less efficient). In this example, DWORD represents 32 bit unsigned words, and WORD represents 16 bit unsigned words.

In machine code terms, this pseudocode is quite inefficient as it involves a 16- to 32-bit word conversion for every addition. This may consume few extra cycles in 32-bit machines, but it may not perform well in 8- or 16-bit machines. Better

```
WORD checksum ( VOID *p, WORD nb)
{
DWORD csum = 0;    // initialize local 32 bit result to zero
WORD   c;          // a scratch variable only used in the last line
WORD* pw = (WORD*)p;  // recast as pointer to WORD array
nb = nb / 2;       // convert count to nr of words (truncated to even)
while ( nb--) csum += *pw++;    // add all the array elements
if (nb & 1)  csum +=*(BYTE*)pw; // special case if odd nr of bytes
// end-around-carry addition
while ((( c = (WORD)(csum>>16))!=0) csum = (csum&0xFFFF)+c;
return csum;
}
```

Figure 7-6: Internet checksum pseudocode

performance could be obtained by writing the function directly in assembler and by making use of the carry bit (which is not directly accessible in C).

Hardware implementations of the checksum computation are described in RFC 1936.

Fragmentation

The lower 13 bits of the fragmentation field indicate the position of the first byte of the payload relative to the original IP buffer. In other words, the offset field represents a pointer to the location of the data carried by the payload in the received stream. A value of zero means the data is to be placed at the beginning of the larger virtual buffer. The three upper bits of the 16 bit word mark the current state of fragmentation. Bit 15 is always zero. Bit 14 is the *don't fragment* flag. This should be set to zero to allow fragmentation and to one to prohibit fragmentation. Bit 13 is the *more fragments* flag. This is set to zero if there are no more fragments following, that is, this packet is the last fragment. The bit is set to one if there are more fragments to come, that is, this is not the last fragment in a series. Systems that do not use fragmentation can set the whole word to the default value of 0×0000. Note that bit 14 can be left as zero as it is only used to notify other systems that the packet can be fragmented elsewhere if necessary. If a datagram received has the *don't fragment* bit set to zero, the receiver must start a procedure for storing, and ordering all arriving datagrams with the same ID into a buffer. It does this by creating an empty buffer into which all the received datagrams will place their sections of data into. The buffer will need to be up to 64 kb in size as this is the maximum value that can be addressed by the offset field. Received datagrams will be placed into the buffer according to their pointer field value. Possible repeated datagrams will overwrite existing memory areas and will have no ill effect. Completion will be detected by the last datagram having bit 13 in the fragmentation field set.

Figure 7-7 shows an example where some of the datagrams have arrived out of sequence. The final datagram (4), which should have its bit 13 reset, has not arrived yet. Note how each of the smaller incoming datagrams has a full complete IP header, all with the same ID field. With fragmentation, the receiver must establish means of storing, and reordering the incoming datagrams. In order to do this, the receiver must implement a state system table and a timeout timer in order to be able to dump the whole buffer in case the final datagram does not arrive.

Many TCP/IP based applications do not require IP fragmentation to transmit large sections of data; this is because they can send series of short TCP segments instead. TCP segments are usually of the right size to push through unchanged, into WAN or LAN physical networks. IP fragmentation is commonly used for conveying stream audio or video data where the packets are large. In most other cases, fragmentation is not needed.

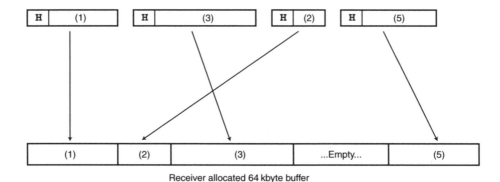

Receiver allocated 64 kbyte buffer

Figure 7-7: Fragments out of sequence

Fragmentation can be a very relevant design issue with small-embedded systems. One design option is just to ignore or disallow fragmented IP datagrams (and maybe reply with an error ICMP message). This may not be much of a problem if the transactions involved are small, for example, a small data logger.

IPv6

The current IP address scheme of 32-bit words is fast becoming inadequate. It would appear that $2^{32} = 4\,294\,967\,296$ combinations of addresses should be enough for everybody, but in practice this is not so. Address ranges are sub-divided into classes, making many subsets of addresses unusable. Furthermore, with the advent of small-scale appliance networking, we shall soon need IP addresses for every component and subcomponent of equipment in an office, factory or the home. The next generation of IP protocols is generically known as version 6, or IPv6. The areas it addresses are described in the following text.

Extended addressing capability. The current 32 bit IP addresses are extended to 128 bits. A more comprehensive hierarchical scheme is also defined to subdivide the address into ranges. Broadcast and multicast addresses are combined into three generic systems: (a) *Unicast*, any packets sent to a unicast address are always delivered only to the interface identified by the address; (b) *Anycast*, an identifier for a set of addresses belonging to different nodes (a packet sent to an anycast address is sent to one of the interfaces described by that address); and (c) *Multicast*, one that identifies a number of interfaces that will typically belong to different nodes (packets sent to a multicast address are delivered to all interfaces identified by that address).

Simplified header format. Many of the fields used in IPv4 are rarely used at present. The new IPv6 header includes only those fields that are necessary (Figure 7-8).

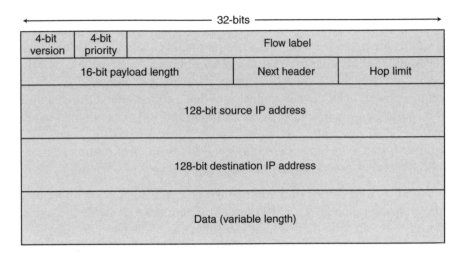

Figure 7-8: IPv6 datagram format

Version: a 4 bit nibble set to six. Priority: the next nibble of 4 bits, which defines the priority of this packet with respect to others. Flow label: a 24 bit field used by the source to identify packets for which special handling may be required. Payload length: a 16 bit field denoting the size of the user payload in bytes. Next header: an 8 bit field identifying the type of header that follows the IP header. Codes here are the same as those used for IPv4, but also include extension headers. Hop limit: a field equivalent to the TTL field in IPv4. Finally, the two 128 bit source and destination addresses.

The way current IP options are encoded have been improved to allow for greater flexibility and to provide a more flexible approach for further options in the future. IPv6 also introduces the concept of series of packets belonging to a traffic flow. This allows sets of packets to have special characteristics such as quality of service and real-time service. Additional extensions are used to allow authentication, data integrity, checking and confidentiality. Some aspects of IPv6 are still under development. The transition between IPv4 and IPv6 will take a long time and is not going to be very easy. Most existing IPv4 systems will be in use for many years to come, so do not expect an overnight switch. Luckily, IPv6 has been designed to coexist with IPv4 and many new designs can carry traffic from both environments and at the same time. It is recommended that any new designs should be 'IPv6 ready'. That is, they should be able to handle both IPv6 and IPv4 traffic. IPv6 is described in more detail in RFC 1883, 2460 and 2373. Mechanisms for transitioning between IPv4 and IPv6 are found in RFC 1933.

ICMP

ICMP stands for Internet control message protocol. This is not a protocol used to transfer user data but rather to provide a form of internal maintenance messaging service. It is mainly used to communicate error messages and other conditions that may require attention by the end nodes or by one of the routers. For example, an ICMP datagram may be returned when an IP packet sent, was not able to reach its destination. ICMP is usually considered as part of the IP network layer, and usually handled by software drivers at the same level. Relevant error returns are then passed to the higher layers as arguments or messages.

Figure 7-9 shows the format of the ICMP message. This is placed immediately after the IP header (and after any IP options). There are four fields in a typical ICMP message: The type field, which identifies one of 15 possible ICMP messages. The code field, which has different meanings for different message types. The 16 bit checksum field, which is calculated over the entire ICMP message (but not the IP header), and the ICMP message data payload. One of the most common messages used in ICMP is a service known as ping. This is a method where a node can query the presence of another by transmitting a special short request message and wait for an echo response (think of submarine echo sounders). The type field for a ping request is 8, with service code 0. A ping reply has message type 0, with service code 0. The data field may contain a variable sized data block, usually containing random data. This is sometimes used to test the capability of the remote to echo long strings of data bytes. The receiver reads the information in the data field and returns it exactly 'as-is' to the sender. To establish data block size limits in a remote node, consecutive ping requests are made with

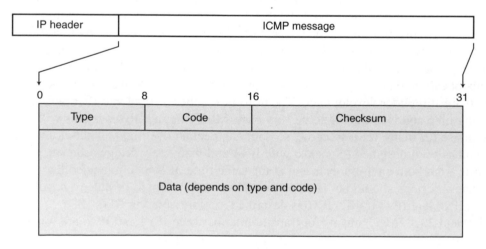

Figure 7-9: ICMP message format

larger and larger data blocks, until the echoed message reports a size error. Ping is an important requirement for any node connected to a network. As a minimum, any embedded implementation should incorporate facilities for responding to ping requests and for echoing back the data block as received. Failing to echo a request, or to echo a request without the right data block sizes and contents may result in the remote not recognizing the node. The Windows OS system uses a nominal ping data size of 32 bytes (the data section is filled with random ASCII text). This should be considered a reasonable minimum for the interim echo storage of ping data in an embedded system.

ICMP messages with type = 3 are destination unreachable messages. These are echoed back to the source when one of the conditions given in Table 7-2 occur.

ICMP error messages always contain the IP header and the first few bytes of the IP datagram that caused the error in the first place. This allows the source to detect the IP datagram that caused the error. Note that most ICMP messages are generated by the gateways and switches on route, and not by the destination node. It is not 100% safe to rely on ICMP messages for error management. They should only be used as an indication of delivery failure. Small embedded systems can happily ignore any ICMP incoming messages (apart from ping). In the same way, they do not need to generate outgoing ICMP messages to report error conditions (ping requests may be an exception).

Other types of ICMP messages are of the request–reply form. That is a node sends an ICMP request to another node expecting a reply. These are mainly used to 'sense' remote nodes and to establish their properties in a large network. Ping is one

Table 7-2: ICMP type = 3 (destination unreachable) codes

Code	Description
0	Network unreachable
1	Host unreachable
2	Protocol unreachable
3	Port unreachable
4	Fragmentation needed
5	Source route failed
6	Destination network unknown
7	Destination host unknown
8	Source host isolated
9	Destination network prohibited
10	Destination host prohibited

of many variations. Please refer to the relevant RFC documentation for the various options.

In summary, as a minimum, a small embedded system can ignore most ICMP messages, but must at least be able to respond to ping requests and have enough storage (at least 32 bytes) to store the data block to be echoed. ICMP is documented in RFC 792, 950, 1812, 1122, 1191, 1256 and 1257.

Implementing ping

Implementing a ping reply to a remote request is a relatively simple task. Assuming we start with a complete IP + ICMP message block that has just arrived and is stored in local memory. The overall procedure is as follows:

1. Look at the first byte of the just arrived IP packet. Multiply the lowest nibble by 4 and store in a variable called 'IP header length' we shall need this value later. Compute the checksum of the IP header only to ensure that it is consistent. This is done by calling a function that performs the checksum over all the 16-bit words forming the IP header, including the checksum field, and also the options field. If the result is not FFFFhex, dump the whole packet and exit altogether (the packet is said to be *silently discarded*). If the checksum was FFFFhex, the IP header is error free. Continue to the next step.

2. Check the destination IP address in the IP header. If this matches with ours, proceed to the next stage. If it doesn't, silently discard the message, the IP packet was not addressed to us. This situation is unlikely to happen in a wired LAN environment, as the Ethernet controller will have filtered out any messages with the wrong hardware MAC address.

3. Check the protocol flag in the IP header. If this is 01hex, proceed with ICMP handling; otherwise, pass the packet to another protocol handler, for example TCP or UDP.

4. Compute the ICMP message length. This is done by subtracting the contents of the datagram-size field in the IP header from the *header length* field (the number obtained by multiplying the lower nibble of the first byte of the IP header by 4). The ICMP size must be computed this way, as it is not transmitted as a field. Do not forget that 16-bit data values are stored most significant byte first.

5. Having isolated the ICMP message, compute its checksum (ICMP header + payload, but not the IP header). If the result is not FFFFhex, dump the whole message and exit altogether. If the checksum was FFFFhex, the ICMP message is error-free. Continue to the next step.

6. Look at the ICMP *type* field. If it is 8, the message was an ICMP ping request. If it is not 8, it is another type of ICMP message, either dump, or

pass to another ICMP handler (we are only handling ping requests in this example).

7. Look at the ICMP *code* field. It should be zero (this stage may be bypassed, the specifications do not cover any other values).

8. We now know we have received a ping request. We must now prepare a reply and send it back to the source. For simplicity we shall assume that we have enough spare RAM to create a separate buffer for the transmitted message (limited RAM systems may have to shuffle the data around and re-use the area occupied by the receiver buffer).

9. First, we create a reply IP header. We use the following fields:

Ver	Set to 45hex
TOS	Set to 00hex
Dgram size	Copy from the same value stored in the received IP header (tx size = rx size)
ID	Set to previously transmitted value +1
Fragment	Set to 00hex
TTL	Set to 80hex
Protocol	Set to 01hex
Checksum	Set to 0000hex (will be properly computed later)
Source IP	Set to our IP address
Dest IP	Copy from Source IP address field in received IP packet.

10. Next, compute the IP checksum over the just constructed IP header by calling the checksum function. Bit invert the result, and place in the checksum field of the IP header. Construction of the IP header is now complete.

11. Construct the reply ICMP message. We start by copying the whole of the received ICMP message into our transmit ICMP message buffer. This is because we want to echo the received data block 'as-is' without adding or taking anything away from it.

12. We then change the *type* field from 08hex to 00hex. This converts the 'request' message into a 'reply' message. All other ICMP header fields can remain the same. However, changing this one field requires the re-computation of the ICMP checksum for transmission. Set the two bytes of the ICMP checksum field to zero. Then call the checksum function to perform the 1's complement addition of all the words in the ICMP message. Invert the resulting 16-bit word, and place back in the checksum field. Those feeling imaginative could simplify checksum calculation by making use of the many shortcut techniques discussed in RFC 1141. In the simplest case, you could try subtracting 8 from the old checksum, and using this

value. However, there is a chance this operation will cause a borrow, and hence an incorrect checksum.

13. The whole message is now ready for transmission (IP plus ICMP). Depending on the data link layer method used, forward this message to the transmitter for delivery to the remote node. You may also need to re-create the MAC frame in the Ethernet controller (by swapping the source and destination addresses).

UDP

UDP stands for user datagram protocol. UDP is a simple transport layer protocol, and is defined as a connectionless, unreliable delivery protocol with no error or flow control mechanisms. In effect, UDP is nothing more than an IP datagram with a few added fields. UDP can be a very effective protocol for the transmission of simple half-duplex style data. Each operation by the application process produces one data block, which is converted to one UDP datagram, which causes one IP datagram to be transmitted. This is unlike connection-based protocols where the amount of data generated by an application bears little resemblance to the data transmitted. To use the correct terminology, UDP provides a connection between *applications* (as opposed to services or nodes). This difference is subtle; applications can run more than one service (or process) over the same connection to the same physical destination.

Sending a UDP message is somewhat like sending a postcard from a holiday resort. UDP is a simple 'shoot and forget' type protocol. It can be very reliable in networks that are reliable to start with such as LANs. UDP is used in these networks for simple file transfers, remote booting of PCs or anywhere where a failure to receive is not disastrous, or where they can be dealt with by simple repeat transmissions. Other forms of error protection can be implemented by the higher layers.

So, why not format our data using simple IP packets? What is the point of using UDP? First, UDP datagrams have network transparency. Most routers and bridges around the world are programmed to pass only certain kinds of packets. Custom designed IP datagrams may be blocked, whereas UDP (and TCP) packets are allowed through. This implies that in order to communicate over the Internet, established formats such as UDP/TCP need to be used, whereas in a local application, either IP or UDP can be used. The overheads of implementing UDP are minimal anyway. The second reason for using UDP is practical. At one stage or other, systems may need to communicate with PCs and workstations. These have software modules (e.g. Winsock in Windows) containing programmer friendly software interfaces (APIs) for program development. Not all these APIs provide facilities for reading or writing to 'raw' IP packets. Most provide interfaces for UDP communications, however.

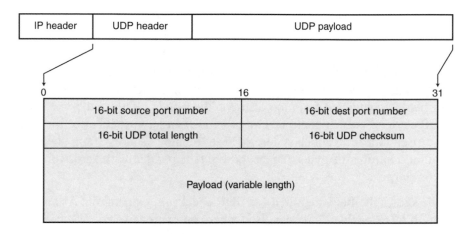

Figure 7-10: UDP datagram format

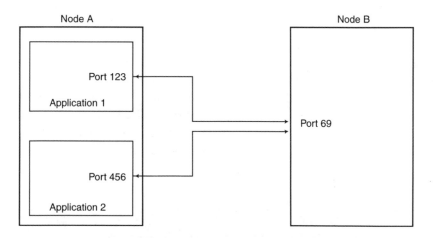

Figure 7-11: UDP ports

Figure 7-10 shows the datagram format. The UDP message immediately follows the IP header and contains an 8-byte header followed by a variable length payload. The source port and destination port fields describe the sending and receiving processes. An IP address can be receiving many communications at any one time; these are de-multiplexed into various processes, each handling one communication. Workstation '192.168.0.31' could be using port 21 to Telnet to another workstation, use TCP on port 80 for web access and use UDP on port 27 for file transfers (see Figure 7-11). Think of ports as telephone extensions working off a main private exchange number. The combination or pairing between a port and an IP address that describes a single one-way communications channel is also known as a *socket*.

The UDP length field is the total size of the UDP header plus the size of the UDP payload in bytes. The minimum value is 8, as sending a UDP datagram with no payload is quite valid. Note that the information in the UDP length field is redundant. The same information could be obtained by subtracting the IP header size from the total data gram size field, which was included back in the IP header. The UDP checksum field is calculated from three arrays: the 8-byte UDP header, the variable length UDP payload (which could be odd in length) and a virtual collection of fields known as a pseudoheader, which is described in the next section. If the payload contains an odd number of bytes, the last odd byte is padded with zeros for computation purposes.

Figure 7-12 shows the fields required for UDP checksum calculation. As an example, an odd length UDP payload has been used where an extra zero byte has been appended for calculation purposes (the pad byte is not transmitted). The pseudoheader is formed by a collection of individual fields copied from other existing headers: the 32-bit source and destination addresses from the IP header, a zero byte, the protocol byte from the IP header (11hex in the case of UDP), and the UDP message length from the UDP header. Note that this length value is repeated twice in the checksum calculations, once in the UDP header, and once in the pseudoheader. The pseudoheader is not a separate array, nor it is transmitted. It is a fictional collection of fields purely used for checksum computations. The reason for adding a pseudoheader to the checksum is to let UDP check that the data has arrived at the correct destination from the right source. UDP will compute its own checksum based on its assumptions on who the sender was.

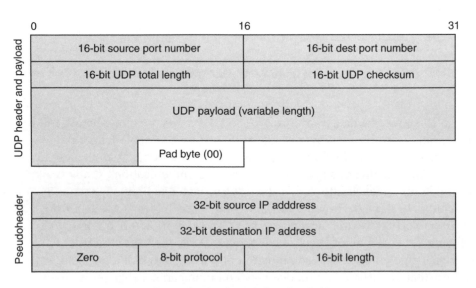

Figure 7-12: Pseudoheader fields

If there is a discrepancy, either the message was in error, or the source address was incorrect.

According to the specifications, a checksum field is not strictly required for UDP. UDP datagrams can be transmitted without a checksum, in which case, the checksum field should be set to 0000hex To cover for cases where a calculated checksum was zero, it is stored as FFFFhex (in 1's complement arithmetic the all zero and the all one fields both denote zero). It is recommended however that checksums should always be enabled by default. In a similar way to IP processing, received UDP datagrams with checksum errors are silently discarded. No error message needs to be generated or sent back. ICMP condition returns may be required when fragmentation problems occur. UDP is used in many protocols such as TFTP, SNMP, etc. UDP is fully described in RFC 768.

Implementing a simple UDP transaction

UDP is a very versatile protocol, and ideal for small embedded systems when used in applications such as data logging, batch transfers, or even general purpose communications. The simplest UDP 'custom' protocol is a demand–return, or client–server, where a client station puts out a request, and the remote server station returns with an answer. The following scheme describes a simple implementation procedure for such a system (see also Chapter 9 for a practical example of a UDP handler). As per example shown in section on 'Implementing ping', we assume that a node has just received a buffer containing an IP header, UDP header and UDP payload. The node will look at this data, and return a response. Each of these 'transactions' is unique, and performed one at a time. This allows the software to respond to requests from many remotes (all having different IP addresses). The essence of the transaction method is that no information is stored between one transaction and the next. Each process is independent of each other. The procedure, starting from the handling of the IP header is as follows:

1. Look at the first byte of the received packet (the first byte of the IP header). Multiply the lowest nibble by 4 and store in a variable called 'IP header length'. Its value will be most likely 20 if no optional extra headers are present. Compute the IP headers checksum to ensure that it is consistent. This is done by calling a checksum function over all the 16 bit words forming the IP header (include any options headers if present). If the result is not FFFFhex, silently discard the message and exit the function (do not generate any error messages). If the checksum was FFFFhex, the IP header is error free. Continue to the next step.

2. Check the destination IP address in the IP header. If this matches with ours, proceed to the next stage. If it does not, silently discard the message, the IP packet was not addressed to us. This situation is unlikely to happen in a

wired LAN environment, as the Ethernet controller will have filtered out any messages with the wrong hardware address.

3. Check the protocol flag in the IP header. If this is 11hex, proceed with the UDP handling; otherwise, pass the message to another protocol handler, for example ICMP or TCP.

4. Compute the UDP checksum. This is done by calling a checksum function over all the 16-bit words of the UDP header plus payload (do not include the IP header). If the payload length was odd, do not forget to add a padding byte of zero to the end of the data area. Save this checksum value, and proceed to compute the checksum of the pseudoheader. This can be done by individually adding each of the 16-bit word fields in 1's complement, or by the use of a special software function dedicated to this. It is most likely that all the required fields will be already available at various dispersed locations in the memory buffer. Use Figure 7-11 to identify the fields to check. Add the two checksums together. If the result is not FFFFhex, silently discard the message and exit the function (do not generate error messages). If the checksum was FFFFhex, the UDP message is error-free, proceed to the next step.

5. Look at the UDP destination *port* number; check that it matches with the one we are expecting. It is not essential to use a port number as a strict addressing mechanism, but this field could be used for other identification purposes. If the fields match, proceed to the next stage; otherwise silently discard the message and exit.

6. We have received a correctly formatted UDP message. Pass the payload in its entirety to the user function; include a payload *length* variable as an argument. Do not throw away the contents of the received UDP or IP buffers; some of the fields will be required for assembling a reply.

7. The application returns to the handler with its reply data array (and its length) to be sent back to the source node. We must now assemble a full IP-UDP message reply and send it back to the originator. We shall also assume that we have enough spare RAM to create a separate buffer for the transmitted message. Limited RAM systems may have to shuffle the data around and re-use the area occupied by the receiver buffer.

8. First, we create a reply IP header. Note that we could pre-compute the total datagram size, as we have all the relevant information on hand: the size of the IP header (20 bytes), the size of the UDP header (8 bytes) and the size of the payload to be sent (supplied by the application). We use the following fields:

Ver   Set to 45hex
TOS   Set to 00hex
Dgram size   Set to 14hex + 8hex + size of tx payload in bytes

ID	Set to previous transmitted value +1
Fragment	Set to 00hex
TTL	Set to 80hex
Protocol	Set to 11hex
Checksum	Set to 0000hex (will be properly computed later)
Source IP	Set to our IP address
Dest IP	Copy from Source IP address in received IP header.

9. Next, compute the IP checksum over the just constructed IP header by calling the checksum function. Bit invert the result, and place in the checksum field of the IP header. Construction of the IP header is now complete.

10. Construct the reply UDP message. We use the following fields:

Source port	Copied from destination port in received UDP message
Dest port	Copied from source port in received UDP message
UDP length	Set to 8 + size of tx payload
Checksum	Set to zero (will be computed later)
Payload	Append the user array data supplied by the application.

11. Compute the UDP checksum (as in item 4 above). Invert the resulting 16-bit word, and place in the UDP checksum field. If this value happens to be 0000hex, replace with FFFFhex.

12. The whole message is now ready for transmission (IP plus UDP). Depending on the data link layer method used, forward this message to the transmitter for delivery to the remote node. Note that you may also need to reconfigure or re-create the MAC frame in the Ethernet controller (by swapping the source and destination addresses).

TCP

TCP stands for transmission control protocol. TCP is a very different type of animal to IP or UDP. TCP is a point-to-point, connection oriented, reliable, byte stream service. Point-to-point means that TCP provides for two-way communications between only two nodes at any one time. Connection oriented means that the two applications must establish a proper connection before they can exchange data, and that they must also close the connection after all data has been exchanged. A reliable byte stream is provided by ensuring each transmitted packet contains ordering, checksum and flow control information. TCP will break the input byte stream into segments ideally sized for optimum transmission, and will provide for efficient methods of acknowledging messages to manage optimum flow control. TCP is used by many of the popular Internet applications such as Telnet, FTP, HTTP and e-mail. The main document for TCP is RFC 793. There is also additional information in RFCs 896, 1122, 1323 and 2018.

By definition, a protocol such as TCP requires receivers to return a certificate of reception by some form of acknowledgment mechanism. Each transmitted segment (in TCP, packets are known as segments) could be acknowledged individually, but TCP goes one better than this. TCP uses a pointer scheme where the receiver acknowledges the position in the stream of the last reliable segment received. In order to do this, each segment carries an index pointer into an imaginary array where the block would belong. This scheme is very convenient, as it allows one acknowledgment segment to refer to more than one transmitted segments. It also allows for transmitted segments to arrive out of order. In other words, there is no need to acknowledge every segment received, a single 'ACK' can be sent after a number of correct transmitted segments have arrived.

In TCP, transmitters and receivers also operate a 'sliding data window' scheme. These tell each other how many more bytes of data each end is willing to accept. The values can be adjusted dynamically, and updates are transmitted as fields on the header. This provides a form of data flow control, enabling the transmitter to stop sending data if the remote cannot immediately take any more data while its buffers are being processed. By constant adjustment of the windows and delays, TCP can tune itself to provide an efficient flow mechanism ideally suited to a particular channel's characteristics. In an ideal situation (assuming one way traffic), the transmitter will be sending data nearly continuously, while communications in the other direction will be restricted to a few ACKs segments every so often. You could see this in practice by observing the TX and RX LED lights on a modem. Inefficient TCP is observed when both TX and RX lamps flash or flicker in opposition, denoting a flurry of transmit data and interrupting ACK replies. Efficient TCP is when the TX light is nearly constantly on (denoting a nearly constant flow) with the occasional flicker of the RX light, denoting a few responding ACKs.

TCP header

The TCP header contains a fixed length section of 20 bytes, and a variable length section containing optional header information. The format is shown in Figure 7-13.

The first two fields are the 16-bit source and destination port numbers. These identify the sending and receiving processes. The combination of a port and an IP address uniquely identifies a one-way connection and is commonly known as a socket. The four-way combination of the two IP addresses (both ends) and the two port numbers uniquely identify a two-way connection (see Section on UDP for more information on port numbers). The next field is a 32 bit sequence number, which is a pointer to the position of the first byte in the segment in the overall stream of data transmitted. The number tells the receiver where to place the received data in its receive 'virtual' buffer. The sequence number is nominally initialised during connection establishment to some random value. It is then incremented by the size of the payload for every segment transmitted (it wraps back to zero after reaching $2^{32} - 1$). There are no

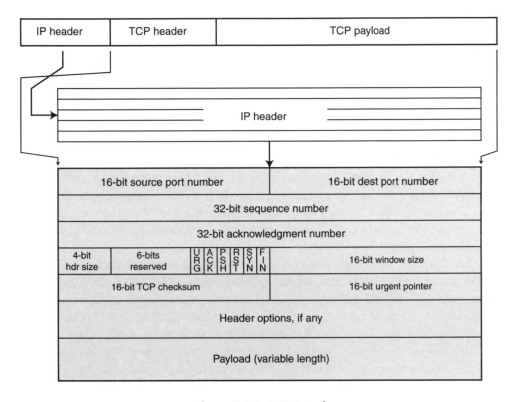

IP header	TCP header	TCP payload

IP header

16-bit source port number	16-bit dest port number
32-bit sequence number	
32-bit acknowledgment number	

4-bit hdr size	6-bits reserved	U R G	A C K	P S H	R S T	S Y N	F I N	16-bit window size
16-bit TCP checksum							16-bit urgent pointer	

Header options, if any
Payload (variable length)

Figure 7-13: TCP Header

special meanings given to specific sequence starting numbers and any starting random numbers could be used as long as they will not be confused with stray packets from previous connections. The only consideration is that a sequence number in one segment does not get mistaken with a similar numbers used in other connections (a rather unlikely situation in practice). The next field is the 32 bit acknowledgment number, which contains the next sequence number that the receiver is expecting. In other words, by sending this number the receiver acknowledges that all data byte positions before this pointer or index value have been received correctly. The combination of sending and acknowledgment sequences allows TCP to use a 'chase and catch' method for error management. The transmitter will know 'up to what byte' the receiver has received data, and can re-transmit old data only from this last point in case of errors. As TCP provides a full duplex service, the sequence/acknowledge mechanism can work in both directions at the same time. The next four bits contain the header length nibble. Multiply this value by 4 to obtain the total TCP header size. This will be 20 bytes plus the size of the optional header, which can be zero length. The next 6 bits are reserved and are usually set to zero. These are followed by 6 bits of flow control flags, these are as follows: URG is the urgent pointer, meaning that the payload data in this segment has priority. This flag is used in conjunction with the urgent pointer field (see later), and is rarely used in normal communications, so it is usually always reset. ACK is a flag indicating that the acknowledge sequence number is valid. This flag should be sensed before the acknowledgment sequence number is read. In practice, this flag is set in most of the segments sent, even if there is no extra data to acknowledge. PSH is a flag warning that the receiver should pass the enclosed payload data to the application as soon as possible. In practice, this is nearly always the case as TCP implementations tend not to buffer too much interim data. In fact, most implementations assume the PSH condition to be set by default whether or not it has been sent by a remote. RST is a flag asking for the connection to be reset. This is a drastic message to send, and means that the remote cannot handle the connection, and is asking for a restart or abort. Data may be lost in some cases, and the receiving end must force itself back to a re-connection condition. SYN is a flag asking to synchronize sequence numbers, and to initiate a connection. This flag is sent by one end when it wants to start a new connection with a remote. FIN is sent when the sender is finished with the session. This flag is set by one end when it wants to terminate the connection with the remote. Note that the receiver must be able to handle not only 'clean' terminations as generated by this flag, but also terminations caused by RST flags, line breaks, aborts and dropouts. The use of all these flags will be described in more detail later. The next 16 bit field is the window size, which advertises the number of bytes that the receiver is willing to accept at this time. This value may change dynamically during a session. It might go up, it may go down, it may stay the same, or it might even go to zero indicating that the receiver is not able to take any more data for the moment. The next field is a 16 bit checksum field that is calculated by the standard IP checksum method by adding the TCP header, the TCP optional headers, the TCP payload data, and the pseudoheader. The pseudoheader is similar to the one already described under UDP, but will *contain the TCP* protocol number field instead (06hex for TCP). The 16 bit urgent pointer is a field valid only if the URG flag is set. TCP urgent mode is a way for a sender to transmit urgent (or supplementary) data to the other end. This facility is rarely used and is usually left as zero.

A number of option fields may immediately follow the TCP header. Every option field begins with a one byte kind indicating the option type, followed by a length len byte and the option data. Fields are terminated with an end of options field; see Figure 7-14. The most common option field is the maximum segment size (MSS) option. This describes the largest 'chunk' of data that TCP should ever send to the other end. The MSS option can only appear in a SYN segment, and is sent once during connection establishment. Do not confuse this with window size, which can change dynamically. The default for MSS, if no field is received, is 576 bytes. Option fields are described in RFCs 793 and 1323.

A simple embedded system implementation should ideally read and store the MSS option field; other option fields can be ignored. However, if the system being

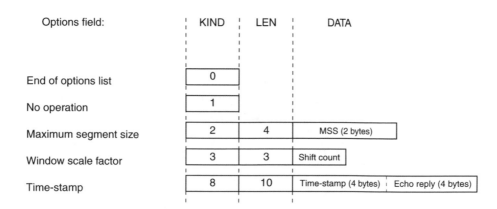

Figure 7-14: Options field

developed is to be used to transmit small items of data, for example, a few bytes at a time, it can safely assume that the MSS is going to be much higher than this and the field can be ignored altogether.

The payload data contains the actual data stream to be passed transparently to the application. The minimum value can be zero if there is no data to be sent, for example, in segments that are used only for connection establishment or acknowledgment. The data field can contain an odd number of bytes, in which case a virtual zero byte should be padded to the last byte for checksum calculations.

TCP states

There are three main stages in a TCP connection: connection establishment, established data flow and connection termination. To implement TCP in software, a state transition table is normally used. This is shown in Figure 7-15 (a more comprehensive diagram, shown in tabular form will be found in RFC 796). Each end of a link will be running its own State Transition Table. A stable situation will be achieved when both ends arrive at one of the two main terminal states: CLOSED or ESTABLISHED. These main states are connected together by transitional (or interim) states, in which each station will wait for some event pending a change to the next state. Events can be valid events, in which the state table will move to the next interim or final state as shown in the diagram. Invalid events, in which an invalid sequence is received (for example, a time-out or receiving an invalid segment during an interim state). User commands are commands initiated by the application, such as Open of Abort, and time-outs, which a state may receive if it has been waiting on an interim state for a long time. The transitions generated by the non-standard events are not shown in the figure, as they would only contribute to cluttering the layout. In practice, all non-standard events should result in graceful terminations of the connection, and a return to the CLOSED state.

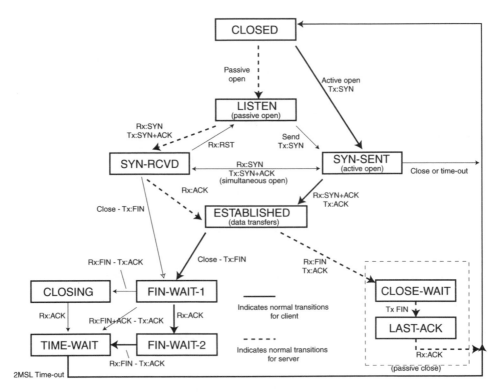

Figure 7-15: TCP state table

Another situation not shown in this state diagram is opening further new connections, that is, when a SYN segment is received, asking a new connection to be opened from a different station on the network, while the system is already dealing with one user. Simple systems that are designed to handle one connection at a time will just ignore these requests.

Connection establishment procedure

A connection must be established (Figure 7-16) before either end can talk to each other. Unlike UDP, TCP software handlers need to maintain a number of local variables and countdown timers during initialisation, and for the duration of the connection. Both stations will nominally start from the CLOSED state. A station wanting to respond to remote data will move to the LISTEN state and wait for a segment to arrive with the SYN flag set, this is called a *passive open*. A station wanting to start a connection will start by sending a SYN segment to the remote and wait for a response, this is called an *active open*. During a passive open, the receiver simply sits waiting for a SYN request segment to arrive. In software terms, this is a blocking call, and any practical implementation should include means of exiting this state in case the remote never sends any data; either with a timeout, or with an abort

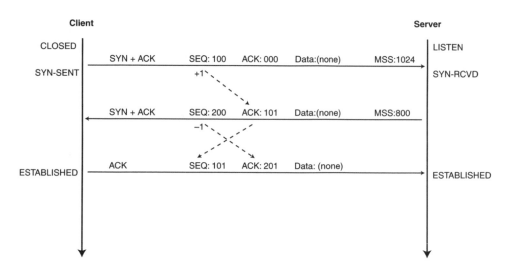

Figure 7-16: TCP connection establishment

routine mechanism. If during a passive open, a SYN segment is received, the receiver will reply with its own SYN segment (this ensures that both ends have sent SYNs to each other). The receiver moves to the interim state SYN-RCVD and waits for the remote to respond with an ACK segment, at which point, it moves to the ESTABLISHED state, where communications can begin. This procedure is known as the *three-way handshake*. During an active open, the prompting station will be in the interim state SYN-SENT waiting for a reply from the called station. The remote will reply with its own SYN segment. When this is received, the station will respond with an ACK segment and move to the ESTABLISHED state, where communications can begin. This is known as the *two-way handshake*. A possibility may occur where both stations want to open communications simultaneously. This is shown in the state table as the line joining the SYN-RCVD and the SYN-SENT state. In a practical implementations designed as client-only or server-only this is unlikely to happen and is usually ignored. Another situation may result if no response is received from the remote end after a time delay, which can be caused by the remote not being available any more, or by the segment getting lost on the way. In which case, the sender proceeds to the termination stage by sending a FIN segment, or silently back to the CLOSED state. This simple description only covers the simplest of details. During all the above transactions, segments will also carry sequence and acknowledgment numbers that need to be checked and stored. Some implementations also allow payload data to be carried as well during the initialization sequences, although in practice this is avoided. As already mentioned, the interim states generate the possibility of blocking if no data is received within a given time period. This should be gracefully handled by the software driver, which should ensure that both

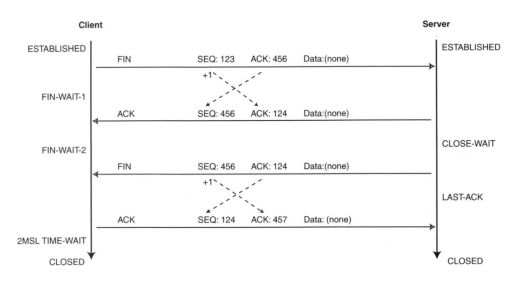

Figure 7-17: TCP connection termination

stations return to the CLOSED state if the two-way and the three-way handshakes are not correctly completed.

Connection termination

There are many ways to terminate a connection (Figure 7-17). Connections can be terminated during a normal session in the established state or even half way through connection establishment. A normal termination is one where a normal close down sequence is implemented. One end will send a segment with the FIN flag set, making the other end shift from its ESTABLISHED state to the CLOSE-WAIT state and send two segments in return: an ACK segment, acknowledging the received FIN message, and its own FIN message, telling the other end that this end wants to close down too. The remote responds with its own ACK segment confirming the four-way termination handshake. The reason for this relatively complex procedure is that one end may not be ready to close down yet, or may have still some data to send. Both ends must agree by sending each other FIN segments, and both must be acknowledged. An *abnormal termination* is caused by one end sending a RST segment. This is a drastic situation where one end tells the other that it cannot carry on any further and wants to reset the connection. There is no guarantee that data will not be lost during a reset, and each end will do the best it can. A timeout termination is caused by either end refusing to respond to any communications; this can be caused by the link going dead, by equipment failure, or by malicious non-standard operation (e.g. SYN attacks). Timeouts in the transition table will ensure both ends return to their CLOSED states cleanly and in due course. Connection termination can also simply be caused by one end simply refusing to send any more data, or by

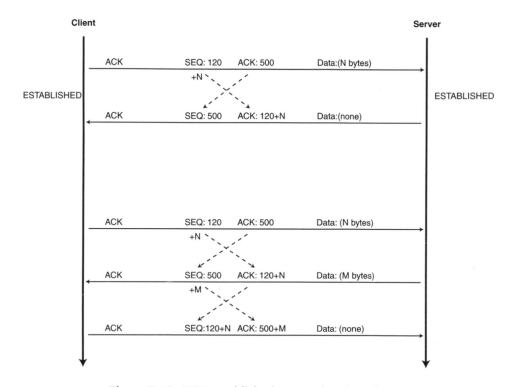

Figure 7-18: TCP established connection data flow

sending a RST segment, and then dropping out. Although this may work in practice, it is not considered good practice as it puts all the termination effort on the software at the other end.

Established data flow

In TCP, data flow (Figure 7-18) occurs in full-duplex mode. However, it is usually easier to describe the transactions when operating in half-duplex mode. That is, with one end sending data and the other end receiving only. Conversion to full duplex is relatively straightforward after this, as data in the other direction is simply added to the segments that would nominally carry acknowledgments. In the general one-way case, end 'A' will send a segment with payload data together with a sequence number pointing to the start of the virtual buffer it belongs to (the segment may also include an ACK to a previous message received from end 'B', but we shall ignore this for now). End 'B' will receive the segment, perform a checksum on the array and check whether the received sequence pointer is the same as the pointer it is expecting. If this is the case, it will transfer the data to the application and increment it's receive pointer by the length of the received payload data, that is, the receiver now points to the next byte it is expecting. End 'B' now owes an acknowledgment to end 'A'. The choice for end 'B' now is whether to send this acknowledgment now or wait for more data segments to arrive, and acknowledge the lot at a later stage. Similarly, end 'A' needs to know whether to wait for an acknowledgment from end 'B' for each segment it has sent, or to simple carry on sending segments and wait for an acknowledgment later on. In the simplest case, end 'B' will send an acknowledgment to 'A' for every segment received. This is very simple, but can be quite inefficient if end 'A' only sends a few bytes of payload data per segment.

Transmitting data involves the notion of a sliding pointer pair. To visualize the concept, imagine the transmitter keeps all data ever to be sent in a very large buffer array. Also imagine two pointers to this array: 'sent' and 'acknowledged'. At the beginning of a transmission, both pointers index to the first element of this array. When the transmitter sends a segment containing n bytes, it moves forward the 'sent' pointer by *n* bytes. When it receives a segment, it checks the received acknowledge number, and moves forward its 'acknowledged' pointer to match. The lag between the 'sent' and the 'acknowledged' pointer is the number of bytes sent, but still waiting to be acknowledged by the remote; when both are the same, the remote has accepted all data sent by the transmitter. Received segments with acknowledge numbers 'stuck' in a lower value, inform the transmitter it needs to retransmit data from that point, possibly because intervening segments have been lost during transmission. The transmitter knows that data up to its 'acknowledged' pointer was received OK, so it only needs to re-send data after this.

It should be noted that TCP is not a constant flow mechanism. If there is nothing to send, there will be no transfers, that is, the line will be quiet. The virtual connection between the two nodes will remain open, but there will be nothing on the line until one end decides to send some data. There is no way for one end knowing that the other end has switched off or crashed for example. A feature known as *keep-alive* may be used to regularly sense the state of the other end in a session by sending 'do nothing' segments. A special state case is known as a half-open connection, this is established if one end has closed or aborted the connection without the knowledge of the other end. This can happen if one of the two ends crashes, for example.

Implementing a TCP transaction

Describing the implementation of TCP in full is a rather complex undertaking, and we may run the risk of confusing the learning process with all the clutter generated by the many options and permutations. Instead, we are going to describe the most basic set of operations required to run a straight version of TCP, ignoring 'special cases' and any other unlikely situations that may arise. The model described here is the simplest client response mode, which describes a server reacting to received messages. User commands or system-initiated actions are not covered. However, these will not be difficult to add to the model once the basics are understood. Document RFC 793 contains a very readable, although lengthy description of the full set of TCP transactions, and should be read after a general mental map of all the operations has been obtained (see also Chapter 9 for a practical implementation of TCP).

All descriptions assume a starting point with a recently received, clean TCP segment. The 'common part' described below shows how to obtain a clean TCP segment from an incoming buffer, and it follows the standard procedures described in previous sections.

Common part – identifying a TCP segment

This part will be commonly used by all sections needing to recognise and accept a TCP segment from scratch. As described in the section on UDP Transaction in, we assume that a node has just received buffer containing an IP header, a TCP header and payload. The software handler will look at this data, and return a valid TCP message.

1. Look at the first byte of the received packet (which should be the first byte of the IP header). Multiply the lowest nibble by 4 and store in a variable called 'IP header length'. Its value will be most likely 20 if no optional extra headers are present. Compute the IP headers checksum to ensure that it is consistent. This is done by calling a checksum function over all the 16-bit words forming the IP header (include any options headers if present). If the result is not FFFFhex, silently discard the message and exit the function (do not generate error messages). If the checksum was FFFFhex, the IP header is error-free. Continue to the next step.

2. Check the destination IP address in the IP header. If this matches with ours, proceed to the next stage. If it does not, silently discard the message (unless the IP address is a broadcast address and we want to handle it).

3. Check the protocol flag in the IP header. If this is 06hex, proceed with TCP, otherwise, pass the message to another protocol handler, for example, ICMP or UDP.

4. Compute the TCP checksum. This is done by calling a checksum function over all the 16-bit words of the TCP header, options header, payload, but not the IP header. If the payload length was odd, add a virtual padding zero byte to the end of the data area. Save this checksum value, and proceed to compute the checksum of the pseudoheader. This can be done by individually accumulating the checksum of each of the special 16-bit word fields. If the result is not FFFFhex, silently discard the message and exit the function (do not generate error messages). If the checksum was FFFFhex, the TCP segment was error free, proceed to the next step.

5. Look at the TCP destination port number; check that it matches with the one we are expecting. If they match, proceed to the next stage; otherwise silently discard the segment and exit.

6. Now, we have a valid TCP segment, pass on to the next stage of processing.

Implementing connection establishment (receive)

This module will emulate the server's side 'listen' function. A listen function is a blocking function that waits for incoming segments discarding all except ones that establish a new connection. It assumes that no current connection is taking place, and a receiver is just waiting for a new connection to be opened. That is, the other end is just about to initiate a connection. The software holds a global constant 'state' initialized to a constant valued, which we associate with the LISTEN state.

1. In the LISTEN state: Read the next incoming TCP segment. If this has the SYN flag set, continue to the next step, if not, go back and wait for the next segment.

2. Store the incoming segment's 32-bit sequence number, in a local variable 'rxSEQ'. In Figure 7-15, this number is shown, for example, as 100. The received SYN segment will most likely have an optional header, which will include a MSS field, store this value in a local variable 'rxMSS'. The MSS is the largest amount of contiguous data the other end will accept from us. We can send smaller data payloads but not larger than the MSS they have specified. We only need to store this value if we think there may be a clash with large data blocks, which is not usually the case in small systems. The default value is usually 1024 bytes. We also create a local sequence number stored in 'mySEQ' and initialise this to a random 32-bit number (in the figure we have initialized to 200). We shall be using this number as our incremental sequence number when we transmit data to the remote.

3. Assemble a reply segment with the following fields: SYN = on, ACK = on, seq(sequence number) = mySEQ, ack(acknowledge number) = rxSEQ + 1, [MSS options] = 800. Set the state table value from LISTEN to SYN_RCVD, and start a 10 s time-out counter. Transmit the segment to the remote, and proceed to the next stage (do not forget to 'swap' the port and the IP addresses source–destination pairs when creating the reply). The ack number sent is just the received seq plus one, as the SYN flag is deemed to be equivalent to one byte of data. We also need to add an options header to our TCP segment containing a MSS field. The MSS field we shall send is the maximum amount of data we are prepared to take from the remote, and will depend on how much RAM memory our system has available. We have set this to 800 bytes as an example.

4. SYN-RCVD state: The receiver now waits for a reply from the remote. At the same time, the countdown timer is ticking down, to ensure the state can be exited if the remote does not respond in time. The next reply from the remote should have ACK = on and its ack field should be set to 'mySEQ + 1', which was our last sent seq number plus one. If this condition is met, we proceed to the next stage. Note that this ack segment may contain actual data, so

provisions should ideally be made to accept this. If the countdown timer times out (no segment received), or if the received ACK was in error or with the wrong sequence number, we drop the transaction (send a FIN, or a RST segment) and return to 1 above. If we receive a RST segment we just drop the transaction, not forgetting to set the state variable to CLOSE, or LISTEN as required.

5. ESTABLISHED STATE: A connection has now been established and communications can take place. This will continue until a segment with a FIN or RST is received, or the connection is lost.

Implementing the established state

This module emulates the 'receive' function. This function blocks waiting for receive data returning or performing an action only when data has been received. For simplicity, we are assuming that data flow is taking place in one direction only (receive only). We are also going to acknowledge each data block received. See also the comments in Chapter 9 on TCP implementation.

1. We assume that the machine is in the ESTABLISHED state, segments received during connection establishment or connection termination stages are handled separately. Segments received during CLOSED state are ignored (unless they have the SYN flag set as previously discussed).

2. The receiver waits for the next incoming TCP segment. As an example, let us assume it contains a data payload with 4 bytes. The received segment will have ACK = on, DATA = [4 bytes of data]. We also assume that just recently we have sent a segment containing 3 bytes of data, and that we are waiting for an acknowledgment to this.

3. If the received segment has the FIN flag set, we proceed to the passive close phase (next section). Alternatively, we proceed to the next stage. Normally, FIN segments do not contain any payload data.

4. If we are expecting an acknowledgement for previously transmitted data, we check whether the received acknowledgment number is in the range between the present and the forward sequence number (in our example, this would be in the range between mySEQ + 1 and mySEQ + 3). If this is the case, our transmit data has been accepted, and we increment our sequence number by the number of bytes acknowledged. If the received sequence number does not correspond, we assume the remote has not yet received our transmit data, and we arrange for a re-transmission of our last data block sent.

5. If a data payload is enclosed in the received segment, we check that the received segment sequence number corresponds to our expected acknowledge number (as stored in myACK). If it is, go to the next section (6). If it is not,

the two sides are out of sequence. This could have been caused by missing segments or by segments arriving out of sequence. The simplest action is to return a segment back to the sender with our 'latest' ack number (in myACK), on the expectation that the transmitter will re-send from that point and normal synchronization will resume. In other words, our response segment will indicate the remote that our acknowledge pointer was not incremented, and that they should re-send the data from that point (see RFC 793 for more advanced options). As we cannot accept the data, we skip (6) and jump directly to (7) below.

6. On a correct seq-ack match, a valid TCP segment has been received. We now peel off the 4 bytes of payload data, and pass them to the application. We increment our acknowledge count by 4 (the received number of bytes). That is, myACK = myACK + 4.

7. We assemble and transmit an acknowledgment segment back with the following fields: ACK = on, seq = mySEQ, ack = myACK. We also update our segment's window size field with the number of data bytes we can still accept depending on the size of our incoming data buffer (this could be zero if we cannot accept any more data). Then go back to (1) to wait for the next segment.

The above description is rather simplistic. It does not consider for factors where the seq and ack numbers have fully 'gone astray' or 'out of sync', where received segments contain unexpected fields such as SYN or RST flags, when one or both sides 'clam up' or in the handling of time-outs and repeated NAKs. A simple implementation could get away by ignoring some of these occurrences, and by performing simple actions (maybe dropping data in the process!). Implementations should at all costs avoid entering into endless NAK loops, and should put a limit to the number of negative ACKs sent back.

Transmitting data is a relatively simple operation (if plenty of spare memory is available). The transmitter needs to maintain a FIFO buffer large enough to keep all data 'in transit'. That is, between sent and acknowledged. The transmitter also keeps two pointers into this array, a 'sent' pointer, and an 'acknowledged' pointer. Every time a segment is sent, the 'sent' pointer is moved forward to point to the last plus 1 byte of data sent, that is to point to the next byte to be sent. Every time an acknowledge segment is received from the remote, the 'acknowledged' pointer is moved forward to match; all data previously held in the FIFO buffer can then be flushed, as it is not needed anymore. If a negative acknowledge is received, the transmitter can simply re-transmit the data held in its buffer ahead of its 'acknowledged' pointer or as requested. A proper implementation should watch for the received announced window size, and not send more data than requested (which could be zero). If the system is memory limited, there are two options: To use a small

FIFO buffer, and transmit only a few bytes per each segment. Or to use only one buffer, and block transmit operations until all data has been acknowledged from the far end.

Implementing the termination state

Termination can take the form of normal or abort. A normal termination is caused by an end receiving a segment with the FIN flag set:

1. During normal connection, the receiver has received a segment from the remote with the FIN flag set. The receiver increments its local myACK variable by one (the FIN flag is deemed as a data byte), and sends an ACK segment back with ACK-on and ack = myACK. The state value is set to CLOSE_WAIT.

2. CLOSE_WAIT STATE: This interim state was defined in order to allow a station to flush out any remaining data. If there is no such data to send, the station can simply transmit a FIN segment immediately after the ACK segment just sent. The segment will contain FIN = on, seq = mySEQ, ack = myACK. The station will also set a timeout counter to a few seconds duration.

3. LAST_ACK STATE: The remote replies with an acknowledgment segment. On receipt of this, both ends are assumed to have closed communications and return to the CLOSE state.

The local station can also cause termination as follows:

1. The local station sends a FIN segment (with no data) to notify the other end that it wants to terminate the connection. It sets its state variable to FIN_WAIT1.

2. FIN_WAIT1 state: The station will wait for an ACK from the remote acknowledging the last FIN sent. If this is received, the state table moves to the FIN_WAIT2 state (3). If a FIN segment is received, the state moves to the SIMULTANEOUS_CLOSE state, where both ends are requesting a close at the same time. After a timeout, both stations return to the CLOSED state.

3. FIN_WAIT2 state: The local station should be able to accept any 'last minute data' sent by the remote, this will be followed by a final FIN segment, to which the local replies with an ACK segment and a return to the CLOSE state.

Van Jacobson header compression

This is a common compression method used in IP/TCP mainly over WAN links such as PPP, and is described in RFC 1144. Note that this method does not apply to any data, but to IP and TCP headers only. Van Jacobson argued that it is possible to make significant savings in bandwidth by simply compressing the headers associated with most common Internet protocols. The basic argument is based on the assumption that datagrams sent are generally short in length, so that a large proportion of their size is made out of headers. In addition, their headers contain mostly redundant information. These two assumptions can be demonstrated by means of an example. In the case of Telnet, we can have a simple situation where every key press on a keyboard, which corresponds to a single byte, generates a single transmission packet of 41 bytes. The IP header has 20 octets, and the TCP header another 20. If we then look at subsequent headers over several transactions, we can notice that only a few fields in the headers have changed value. We can appreciate that substantial savings can be made if we had a method of recalling previous headers, and only transmitting the differences. Furthermore, many of the changing fields are quite predictable (i.e. a field value is incremented by a fixed number on every transmission). Of course, in order to preserve quality, some fields such as overall checksums, will need to be transmitted unchanged on every transaction. The Ven Jacobson algorithm transmits a bit mask indicating which fields have changed and by how much.

CHAPTER 8

Application Layer Protocols

Having gone through all the trouble of implementing a TCP/IP stack, it may be reassuring to know that some of the more advanced application layer protocols do not require large amounts of extra software.

This chapter neither contains any ready-made computer listings, nor does it describe any special techniques or short cuts for implementing the protocols using a particular compiler or any other method. This is because the implementation of these protocols is relatively straightforward and detailed listings would only serve in cluttering the pages of this book. Along the same lines, the chapter does not contain full descriptions of the protocols, only those items most relevant for an implementation in small embedded systems. For detailed information, the reader is directed to the various RFC documents mentioned.

The main purpose of this section is to allow the software designer to get a mental map of the higher-layer protocols, how they operate and how to implement them. There are enough pointers and relevant information supplied here to allow a competent programmer to write working software. It is recommended that the reader working on any of these implementations should also refer to the relevant RFC documents to get the fuller picture.

Telnet

Telnet provides a very useful byte-by-byte, simple two-way communication path between two stations. Telnet gives users the illusion that they have a single, dedicated connection to another user or computer. It is the nearest thing to a simple, plain RS-232 style serial link between two stations. Telnet can be a very useful protocol for providing simple communications between an embedded system and a host computer such as a PC or mainframe. Nearly all operating systems for PCs include built-in Telnet terminal emulators, this allows any PC to communicate with a remote embedded system that supports Telnet. Operation is very simple: whatever the user types in their keyboard arrives at the other end exactly as sent. That is, as a sequential string of characters. In the same way, all characters sent by the remote node arrive one by one, as sent. The only perceived difference between Telnet and a direct connection is the timing of the arrivals: characters may arrive one by one as sent, or bunched together sometimes later. One 'limitation' of Telnet is that it does not preserve the timing separation between data bytes sent. Telnet is fully described in RFC 854. Its many additions and updates are also covered in RFCs 856–860, 885, 1091, 1096 and 1184.

Establishing a link

In order to establish a Telnet link, the two stations must first open a standard TCP connection. The commonly agreed port for a Telnet 'called station' is 23 (17hex). The caller can declare any port they like for a response, so that communications in the 'caller-to-called' direction will be to port 23, communications in the other direction will be to whatever port the 'caller' declared during TCP initialization. Once the TCP connection is established, the two sides start to communicate transparently via string character sequences. All user data is transmitted as standard characters, which can be inter-mixed with control characters to provide various link management functions. Telnet uses the concept of an imaginary network virtual terminal (NVT). This standard configuration defaults to a set of basic terminal characteristics, known as a minimum common denominator set. This allows either end to map their own terminal to the common denominator, or to improve on them by negotiation. This allows for transparent transmission between the two systems even if no alternative mapping has been agreed. The NVT is nothing more than a character-based device with a keyboard and a printer (or screen) and a standard basic character set. No storage or third-party devices are assumed. Data typed by the user is sent to the other user's screen, and that is it.

The term NVT-ASCII refers to the 7-bit US variant of the ASCII character set (as used throughout the internet protocol suite). The eighth bit is nominally set to zero. To extend performance, Telnet uses in-band signalling in both directions for control purposes. In other words, extra non-display commands are added to normal transmission for this purpose. All control commands are preceded by the byte FFhex (255 decimal). This is called IAC or 'Interpret as Command' The next byte will be interpreted as the actual command byte. The 2-byte escape sequence <FFhex-FFhex> is used to transmit the byte FFhex if it were to occur as data in the normal data stream. Table 8-1 shows a list of TELNET commands.

At the start of a Telnet session, that is, just after the TCP link on port 23 has been established, both ends assume a plain NVT connection. The two ends can simply start communicating in the default style, which is plain NVT-ASCII and half-duplex mode. This is good enough for normal communications, but in many cases, one of the two ends may prefer to start negotiating options. In other words, request a

Table 8-1: List of TELNET commands

Name	Code (decimal)	Description
EOF	236	End of file
SUSP	237	Suspend current process
ABORT	238	Abort process
EOR	239	End of record
SE	240	Suboption end
NOP	241	No operation
DM	242	Data mark
BRK	243	Break
IP	244	Interrupt process
AO	245	Abort output
AYT	246	Are you there?
EC	247	Escape character
EL	248	Erase line
GA	249	Go ahead
SB	250	Subscription begin
WILL	251	Option negotiation
WONT	252	Option negotiation
DO	253	Option negotiation
DONT	254	Option negotiation
IAC	255	Data byte 255

number of extra 'facilities' to be provided; full duplex, echo characters, set window sizes, terminal emulation type, etc. It is not essential that the other end agree to the requests (it may not be able to implement them). A very simple implementation of Telnet in a small microcontroller for example, may just reject all requests, and operate only at the default settings. It is important however, that all remotes are able to respond to requests in one way or the other, even if they are all denials. Options can be negotiated anytime during a session. The method of negotiation is to have either party initiate a request that some specified option should take effect. The other end may either accept the request or reject it. Some of the options are given in Table 8-2.

Negotiating options

Option negotiation is symmetric – either end can send a request to the other. The four basic requests/reply methods are organized as 'verbs':

- WILL   The sender wants to enable the option itself.

- DO   The sender wants the receiver (other end) to enable the option.

- WONT   The sender wants to disable the option itself.

- DONT   The sender wants the receiver to disable the option.

Table 8-2: Options that can be negotiated during a Telnet session

Option (decimal)	Name	RFC
1	Echo	857
3	Suppress go ahead	858
5	Status	859
6	Timing mark	860
24	Terminal type	1091
31	Window size	1073
32	Terminal speed	1079
33	Flow control	1372
34	Line mode	1184
36	Environment variables	1408

For example, a sender wants to enable an option, say a particular terminal type. It starts negotiation by sending the request sequence <IAC><WILL><24>. This tells the remote that the sender wants to enable a particular terminal type, (note that the actual terminal type has not been specified yet). The remote could reply with a <IAC><DONT> meaning that it will not accept the request. The remote perhaps does not know anything about terminal types, nor does it want to emulate one. From this point on, the sender's only option is to carry on using the default NVT-ASCII sequences or abort the session. If on the other hand, the remote replied with a <IAC><DO><24>, it would tell the sender that it is capable of negotiating terminal types. Note how the number 24 (the code for 'terminal type') is also returned. This is used identify or match the current negotiating option 'ID', as more than one negotiation can be going on at any one time. The sender can now go to the next stage of the negotiation by sending something like: <IAC><SB><24><1><IAC><SE>. Note how command parameters are always encapsulated in 'Subscription Start' <IAC><SB> and 'Subscription End' <IAC><SE> byte pairs. The actual request <24><1> tells the remote to return the 'type' of terminal it is emulating now. The remote may return, for example, with <IAC><SB><24><0><'ADM33'><IAC><SE> to notify the sender that it is emulating an ADM33 terminal type.

Most embedded applications may not need any of the advanced Telnet options and will happily communicate using the default settings. There are, however, some options worth noting, which may have an effect on overall performance.

Half/full-duplex

Half-duplex is the default mode. The default NVT-ASCII terminal is a half duplex device that ideally waits for a GO AHEAD command <IAC><GA> to be sent from the other end before transmitting its data to the line. In half-duplex, only one terminal sends data at a time. User input is locally echoed to the screen as soon as typed and stored in a local buffer. Only when the line is completed (or after a time-out) the buffer is sent to the other end as a single TCP segment. In practice, this is not necessary, and characters can be sent and received at any time, with each character possibly occupying one full TCP segment if they are typed slowly enough. Segment transmission also implies a duplex switch, so there is no need to handle the GO AHEAD commands for simple systems. The alternative to half-duplex is full-duplex, where both terminals can communicate in both directions at the same time. To enable full duplex, ECHO (described in RFC 857) and SUPPRESS GO AHEAD (described in RFC 858) must be enabled at both ends (responses from the remote are shown indented for clarity purposes):

<IAC><DO><3>	Send DO SUPRESS GO AHEAD to other end
<IAC><WILL><3>	Receiver WILL SUPPRESS GO AHEAD
<IAC><WILL><1>	Receiver usually also enables ECHO by default

Character at a time transmission

When this option is enabled, each character the sender types is immediately sent to the remote (without waiting for a go ahead or line end). IF ECHO is enabled, the remote will return the same characters back to the sender. This mode will be automatically enabled if both SUPRESS GO AHEAD and ECHO are enabled at both ends, that is, when in full-duplex mode. Character-at-a-time gives the most realistic response to a Telnet link, as echoing is almost immediate. One disadvantage of this method, especially when used with TCP, is that each key pressing will generate a string of TCP packets in both directions, each containing at least 20 bytes of overhead (to carry just one byte of payload). This of course can cause delays and be very inefficient.

Line at a time

In operation, lines are not transmitted to the remote until the 'return' key is pressed on the terminal. A useful addition to this feature is adding a timer to transmit the buffer say if no keys have been pressed for a given time. This is described in RFC 1184. In Telnet, a line end (or end-of-line) is transmitted as the two-character sequence <CR> <LF>, this is the same as the sequence '\r\n' used in programming software, or 0Dhex, 0Ahex in hex notation. A carriage return on its own is usually transmitted as the two character sequence <CR><NUL>, same as '\r\0' or 0Dhex, 00hex.

Summary

Telnet is a very simple protocol for implementing in embedded systems. There is no need to include any of the advanced features, and a most basic 'no-options' implementation will operate perfectly well. However, an embedded implementation should ideally provide for facilities for at least rejecting all negotiating requests made by a remote. The steps for a simple Telnet session are:

1. Client opens a TCP connection on port 23 with the remote.

2. When the connection is open, the client can send (and receive) plain NVT-ASCII sequences as described above, either in groups, or one character at a time. If transaction speed is important, the client can negotiate other options.

3. In small systems, include software to negate any negotiation requests from a remote by sending the <IAC><WONT> response for any requests.

4. On termination, the client can then drop the connection, either by closing the TCP connection, or more crudely, by simply dropping the line.

Electronic Mail

Electronic mail (e-mail) is one of the most convenient ways for sending simple messages over a LAN or over the Internet. E-mail can be sent over a LAN to a host running e-mail server software, or it can be sent over telephone via an Internet service provider (ISP) to another user on the Internet. E-mail is simple to implement. An embedded data logger can use e-mail to transmit updates over the Internet anywhere round the world, the only thing it needs is a dial-up modem and an ISP account.

Superficially, it may appear that e-mail is passed directly from a sender to a recipient. This is not always true; a typical e-mail may pass through several computers during its lifetime. This happens because many organizations have dedicated machines in their networks to handle mail only. These are called mail servers. The information from the sender will first go through the local mail server, which will store it, and eventually send it to the recipient organization's mail server, from which the remote users can download their mail. In the case of an ISP, where users dial in from their home computers, the 'client' is the user's machine, and the 'server' is one of the ISP's machines, often dedicated purely to mail tasks. When a user sends mail, they compose the message offline on their own computer, and then send it off over the telephone line to their local ISP's mail server. From this point on, the user's computer has finished with their job, but the mail server at the ISP still has to deliver the message. It does this by finding the recipient's mail server, communicating with that server and delivering the message to it. The ISP may decide to send the mail item immediately, or at a later time, when costs are less. The message, after arriving at the remote mail server, will wait there, until the final recipient logs on to their system and retrieves their mail, deleting it from their own mail server in the process. The original client may have used the SMTP or POP3 protocols to upload the electronic mail message to their local server. The remote recipient used the POP3 protocol to retrieve, delete and manage their mail items.

SMTP

The simple mail transfer protocol (SMTP) is defined in RFC 821, and is used for simple e-mail transmission; SMTP can only be used to transmit mail. A different protocol, post office protocol 3 (POP3) is required for more advanced operations such as receiving, deleting, enumerating and managing mail items. Most ISPs provide both SMTP and POP3 hosting services on their dial-up lines.

In order to use e-mail with an ISP, a client must have an e-mail account with the ISP arranged. During a dial-up session, the PPP protocol is used to authenticate the client (by sending its password and user number), and for the server to allocate an IP number to the client, which is valid for the duration of the session. Once the IP connection to the ISP is established, the client opens a TCP connection on port 25, the nominal port allocated to SMTP. Once the TCP link on this port is established, all subsequent two-way communication on the line is via standard NVT-ASCII characters.

Operation follows the standard client–server model, where the client originates a response from the server. Requests are made in the form of SMTP Commands. All commands follow a simple character format structure known as the 822-header format (after the RFC standard that defines it, RFC 822). This format uses standard NVT-ASCII characters delimited by normal carriage return – line feed character pair sequences <CR-LF>. This 'standard' text header format is also used in various other Internet application layer protocols. An SMTP transaction is straightforward, and easily implemented on a small micro. The general sequence of operations is as follows:

1. The caller establishes a TCP connection on port 25 with the host (the caller itself may use for response any port it wishes). The host (ISP) may reply with a welcome text message as follows (note the first three digit number or response code):

```
220 Sat, 28 Jan 2002 MYISP.COM Mail server. Welcome
```

2. The client logs onto the SMTP server by sending the following text string:

```
HELO myname <CR><LF>
```

Note the single 'L' in 'HELO' This is followed by your registered e-mail 'id', followed by a single carriage return – line feed pair. Some hosts will require just the id, some others will want your full e-mail address, and some others may just accept the HELO string without a senders address at all, that is:

```
HELO <CR><LF>
```

3. The client now needs to wait for a reply. The reply from the server will also be in ASCII form and typically will contain the following message:

```
250 post - welcome myname@myisp.com
```

The three-digit number is a unique reply code. The text following it contains the corresponding plain text explanation for human consumption. Client software only needs to check the three digits against a list (full details in the RFC). Code 250 for example is a general OK response. This indicates that the server has accepted the command and that the client can proceed to the next stage. Simple client end software could just respond to 250 codes and ignore the rest, aborting the session otherwise. In any case, the client must wait for a reply before proceeding to the next stage. Not waiting for a response from the server may cause it to ignore the rest of the commands.

4. On receipt of the correct error code, the client can now send the e-mail message envelope (which contains the sender and recipient addresses). The information in this envelope is required by the server in order to route the message to the final recipient. A typical envelope transaction is as follows:

```
MAIL FROM: myname@myisp.com<CR><LF>
   250 OK
RCPT TO: yourname@yourisp.com<CR><LF>
   250 Recipient OK
RCPT TO: elsesname@yourisp.com<CR><LF>
   550 No such user
RCPT TO: elsename@yourisp.com<CR><LF>
   250 Recipient OK
DATA
   354 Start Mail input
```

Note that the server acknowledges every line sent individually (returned lines are shown here indented for clarity). The client must wait for every reply before proceeding to the next command. Multiple RCPT TO headers have been used here to show how the same e-mail can be sent to more than one recipient in one session. In a real message, at least one recipient address is required. Note how the server checks every address entry as it arrives, and notifies the sender whether it can or cannot recognise the destination. Many other envelope commands are available, please refer to the RFC for more information. The last line of the envelope contains the command DATA on its own. This tells the server that any text following this command will be the body of the text message.

5. The client can now send the text of the message. It is common practice to add a message header at the beginning of the message body. Message headers are used by receivers and browsers to classify message received and for displaying to remote users. They are not strictly necessary, and they do not need to be present for a message to reach its destination.

```
FROM: eddy <myname@myisp@com><CR><LF>
TO: fred <yourname@yourisp.com><CR><LF>
```

```
SUBJECT: test message <CR><LF>
Text message goes here <CR><LF>
More text goes here <CR><LF>
This is the last line <CR><LF>
.<CR><LF>
```

The FROM command is followed by the common name and the e-mail address of the sender. They could be anything you like; they are only used for display purposes as the host will simply pass them on without processing. The second header command TO, takes the common name and the e-mail address of the recipient. Again, this information is used by the recipient's browser or e-mail manager, and not processed by the mail system. The SUBJECT line can be used to carry optional header information, which may be of use to a recipient browsing through a long list of incoming mail messages. Information on headers can be very confusing and misleading as every computer in the chain may append its own piece of text to the header. This is done so that a recipient can track the sequence of events back to the sender. Unfortunately, misleading information can be added to headers by spammers to confuse the recipient as to who the original sender was. The body text follows the headers next. It is common practice to send text in plain 7-bit ASCII. It is also possible to encode sections of text in different character formats by using MIME type encoding. This allows the inclusion of characters in non-standard character sets, special punctuation marks and special symbols. Computer or graphics files can also be sent as attachments, where text or binary files are converted using compression and other encoding algorithms into character sets compatible with NVI-ASCII, without including characters that may upset transmission. RFC 1522 specifies one way of sending non-ASCII characters in RFC 822 message headers. The main use of this is to allow additional characters in the sender and receiver names, and in the subject lines. With this method, encoded characters are sent as multiple-character encoded sequences, for example, the sequence *=?ISO-8859-1?Q?Andr=E9?=* results in the text *André* (note the addition of an accent in the last letter). The text after the first question mark *ISO-8859-1* specifies one of many character sets to be used (valid values are 'us-ascii' and 'iso-8859-X' where X is a single digit, as in ISO-8859-1), *Q* denotes 'quoted printable' that is, characters are sent as the combination of the character '=' followed by two hexadecimal digits corresponding to the wanted character position in the relevant table. For example, the character é (accented e), corresponding to the 8-bit character 0xE9, is sent as the sequence '*=E9*'. Spaces can be sent as an underscore or the three character sequence '*=20*'. The British pound currency sign is sent as '*=A3*'. An alternative to *Q* is *B*, which means *base-64 encoding*. In base-64 encoding, three consecutive bytes of original text (24 bits) are encoded as four 6-bit values. The 6-bit values are mapped to a standard ASCII table of numbers and upper/lower case letters. In this way, text and data composed of 8-bit characters can be sent as a limited character set.

Multipurpose Internet mail extensions (MIME) encoding is covered in RFC 1521. This applies mainly to the body of the text (as opposed to the headers). The purpose of MIME is to add extensions, in the form of command lines, to the body of a mail message to add some form of structure to it. In practice, MIME just adds some new RFC-822 style headers to the text, telling the recipient the structure of the body to follow. RFC-1522 encoding is normally applied to ensure the body is transmitted using plain ASCII (NVT ASCII) characters in case some of the original material contains 8-bit data (i.e. binary files or images). A typical set of MIME headers are:

```
Mime-Version: 1.0
Content-Type: TEXT/PLAIN; charset=US-ASCII
Content-Type: image
Content-Transfer-Encoding: Quoted printable
Content-Type: audio/x-wav; name = sound.wav
Content-Transfer-Encoding: base64
Content-ID: <T1m10V>
```

More information on character and graphic encoding can be found in the respective RFCs. The last item of body text must have a full stop (period) character in a line of its own. That is, the termination sequence <CR><LF><.><CR><LF> notifies the server that the message text is completed and message transmission is over.

6. The client now waits for the host to send an acknowledge message. The reply will usually contain a unique message number

```
 250 submitted and queued (msg.12345678)
```

7. The client can now close the e-mail session, close the TCP connection, or attempt to send another e-mail message if needed. The client does this by sending the QUIT command on a line of its own:

```
QUIT<CR><LF>
250 myisp.com closing transmission channel
```

Tables 8-3 and 8-4 give a list of SMTP commands and reply codes, respectively.

POP3

While SMTP can only be used only for sending e-mail messages, POP3 is used to retrieve messages from an ISP. POP3 can also be used to enumerate waiting messages and to manage the message queues. There are commands for deleting, listing, re-transmitting messages, etc. POP3 is described in RFC 1939, with additions and enhancements in RFCs 1957 and 2449.

Handling a POP3 transaction follows similar steps to SMTP, but the TCP port used is 110. When the TCP connection is established, the POP3 server starts by sending a

Table 8-3: List of SMTP commands

Command	Argument	Description
HELO	Sender's host name	Used for logging on
MAIL	Sender of message	Used to identify the sender and therefore define the revere path back to the sender (also MAIL FROM)
RCPT	Intended recipient	The forward path to one or more final recipients
DATA	Body of message	Message is terminated with a full stop on a single line of text
SEND	Intended recipient	Used to initiate a mail message that should be delivered directly to a user if they are currently logged on to the system
RSET		The current mail transaction should be aborted, and that any stored messages should be deleted
VRFY	Recipient to be verified	Used to confirm the identity of the user passed as an argument, this can be used to check if the user actually exists in the hosts list.
NOOP		Used to solicit an OK response from the remote
QUIT		Specifies that the host should send an OK response, and then close the communications channel.
TURN		Command the host to return an OK reply and then reverse the roles of the machines in order to send mail the other way

Table 8-4: SMTP reply codes (please refer to RFC 821 for complete definitions)

Code	Description
211	System status or system help reply
214	Help message
220	Service ready
221	Service closing transmission channel
250	OK, service action accepted
251	User is not local, will forward to given path
354	Start mail text input
421	Service not available – closing communications channel
450	Requested action not taken, mailbox unavailable
451	Requested action not taken, local error in processing
452	Requested action not taken, insufficient storage
500	Syntax error – command unrecognized
501	Syntax error in parameters or arguments
502	Command not implemented
503	Bad sequence of commands
504	Command parameter not implemented

greeting. The client and POP3 server then exchange 822 header style commands and responses until the connection is closed or aborted. Operation follows the standard client–server model, where the client originates a response from the server. In the same way as SMTP, requests are made in the form of POP commands using the standard 822-message structure described in the previous section. An example POP3 session (taken from RFC 1939) is as follows. The client has just opened a TCP connection on port 110 and returned messages from the POP3 server are shown indented.

```
  +OK POP3 server ready <mailserver@myisp.com>
APOP myname c4c9334bac560ecc979e58001b3e22fb
  +OK myname maildrop has 2 messages (320 octets)
STAT
  +OK 2 320
LIST
  +OK 2 messages (320 octets)
  1 120
  2 200
RETR 1
  +OK 120 octets
  <the POP3 server sends message 1>
DELE 1
  +OK message 1 deleted
RETR 2
  +OK 200 octets
  <the POP3 server sends message 2>
DELE 2
  +OK message 2 deleted
QUIT
  +OK dewey POP3 server signing off (maildrop empty)
<close connection>
```

The strange-looking code after the first APOP command is known as a MDS digest string. A digest string is a form of secret password, computed at both the client and the server (from items such as the time stamp and a shared secret word only known to the client and the server, possibly related to the user's ISP password). This avoids sending passwords in the open. The actual algorithm is defined in RFC 1321 and is also discussed in RFC 1734. Some hosts do not require digests strings. An alternative form of logging in is by using the USER/PASS combination.

The STAT and LIST commands are used to enumerate the number of mail items pending. The DELE is used to delete messages, and RETR to download them. In this example, the client has first obtained information about all the e-mail messages waiting to be retrieved. Then it proceeds to retrieve and delete the first and second message (note the difference in reply codes from SMTP). Also note how multi line messages always use the full stop (period) on a single line as terminators.

In POP3, all reply codes start with one the two forms '+OK' or '-ERR'. These are known as status indicators. These are always in upper case. Table 8-5 summarizes the

Table 8-5: The main POP3 commands

Command	Argument	Description
APOP	User name followed by MDS digest string	Used to log on
USER	String identifying a mailbox	Used for authentication using the USER and PASS command combination, the client must first issue the USER command. If the POP3 server responds with a positive status indicator ('+OK'), then the client may issue either PASS to complete authentication, or the QUIT to terminate the POP3 session
PASS	Valid server/ mailbox password (required)	When the client issues the PASS command, the server uses the argument pair from the USER and PASS commands to determine if the client should be given access to the appropriate maildrop. Since the PASS command has exactly one argument, a POP3 server may treat spaces in the argument as part of the password, instead of as argument separators
STAT	None	The server issues a line containing information for the maildrop. This line is called a *drop listing* for that maildrop. In order to simplify parsing, all POP3 servers are required to use a certain format for drop listings
LIST	Message number, or none	If a valid argument was given (the message exists) the server issues a line containing information for that message. This line is called a *scan listing* for that message. If no argument was given, the server issues a a multiline response with information for each message available for downloading. The last line of the multiline message will contain a full stop (period) on its own
RETR	Message number (obtained from LIST)	If the message number is valid, the server issues a multi-line response consisting of a line containing the number of octets in the message, followed by the message contents. The last line of the multiline message will contain a full stop (period) on its own

| DELE | Message number | The server marks the message as deleted. Any future reference to the message number associated with the message in a POP3 command generates an error. The POP3 server does not actually delete the message until the POP3 session enters the UPDATE state |
| QUIT | None | Used to terminate the transaction. QUIT has slightly different meanings depending at what point in the transaction it was called, refer to the RFC documentation |

main POP3 commands. Please note that some of these commands only apply at certain points during the transaction (called states in RFC parlance). For more information refer to the relevant RFC document.

Summary

SMTP is much simpler than POP3 and is ideal for embedded systems for sending e-mail messages. It is also appealing because all messages can be small, and easily handled by RAM limited systems. The steps required for a simple mail dial-up transaction are:

1. Client (assumed the embedded system) contacts the ISP over a dial-up telephone connection. The client uses AT commands to enable the modem dial the number and establish the connection.

2. The ISP will answer with a PPP (or SLIP) initialization sequence. The client will negotiate a convenient protocol using PPP commands. In the case of an embedded system, these could be the minimum necessary. During negotiations, the client will send its logon ID and password. If accepted, the ISP will return an allocated IP address for the session. The client will effectively become this IP address for the duration of the call.

3. Having negotiated PPP parameters, the client can now talk directly to the mail server. The first thing it will do is to open a TCP connection (port 25 for SMTP, port 110 for POP3).

4. When the connection is open, the client will send commands and e-mail body text sequences as described in the previous section, always waiting for replies.

5. At the end of the transaction, the client can drop the connection, either by closing the TCP link, or more crudely, by simply dropping the phone line.

Reading Email Headers

Here is a brief analysis of the life of a piece of email. This background material may be important for understanding how emails are transmitted, especially for automatically generated emails such as may be used in an embedded system. Let us assume that user **myname@myisp.com** wants to send a simple email to **yourname@yourisp.com**. Let's further assume that the remote system is using a mail handler program called **supermail** (the IP addresses shown are fictitious). When **myname** wants to send an email to **yourname**, he or she composes it at their PC workstation, which is possibly connected to the **myisp** network via a dialup line. The computer at **myname** contacts the ISP via a dialup line (assume the web name of the mail handling system at the ISP is **mail.myisp.com).** The mail server, now seeing that it has a message to forward to another computer, contacts the mail server at the remote location and delivers it (assume this is called **mail.yourisp.com**). The remote destination user **yourname** retrieves the message by logging in to **yourisp.com** and downloading the message. During this processing, headers will be added to the message at least three times: At composition time, by whatever email program **myname** is using. When the message passes through **mail.myisp.com**, And at the transfer between **myisp.com** to **yourisp.com**. Sometimes, the remote ISP program that downloads the messages may add a further header. At composition time, the message header is:

From: eddy <myname@myisp@com><CR><LF>

To: fred <yourname@yourisp.com><CR><LF>

Date: Tue, Jan 1 2002 10:06:14 GMT

X-Mailer: Supermail V1.0

Subject: test message <CR><LF>

Text message goes here <CR><LF>

.<CR><LF>

Note: The two command lines **Date:** and **X-Mailer:** were not included in the original sender's text. These are usually added by user mail applications. When **myisp.com** processes the message for sending to **yourisp.com**, the headers have now become:

Received: from myisp.com (myisp.com [192.123.1.11]) by mail.myisp.com

(1.1.2) id 00421: Tue, Jan 01 2002 10:06:17 (GMT)

From: eddy <myname@myisp@com><CR><LF>

To: fred <yourname@yourisp.com><CR><LF>

Date: Tue, Jan 1 2002 10:06:14 GMT

Message-Id:<myname01012002100614-0000179@mail.myisp.com>

X-Mailer: Supermail V1.0

Subject: test message <CR><LF>

Text message goes here <CR><LF>

.<CR><LF>

When the message is received at **yourisp.com** the headers have now become:

Received: from mail.myisp.com (mail.myisp.com [192.123.1.12]) by mail.yourisp.com (SM-1.1.2) with SMTP id LAA2001 for<yourname@yourisp.com>; Tue, 01 Jan 2002 10:07:24 (GMT)

Received: from myisp.com (myisp.com [192.123.1.11]) by mail.myisp.com

(1.1.2) id 00421: Tue, Jan 01 2002 10:06:17 (GMT)

From: eddy <myname@myisp@com><CR><LF>

To: fred <yourname@yourisp.com><CR><LF>

Date: Tue, Jan 1 2002 10:06:14 GMT

Message-Id:<myname01012002100614-0000179@mail.myisp.com>

X-Mailer: Supermail V1.0

Subject: test message <CR><LF>

Text message goes here <CR><LF>

.<CR><LF>

This last set of headers is what the recipient sees on his email text. The first extra line (note the word wrap, it is all in a single line) shows that this email was received from a machine calling itself **mail.myisp.com** (i.e. the first reference to **mail.myisp.com** in the line). The next entry in brackets show who the real sender was. In this case the sender was IP address 192.123.1.12, which just happens to correspond to **mail.myisp.com**. (the system will do a reverse check). The same line shows that the machine that did the receiving was **mail.myisp.com**, and that is running a **Supermail** program version 1.1.2. The receiving machine assigned ID number LAA2001 to the message, this is used internally by the system for logging and administration purposes. The line also shows the message was destined for **<yourname@yourisp.com>**. Note that this header is not related to the To: header. The second extra line shows the similar information but related to the previous hop. That is at the point between **myisp.com** and **yourisp.com**. Note the differences in travel times for the messages., and the repeated entries for source and destination machines. This seemingly irrelevant repetition of addresses only makes sense when considering **Relays**, these are intermediate machines in the transmission path. A message may not go directly from machine **A** to **B**, but possibly from **A** to **C**, then to **D** and finally to **B**. The third extra line is a Message Id line added by the first mail sender to identify it, and to be able to track it during its lifetime.

The situation above is rather simplistic. In reality, a message may pass through several more machines (including firewalls and relays) each adding an extra header to the message. This contributes to the strange system addresses found on some email messages.

HTTP

The hypertext transfer protocol (HTTP) was first defined in RFC 1945, although it existed in various other fashions since the beginning of the 1990s. The first version has now been upgraded to HTTP/1.1, described in RFC 2068 and RFC 2616. HTTP is the basic communication method used on the Internet by web servers to deliver pages, images, sounds and other types of files. HTTP follows a simple client–server (or request/response) methodology. The server simply sits there waiting until a client makes a request, and then supplies the requested information. HTTP requests are presented in standard RFC 822 header message format (see previous section for a definition).

All HTTP requests are handled one at a time, and are responded individually. In other words, requests are independent of each other. One transaction does not link to the next. In HTTP/1.0, the TCP connection is opened before a request, and then closed after it has been serviced. That is, each request results in a full opening and closing of a TCP connection. HTTP/1.1 includes enhancements to allow the TCP connection to remain open between transactions, greatly improving protocol performance. HTTP nominally uses TCP port 80 for communications, although it is possible to specify other ports for special applications. Special PC programs called browsers are used to access web pages using the HTTP protocol. Most browsers will support all versions of HTTP, new and old. Simple embedded systems acting as servers can limit themselves to HTTP/1.0 commands, simplifying their design.

HTTP is an inverted pyramid of complexity. At the lowest level, commands are available to transfer simple formatted web pages between a host and a web browser. HTTP has many options an additions, in order to transfer complex objects such as images. In order to understand the basics, we must first go back and see how things function from the browser's point of view.

The HTTP transaction

When you fire up your Internet browser on your PC and request a web page, a number of events will take place. Firstly, a full TCP connection on port 80 is established between the PC and the remote server. Once the TCP link is open, the browser and server can exchange data. To request a page, the browser sends a 'GET' command string in plain text, usually followed by a file name and maybe a few other parameters in plain text.

```
GET /Welcome.htm HTTP/1.0<CR><LF>
or:
GET HTTP/1.0<CR><LF>
```

The above can be optionally followed with a number of extra RF C822 style command lines, for example:

```
GET /Welcome.htm HTTP/1.0<CR><LF>
User-Agent: Mozilla/4.5<CR><LF>
```

```
Accept: image/gif, image/jpeg<CR><LF>
Accept-Encoding: gzip<CR><LF>
Accept-Charset: iso-8859-1<CR><LF>
<CR><LF>
```

These commands notify the host what type of information the browser can accept. This allows the server software to format pages correctly. Note how the last line is terminated on a blank line, that is, two CRLF sequences <CR-LF-CR-LF> and not with a single full stop. On receipt of a request from the client, the server will reply with the contents of the requested file (in this case, the stored text file 'welcome.htm'). Web pages are made up of plain NVT-ASCII text, and use a formatting language known as Hypertext markup language (HTML), which allows for the inclusion of text formatting commands, font and colour changes by the use of pre-defined bracketed 'tags' within the text. If no filename is supplied, a default name such as 'Welcome.html' or 'Index.htm' is always substituted instead. Some servers have case sensitive formats, others do not. When the file has been fully transmitted, the server closes the TCP connection, and that is the end. A typical reply from the server would be:

```
HTTP/1.0 200 OK<CR><LF>
Last-modified: Wed, 2 January 2002 10:10:43 GMT<CR><LF>
Server: Apache/1.1<CR><LF>
Content-type: text/html<CR><LF>
Content-length: 1892<CR><LF>
<CR><LF>
contents of requested file here....
```

The end of the command sequence is delimited by a blank line on its own <CR-LF-CR-LF>. The contents of the file are sent 'as is' whatever they may contain. To get another page, the browser must open another TCP connection, and send another GET command with the name of the new file. If the page requested does not exist, the first line is replaced with the well-known 'page does not exist' 404 error code.

```
HTTP/1.0 404 Not Found<CR><LF><
<CR>LF>
```

Most user-friendly servers will send a more comprehensively edited message, perhaps using HTML encoding:

```
HTTP/1.0 404 Not Found<CR><LF><
<CR><LF>
<HEAD><TITLE>File Not Found</TITLE></HEAD><CR><LF>
<BODY><H1>File Not Found</H1><CR>LF>
ERROR 404 - The requested URL was not found<CR><LF>
<P></BODY><CR><LF>
<CR><LF>
```

A typical web site on a server may contain many HTML files. There is usually one 'base' default file, usually called 'welcome.html' or 'index.html' and various other support files: bitmap images, sound files, java applets, etc. In a standard page request, the browser will first request (and display) the main page. Then it will scan through the contents of this page looking for links to other files. For each link it finds, it will make further GET requests for each, one after the other. As the files arrive, they are presented to the user in the same order. If they are bitmaps, for example, they are displayed at their correct location on the screen. Text files are very short and can display very quickly. Images, even compressed ones, are bigger and can take more time to download. The HTTP/HTML scheme allows the various parts of a file to be displayed in any order, and give an impression of speed. Following this logic, it is easy to understand why some web pages can load and display very quickly (text only) and why some pages display a blank rectangle while the image that goes within is still being downloaded. It should also be clear now how straightforward it could be to implement a web server using an embedded system. The server only needs to respond to GET requests, send file contents, and just ignore any other commands. The page data can be stored in PROM, disk, or any other non-volatile device.

Formats, images and other files

HTTP transactions do not need to contain only HTML pages. A 'GET' could result in the transmission of a plain text page (or even binary data). This is not much use for a browser, which will be expecting special HTML tags (plain data would be displayed as black text of standard size on white background) but could be useful for other kinds of transactions. The advantages of HTML are many, and for the sake of a few extra ASCII characters forming the HTML headers, worth having in all transactions. Another formatting option is WAP pages, which may be aimed at wireless browsers and for cell phone access. Another 'advanced' data format that is gaining acceptance is XML. The value of XML and similar codes is in the use of schema. A schema defines the type of data a device collects and how it sends it, it is a form of classifying the data contained within a page or set of pages, and can be used in automated or semi-automated web access systems.

Summary

The design of embedded servers is relatively simple. Using the client–server model, the embedded system only needs to wait for commands from remotes and serve them individually. Simple embedded systems acting as servers can also limit themselves to HTTP/1.0 commands, simplifying their design. A typical web server HTTP transaction is as follows:

1. The server (assumed an embedded system) waits (LISTENs) on port 80 until a client opens a connection on that port. If service to multiple clients is

required, the server must dedicate the connection to the session, and open another LISTEN port 80.

2. The server parses the received string (the GET command) A small web server only needs to respond to GET commands and ignore others. From the parsing sequence, a file name will be retrieved.

3. The server transmits the contents of the file. The file will generally contain a formatted HTML page, but it can also contain plain text, graphics, java scripts or any other data aimed at HTML, or even non HTML browsers.

4. After sending all the bytes of the page, the server closes the TCP connection and opens another LISTEN on port 80.

A typical web client HTTP transaction is as follows:

1. Client (assumed the embedded system) establishes a connection with the host, maybe by first contacting the ISP over a dial up telephone connection. The client uses AT commands to enable the modem dial the number and establish the connection.

2. The ISP will answer with a PPP initialisation sequence. The client will negotiate protocol using PPP commands. The client at this stage will send the ISP logon ID and password. If accepted, the ISP will allocate and return an IP address, which will be used for the transaction. The client will effectively become this IP address for the duration of the call.

3. Having negotiated PPP parameters, the client can now communicate with the server. The first thing it will do is to open a TCP connection on port 80.

4. When the connection is open, the client will send the HTTP GET sequence followed by the page filename wanted, plus any optional command messages.

5. The client waits for the page to arrive, storing it in local memory.

6. The server (or client) will close the TCP connection (assuming HTTP/1.0).

7. The client now scans through the HTTP page contents. If further page requests are found within the text. The client will make further GET requests via further TCP open/close connections. The received data (usually images) are then displayed at their correct locations on the screen.

FTP

File transfer protocol (FTP) was one of the original protocols developed for the Internet. It was developed for the transmission of files and fixed blocks of data. FTP is described in RFCs 412, 959 and 1635. FTP is also based on a client–server model. It requires a reliable transport mechanism, so TCP connections are used. The FTP process running on the computer that is making the file transfer request is called the

FTP client, The FTP process running on the computer that is receiving the request is called the FTP server.

Format

Two TCP connections are required during an FTP session: a TCP data connection on port 20, and a TCP control connection on port 21. The control connection must remain open at all times when data or commands are sent. The data connection is only open during an actual data transaction. The general sequence of operations is as follows:

1. The FTP client opens a TCP connection to the server on port 21. This is known as the control connection. It will be used to transfer commands, and not data. This control connection will be open for the duration of the full session, and is effectively a Telnet type link between the two systems.

2. The FTP client forwards information such as user name, passwords to the server for authentication. The server will reply with accept or reject codes to these requests.

3. The client sends further commands with file names, data types etc to be transferred, plus data flow (i.e. file transfers from client to server or vice versa). The server responds with accept or reject codes.

4. Once ready for data flow, the two sides open a TCP connection on port 20.

5. Data can now flow between client and server on port 20. Data transferred is encoded in a number of specified formats including NVT-ASCII or binary.

6. When the whole file has been transferred, the sending FTP process closes the data connection (port 20), but retains the control connection on port 21.

7. The control connection can now be used to establish another data transfer, or to close down the link.

FTP commands on the control port are sent as text headers, and in standard RFC 822 format. Each protocol command consists of a four character ASCII sequence terminated in a <CR><LF> sequence. Some commands also require parameters. Commands are roughly divided into service, transfer and access control. A list of the most useful commands is given in Table 8-6.

A manual interactive Telnet could be used for hand transmitting the commands. In which case, the connection will not be too different from a DOS command prompt session. The reply codes are many, the format for the replies is given in Table 8-7.

Here 'y' and 'z' are the second and third digits. The second digit provides more information about the reply. The third digit also provides more information, but the exact meaning may vary between installations (Table 8-8).

Table 8-6: Most useful FTP commands

Command	Argument	Description
USER	username	User name allocated by ISP
PASS	password	Password (allocated by ISP)
ACCT	account info	User account
CWD	pathname	Change working directory
CDUP	none	Change to parent directory
SMNT	pathname	Structure mount
REIN	none	Terminate and re-initialize
QUIT	none	Logout FTP
RETR	pathname	Retrieve file from server
STOR	pathname	Store data to server
RNFR	pathname	Rename 'from'
RNTO	pathname	Rename 'to'
DELE	pathname	Delete file
RMD	pathname	Remove directory
MKD	pathname	Make directory
LIST	pathname	List files or text
STAT	pathname	Status
HELP	subject	Print help on
PORT	host-port	Specify port for transfer (non-default)
TYPE	type code	Type of transfer (ASCII, image, etc.)
MODE	mode code	Transmission mode (stream, block, etc.)

Table 8-7: Format for replies in manual interactive Telnet

Reply	Description
1yz	Action initiated. Expect another reply before sending a new command
2yz	Action completed. Can send a new command
3yz	Command accepted, but on hold due to lack of information
4yz	Command not accepted or completed. Temporary error condition exists. Command can be re-issued
5yz	Command not accepted or completed. Do not re-issue – reissuing the command will result in the same error.

It is important to note that in FTP, requests are not necessarily implemented in the same sequence as sent, and that transactions and replies may be interleaved.

Summary

FTP is the standard method for transferring files on the Internet. Unfortunately, it requires two TCP connections to be opened at the same time, something that not all

**Table 8-8: Some meanings for the third digit,
represented by 'z'**

Value	Description
X0z	Syntax error or illegal command
X1z	Reply to request for information
X2z	Reply that refers to connection management
X3z	Reply for authentication command
X5z	Reply for status of server

embedded implementations may be able to support. Resource-limited systems may prefer to use a simpler protocol such as TFTP.

TFTP

The trivial file transfer protocol (TFTP) is described in RFC 1350. This is a less sophisticated version of FTP, and quite suitable for transferring files in simpler systems. TFTP is typically implemented in ROM form in the boot section of diskless machines such as point of sale terminals. It is generally used for power-on remote system bootstrapping. TFTP does not contain authorisation controls and little error correction, which should be provided by the application. A diskless station would normally use a protocol such as BOOTP (see next section) to establish its address and identity on the network, then use TFTP to download the data and program code from the server. TFTP uses a UDP connection on port 69. Simple time-outs and retransmissions methods are used to ensure data delivery.

Format

Each exchange between the client and the server starts with the client asking to read a file or to write a file. Data is relayed in consecutive addressed blocks of up to 512 bytes. Each block is acknowledged individually using the block number in the message header, before the next block can be transmitted. A block of less than 512 bytes indicates an end of file. A block is assumed lost and re-sent if an ack is not received within a certain time limit. The receiver also sets a timer, and if the last block received was not the end of file block, on timeout, the receiver will re-send the last acknowledgment message. On complete failure, the whole transaction is usually re-started. UDP TFTP payloads are known as TFTP packages. There are five different TFTP package types, depending on the opcode.

Read request/write request frames (RRQ/WRQ): RRQ frames have a 2-byte opcode of 0001, WRQ frames have opcode 0002. The Filename field specifies the pathname the file will be saved as. The format will be of course, system dependent. The Mode field specifies the method of transfer; the options are 'Netascii', 'Byte' (for binary files) and 'Mail' (where the pathname is a destination address rather than a file name).

Op Code	Filename	Mode
0001/2	(zero terminated string)	(zero terminated string)

Data frames: The 2-byte opcode is 0003 to indicate a data frame. The block number is allocated sequentially starting with zero. A maximum of 65536 bocks are allowed for a complete file transfer, so the maximum file transfer size in a TFTP transaction is 32 Mb. Data blocks are always 512 bytes except for the last one, which indicates the end of file block.

Op Code	Block Number	Data
0003	(2 bytes)	(1–512 bytes)

ACK frames: The 2-byte opcode for an Ack frame is 0004. The Block number refers to the received block being acknowledged. The Ack frame is sent by the receiver to acknowledge each block received.

Op Code	Block Number
0004	(2 bytes)

Error frames:

Op Code	Block Number	Error Message
0005	(2 bytes)	(zero terminated string)

The Opcode is 0005. The error code can be one of the several shown in Table 8-9, with the error message field describing the error in human-readable form.

Table 8-9: Error codes and their description

Error Code	Description
0	Not defined
1	File not found
2	Access violation
3	Disk full/memory limit
4	Illegal operation
5	Unknown operation
6	File already exists
7	No such user

Summary

TFTP is a very convenient protocol for small systems to transfer files, and other similar information. Because it is UDP based, it does not need the added complexities of a TCP stack, and it will only require a small amount of extra code for implementation. The limited but effective error control will be quite acceptable in most environments.

BOOTP

BOOTP is not strictly an application layer protocol, as it is conducted mainly at the lower data link layers. BOOTP is similar to ARP and RARP in operation: when a diskless workstation (client) is powered up, it broadcasts a BOOTP request to all on the network. A BOOTP server hears the request, looks up the requesting client's MAC address in its files, and returns the following three items of information:

- The IP address allocated to the client (maybe allocated on a session by session basis).

- The IP address of the server.

- The pathname of a file on the server that is to be loaded to the client (the bootstrap file).

In BOOTP, messages are carried as payloads in UDP datagrams. Port 67 is used for the client, and port 68 for the server. BOOTP is very simple to implement and can be hardwired into the ROM space of almost any microprocessor system. BOOTP is described in RFC 951, with more information and extensions described in RFCs 1532 and 1533.

Format

The BOOTP message is contained as a UDP payload, and has 300 bytes, the format is shown in Figure 8-1. The Opcode field (8 bits) can have two values: 01 for a boot request (from the client); and 02 for a boot reply (from the server). The Hardware type field (8 bits) corresponds to the same field used in ARP, and is 1 for a 10 Mbps Ethernet connection. Similarly, the Hardware length field (8 bits) is 6, corresponding to the size of a standard MAC address in bytes. The Hop count is set to zero by a client, but is also used by relay agents when booting remotely. The Transaction ID (32 bits), also called XID, is a tracking number similar to the sequence numbers used in IP and TCP. The client sets this to a random number, and the server responds with the same number. The Number of seconds field (16 bits) is the time elapsed since the client started to boot. The Client IP address (32 bits) is set by the client to its IP address (if known) or zero if it is requesting one. The Your IP address (32 bits) is set by the server to the allocated IP address to the client, if client is requesting for one. The Server IP address (32 bits) is set by the server to its own IP address.

Operation (8 bits)	Htype (8 bits)	Hlen (8 bits)	Hops (8 bits)
Transaction ID (32 bites)			
Seconds (16 bits)		Unused (16 bits)	
Client IP address (32 bits)			
Your IP address (32 bits)			
Server IP address (32 bits)			
Gateway IP address (32 bits)			
Client hardware address (16 bytes)			
Server host name (64 bytes)			
Boot filename (128 bytes)			
Vendor specific (64 bytes)			

Figure 8-1: Bootp format

The Gateway IP address (32 bits) is set by a proxy server, if one is being used, otherwise left as zero. The Client hardware address is set by the client when making a request. The Server hostname is a null terminated string that is optionally filled in by the server. The Boot filename is also a null terminated string filled in by the server, this is the name of a file in the server that the client will be using when downloading its bootstrap information. The Vendor specific area (64 bytes) is used for DHCP options, see RFC 1531.

BOOTP was mainly designed for authenticating workstations on power up before bootstrapping their OS files using TFTP. Servers implementing BOOTP include facilities for dealing with multiple requests, and for handling multiple servers on the one network.

Summary

BOOTP is an enhancement to RARP and can be used in embedded systems to provide authentication and as a simple form for dynamically allocating IP addresses. Its main advantage is that it can be used at the very low levels using UDP only transactions.

DHCP

The dynamic host configuration protocol (DHCP) was developed as an enhancement out of BOOTP in an effort to centralize and streamline the allocation of IP addresses in a network. The purpose of DHCP is to control and allocate IP-related information centrally thus eliminating the need to keep individual tracks of where individual IP addresses are allocated. DHCP is defined in RFCs 2131 and 2132.

In a DHCP-enabled network, when a client is powered on, it broadcasts a special message requesting an IP address and a subnet mask from a server (there can be more than one DHCP server in a network). The DHCP server, checks its database, and replies with a message allocating the addresses to the client. This IP address allocation is only given for a limited period, and is called a *lease*. The first step from a client in obtaining an IP address is called an *IP lease request*. A client that has just connected to the network, or just switched on will attempt to obtain an address automatically from the DHCP server as part of its boot up procedure. Since the client is not aware of its own IP address, (or that belonging to the server), it performs the request using addresses 0.0.0.0 and 255.255.255.255, respectively. These are known as DHCP *discovery messages*. The broadcast is made on UDP port 67 (same as BOOTP client) and port 68 (same as BOOTP server). The message will contain the MAC address of the client in order for the server to be able to identify the source of the request. If no DHCP server responds to this initial broadcast, the request is repeated three more times at 9, 13 and 16 second intervals, plus at a random time after that. If there is still no response, the broadcast is repeated every five minutes until something is received. If no DHCP server ever becomes available, the client cannot be enabled.

The next stage is called *lease offer*. This corresponds to the message sent by the server and the information offered to clients. This message consists of an IP address, subnet mask, lease period (in seconds), and the IP address of the server itself. The server can identify the request source, because of its MAC address. The offered IP is reserved temporarily until accepted, to prevent it from being been offered to other machines that may be generating lease requests at the same time on the system. The next stage is *lease selection*. It is quite possible, especially in a network with multiple DHCP servers, for a client to receive more than one lease offers. The client nominally accepts the first lease offer it receives. The client replies by broadcasting an acceptance message, requesting to lease that particular IP and related information. Just as in the first stage, this message will be broadcast as a DHCP request, but this time, it will also include the IP address now accepted by the client. This allows other DHCP servers in the network to add this 'already allocated' IP number to their internal lists, and stop making further lease offers on this number. The last stage is *lease acknowledgement*. The accepted DHCP server notes the acceptance from the client, adding the IP address to its own list, and returns an acceptance message to the client. This is called a DHCP ACK. Occasionally a negative acknowledgement may be sent (a DHCP NACK). This can happen for example, if there are timing irregularities in the allocations, or an IP has time lapsed and has been reallocated elsewhere. Before the lease period elapses, the client will send a *lease renewal* message to the DHCP host. If the DHCP server is active, it will just send a

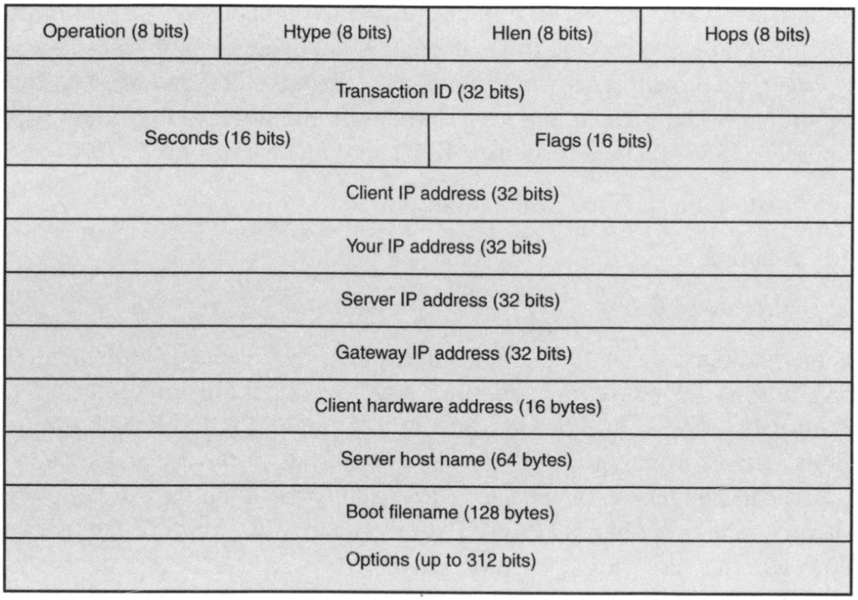

Operation (8 bits)	Htype (8 bits)	Hlen (8 bits)	Hops (8 bits)
Transaction ID (32 bits)			
Seconds (16 bits)		Flags (16 bits)	
Client IP address (32 bits)			
Your IP address (32 bits)			
Server IP address (32 bits)			
Gateway IP address (32 bits)			
Client hardware address (16 bytes)			
Server host name (64 bytes)			
Boot filename (128 bytes)			
Options (up to 312 bits)			

Figure 8-2: DHCO format

reassuring acknowledge message to the client, resetting the lease time. If the DHCP server is not active, the client will send a further renewal message nearer its lease termination time. Any other available DHCP servers could respond to the message by allocation a new IP address to the client. If the client wishes to terminate a session, it can do a *lease release*. Alternatively, it can allow the lease period to expire normally.

Format

A single DHCP message format is used for all transactions. This is based on the BOOTP format and sent as a UDP payload. The DHCP message fields are similar to those in BOOTP (see previous section), except for the message type of which there are many. The options field (up to 312 bits) is described in RFC 2132. The format is shown in Figure 8-2.

Summary

BOOTP is a simpler scheme for simple network IP allocation in embedded outstations. However, if embedded systems need to co-exist with other users in a LAN, they must be able to implement protocols such as DHCP.

RTP/RTCP

The real-time transport protocol (RTP) is not so much a specific protocol, but a building block on top of which other protocols can exist. RTP protocols are of interest to embedded systems as they can be used for the transmission of real-time information. RTP was designed to allow receivers to compensate for the timing discrepancies and de-sequencing introduced by IP networks (sometimes called network *jitter*). RTP is aimed at continuous data streams. RTP can be used for any real-time stream of data, voice, video etc. where timing order is important. RTP is defined in RFC 1889. RTP packets use UDP and include extra fields for:

- information on the type of data transported,
- time-stamps,
- sequence numbers.

RTCP is the feedback mechanism, and is used often in advanced implementations of RTP. RTCP allows the conveyance of control and feedback information such as signal quality, data losses and participants information. RTP and RTCP allow receivers to recover from network 'jitter' by appropriate buffering and sequencing. Lost packets can be ignored or repeated. It is usually assumed that streamed data can allow for such data dropouts. RTP/RTCP design can work on top of any network layer. However, they are mostly used on top of UDP because TCP is not well adapted for low-latency data situations. Traditionally, RTC is assigned an even UDP port, and the corresponding control RTCP protocol, the next port up. RTP can be carried by multicast IP packets, that is, packets with a multicast destination address. An RTP stream generated by a single source can reach several destinations. Each RTP packet carries a sequence number and a time-stamp. Depending on the application, they can be used in a number of ways. A video receiver for example, can deduce which part of the screen (i.e. which TV line) is described by the packet. Even if it has still not received the packets before it (due to network desequencing), the receiver can still make use of the information. An audio application will place the packet in a received buffer. Since audio requires a constant stream, the receiver will decide what to do if spaces in the buffer have not been filled, maybe by packets not arriving or arriving in error. The receiver may decide to send a section of silence, or more often, fill the missing slot with a copy of the previous audio section, on the assumption that this would be the least objectionable to a listener. For telephone, that is, two-way communications, it is not wise to use too long a buffer, as the delays may be to noticeable for the users, so the receiver may keep a short buffer instead. Each RTP packet also carries a payload type. This is a code for the real-time information carried in the packet. This allows interleaved packets to be sent to the same destination, for example, audio and video, or data and audio. It also notifies the receiver which type of decompressing scheme to use. Table 8-10 shows some of the current codes in use for H323 (the current standard used for voice and voice over IP).

Format

The format is carried as a UDP payload and is shown in Figure 8-3. The first 16-bit word is sub-divided into a number of fields: the first two bits (V) define the RTP

**Table 8-10: Some of the current codes in use
for H323**

Payload Code	Codec	Type
0	PCM, u Law	Audio
8	PCM, A law	Audio
9	G.722	Audio
4	G.723	Audio
15	G.728	Audio
18	G.729	Audio
34	H.263	Video
31	H.261	Video

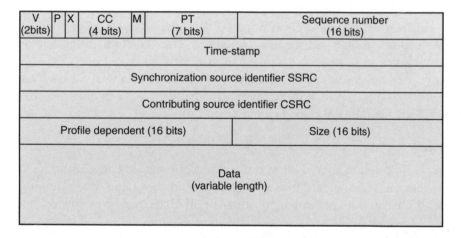

Figure 8-3: RTP format

version (currently 2). A padding bit (P) indicates whether the payload has been padded for alignment purposes. A padded payload (P = 1) has as its last byte, the number of bytes appended as padding to the original payload. An extension bit (X) indicates the presence of optional extensions after the CSRS of the fixed header. Extensions use a three-field format comprising of a code, their length, and the header extension information itself. Extensions are always a multiple of 4 bytes in length. The 4-bit CSRC count (CC) tells how many CSRC identifiers follow the fixed header (usually none) and CC = 0. The marker bit (M) is defined by the format. For example, in H225.0 this bit is used to denote the end of a silence period. The payload type (PT) has been defined earlier. It consists of 7 bits, and a full list will be found in RFC 1889. See also the specifications for H332 and H225 for more payload codes. The sequence number is a 16-bit count incremented with each packet sent. This number can either start at zero or at some other random number. The time-stamp is a complex 32-bit number denoting real time and reflects the sampling time of the first byte on the payload. In other words, the time point the first byte relates to. Its exact use will depend on the payload type. For example, in telephone audio work, the RTP clock frequency is set to 8 kHz. For video work, the time-stamp is the tick count of the display time of the first TV frame encoded. The clock can be initialized with a random value. The time-stamp is related to the wallclock, a nominal clock formatted in the standard network time protocol (NTP) format. This is defined as the number of seconds since first of January 1900 at zero hours. This uses 32 bits for the integer part, and 32 bits for the decimal part (in $1/(2^{32})$ s). A compact format is also exists with only 16 bits for the integer part and 16 bits for the decimal part. The first 16 bits of the integer part can usually be derived from the current day; the fractional part is simply truncated to the most significant 16 bits. Wallclock time (absolute time) is represented using the time-stamp format of the NTP, which is in seconds relative to zero hours UTC on 1 January 1900. The SSRC field denotes the source of a RTC stream. This is identified as a 32-bit word. All RTP packets with a common SSRC will have a common time and sequence reference. The CSRS identifier denotes a 'contributory stream source'. A given stream may be formed out of the combination (or mixing) of several sources along the way. One CSRS is tagged for each additional source of material mixed in with the signal stream. Streams with only one source will have no CSRS field. RTCP packets are defined fully in RFC 1889.

Summary

This simple description should allow embedded designers consider using RTP in their application. The standard uses of sequence numbering and time stamping make RTP useful for real time control applications of all kinds, not just voice or video.

NTP/SNTP

The NTP and the simple network time protocol (SNTP) are used to synchronize clocks in a network. SNTP is a simpler version of NTP, and can be used when the full performance is not required. NTP is described in RFC 1305 and SNTP in RFC 1769.

NTP is used to synchronize computer clocks in the Internet. It provides for full mechanisms to access national and international time and frequency dissemination services, and adjust the local clocks in all nodes in a network. Even though the national services use atomic clocks, because of delay paths and other problems NTP can only provide an overall accuracy of 1–50 ms. To improve on these accuracies, a number of algorithms need to be implemented in the software running the protocol to compensate for path delay. In many cases, these small inaccuracies (in the order of milliseconds) are not important, and simpler versions of the protocols can be used. Both NTP and SNTP operate in unicast (point to point) and broadcast (point to multipoint) modes. A unicast client sends a request to a server and expects a reply from which it can determine the clock time. The information provided by the server may allow the round trip delay to be calculated, and the client may be able to estimate the local time with more precision.

A broadcast server periodically sends a message to a designated IP address or to an IP multicast group. It will not expect any replies from the receivers. A broadcast client (receiver) listens on a particular port for broadcasts from a time server, and sends no requests. The protocol allows broadcast clients to respond to a time broadcast, and the broadcast server to respond with path delay information. Broadcast servers use the IP multigroup IP address 224.0.1.1. However, to ensure the broadcasts are limited in range (i.e. not over the whole of the Internet), measures are put in place to limit this range. Please refer to RFC 1769 for more details.

Format

This format used for sending time and clocking information is the same as used in other protocols (i.e. RTP). This is described in RFC 1305. Time data stamps are implemented as a 64-bit unsigned fixed-point number, corresponding to the total number of seconds elapsed since 1 January 1900. The integer part is in the first 32 bits, and the fraction pert in the lower 32 bits. In the fraction part, the non-significant low-order should be set to zero. The precision of these stamp system is about 200 ps. Systems that only require second precision, only use the top 32 bits, and assume the lower-order bits (fractional part) is zero. Both NTP and SNTP use UDP datagrams using port 123 at both ends. The UDP payload is shown in Figure 8-4.

In SNTP, most of these fields are pre-initialized with fixed data. The LI Leap Indicator (2 bits) is a 2-bit code warning of an impending leap second to be

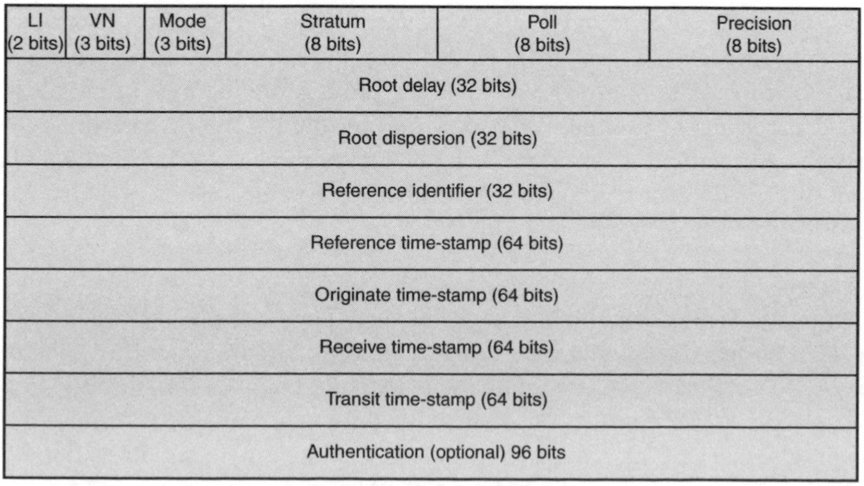

LI (2 bits)	VN (3 bits)	Mode (3 bits)	Stratum (8 bits)	Poll (8 bits)	Precision (8 bits)
Root delay (32 bits)					
Root dispersion (32 bits)					
Reference identifier (32 bits)					
Reference time-stamp (64 bits)					
Originate time-stamp (64 bits)					
Receive time-stamp (64 bits)					
Transit time-stamp (64 bits)					
Authentication (optional) 96 bits					

Figure 8-4: SNTP format

inserted/deleted in the last minute of the current day. The VN version number (3 bits) contains the current version of the protocol; the current version is 3. The Mode field (3 bits) indicates the purpose of the information: broadcast datagrams use 5; unicast servers 4; and unicast clients 3. The Stratum field (8 bits) is an unsigned integer indicating the 'quality' or stratum level of the clock. Primary references such as radio clocks use 1, secondary references use 2. The Poll Interval field (8 bits) is a signed integer indicating the maximum interval between successive messages, in seconds to the nearest power of two. The Precision field (8 bits) is a signed integer indicating the precision of the clock, in seconds to the nearest power of two. The Root Delay field is a 32-bit signed fixed point number indicating the total round trip delay to the primary reference source, in seconds, with fraction points between bits 15 and 16. Typical ranges are between zero and a few hundred milliseconds. The Root Dispersion field is a 32-bit unsigned fixed-point number indicating the nominal error relative to the primary reference source. This is in seconds with bits 15 and 16 denoting the fractional point. The Reference Identifier field is a 32-bit code denoting the particular reference source. This directly identifies sources such as National Bureau of Standards, and other atomic clock sources. It can also be used to store the IP address of a local clock. The Reference Time-stamp field is the last time in NTP64 bit format, at which the local clock was set or corrected. The Originate Time-stamp field is the time in NTP64 bit format, at which the request departed the client for the server. The Receive Time-stamp field is the time in NTP64 bit format, at which the request arrived at the server. The Transmit Time-stamp field is the time in NTP64 bit format, at which the reply departed the server for the client. The Authenticator field carries optional authentication information as defined in RFC 1305.

General operation

In unicast mode, the client sends a client request (mode 3) to the server and waits for a server reply (mode 4). The client uses the information in the time fields to calculate the local clock from the nominal clock and the propagation delays. In broadcast mode, the server regularly sends out broadcast timestamps (mode 5). This information can originate from more than one server in a network. The client has no sufficient information for calculating the propagation path.

SCTP

Many applications need reliable message delivery. They can do so by using a TCP stream. TCP ensures both strict byte ordering and full stream reliability, which can add heavily to overheads. Many applications may not need such reliability. For example, simple HTTP transactions, where we only want reliable transmission for individual 'chunks' of files requested. A constant reliable byte stream is not a necessity. In addition, in systems such as embedded data loggers we are only interested in the reliable transmission of sections of short data. In this case, each of the sections themselves need to be transmitted reliably, but where ordering, or even delivery of all segments may not be so important.

The stream control transmission protocol (SCTP) was originally designed to provide PSTN signalling over IP networks. It is a reliable transport protocol operating on top of IP. SCTP is message oriented and offers acknowledged error-free non-duplicated transfer of datagrams. Detection of data corruption, loss of data and duplication of data is achieved by using checksums and sequence numbers. A selective re-transmission mechanism is applied to correct loss or corruption of data. The relevant RFC number is RFC 2960. There is also a website at *www.sctp.org*.

Concepts

SCTP introduces the concept of an *association* instead of a connection. An association is a relationship between two end points where a list of connections is specified. In other words, an association can have multiple streams or connections to a single destination. SCTP is connection oriented in nature, but the SCTP association is a broader concept than its TCP counterpart. Each SCTP end point is associated with a remote end point with a list of transport addresses (i.e. multiple IP addresses). An essential property of SCTP is its support of multihomed nodes, that is, nodes that can be reached under several IP addresses. If the SCTP nodes and the according IP network are configured in such a way that traffic from one node to another travels on physically different paths if different destination IP address are used, associations become tolerant against physical network failures and other problems.

The SCTP Transport Service (Figure 8-5) has the following tasks:

- *Association startup and takedown*: Tasks needed for setting up and closing an association. A four-way handshake is used to set up the channel. SCTP supports for both graceful closedown, or ungraceful close (abort).

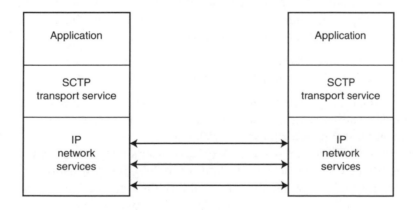

Figure 8-5: SCTP transport

- *Sequenced delivery within streams*: Where in TCP a stream is referred to as a sequence of bytes, an SCTP stream represents a sequence of messages. The number of streams supported during an association is negotiated with the remote end during setting up. Internally, SCTP assigns a stream sequence number to each message passed to it by the SCTP user. On the receiving side, SCTP ensures that messages are delivered to the SCTP user in sequence within a given stream. However, while one stream may be blocked waiting for the next in-sequence user message, delivery from other streams may proceed. SCTP also provides a mechanism for bypassing the sequenced delivery service. User messages sent using this mechanism are delivered to the SCTP user as soon as they are received.

- *User data fragmentation*: When needed, SCTP fragments user messages to ensure that the SCTP packet passed to the lower layer conforms to the path MTU. On receipt, fragments are reassembled into complete messages before being passed to the SCTP user.

- *Acknowledgement and congestion avoidance*: SCTP assigns a transmission sequence number (TSN) to each user data. The TSN is independent of any stream sequence number assigned at the stream level. The receiving end acknowledges all TSNs received, even if there are gaps in the sequence. In this way, reliable delivery is kept functionally separate from sequenced stream delivery. The acknowledgement and congestion avoidance function is responsible for packet retransmission when timely acknowledgement has not been received. Packet retransmission is conditioned by congestion avoidance procedures similar to those used for TCP.

- *Chunk bundling*: The SCTP packet as delivered to the lower layer consists of a common header followed by one or more chunks. Each chunk may contain either user data or SCTP control information. The SCTP user has the option to request bundling of more than one user messages into a single SCTP packet. The chunk bundling function of SCTP is responsible for assembly of the complete SCTP packet and its disassembly at the receiving end.

- *Packet validation*: SCTP uses a 32-bit Adler checksum. The receiver of an SCTP packet with an invalid checksum silently discards the packet.

- *Path management*: The sending SCTP user is able to manipulate the set of transport addresses used as destinations for SCTP packets. The SCTP path management function chooses the destination transport address for each outgoing SCTP packet based on the SCTP user's instructions and the currently perceived reachability status of the eligible destination set. The path management function monitors reachability through heartbeats when other packet traffic is inadequate to provide this information and advises the SCTP user when reachability of any far-end transport address changes. The path management function is also responsible for reporting the eligible set of local transport addresses to the far end during association startup, and for reporting the transport addresses returned from the far-end to the SCTP user.

Format

An SCTP packet is sent as a UDP payload and is composed of a common header and a sequence of chunks; see Figure 8-6. A chunk contains either control information or user data. The common header has four fields: source and destination port numbers. A 16-bit verification tag is used by the receiver to validate the sender of this SCTP packet. This is initially set by the transmitter to the value of the initiate tag received during association initialization. The fourth field is a 32-bit checksum. Checksums are computed using the Adler 32 algorithm as described in RFCs 1950 and 2960. The chunk sections contain four fields: a chunk type field, identifying the type of information contained in the chunk: this could be payload data, initiation information, initiation acknowledgment, heartbeats, abort, error and many others. Chunk types are encoded so that the high 2 bits denote the main action to be taken, just in case the end point does not recognise the full type code. The chunk flag field

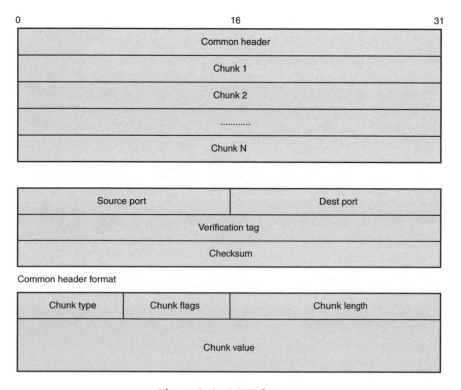

Figure 8-6: SCTP format

depends on the chunk type field, it is usually set to zero. The 16-bit chunk length represents the size of the chunk in bytes, including the field of the header plus data. The variable length chunk value contains the actual information to be transferred with the chunk. The total length of a chunk must be a multiple of 4 bytes. Zero padding must be used to ensure this.

Connection

The first step is the SCTP association. The procedure uses a state table with two main states CLOSED and ESTABLISHED. At any time, the state will return to CLOSED if an ABORT message is received. From the CLOSED state, the system will pass to the ESTABLISHED state by means of a four-way handshake, and the exchange of cookie messages. Return to the CLOSED state is also possible via an established SHUTDOWN exchange procedure.

During ESTABLISHED mode, data transfers can take place. The endpoint must always acknowledge the reception of each valid data chunk.

CHAPTER 9

A Simple Implementation

This chapter shows how a simple TCP/IP stack could be developed. In order to make the exercise useful, the text contains many descriptions on how the modules can be expanded or simplified as necessary. The sections of code shown here are not a complete off the shelf solution, but a set of building blocks. The emphasis is on understanding the techniques and limitations rather than supplying pages and pages of ready-made code. This should allow the reader to understand what is going on, and to have the confidence and expertise to add extra facilities or modify the code as required.

The modules handle ARP, ICMP (ping), UDP (block mode) and TCP (stream mode). UDP received data is passed in block mode to a user function. TCP received data ends up in stream mode and passed to a user function. Readers can add their own functions to implement simple block or serial byte mode handling. Protocols such as Telnet and HTTP are therefore easy to implement, the major limitations being the amount of RAM space available in the system being used. The modules have enough flexibility and are commented so that readers can use them as the basis for implementing custom-based protocols, variations, or add on to existing protocols.

Please note that the author retains full copyright to the software, and that it may only be distributed in conjunction with the book. Any commercial use will require a license; please contact the author at `tcpip@eixltd.com` for more details.

Introduction

The target architecture is a small, resource-limited microprocessor such as Microchip's PIC, Intel 8051 core, or a small custom 8-bit FPGA core. These devices have common limitations in their instruction sets and memory space. Data RAM for example, is usually limited to 400 bytes or less, which generates interesting challenges when writing code for these devices. The Ethernet controller used in this example is the Realtek RTL8019AS. From the background provided in this book, and with the relevant data sheets, any competent designer should be able to transpose the code sections for use with other similar CPUs and controllers. The main advantage of using the Realtek device is that it contains a very useful 16 kb circular FIFO buffer, which is very convenient when interfacing to slow microprocessors. Another very useful advantage is that this device is available in packages large enough for hand soldering, a definitive plus when wiring prototypes.

Software listings

All the code is written in the C language using plain 'vanilla' conventions. In other words, techniques particular only to the 'C' language are avoided as much as possible, and program listings are shown in a standardized form that should be easily understood by readers not familiar with C. Many novice readers cannot sight-read computer listings, and their mental map of a process may be disrupted by too much clutter caused by language specific constructs. Expert programmers should bear this in mind when noticing the more obvious 'features'. For example, code that would be normally written as a single C complex statement may be opened up into several lines, possibly using intermediate variables to emphasize the point (and allow readers to add their own extra code). The purpose of the listings shown here is not to produce the neatest or most compact code, but to illustrate the processes involved. It is left to the individual programmer to optimize the code in his or her own way. Error handling is also covered generically; most of the functions will return various forms of error codes, but nothing specific is included to handle these. This avoids cluttering the text with lengthy error-handling sections. It is up to the user to generate the extra coded required to handle error conditions. Some compiler specific instruction, such as direct I/O to ports, also had to be included. These instructions will depend on the compiler used, and different compilers will use different constructs, but their meaning should be clear from the listings and the comments.

We have also made some assumptions regarding the variables used. Some compilers use `into` to denote 8-bit variables; others use `int` to denote 16-bit variables. In order to standardize the format, we have used the generic forms as follows:

u8   an unsigned 8-bit char

u16   an unsigned 16-bit word

u32   an unsigned 32-bit word

The modules are divided into sections and organised as separate source text files that are 'included' together. Readers who are only interested in part of the system, for example, only access to the Ethernet driver, or simple UDP handling, can choose to use only that module or section of code. Considering such a small demonstration, the code takes up to 5 kb of code space, and nearly 200 bytes of RAM. However, there is quite a lot of scope for improvement and code compaction.

The 'Main' Program

Referring to the listing, the main program is very simple; it just loops forever polling the Ethernet controller until a frame has been received. Within this loop, other user operations could be included (these are not shown here). This is an example of a round-robin design as discussed in Chapter 2, and although inefficient, it provides for a simple workable demonstration. More effectively, we could redesign the program to respond to an interrupt from one of the I/O lines connected to the interrupt pin at the Ethernet controller. In either case, the function `nic_Poll()` will be called within the interrupt handler; this will be used to determine whether the controller has received a valid Ethernet frame.

The program listing is divided into modules, each handling a specific network task, and organized as a number of include text sources (Figure 9-1). Each module includes an initialization routine, which does nothing much more than set various internal variables to starting values.

The first part of `main()` is used to initialize the environment for the PIC device and its various constants. This section is very processor dependent and will not be discussed here in any detail. Readers will need to refer to the particular assembler or compiler they are using for more information. In this demonstration, the program initializes a global timer, and other global PIC variables for general use. The I/O port initialization required specifically for the controller hardware is done in

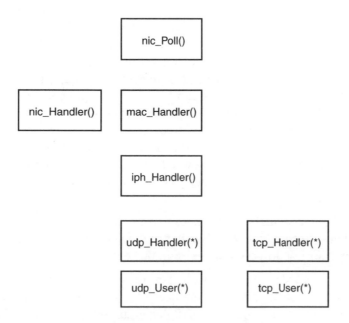

Figure 9-1: Program components

function `nic_Init()` within the `nic-lib.c` module. This maintains a level of encapsulation unique to a particular hardware interfacing method. During the main program initialization stage, the initialization function in each of the modules is called. Lastly, the section sets common global variables such as MAC and IP addresses to pre-determined constant values.

The second part of `main()` contains the do forever loop. The function `nic_Poll()` is called at the beginning of each loop, this will return a non-zero value if a valid Ethernet frame has been received, denoting that it is now available and stored within the DMA area of the controller. If this is the case, function `mac_Handler()` is called. This function reads the Ethernet frame header and performs first-level processing. That is, handling ARP internally, or alternatively, passing the frame on to the next function handler if it happened to be an IP formatted packet. The function will return a value depending on the action performed. For example, if the frame was an ARP frame and was handled internally, it returns the value 10 decimal. If the frame was an IP packet that needs to be passed on, it returns the value 20 decimal (there is no special significance in these values, they are just identifier constants, written here as numbers to avoid introducing extra mnemonic terms). If there was an error, or the frame could not be handled, the function will return an 'error' value. In this simple demonstration, we shall be ignoring (dumping) any packets other than IP, so the next module handler will be receiving only correctly formatted IP frames, any other received messages will be ignored, and program will just return to the beginning of the forever loop. If an IP packet has been received, the program calls function module `iph_Handler()`. This function will handle IP formats such as ICMP (ping only in this case), and return different values depending on the operation performed. The three returns of interest for our demonstration are UDP (40 decimal) and TCP(50 decimal). There is no need to do any further handling on ICMP (return code 30 decimal) as the only operation we were interested in (ping) will have already been handled by `iph_Handler()`. The final part of `main()` simply calls either the UDP or the TCP handler depending on the return of the previous handler. These functions will check the received packets, and if correct, call a 'user' function, which presents the final payload to the application. For this demonstration, the UDP 'application' simply returns a datagram (with different data) for every datagram received. The TCP 'application' also returns (echoes) data to the source. Readers can add their own handling routine here.

The `main()` module also includes a timer interrupt. This provides a rough 'one second tick' that is used by the TCP handler (but could be used by others). The timing handler does not do very much else in this demonstration.

The modules also include a number of 'helper' functions that can be used to create transmit packets, and other requests from users. For example, an application can generate a ping request, or transmit a UDP datagram, by just calling a function providing a number of arguments.

To demonstrate the program, we can run Telnet from a PC, and open a connection on IP address '192.168.0.13' on port 23. Everything we type on the screen will be responded with an 'OK'. We now describe in more detail each of the modules, starting from the lowest level, the hardware interface.

Driving the Network Interface Card

With so many different types of hardware interface, chips and formats, it would seem logical to develop a set of hardware independent software interfaces roughly corresponding to the PHY layer definitions. In Chapter 4, we mentioned recommendations for interface naming conventions between layers, these included methods and events generally referred to as requests, indications, responses and confirms. In real life, we would like to stick to these concepts not forgetting that by interpreting too many (unnecessary?) rules, we may end up with too much program code. The listings included here show the procedures for a 16F8XX PIC driving the Realtek 8019AS controller using I/O mapping, these are all encapsulated in module `nic-lib.c`. When porting to other hardware, only the contents of this module will need to be changed. The interfaces and entry points (function names and arguments) will remain the same, but the code within, will need to be rewritten accordingly. The interface has four major components: initialise (Network Interface Card and its registers) read data from the line, write data to the line, and obtain status on operations.

Direct hardware interfacing (helpers)

Helpers are functions used locally not generally available to callers outside the module. Here are all the functions that communicate directly with the hardware and are called by other functions in the module. These are the real 'hardware-dependent' functions, which perform actual writes and reads from the interface and I/O pins. These functions will most likely have compiler and microcontroller-dependent statements and macros, as the C language does not offer standard constructs for these operations. Encapsulating function calls this way has advantages and disadvantages: changes to physical interfaces, controllers or compilers can be done by simply changing the code within the helper functions. However, writing helpers as functions (as opposed to inline code) may slow down transfers, as an extra layer of function calls will be required, using scarce resources such as memory and stack space. The three main direct hardware helpers are:

```
void nic_CmdRst()
```

This function is used only to hard-reset the controller chip. It raises the reset pin on the controller for a few milliseconds, causing an internal hardware restart. Most ISA bus compatible Ethernet controllers have dedicated reset pins, although the wait (settling) time may be different for different devices. The microcontroller will also need to dedicate an I/O port pin for the reset function. The function is non-time critical and can be implemented as a separate function or as an inline operation, as shown in the listing. Note how the device dependent macro calls OUTPUT_HIGH(PIN_EO), OUTPUT_LOW(PIN_E0) and DELAY_MS(25) have been used to toggle the pin (their meaning should be obvious). Some controllers allow for alternative methods for generating a hard reset, such as writing into one of the registers (this is also shown in the listing as an option).

```
u8 nic_CmdRd(u8 register)
```

This function reads a byte from one of the internal controller registers. The RTL8019AS is organized as 32 paged registers, with each page relatively addressed from 00hex to 1Fhex. This function can also be used to read data from the DMA area by reading sequentially from the same location at 10hex. The internal pointer to the DMA area can be set independently (by writing to registers RSAR0 and RSAR1) and has an autoincrement facility; repeated reads from the same port results in sequential DMA data being read back. This function is used very often throughout the program, and is quite time critical, good effort should be put into maximizing its efficiency. The example here shows one way of implementing this operation, in this case I/O mapping. The code shown is not particularly efficient, and readers should employ no effort in improving on this. Additionally, some of the resulting code can be simple enough to be defined as a macro and added inline to user code, saving on one subroutine stack level. Many compilers also allow compile time commands to force the function to be interpreted automatically inline irrespectively.

```
void nic_CmdWr(u8 register, u8 data):
```

The function writes one byte to one of the internal registers. This follows more or less the same procedures as with the read function described above. Again, the resulting code can also be simple enough to be defined as a macro.

Controller initialization and status sense

```
u8 nic_Init(u8 options, u8* myHA)
```

This function is used to initialize the hardware interface and controller chip. It will normally be called once at the start of the program, although it should be possible to call it again at any time, maybe to re-initialize the hardware or after a catastrophic crash or major error. At least two arguments are required with the call. An 'options' value used to set initial conditions (in this example, there are only two options, normal mode and promiscuous mode), and a pointer to a 6-byte array containing our hardware or MAC address. All network interface chips need to have their MAC address programmed in during initialisation. In a standard PC card installation, the controller downloads the MAC address directly from a flash EPROM during its reset sequence. Systems without such a facility need to have the MAC address written 'by hand'. After calling the initialization function, the interface chip will be in a position ready to receive and transmit data. In some situations, and for some applications, there may be benefits in adding extra software functions to switch off the Ethernet interface, or to render it inactive. This function could be called `nic_Stop()` or `nic_Exit()`, for example. To re-start the device, we would call `nic_Init()` again. This option is not so necessary in a simple embedded system, which is assumed to be enabled all the time.

The listing shown is specific for the Realtek 8019AS. Procedures for other devices will be rather similar, that is, writing a series of bytes to a number of registers in a specific order (see also section titled 'Initialization,' Chapter 5). The code starts with a chip reset; the listing shows two alternative methods of resetting the chip, either by raising the reset pin high for a few milliseconds, or by writing a reset vector into one of the internal registers. Either method is valid, and both are shown for demonstration purposes (only one is needed). A simple chip validity check follows. This is used to ensure that the controller is present and is working properly. Conveniently, the Realtek chip has the two constants 'P' and 'p' hardwired into two of its registers. If the function does not find these bytes in the right place, it returns with an error code. Note how the helper function `nic_CmdRd(reg)` is used to read one byte of data at a time from each register. All register operations are eight byte regardless of whether data transfers have been organized in either eight or sixteen bit mode. The next command 'stops' the controller. That is, removes its connection from the line to stop the controller interfering with other outside Ethernet nodes during initialization. This is followed by a number of register settings that define how the controller should behave. The entries shown here provide for the most basic facilities, readers should refer to the device data sheets for more information on what each of the registers do. Next, we set the page boundaries. The circular DMA buffer in the Realtek device is arranged as a number of 256-byte pages (or 128 bytes per page if the device was set to work in 8-bit mode) numbered from `40hex` to `7Fhex`. We allocate pages `40h–72h` for receive, and pages `73h–7Fh` for transmit. This gives a transmit allocation of 1664 bytes, big enough for a maximum size Ethernet frame. The remaining 51-page receive buffer is automatically arranged as a circular FIFO buffer, with a write pointer and a read pointer. These are all initialized to point at the first page for the moment. These pointers will be updated automatically as data is received or removed from the FIFO area. We then set the command register with options 'normal' or 'promiscuous'. Promiscuous mode is only used if we want to use the system as a network tester or sniffer; the default is normal mode. Lastly, we copy our supplied MAC address into the address check register. This will be used for comparing against the address of incoming frames. The last two instructions re-start the chip, making it ready to receive and transmit frames.

`u8 nic_Status()`

This function returns various status flags or 'last error' codes. These include transmit status, receive status, and various other flags. For code compatibility, the return byte is assembled from a number of register reads. The returned values could be read after an error situation to determine exactly what caused a read or write error. This function is not being used in our simple demonstration, and returns a token error value.

Receiving data

One aim of this demonstration is to develop code that can be used by embedded systems with very limited memory. Our embedded core or microcontroller may not have enough local memory to store a full received frame, which can be about 1500 bytes in length. There are a number of ways we can deal with this situation. The option chosen here is to split the receive operation into a sequence of functions (A start; a number of reads, and an end). This method will allow us to peel data from the DMA in variable sized 'chunks'. The approach used here retrieves data in one direction only; there is no software pointer 'rewind', once the data has been read, it cannot be read again. Not all controllers allow their DMA pointer to be relocated anywhere in the DMA area, and we are taking the minimum common denominator and assuming this is not possible.

`u8 nic_Poll()`

This provides a quick means of detecting whether an Ethernet frame has been received. This function checks for incoming data by polling the 'receive data available' flag in the receive status register. The function will return TRUE (i.e. a logic '1', or a non-zero value) if data is available for collection in the DMA receive buffer, or FALSE (logic '0') if no data is available. When TRUE is returned, the main program will call the next function set to peel additional data off the DMA buffer. A simple network program will call the polling function regularly, maybe within an infinite loop somewhere in the main program. This method of operation is quite acceptable, although inefficient in terms of overall timing. A more effective way is by using interrupts as already mentioned. `nic_Poll()` is nothing but a special case of `nic_Status()`. Most controllers offer more than one way of detecting whether data is present in the DMA. The method used in the listing just compares the write and the read pointers, if they are the same it assumes that no new data has arrived. Other methods are just as effective.

`u8 nic_RxBeg()`

This function initializes the 'read' sub-system for removing data off the DMA area. This must be called soon after `nic_Poll()` returns TRUE. The job of this function is to initialize registers, pointers, and allocate resources such as memory blocks for receiving the data. In the case of the Realtek device, the function also reads the first four bytes off the DMA buffer. These contain a status byte, a 16-bit word containing the length of the received frame in bytes, and a pointer to the next available DMA page. These variables are stored locally for later use. The other bytes now left in the

DMA buffer contain the full Ethernet frame, for example, header and payload. The controller's internal hardware will have already dealt with the preamble and the FCS checksum, which are not available to the user. Depending on how it is programmed, the controller will completely ignore frames with checksum errors, or present them as invalid to the user. Our initialization sequence has programmed the chip to dump frames with bad checksums, `nic_Poll()` will just return a FALSE if a bad frame was received, just as if none had ever arrived.

```
u16 nic_RxDMA (u8* buffer, u16 nbytes)
```

After `nic_RxBeg()` has been called, the read interface is ready to collect data from the DMA area. We can read all remaining bytes at once, or in smaller, more manageable chunks. This approach makes sense when considering that most protocols contain meaningful information in compact headers placed ahead of data blocks. We can make use of this partly read information in order to know what to do next. In other words, there is no real need to read the entire Ethernet frame at once. The function argument *nbytes* specifies the number of bytes to be read off the DMA, and *buffer* specifies a pointer to the RAM location within the microcontrollers memory space where these are to go. Reading from the DMA buffer is a self-incrementing operation, so there is no need to maintain an external address pointer; this is done automatically within the interface chip. Note how nbytes is cast as a 16-bit unsigned word. If we never intend to read more than 256 bytes at a time from the DMA buffer, we could recast this argument as a byte, and save a nominal amount of space. Some compilers are not too happy when passing pointers to memory, and the function could be rewritten to include an index to a memory area rather than a full pointer to it. Many small microcontrollers do not have serious support for large pointers to RAM memory areas, and this minimalist approach may make sense. The function returns with the number of bytes still left in the DMA buffer (bytes still to be read). Such a return implies a PENDING condition, that is, that we have not yet finished reading all the bytes in the DMA buffer. A zero return implies a FINISHED or OK condition, that is, that all bytes in the DMA buffer has now been read. In practice, this length information can be misleading. Received Ethernet frames may contain large number of padding bytes, which are of no use to us, but are still received, and stored in the DMA. To obtain best results, frame sizes must be derived from the fields within the protocols, and not from the overall received size count returned by the Ethernet controller. In other words, user software should not depend on this return value for calculating how many bytes are still to be read. In any case, no harm will be done if read operations are under-run or over-run, that is, when more bytes are read than are available. The data returned from these calls will of course, be meaningless.

```
void nic_RxEnd()
```

This function needs to be called after all required bytes have been read from the DMA. The function will deallocate memory, and release any other resources associated with the read functions. The function can be called at any time, even if not all the bytes in the DMA have been read. In effect, this function terminates the current DMA read session, and sets the chip interface ready for the next DMA transfer. The reason why chip resources have to be managed this way is because some controllers have only limited forms of DMA sharing.

Transmitting data

`u8 nic_TxBeg()`

This function initializes the 'write' subsystem, and needs to be called before a frame is to be sent. The function initializes the transmit registers, and allocates any memory and resources required within the interface chip.

`nic_TxDMA(u8* buffer, u8 nbytes)`

This function will place nbytes of data from the given microprocessor's buffer RAM area into the controller's transmit DMA area (we have programmed this area to be different to the receive DMA area). No data will be transmitted to line yet. This function is used to assemble a frame for transmission in sections. A normal user program can call this function once, or a number of times, in order to assemble a frame sequentially out of many blocks for transmission. See also section on `nic_RxDMA()` for other relevant comments.

`nic_TxEnd(u8 op)`

This function instructs the interface chip to transmit the frame already assembled in the transmit DMA buffer. The argument *op* offers two options: Start transmitting now, and do not return until the whole frame has been transmitted, or start transmitting now and return immediately. In the latter case, the user must check the transmit status flag, either directly, or using the `nic_Status()` function in order to determine whether a packet has finished transmitting or not.

Data Link Layer

The purpose of the data link layer is to handle addressing, verification of data integrity, and the generation of correctly formatted frames. All functions have been encapsulated in the one source file `mac-lib.c`. Ethernet needs for data link layer management are simple, and this module has little to do. Other network types such as wireless are rather more complex and will require more functionality at this level.

The most common protocol implemented at this level is ARP (and sometimes RARP). Other than this, the module only needs to recognize IP packets and pass them on to the next layer. Implementing ARP protocol is simple; just reply to an external ARP query with another ARP frame containing locally generated information (namely our IP and MAC addresses), see also Chapter 6 for more details. A more advanced implementation of ARP would include local storage for all handled MAC/IP pairings, which would be used as 'phone book' entries to higher layers next time a query is made. This is useful, as it avoids re-sending ARP request frames every time a new user needs to be accessed; the lists are upgraded by flushing unaccessed entries every few minutes. These facilities are not necessary for smaller embedded systems, especially if there is plenty of spare time allowed for sending fresh ARP requests every time.

MAC handler software

This is implemented within the function `mac_Handler()`. On entry, the controller's DMA will contain the full Ethernet frame, as indicated by a TRUE return from a previously called `nic_Poll()` function. The operation of the handler is simple; IP type frames are passed on, and ARP frames are acted upon locally. The stages are described in the following text.

Read the Ethernet header

First, we read the first 14 bytes from the DMA buffer into local memory. These contain destination and source MAC addresses plus the type field (or length field for 802 frames). We are storing these in a 'C' defined structure S_ETHHDR, which conveniently allocates the 14-byte array as two 6-byte field addresses, plus a 2-byte protocol field. The first field (corresponding to the first six bytes retrieved from the DMA) are the 6-byte destination MAC address; this address will have already been checked by the hardware, so only frames arriving with the same address as our MAC address, or have Ethernet multicast or broadcast addresses will be present here. The second field is the source address, that is, the address of the sender. We shall need this number later on to know who to reply to. The third field is the payload frame type (in Ethernet II frames) or the frame length (in IEEE 802 frames). We compare this number against `0600hex`. If greater, the field is a protocol type and we save it as such. If less, the frame is IEEE 802, we need to move the pointer forward 6 bytes, and read the protocol field again. We do this by reading (and dumping) the next 6 bytes from the DMA buffer, then read the next 2 bytes and place the result in the 'type' variable of the S_ETHHDR structure. The protocol types we are interested in are `0800hex` (IP frames) and `0806hex` (ARP frames). Frames with other protocols are just ignored this stage. Refer to Chapters 5 and 6 for more details.

At this point, it should be worth mentioning that the 2-byte field value is stored in network-order as received, with the most significant byte first, and that we are not performing any byte reordering operations here (mainly to save code and time). Because of this, these values must be compared with byte-inverted versions of the frame type. Be aware of this when porting to other systems that may be storing data in different orders. Once the comparison is made, the action to be performed is as follows:

> *If protocol field is 0x800*: This denotes the rest of the frame is an IP frame (or packet). We want to pass this on to the next layer. We store the sender's MAC address in a global variable (we need to know who to reply to!), and return the

function with a known return code to let the next function know this was an IP packet. We might also first want to check that the destination MAC address is not a broadcast 'all FFs' address (unless we are also interested in broadcast frames). Storing the sender's MAC address in a global variable is not such a good idea if our system needs to handle multiple connections. Ideally, this address should be passed on dynamically as a function argument.

If protocol field is 0x806: This denotes the incoming frame was an ARP frame. We shall be processing this protocol locally. We read the next 28 bytes from the DMA into a local 'C' defined structure S_ARPPKT. The structure will now contain the full ARP request including header plus payload. We then check the OP field in the structure that contains the ARP requested function. If the OP field is an ARP request (0x0001), a remote node is asking for our IP address; we assemble a response ARP frame that includes our MAC and IP addresses and transmit it back to the remote as soon as possible. Having done this, we terminate the function with a zero return. We do not need to store any interim variables or do anything else. If the OP field is an ARP reply (0x0002), a remote must be telling us their MAC address, we need to store this for later use. This reply will only happen because at some point in the past our system must have broadcast an ARP request (in an ARP request we broadcast a message saying 'whoever has this IP address, please tell me your MAC address'). After this, we terminate the function with a known return to indicate the rest of the system that a remote IP/MAC address pair has been received, beyond that we do not need to do anything else. Ideally, we should return the MAC/IP pair as arguments or flagged messages, but in a small system, we may only have the option of storing these as global.

If frame field is 'other codes': Our system could be enhanced to process other link level protocols such as RARP, if needed. Otherwise, we just return the function with a zero for no further action to be taken.

Sending ARP requests

This is something we may need to do when we want to find out the hardware MAC address of a remote machine (assuming we know its IP address). In other words, when we need to send an ARP request ourselves. We create a transmit packet by assembling an ARP request packet in a locally defined structure S_ARPPKT and a MAC header packet in a locally defined structure S_ETHHDR. We then send both to the nic module transmit function. The data in both structures need to be filled as follows.

The 14 bytes of the Ethernet header (in structure S_ETHHDR):

hadest	0xFFFFFF	Denotes a broadcast MAC address
hasurce	myHA	My own 6-byte MAC address goes here
frame	0x0806	Denotes ARP request

This is followed by the 28 bytes of the ARP frame (in structure S_ARPPKT):

hw	0x0001
prot	0x0800
hs	0x06
ps	0x04
hasndr	myHA (my own MAC hardware address)
ipsndr	myIP (my IP address)
hatrgt	0x000000
iptrgt	the IP of the target we want to query.

We transmit the packet, and then we wait for an ARP reply, the reply will contain the remote's hardware address. Helper function `mac_ReqArp()` has been included, which performs all these actions under one entry point. Note how the protocol constants are specified in network compatible big-endian fashion. This is to avoid an unnecessary format conversion call. As mentioned, care should be taken when porting this part of the program to other compilers or machines. The listing also shows a local helper `mac_FillHdr()`, which is used to assemble an Ethernet frame for transmission. This function is also called by other modules when preparing their own frames for transmission.

Network Layer – IP

Valid frames returned by the mac handler will be IP frames. The data still left in the DMA will contain full IP packets starting from the first byte. IP frames (also called packets or datagrams) are at the core of IP centred network design. The advantage about the IP protocol is that it is completely hardware and network hardware independent. From now on, all references are completely independent of how the datagrams arrived at their destination; whether by LAN, WAN, wired or wireless networks. In other words, we could replace the code in previous sections with alternative code that generates IP frames by other methods, that is, a wireless network, or a WAN link using the PPP protocol. All IP packets will look the same and be compatible with each other.

There is one small complication. In a properly written network driver, MAC to IP address relationship is handled automatically. This is done by managing local directory lists, and by automatically sending ARP requests when no entries are found. In our small system, we have no provisions for storing past histories of MAC/IP bindings. Therefore, if we want to communicate with a remote, we must first collect their MAC address, possibly by preceding every new user message with an ARP request. This is not too bad in practice. However, it implies that the upper layers must be aware of ARP, breaking the neat transparent protocol layer scheme.

The job of the IP handler is as follows:

- check consistency by calculating checksums,
- perform fragmentation and defragmentation,
- handle some ICMP here; pass the rest on to higher layers,
- pass on UDP, TCP and other ICMP to higher layers.

The checksum is calculated over the header only, and should be easy to do as the header (plus options) can be read as one into local memory without bringing in the payload. Handling fragmentation and de-fragmentation is rather costly in terms of system resources. To handle fragmentation properly, a receiver must open a provisional RAM buffer (which must be up to 64 kbytes to handle worst cases) on receipt of the first fragmented datagram. Subsequent fragmented datagrams write into this buffer at their correct locations. The last fragment causes the receiver to assemble the whole array into a single, bigger datagram for passing on. The receiver must also initialize a temporary countdown timer to handle error situations where the last fragment is lost (hanging the operation forever, as it waits to be completed). The receiver will also need to perform this strategy for data from different sources if it is to handle multiple users at any one time. In most practical LAN situations, IP level fragmentation is rarely used, and it may be safe to conclude that fragmentation can be handled in small systems by just ignoring any fragmented frames.

The ICMP protocol is mainly used for network management, and its use in an embedded local network system is limited. ICMP messages are returned to sources when routers find problems when addressing IP datagrams. This allows the source to find alternative paths, or try other strategies. A simple system that ignores ICMP messages altogether will not benefit from these helpful 'hints' but at the same time, no real harm is done by not implementing a comprehensive ICMP handling strategy (especially in closed local networks). The only ICMP protocol worth implementing at this level is PING. Ping is extensively used by nodes on network to find out about each other. It would be advantageous if not essential, that any embedded node in a network should include facilities for replying to ping requests.

The IP handler

The function `iph_Handler()` is called after the previous function `mac_Handler()` has returned a value of 20 decimal denoting an IP packet is now present in the DMA buffer. The steps are:

Read the IP header: Read the next 20 bytes from the DMA area into a local IP header structure S_IPHHDR. This will contains the main section of the IP header only to start with (20 bytes). IP specifications state that an 'options' header may follow the main header, so we must check whether we should be reading this extra header as well. This information can be derived from the low nibble of the first byte of the header, which contains the total number of 4-byte words in the header. If an optional header is present, this is read by reading further bytes from the DMA area (see Chapter 7 for more information). The limit for the optional area is 40 bytes, so that the maximum number of bytes we may need to read in this operation is 60. Most IP transmissions will not contain optional headers, and it may be tempting just to ignore this block and use the RAM for something else. A more viable strategy is to store the options header, and then dump, or recover the memory when it has been established that it is not required (and after any checksums have been calculated).

Header checksum calculation: At this point, the header checksum can be checked for consistency as all the relevant data (IP header and optional header) are now in user memory. A number of helper functions are provided to calculate the checksum over an array in memory, or over single numbers. The checksum of all the elements in the IP header should add to FFFFhex. We do this by calling the helper function iph_ChkBlock(). The number of bytes in the argument is the size of the IP header, and the pointer points to the start of the IP header area. If any errors are detected, we just dump the whole packet and return an error value of FFhex.

Store datagram size and header size in global memory: We shall need these values later on. The total datagram size is a 16-bit unsigned value obtained from the third field in the IP header. The total header size is calculated by multiplying the low nibble of the first byte by four (as discussed before). The payload size is just the difference between these two. We do not need to store this last value as it can be calculated on the fly as required.

Check destination IP address, and store source IP address: Considering that the frame handled by the MAC layer contained our MAC address, it is likely that the datagram will be addressed for us, and that the destination IP (field 10 of the IP header) address will most likely correspond with our own IP address. Nevertheless, it is wise to check for this match, and to check for broadcast addresses if we want to use them; we then dump the whole datagram if they do not match. If successful, we also need to store the source IP address, which together with the already stored source MAC address, will be used later on to assemble reply packets.

Handle other fields: A simple embedded application will not need to make use of the other IP header fields. The ID field could be checked for sequential consistency, but this is not essential. Similarly with the TOS and TTL fields, but again, this is not so important. Fragmented packets are discarded, as our system cannot handle them.

Handle protocol field: The protocol field will tell us what the included payload contains. If it is either UDP or TCP we just terminate the function with a return code notifying the following function to handle the payload. If the datagram is ICMP, we handle it locally if it is a ping request, or pass it on to an external ICMP handler. Protocols other than UDP, ICMP or TCP are ignored, and the datagram is discarded.

Handling ICMP requests – ping

Having decided to handle ping locally, we need to read at least part of the ICMP payload, which nominally follows the IP header. The ICMP payload contains its own checksum, which should be calculated for consistency. For a simple application, we could ignore it, as the Ethernet frame passed its CRC check already, so there is a very good chance the datagram data is correct. However, this does not constitute best practice. We read the first byte of the ICMP header. This corresponds to the TYPE field. If TYPE is 0x0001 (first field of ICMP header), the ICMP datagram is an ICMP 'request' in other words, a ping request. A remote machine is querying us. We need to assemble and return a packet. This nominally containing the same data as was sent to us and assembled as follows (all other fields the same as received):

Ethernet header:	HADEST	HA address of remote. get this from the received header
	HASRCE	myHA
	FRAME	0x0800
Ip Header:	IPSRCE	my IP address
	IPDEST	IP address of remote, get this from just received IP Header
ICMP data:	TYPE	0x08
	CHK	recomputed (or add 0x800 to existing)
	DATA	same number of bytes as received

It is normal practice for ping requests to echo the payload received in the original ICMP request. In order to do this, we must read the whole of incoming payload, which can be of any size, and copy it to the transmit buffer. We do not usually know how big the ICMP payload is, so we need to make a decision involving how much memory we have available. If memory size is a limitation, we could impose a limit on memory, and just dump or ignore ICMP request large than this. Alternatively, we could implement more complex code and break the buffer into small sections.

A convenient size value is 32 bytes, as this is the default payload size used in the standard Windows 'ping.exe' program. Having read the whole of the incoming ICMP payload, we can now compute the ICMP checksum. This is the checksum of the ICMP header (16 bytes), added to the checksum of the payload, added to the checksum of the pseudoheader (see Chapter 7 sections titled 'The IP checksum' and 'ICMP'). There are local helpers functions provided to do all this.

Transmitting a ping request

This is something we may need to do in order to find out something about a remote machine or about the routers on line. Note that we may need to send an ARP request first to obtain the MAC address of the remote. To send a Ping request, we create a transmit packet as follows:

Ethernet header:	HADEST	HA address of remote
	HASRCE	myHA
	FRAME	0x0800
IP header:	IPSRCE	myIP address
	IPDEST	IP address of remote
	DSIZE	20 + 4 + size of ICMP data area
	CHK	Must compute
	OTHERS	normal values
ICMP data:	TYPE	0x00
	CODE	0x00
	CHK	Must compute after assembly
	DATA	any number of (random) data we may care to use

We transmit the datagram, and then we wait for a ping reply, which can take some time to arrive. It is wise to add a time-out counter to provide a way out in case a reply does not arrive (perhaps re-send three times). This is mainly an application specific task. The listings do not contain a specific ping request function, but this can be deduced from the function used to return a ping reply.

UDP

The UDP handler is implemented within function `udp_Handler()`. On arrival, the DMA points to the first byte of the UDP header. From previous functions, we have already collected the following information:

- the remote MAC address,
- the remote IP address,
- the total size of the datagram,
- the size of the IP header (including options header),
- the contents of the IP options header (if applicable).

In our simple system, these variables are stored globally, implying that transactions can only handle one user at a time. This is not much of a problem with UDP, as datagrams are independent of each other, but may be a problem with other protocols such as TCP.

The UDP handler

The procedure for handling UDP is as follows (see also Chapter 7 for more details):

Read the UDP header: The function reads the first 16 bytes of the UDP header. This gives us information about the source and destination ports. From the information already gathered by previous handlers (see above) we can compute the size of the UDP header plus its payload (datagram size − IP header size), or we can also read it directly from the third field of the UDP header (they both contain the same information).

Store the source port number: We need to store the source port, as it will be used when assembling a reply. Note that the source port may change on a per session or per message basis, so we need to use the most recently arrived version.

Check the destination port: The handler compares the destination port with our own 'expected' port number. This ensures that a datagram sent to a specific port at our IP address will be handled correctly. Such extended form of addressing may not be required in simple custom systems, and port comparison may be simplified or ignored altogether.

Compute and store intermediate checksum: In order to check the consistency of the UDP header, we must compute the checksum, which implies reading the rest of the DMA area, which can be of any size. To avoid this, we can compute the checksum of the header, add the checksum of the pseudoheader (all this information is already available), and store it for further processing by the user handler.

Handle user data: At this point, the DMA buffer is pointing to the first byte of the user payload. The UDP handler can pass control to the user application program `udp_User()`. This needs to:

- Read user data from the DMA area, maybe one byte at a time. The total number of bytes to read is the size of the payload already calculated, that is the size of the UDP datagram minus the size of the UDP header (always 16).

- For every byte read, calculate the accumulated checksum. Helper functions are available to add one byte at a time to an accumulated checksum.

- At the end of the read, make a decision on the final checksum. If the checksum was invalid, the user application should discard the data. Note the small problem: the application will only know the result of the checksum after it has read all the user data from the DMA, at which time it might have been used (unless it is buffered first).

- If the user application wants to generate a reply, it must create a data array, and call the function `udp_Tx()`, which is described in the next section.

Sending UDP datagrams

Helper functions are provided for transmitting a UDP datagram. The only arguments that need to be provided are a pointer to the user data payload in memory and the number of bytes. All other variables such as destination addresses and ports are taken from global memory. These would normally be filled on receipt of a previous UDP datagram. Therefore, in order to send a response to a just received datagram, no other calculations are necessary.

TCP

TCP provides a link layer service known as 'connection oriented service'. Unlike UDP, and other previous formats, TCP requires the system to maintain status conditions throughout a session. Sessions need to be started and terminated properly, and a timer clock has to be kept to maintain order. TCP is usually handled with a state table variable, which controls actions that need to be taken for establishing a connection, flow of data between the two stations, and termination of the connection. The state transition table described here also includes limited options for dealing with timeouts, errors and other problems such as sudden disconnections. This section should be read in conjunction with Chapter 7, section titled 'TCP' which describes the implementation of TCP in more generic detail.

The TCP handler

On entry to the function `tcp_Handler()`, the DMA read pointer is indexing the first byte of the TCP header. From previous functions we have already stored:

- the remote MAC address,
- the remote IP address,
- the total size of the datagram,
- the size of the IP header (including options header),
- the contents of the IP options header (if applicable).

As already mentioned under UDP, these variables are stored globally, and that TCP transactions in this demonstration will only be able handle one user at a time. Multiple users are more of a problem with TCP than UDP, as connections can remain open for long periods, as new users try to contact our station. The demonstration program ignores such requests until the first (and only) user has terminated its connection. The handler function reads the first 20 bytes of TCP header into a local structure S_TCPHDR. The header size is computed, and the options header loaded if present (the options header will contain useful information when a SYN segment has been received). The handler then compares port numbers and starts to compute the partial checksum of the header, options header and pseudoheader. If everything is OK at this point, the flow is divided into a number of streams depending on whether the segment contained a SYN, FIN or ACK flags. Not all possible states are implemented, only those required for a most basic TCP transaction. Chapter 7, section titled 'TCP states' and 'Implementing & TCP transaction' describe the operation of the states in more detail. Note that the program includes a very simple form of timeout handling.

If a SYN segment was received

After performing some simple validity checks, the handler stores the incoming MSS value in global variable tcp_rxmss (this simple demonstration does not do anything with this value). Initiates the local acknowledge number value to the received sequence number value plus one (the SYN flag is deemed as one data byte). Initiates the local sequence number value to a random number (in this case to a fixed constant!), and sends back a segment with the SYN flag set. The handler then sets the current state value to SYN_RCVD and returns the function, as nothing else needs to be done.

If a RST segment was received

The state is returned to the CLOSED state. Nothing else is done.

If a FIN segment was received

This simple implementation just returns an ACK segment followed by a FIN segment, then returns to the CLOSED state. It does not wait for a returned ACK, nor does it bother with flushing any data remaining.

If a normal ACK segment was received

The next set of actions will depend on the current state of the machine. If the state is SYN_RCVD, the received segment is an acknowledgment to our previously sent SYN segment during connection establishment. The handler simply moves the state to ESTABLISHED, and returns the function, as nothing else needs to be done. It is theoretically possible that this incoming segment may contain data, so provision should ideally be made to handle this. This simple implementation ignores this case, and the sender will be asked re-transmit this first data block if present, as the handler will not have incremented its own acknowledge number.

Remaining segments are only accepted if the system is in the ESTABLISHED state. If we are expecting an acknowledge to data we have previously sent (we know this is the case when variable tcp_ndata is non-zero), we check for a match between the received acknowledge number and our forward sequence number. If this is within the range, the remote has accepted our data. If this is not the case, we set for a re-transmit request (the handler uses a local flag `tx` to mark whether an assembled segment should be sent back or not).

After this point, incoming segments with no data are not responded to, and in this simple example, ignored (a plain ACK segment should not be responded with another ACK). If the incoming segment contains data, the received sequence number is compared with our expected acknowledge number. If there is a match, we then read the incoming payload data and pass it on to the user application. Note that in this simple non-buffered implementation, the checksum on the payload still needs to be calculated. The user application must include facilities for doing this, and return an error value if the total accumulated checksum was not FFFFhex as expected. If the checksum was OK, the local acknowledge variable is incremented by the number of bytes received and an acknowledge segment is returned. If for various reasons (checksum not OK, inconsistent seq-ack numbers, etc.) the received segment is bad, the data payload is not read, and a NACK segment is sent back containing the original acknowledge number, prompting the remote to re-send.

A simple time-out handler is also included in this example. This is generated by a 1 s interrupt routine in the main program, and the function `tcp_Timer()` is called about every second or so. Note the simple semaphore mechanism used in the main program to ensure the function is not called during a hardware interrupt, but as part of the round-robin cycle. The timer functions handles non receipt of ACK segments during the SYN_RCVD state, and after transmission of data segments. Note that this simple handler does not include advanced facilities for limiting the number of tryouts sent.

User handler

The user handler is a very simple demonstration program that prints the received characters one at a time. It also generates a simple 'OK' or 'NOK' reply to be sent back. Readers should add their own code in this section as required.

Sending TCP data

The listing includes helpers for transmitting a TCP segment: `tcp_Tx()` and `tcp_Putch()`. The latter function is used to push single characters, one at a time, into a transmit buffer. Because this simple implementation only uses a small buffer, the function will return an error when the buffer is full. The function maintains three 8-bit pointers, these are related to the current transmit states: 'acknowledged', 'transmitted, but not acknowledged' and 'data in buffer, but not transmitted yet'. A more formal version of this function will use the incoming window size to determine whether to transmit the segment or not.

Software Listings

```
main.c
```

```
//***********************************************************************
//***********************************************************************
//      main.c
//      - Copyright 2002 eixltd.com
//      - The main program
//.....- This version uses the CCS compiler for a PIC 16F877
//
//***********************************************************************
//***********************************************************************
#include ,main.h.              // standard .h file from CCS compiler
#use rs232(baud=9600 ,xmit=PIN_C6,rcv=PIN_C7)
#include ,nic-lib.c.
#include ,mac-lib.c.
#include ,iph-lib.c.
#include ,udp-lib.c.
#include ,tcp-lib.c.

//***********************************************************************
//**     Variables used here:
u8      HA[6]={0x01,0x02,0x03,0x04,0x05,0x06};  // my MAC address
u16     main_tout;                               // timeout counter
u1      main_itim;                               // timeout semaphore
//***********************************************************************

//***********************************************************************
//***********************************************************************
main()

{       u8 b; u16 cs,nb;

//****   Initialise PIC HW PORTS (PIC specific)..........................
        setup_counters(RTCC_INTERNAL,RTCC_DIV_128);
        setup_port_a(NO_ANALOGS);
        setup_adc(ADC_OFF);
//......................................................................

//****   Initialise Timer. One second "tick" interrupt counter...........
        enable_interrupts(RTCC_ZERO);
        enable_interrupts(GLOBAL);
//......................................................................

//****   Initialise local Hardware Interfaces............................
        for (b=0; b<6; b++) myHA[b]=HA[b];
        myIP=           0x0D00A8C0;              // "192.168.0.13"
        udp_myPT=       0xF401;                  // my UDP port 500
        tcp_myPT=       0x1700;                  // my TCP port 21 (telnet)
        nic_init(0,HA);
        iph_Init();
        mac_Init();
```

```
            udp_Init();
            tcp_Init();
            main_itim=      FALSE;                   // timer interrupt vars
            main_tout=      0;
//..........................................................................


//****    Do the Forever Loop........................................
        while (TRUE)
        { //** Ethernet Controller handler...........................
            if (nic_Poll())         // poll controller for rx frame
                { // Handle ARP, return 20 if frame was IP
                    b=mac_Handler();
                    if (b==20)
                        { // Handle IP, ret 40 if UDP, 50 if TCP, 32 if ping
                            b=iph_Handler();
                            //
                            // handle UDP
                            if (b==40) { udp_Handler(&cs,&nb);
                                        if (nb.0) udp_User(cs,nb);
                                        }
                            //
                            /// Handle TCP
                            if (b===0) tcp_Handler();
                        }
                }
            //.............................................................
            //** Timeout operations.......................................
            if (main_itim)
            { tcp_Timer();          // here every sec or so
              main_itim=FALSE;
            }
            //.............................................................


            //** Other user application round-robin operations go here...
            //
                //.........................................................
        }
//..........................................................................
}
//==========================================================================
//==========================================================================


//**************************************************************************
//**************************************************************************
//**    Timer interrupt
//      - Only used to generate a one second tick
//      - Every second a global flag (semaphore) is set
//      - This is tested during main program loop in order to do some op
//          thus avoid calling functions from the interrupt program itself
//**************************************************************************
```

```
#INT_RTCC
rtcc_handler()
{
//**      One second timer.........................................
         if ((main_tout--)==0)
             { main_itim=TRUE;        // set this flag approx once per second
               main_tout=100;         // countdown to 1 sec
             }
}
//=========================================================================
//=========================================================================
```

nic-lib.c

```
//*************************************************************************
//*************************************************************************
//      nic-lib.c
//      - Copyright 2002 eixltd.com
//      PHY Layer Network Card Low level interface Driver
//      - This version for PIC 16F877 and RTL8019AS Ethernet controller
//
//*************************************************************************
//*************************************************************************
#if !defined    (NIC-LIB_C)     // allows file to be multiply included
#define         NIC-LIB_C
//=========================================================================


//*************************************************************************
//   Hardware Connections between PIC and RTL controller:
//
//   8019AS       PIC
//   ======       ===
//   D0-D7        RD0-RD7
//   A0-A4        RB0-RB4
//   RES          RE0
//   IOW          RE1
//   IOR          RE2
//   AEN          gnd
//   IOCHRDY      n/u
//
//*************************************************************************
#USE FAST_IO(B)                    // allows direct I/O instructions
#USE FAST_IO(D)
#USE FAST_IO(E)
//
//*************************************************************************
//**     Prototype declarations
//
u8      nic_Init          (u8 opts, u8* pHa);
//                         - Call this once to initialise interface chip
```

```
//                          - Can be recalled at any time
//                          - 'opts'  1= Normal mode
//                                    0= Promiscuous mode
//                          - 'pHA'   pointer to 'my' 6 byte MAC address
//
u8       nic_Poll          ();
//                          - Call this regularly to test RX.
//                          - Alternatively call on rx interrupt to ensure
//                              data was rcvd from line.
//
u8       nic_TxBeg         ();
//                          - Call this first before sending a data block
//                          - returns 0 if it can be done, 1 if not.
//
u8       nic_TxDMA         (u8 *pbuf, u16 nb);
//                          - Then, call this n times to move data to the
//                              controller's DMA buffer.
//
u8       nic_TxEnd         (u8 op);
//                          - Lastly, call this to transmit frame
//                              if op=3 send immediately, block till done.
//
//
u8       nic_RxBeg         ();
//                          - Call this before reading any data from the
//                          DMA area.
//
//
u8       nic_RxDma         (u8 *pbuf, u16 nb);
//                          - Call this N times to read DMA data
//                              up to a total of 'nic_size' byte transfers
//
u8       nic_RxEnd         ();
//                          - Lastly, call this when finished reading.
//
//
//**      Local hardware access helpers................................
//       nic_CmdRd         (u8 raddr);         // read from chip register
//       nic_CmdWr         (u8 raddr, u8 d);   // write to chip register

//**      Local RAM storage used only in this module.....................
u8       nic_cpage;                            // current read DMA page
u16      nic_size;                             // tx/rx frame size (shared)
//================================================================


//********************************************************************
//**         RTL8019AS Register defines
#define   CR        0x00
#define   PSTART    0x01          // page 0-W   page 2-R
#define   PAR0      0x01          // page 1-RW
```

```
#define      PSTOP      0x02        // page 0-W   page 2-R
#define      BNRY       0x03        // page 0-RW
#define      TSR        0x04        // page 0-R
#define      TPSR       0x04        // page 0-W   page 2-R
#define      TBCR0      0x05        // page 0-W
#define      TBCR1      0x06        // page 0-W
#define      ISR        0x07        // page 0-RW
#define      CURR       0x07        // page 1-RW
#define      RSAR0      0x08        // page 0-W
#define      RSAR1      0x09        // page 0-W
#define      RBCR0      0x0A        // page 0-W
#define      RBCR1      0x0B        // page 0-W
#define      RSR        0x0C        // page 0-R
#define      RCR        0x0C        // page 0-W   page 2-R
#define      TCR        0x0D        // page 0-W   page 2-R
#define      DCR        0x0E        // page 0-W   page 2-R
#define      IMR        0x0F        // page 0-W   page 2-R
#define      DMA        0x10
#define      RESET      0x1F
#define      KPBEG      0x40        // DMA RX start   page
#define      KPEND      0x71        // DMA RX end+1   page
#define      KPTXD      0x71        // DMA TX page
//=========================================================================
//=========================================================================



//*************************************************************************
//*************************************************************************
//** Local Helper: Write one byte to Ethernet Controller Register
//      - Hardware dependent call
//      - Loads of room for improvement!
//
//    IN:   'addr'       Register address <00-1F>
//          'd'          Byte to write
//
//*************************************************************************
u8      nic_CmdWr(u8 raddr, u8 d)
{
//**     This code specific to PIC and CCS compiler
        OUTPUT_B     (raddr);       // output register address
        SET_TRIS_D (0x00);          // set port D for write
        OUTPUT_D     (d);           // output data
        OUTPUT_LOW (PIN_E1);        // clock IOWR low
        OUTPUT_HIGH(PIN_E1);        // clock IOWR high
        //
        return 0;
}
//=========================================================================
//=========================================================================
```

```
//**********************************************************************
//**********************************************************************
//** Local Helper: Read one Byte from Ethernet Controller Register
//      - Hardware dependent call
//      - Loads of room for improvement!
//
//      IN:  'addr'       Register address <00-1F>
//      RET:              Register data
//
//**********************************************************************
u8      nic_CmdRd(u8 raddr)
{       u8    c;
        //
//**     This code specific to PIC and CCS compiler
        OUTPUT_B    (raddr);      // output register address
        SET_TRIS_D (0xFF);        // set port D for write
        OUTPUT_LOW (PIN_E2);      // clock IORD low
        c=INPUT_D();              // input data
        OUTPUT_HIGH(PIN_E2);      // clock IORD high
        //
        return c;
}
//======================================================================
//======================================================================


//**********************************************************************
//**********************************************************************
//**     Initialise the Ethernet Controller Chip
//        - Call once at beginning of program
//        - Could also be called again at any time
//        - leaves chip ready to receive and transmit
//
//      IN:      'opts'        0= Normal mode
//                             1= Promiscuous mode (network sniffer mode)
//               'pHA'         pointer to our 6 byte MAC address
//
//      RET:     0 if OK
//               1 if chip does not exist or cannot be initialised
//**********************************************************************
u8      nic_Init(u8    opts, u8  * pHA)
{       u8    c;

//**     Initialise relevant I/O ports and directions...................
        SET_TRIS_D(0xFF);
        SET_TRIS_B(0xE0);
        SET_TRIS_E(0xE8);
        OUTPUT_E   (0x6);              // -IORD=1 -IOWR=1 RESET=0
```

269

```
//**     Reset controller (two methods: hardware and software, use either)...
         // This section could also be implemented as a separate function
         OUTPUT_HIGH(PIN_E0);      // Hardware reset
         DELAY_MS(250);            // send pin high for 250mS
         OUTPUT_LOW(PIN_E0);       // PIC pin E0 is the reset pin
         DELAY_MS(25);
         //
         DELAY_MS(25);             // Alternative method of reset
         nic_CmdWr(RESET ,0xFF);   // using software to write to a register
         DELAY_MS(25);

//**     Perform a simple validity check on the chip....................
         // the two registers should return constants for the RTL chip
         if ('P'!=nic_CmdRd(0x0A)) return 1;   // should be 'P' for RTL8019AS
         if ('p'!=nic_CmdRd(0x0B)) return 1;   // should be 'p' for RTL8019AS

//**     Initialise controller chip registers..........................
         nic_CmdWr(CR     ,0x21);   //// page 0, stop chip
         nic_CmdWr(DCR    ,0x48);   //   Set byte mode and byte order
         nic_CmdWr(RBCR0  ,0x00);   //   Clear remote byte count register
         nic_CmdWr(RBCR1  ,0x00);   //   Clear remote byte count register
         if ((opts&0x01)==0) c=0x04; else c=0x1E;
         nic_CmdWr(RCR    ,c  );   //   Set Normal/Promiscuous
         nic_CmdWr(TCR    ,0x02);   //   l/back to avoid upsetting wire
         nic_CmdWr(ISR    ,0xFF);   //   Clr interrupt Status register
         nic_CmdWr(IMR    ,0x00);   //   Clr interrupt Mask reg (no ints)

         nic_CmdWr(PSTART,KPBEG);   //   Start page for receive: DMA=0x4000
         nic_CmdWr(PSTOP ,KPEND);   //   End   page for receive: DMA=0x7100
         nic_CmdWr(BNRY   ,KPBEG);   //   Boundary page

         nic_CmdWr(CR     ,0x61);   //// page 1, stop chip
         nic_CmdWr(CURR   ,KPBEG+1); //   current page pointer

         nic_CmdWr(PAR0   ,pHA[0]);  //   My Ethernet MAC address
         nic_CmdWr(PAR0+1,pHA[1]);  //   My Ethernet MAC address
         nic_CmdWr(PAR0+2,pHA[2]);  //   My Ethernet MAC address
         nic_CmdWr(PAR0+3,pHA[3]);  //   My Ethernet MAC address
         nic_CmdWr(PAR0+4,pHA[4]);  //   My Ethernet MAC address
         nic_CmdWr(PAR0+5,pHA[5]);  //   My Ethernet MAC address

//**      Start controller..............................................
         nic_cpage=KPBEG+1;         //   current read page
         nic_size=0x0000;           //   Init current frame size to zero
         nic_CmdWr(CR     ,0x22);   //   Page 0, start chip
         nic_CmdWr(TCR    ,0x00);   //   Set to normal
         return 0;
}
//=======================================================================
//=======================================================================
```

```
//*************************************************************************
//*************************************************************************
//** Peek Ethernet chip for data
//    - User program should call this regularly
//    - Alternatively, use interrupt routine before calling
//    - This version compares rd vs wr pointers, other alternatives possible
//
//    IN:     none
//    RET:    1=    Ethernet frame has been received and is now in DMA buffer
//            0=    No data in DMA buffer, no frames received
//*************************************************************************
u8    nic_Poll()
{     u8    b;
//**   Check if RD page = WR page....................................
      nic_CmdWr(CR,0x62);                         // Set Page 1
      b=nic_CmdRd(CURR);                          // read current ptr CURR
      nic_CmdWr(CR,0x22);                         // Set Page 0
      if (b!=nic_cpage)             return 1;  // data available
      //if (0x01 & nic_CmdRd(ISR) ) return 1;  // alternative version
      return 0;                                   // no data available
}
//========================================================================
//========================================================================


//*************************************************************************
//*************************************************************************
//** Set Up for rx DMA Read
//    - Call this when a previous call to nic_Poll() returns '1'
//    - This function used to set up buffers, set up chip for DMA xfers etc.
//    - User can then call rdDMA functions until all data hase been read
//    - Do not forget to call nic_RxEnd() to restore chip to normal mode.
//
//    IN:       none
//
//    GLOBALS: 'nic_rsize' stores nr of bytes in DMA still to read.
//
//    RET:      0  Read OK, user can now read DMA data via nic_RxDma() calls
//              1= Error. Cannot open DMA area, perhaps busy or lost sync
//*************************************************************************
u8      nic_RxBeg()
{       u8    st,b;

//**     Init pointers and read first 4 bytes from current DMA page.......
        // First 4 bytes contain status, next page, and RX frame size
        nic_CmdWr(CR     ,0x22);      // Stop the chip.
        nic_CmdWr(RSAR1 ,nic_cpage); // point to current page.
        nic_CmdWr(RSAR0 ,0x00);
        nic_CmdWr(RBCR0 ,0xFF);       // Could set these to exact nr of bytes
        nic_CmdWr(RBCR1 ,0xFF);       // to read, but this is not necessary.
        nic_CmdWr(CR     ,0x0A);      // DMA read command.
        //
```

```
        st=nic_CmdRd(DMA);           // get status, same as RSR register
        if ((st&0x0F)!=0x01)         // Check for Error (bad data)
            { nic_CmdWr(CR,0x62);    // - If so, realign all the pointers
              b=nic_CmdRd(CURR);     //    get CURR page (last valid page)
              nic_CmdWr(CR,0x22);    //
              nic_cpage=b;           //    reset current read page
              nic_RxEnd();           // - could do further checks here!
              return 1;              // error return, dump frame
            }

//**     Set up resources.........................................
        nic_CmdWr   (ISR,0xFF);                      // Reset Interrupt flag
        nic_cpage=  nic_CmdRd(DMA);                  // Store next DMA page
        nic_size=   nic_CmdRd(DMA);                  // get LSB of rx fr size
        nic_size+=  (256*((u16)nic_CmdRd(DMA)));     // get MSB of rx fr size

//**     A further error check........................................
        if (nic_cpage<KPBEG)
            { nic_RxEnd();
              return 1;
            }
//**     All OK.......................................................
        return 0;
}
//=============================================================================
//=============================================================================


//*****************************************************************************
//*****************************************************************************
//** Transfer DMA data to RAM in uP
//     - User program can use this function to read bytes from the DMA area
//         and copy to own RAM memory
//     - User program can read as many bytes as required, noting that global
//         var 'nic-rsize' contains the max number of valid bytes in frame.
//     - The use of RAM pointers as arguments can be inneficient. If speed
//         is a consideration, function could be rewritten avoiding pointers.
//     - Note that optimising compilers may remove code it thinks it doesn't
//         need, i.e. repeated accesses to the same register
//
//     IN:    'pbuf'   pointer to RAM area in uP
//            'nb'     number of bytes to copy
//
//     RET:    0       If read OK
//*****************************************************************************
u8      nic_RxDma (u8 *pbuf, u16 nb)
{       u16 w;  u8* p;

//**     Cast local pointer.(required by some compilers).................
        p=(u8*)pbuf;
//**     Read byte by byte.............................................
        // Could be rewritten inline for speed
        for (w=0; w<nb; w++) *p++=nic_CmdRd(DMA);
```

```
//**    End bits.................................................
        nic_size -= nb;           // tally of bytes read (not really used)
        return 0;
}
//========================================================================
//========================================================================

//************************************************************************
//************************************************************************
//** End the rx DMA transfer
//    - User program calls this when it has finished reading data from the
//        DMA area in the Ethernet chip, and wants to finish Rx xfers.
//    -
//    IN:    none
//    RET:   none
//************************************************************************
u8      nic_RxEnd()
{       u8 b;

//**     Reset Boundary pointer.to next in circular buffer..............
        if (nic_cpage>KPBEG) b=nic_cpage-1;
        else                 b=KPEND-1;        // wraparound condition
        nic_CmdWr(BNRY,b);

//**     Restore chip to normal.....................................
        nic_CmdWr(RBCR0 ,0x00);
        nic_CmdWr(RBCR1 ,0x00);
        nic_CmdWr(CR    ,0x22);
        return 0;
}
//========================================================================
//========================================================================

//************************************************************************
//************************************************************************
//** Set Up for Transmission
//    - User program calls this function before moving data to DMA area
//    - After this, call nic_TxDMA() to move data to the chips DMA area
//    - When all data has been sent, call nic_TxEnd()
//
//    IN:    none
//************************************************************************
u8   nic_TxBeg()
{
//**  Ensure Rx is closed (just in case, some DMAs cannot read and write).
        nic_RxEnd();

//**  Init registers for Transmission...............................
        nic_CmdWr(CR    ,0x0A);  // Set for DMA read
        nic_CmdRd(RSAR0);        // Dummy rd (see data sheets for reason)
        nic_CmdWr(RSAR0 ,0x00);
        nic_CmdWr(RSAR1 ,KPTXD);
        nic_CmdWr(RBCR0 ,0xFF);
```

```
          nic_CmdWr(RBCR1  ,0xFF);
          nic_CmdWr(CR     ,0x12);      // Set for DMA write
          nic_size=0;                   // Init tx byte counter
          return 0;
}
//========================================================================
//========================================================================


//************************************************************************
//************************************************************************
//** Xfer xdata in uP to DMA
//    - Call this function to write 'nb' bytes to controller's DMA area
//    - User program can write as many bytes as required, noting limitations!
//    - Note that optimising compilers may remove code it thinks it doesn't
//       need, i.e. repeated accesses to the same register
//
//    IN:    'pbuf'  ptr to area in uP containing data
//           'nb'    nr of bytes to transfer to DMA
//************************************************************************
u8      nic_TxDma (u8 *pbuf, u16 nb)
{       u16 w;   u8* p;

//**     Cast local pointer.(required by some compilers)..................
        p=(u8*)pbuf;

//**     Read byte by byte............................................
        // Could be rewritten inline for speed
        for (w=0; w<nb; w++) nic_CmdWr(DMA,p[w]);

//**     End bits......................................................
        nic_size += nb;          // tally nr of TX bytes
        return 0;
}
//========================================================================
//========================================================================


//************************************************************************
//************************************************************************
//** End of Tx session (transmit frame)
//    - Call this function when all data hase been moved to the
//       Ethernet chip DMA, and want to transmit.
//
//    IN:    'op'      1    Transmit now, block until finished
//                     0    Transmit now, return immediately
//
//    RET:             0    if OK, no errors
//                     1    Error during Transmit
//                            (could be still sending previous frame)
//                     2    PENDING code (still transmitting)
//************************************************************************
```

```
u8      nic_TxEnd(u8 op)
{       u8 c;

//**    Init registers.............................................
        nic_CmdWr(RBCR0 ,0x00);
        nic_CmdWr(RBCR1 ,0x00);
        nic_CmdWr(CR    ,0x22);

//**    Is it still transmitting previous frame?, if so wait or exit.....
        if (op==0) { if ((4 & nic_CmdRd(CR))) return 2; } // exit now
        else       { while ((4 & nic_CmdRd(CR))) {;}    } // wait till sent

//**    validate frame size (short frames are padded to at least 64 bytes)..
        nic_size += 12;                     // compensate for hdr size
        if (nic_size<64) nic_size=64;       // pad to at least 64

//**    Tx frame ..................................................
        nic_CmdWr(CR,       0x22);          // Reset remote DMA status
        nic_CmdWr(TBCR0,    nic_size&0xFF); // LSB bytes to send
        nic_CmdWr(TBCR1,    nic_size/256 ); // LSB bytes to send
        nic_CmdWr(TPSR,     KPTXD );        // start page address
        nic_CmdWr(CR,       0x1E);          // Set TX command

//**    Block/wait until all packet has been txted (max 1.2mS)..........
        if (op!=0) while (4 & nic_CmdRd(CR)) {;}   // block till txted

//**    Test Transmission quality (could add more checks here)..........
        c=nic_CmdRd(TSR);
        if (c&0x01) return 0;               // txted OK
        return 1;                           // error return
}
//========================================================================
//========================================================================

//************************************************************************
//************************************************************************
//**    Local Helper
//      - For test or debug uses only
//      - Used to print the contents of the TX DMA buffer
//      - avoids using printf()
//************************************************************************
void    nic_PrintTxDMA(u8 nb)
{       u8  b,a;

//**    set DMA to read from page KPTXD.................................
        nic_CmdWr(RSAR0 ,0x00);
        nic_CmdWr(RSAR1 ,KPTXD);
        nic_CmdWr(RBCR0 ,0xFF);
        nic_CmdWr(RBCR1 ,0xFF);
        nic_CmdWr(CR    ,0x0A);
//
//**    print array (avoids using printf)..............................
        putchar ('[');
        putchar ('T');
        putchar ('X');
```

```
                while (nb--)
                { nic_RxDma(&a,1);
                  putchar (' ');
                  a=(a/16)&0x0F; if(a>9) a=a+7; putchar(a+0x30);
                  a=(a    )&0x0F; if(a>9) a=a+7; putchar(a+0x30);
                }
                putchar (']');
                //
                nic_RxEnd();
}
//==========================================================================
//==========================================================================

//==========================================================================
//==========================================================================
#USE STANDARD_IO(B)
#USE STANDARD_IO(D)
#USE STANDARD_IO(E)
#endif // !defined (nic-lib.c)
```

mac-lib.c

```
//*********************************************************************
//*********************************************************************
//        mac-lib.c
//        MAC level handler demo
//        - Copyright 2002 eixltd.com
//        - Handles ARP here
//        - Passes on IP packets
//
//*********************************************************************
//*********************************************************************
#if !defined    (MAC-LIB_C)      // allow3s file to be multiply included
#define         MAC-LIB_C
#include         "nic-lib.c"
#define          IPHFRAME       0x0008        // 0x0800 INTEL ORDERING
#define          ARPFRAME       0x0608        // 0x0806 INTEL ORDERING
#define          ARPOPREQ       0x0100        // 0x0001 INTEL ORDERING
#define          ARPOPREP       0x0200        // 0x0002 INTEL ORDERING
#define          ARPPROT        0x0008        // 0x0800 INTEL ORDERING
#define          ARPHW          0x0100        // 0x0001 INTEL ORDERING
//*********************************************************************
//
//
//   Prototype Functions
//   ===========================
//
//   mac_Init();   // Call once to initialise system
//                 - Must call after nic_Init()
//
//
//   mac_Handler();
//                 // Call this on TRUE return from nic_Poll()
```

276

```
//                      - Reads MAC header & protocol field
//                      - Handles ARP if present
//                      -- Otherwise returns for next call to read IP packet
//                      - Return code (even codes=OK, odds=error)
//                            .  00  No data to process, dump
//                            . 255  Problem reading data, dump
//                            .  10  ARP REQ rcvd, ARP reply sent OK
//                            .  13  ARP REPLY rcvd, but not for the IP I wanted
//                            .  14  ARP REPLY rcvd, remote HA stored in tuHA, OK
//                            .  15  ARP received, but unknown frame code
//                            .  17  ARP rcvd  but not for my IP addr
//                            .  19  Unknown frame rcvd, nor ARP, nor IPH, dump
//                            .  20  Frame is IP, process next!
//                            .  27  Frame is IP, but not for my HA
//
//   mac_ReqArp ();
//                  // Call this to broadcast an ARP request
//                   - before calling, set 'rqIP' to remote IP addr wanted
//                   - Function clrs a valid flag 'mac_arpvalid'
//                   - When ARP reply is received later, flag is set
//                   -  and Global 'rqHA' is filled with remote HA address
//
//
// EXAMPLE:
// Loop: if (nic_Poll())
//          { e=mac_Handler();
//              // check if frame was IP
//            if (e==20)
//              { iph_Handler()
//                 .....
//
//    HELPERS (word conversion network <-> host)
//    =================================================
//u16   mac_htons       (u16 w);
//u16   mac_ntohs       (u16 w);
//u32   mac_ntohl       (u32 i);
//u32   mac_htonl       (u32 i);
//
//u8    mac_FillHdr (u16 pcol);  // Fills tx DMA with Ethernet2 MAC header
//
//***************************************************************************

//***************************************************************************
//**      Structure definitions
//**      Ethernet Frame Header (14 bytes).................................
struct   S_ETHHDR
{        u8    hadest[6];
         u8    hasrce[6];
         u16   frame;
};
//..........................................................................
//
```

```
//      ARP Frame Header (28 bytes)....................................
struct  S_ARPPKT
{       u16    hw;
        u16    prot;
        u8     hs;
        u8     ps;
        u16    op;
        u8     hasndr[6];
        u32    ipsndr;
        u8     hatrgt[6];
        u32    iptrgt;
};
//................................................................
//
//**    RAM area Used by this module.............................
u8      myHA[6];               // GLOBAL: my MAC address (pre-initialised)
u32     myIP;                  // GLOBAL: my IP  address (pre-initialised)
u8      tuHA[6];               // stores last MAC address received
//      RAM area, used only for ARP Request & remote reply
u32     rqIP;                  // requested IP (for ARP req)
u8      rqHA[6];               // returned MAC (for ARP req)
u1      mac_arpvalid;          // wait flag    (for ARP req)
//................................................................

//============================================================================
//============================================================================

//****************************************************************************
//****************************************************************************
//** Initialise
//    - Call once at start of user program
//    - Assumes 'myIP' and 'myHA' have been defined
//****************************************************************************
u8      mac_Init()
{
//**    Init our vars......................................
        mac_arpvalid=   0;        // the ARP request wait flag
        return 0;
}
//============================================================================
//============================================================================

//****************************************************************************
//****************************************************************************
//** MAC Handler
//    - Call this on <>0 return from nic_Poll()
//    - Processes EthernetII frames only, extra mods needed for 802 frames
//    - Stores 'tuHA[6]' for last MAC address received
//    - Handles rx packet in the DMA buffer
//    - - ARP request: returns ARP reply with our information
//    - - ARP reply:   stores return HA address in rqHA[6]
//    -
```

```
//    - Important: Caller must ensure that receiver is closed before
//      - returning to loop, i.e. by calling nic_RxEnd() when no more
//        bytes  are needed from DMA.
//
//    IN:     None
//    RET:    Error (odd), or Process code (even). See list
//*******************************************************************
u8     mac_Handler()
{      u8 b;
       struct S_ARPPKT arppkt;
       struct S_ETHHDR ethhdr;

//**    Init vars.....................................................

//**    Init reader to get data from DMA ............................
       b=nic_RxBeg();
       if (b!=0) return 0xFF;  // can't initialise, exit!

//**    Read Ethernet Frame header (first 14 bytes) ...................
       nic_RxDma((u8*)&ethhdr,14);
       //   At this point, 'hadest' can only be 'FFFFFF' or 'myHA'

//***   Extra software for recognising 802.3 frames goes here...........
       //   If frame<0x600, skip 6 bytes, then read again

//***   Is received Frame an ARP? ....................................
       if (ethhdr.frame==ARPFRAME)
       { // Yes, Read the full ARP packet (next 28 bytes) to RAM
         nic_RxDma((u8*)&arppkt,28);
         nic_RxEnd();          // no more DMA reads needed, so end receiver
         //
         // Does the ARP frame contain my IP addr?
         if (arppkt.iptrgt!=myIP) return 17;  // No, drop the frame
         //
         // ARP frame was for me. Is it an ARP request?
         if (arppkt.op==ARPOPREQ)
            { // It is, prepare an ARP reply frame and tx it back
              ethhdr.frame= ARPFRAME;
              for (b=0; b<6; b++) { ethhdr.hadest[b]= arppkt.hasndr[b];
                                    arppkt.hatrgt[b]= arppkt.hasndr[b];
                                    ethhdr.hasrce[b]= myHA[b];
                                    arppkt.hasndr[b]= myHA[b];
                                  }
              arppkt.iptrgt= arppkt.ipsndr;
              arppkt.ipsndr= myIP;
              arppkt.op=     ARPOPREP;
              //
              // transmit to line
              nic_TxBeg();
              nic_TxDma((byte*)&ethhdr,14);    // send Eth Header
              nic_TxDma((byte*)&arppkt,28);    // send ARP packet
              nic_TxEnd(3);                    // Tx it now
```

```
                    return    10;                        // OK return!
                }
            //
            // Is frame an ARP reply?
            if (arppkt.op==ARPOPREP)
                { // is it a reply for an IP address I wanted?
                    if (arppkt.ipsndr!=rqIP) return 13; // No, drop and exit
                    //
                    // Yes, it is for the IP I wanted, store the HA recevd
                    for (b=0; b<6; b++) rqHA[b]=arppkt.hasndr[b];
                    mac_arpvalid=1;          // set valid flag
                    return 14;               // report ARP reply received
                }
            //
            // Is frame other ARP codes?
            return 15;                       // ARP rcvd, but unknown code
        }
//..............................................................................
//**    Is received frame an IP datagram?................................
        // and is it for me? (not essential to check)
        if (ethhdr.frame==IPHFRAME)
            { for (b=0; b<6; b++) { if(ethhdr.hadest[b]!=myHA[b]) return 27;}
                for (b=0; b<6; b++) tuHA[b]=ethhdr.hasrce[b];
                return 20;   // return OK, frame is IP/ICMP and it is for me
            }
//..............................................................................
//***    Is received frame "other" type?...............................
        nic_RxEnd();
        return 19;                           // unknown frame type
}
//============================================================================
//============================================================================


//****************************************************************************
//****************************************************************************
//**    Helper Function
//     - This function is used to send an ARP request
//     - function will clr flag 'mac_arpvalid' while waiting for reply
//     - (flag will be set when reply is received from remote)
//
//     GLOBs:  'rqIP'      Must be Filled with wanted IP address
//             'rqHA'      Eventually filled with remote's HA address
//             'mac_arpvalid' Set to 0 on this call, set when reply rcvd
//****************************************************************************
u8      mac_ReqArp ()
{       u8 b;
        struct S_ARPPKT arppkt;
        struct S_ETHHDR ethhdr;

//**    fill a ARP structure.with a request message....................
        arppkt.hw=      ARPHW;
```

```
          arppkt.prot=      ARPPROT;
          arppkt.hs=        0x06;
          arppkt.ps=        0x04;
          arppkt.op=        ARPOPREQ;
          for (b=0; b<6; b++) { arppkt.hasndr[b]=myHA[b];
                                arppkt.hatrgt[b]=0xFF;
                         }
          arppkt.ipsndr=myIP;
          arppkt.iptrgt=rqIP;
//**      fill MAC structure with broadcast.message.....................
          for (b=0; b<6; b++) { ethhdr.hadest[b]=0xFF;
                                ethhdr.hasrce[b]=myHA[b];
                         }
          ethhdr.frame=ARPFRAME;
//**      Now TX the ARP request....................................
          nic_TxBeg();
          nic_TxDma((u8*)&ethhdr,14);      // send Eth Header
          nic_TxDma((u8*)&arppkt,28);      // send ARP packet
          nic_TxEnd(3);                    // Tx it now
          mac_arpvalid=0;                  // Clr wait flag, set on rx reply
          return 0;
}
//=======================================================================
//=======================================================================

//***********************************************************************
//***********************************************************************
//**      Helper Function. Called from other modules
//          - Used by other modules when preparing their frames for transmission
//          - Fills DMA with Ethernet header: 2xaddresses and protocol field
//          - User must fill myHA[6] and tuHA[6], then call nic_TxBeg()
//          - mac_FillHdr must be the first call after nic_TxBeg()
//          - Note: protcol word must be byte inverted! ie. 0008 for IP (0800)
//
//      IN:                  'pcol'          protocol word <IPHFRAME,ARPFRAME>
//
//          GLOBALS: uses    'tuHA[6]'       Dest MAC address, must fill
//                           'myHA[6]'       my   MAC address, fixed
//***********************************************************************
u8        mac_FillHdr (u16 pcol)
{
          u8 b;
          struct S_ETHHDR ethhdr;
          for (b=0; b<6; b++) { ethhdr.hadest[b]=tuHA[b];
                                ethhdr.hasrce[b]=myHA[b];
                         }
          ethhdr.frame=pcol;                  // byte inverted!
          nic_TxDma((byte*)&ethhdr,14);    // Eth Header
          return 0;
}
//=======================================================================
//=======================================================================
```

```
//**************************************************************************
//**************************************************************************
//**     Helpers: called from other modules
//         - Convert data formats from network to host order
//         - Network order is big-endian (i.e. motorola format)
//         - KEIL order is     big-endian, so no conversion required
//         - CCS  order is     lil-endian, conversion is required
//
//         'htons'           Host to Network short (u16)
//         'ntohs'           Network to Host short (u16)
//         'htons'           Host to Network long  (u32)
//         'ntohl'           Network to Host long  (u32)
//
//         IN:      'w'                word to convert
//         RET:                       converted word
//**************************************************************************
u16     mac_htons  (u16 w)
{        return MAKE16(MAKE8(w,0),MAKE8(w,1));
}
//**************************************************************************
u16     mac_ntohs  (u16 w)
{        return MAKE16(MAKE8(w,0),MAKE8(w,1));
}
//**************************************************************************
u32     mac_ntohl  (u32 i)
{        return (MAKE32(MAKE8(i,0),MAKE8(i,1),MAKE8(i,2),MAKE8(i,3)));
}
//**************************************************************************
u32     mac_htonl  (u32 i)
{        return (MAKE32(MAKE8(i,0),MAKE8(i,1),MAKE8(i,2),MAKE8(i,3)));
}
//======================================================================
//======================================================================


//======================================================================
//======================================================================
#endif      // !defined (mac-lib.c)
```

iph-lib.c

```
//**************************************************************************
//**************************************************************************
//       iph-lib.c
//         - Copyright 2002 eixltd.com
//         - IP/ICMP handler demo
//         - Handles ICMP-ping
//
//**************************************************************************
//**************************************************************************
#if !defined    (IPH-LIB_C)       // allow3s file to be multiply included
#define         IPH-LIB_C
```

```
#include        "nic-lib.c"
#include        "mac-lib.c"

#DEFINE  OPTSIZE   40                // Otions header size
//*******************************************************************
//
//   PROTOTYPE DECLARATIONS
//   =====================
//
//u8  iph_Init();   // Call once at beg of program to initialise system
//                   - Call after nic_Init()
//                   - Can be recalled at any time
//
//u8  iph_Handler();// Handle ICMP (ping)
//                   - Call this on return from mac_Handler()
//                   - recovers 'iph_dsize, iph_hsize, tuIP'
//                   - return codes:
//                      Error code (odd), or status after an op (even):
//              .  00  No data to process, dump frame!
//              .  FF  General error, dump frame!
//              .  21  IP rcvd, but wrong header (version) type, dump
//              .  23  IP rcvd, but not for our IP, dump
//              .  25  IP rcvd , but failed IP hdr checksum, dump
//              .  29  IP rcvd , unknown protocol
//                 33  ICMP PING rcvd.  Array too big, dump
//                 39  ICMP ???  rcvd  Unknown type, dump
//                 32  ICMP PING rcvd.  PING req replied OK
//                 30  ICMP rcvd.  call handler next..
//                 40  UDP  rcvd.  call handler next..
//                 50  TCP  rcvd.  call handler next..
//
//
//   HELPERS
//   =======
u8      iph_FillHdr     (u16 psize, u8 pcol);
u16     iph_ChkBlock    (u8* ptr,    u16 nb);
u16     iph_ChkAddI     (u16 chksum, u32 i);
u16     iph_ChkAddW     (u16 chksum, u16 w);
u16     iph_ChkAddB     (u16 chksum, u8 b, u8 odd);
//*******************************************************************

//*******************************************************************
//**     Local RAM areas
//
//**     IPH Header (20 +40 bytes).........................................
struct  S_IPHHDR
{       u8      hdr;
        u8      tos;
        u16     dsize;
        u16     id;
        u16     frag;
        u8      ttl;
```

```
        u8      pcol;
        u16     chk;
        u32     ipsrce;
        u32     ipdest;
        u8      opt[OPTSIZE];    // Options header
};
//
//*************************************************************************


//*************************************************************************
//**     Local GP RAM area.........................................
u32     tuIP;                   // GLOBAL last received remote IP address
u16     iph_hsize;              // GLOBAL Stores size of IP header+opts
u16     iph_dsize;              // GLOBAL Stores size of full datagram
u16     iph_idnum;              // local: IP ID (++ on every IP sent)
u16     iph_chksum;             // local: Stores checksum
//
//.........................................................................


//=========================================================================
//=========================================================================


//*************************************************************************
//*************************************************************************
//** Initialise
//    - Call once at start of user program
//    - Assumes 'myIP' and 'myHA' have been initialised
//    - Assumes PHY and ETH drivers have been initialised
//*************************************************************************
u8      iph_Init()
{
//**     Init our vars...............................................
        iph_idnum=0x0101;        // Init ID to some random number
        return 0;
}
//=========================================================================
//=========================================================================


//*************************************************************************
//*************************************************************************
//**     IP Handler
//    - Handles ICMP (ping)
//    - Call this on 20 return from mac_Handler()
//    - Recovers 'iph_dsize, iph_hsize, tuIP'
//    - Recognises UDP and TCP frames for processing elsewhere
//    - a local ram area of 34 bytes has been allocated to store incoming
//       ICMP ping messages. This can be made larger or smaller as required
//    - Note: caller must ensure that receiver is closed before returning!
//       - i.e by calling nic_RxEnd()
```

```
//
//    IN:          None
//    RET:         Error (odd), or Process code (even). See list
//*************************************************************************
u8      iph_Handler()
{       u16 w;
        u8 ram[34];       // local ram used to store incoming ICMP packet
        struct S_IPHHDR iphhdr;

//***    Frame is IP, so read the first 20 bytes of IP header............
        nic_RxDma((u8*)&iphhdr,20);
        //
//**     Do a few simple vaildity checks on the IP header & dump if bad....
        if ((iphhdr.hdr&0xF0)!=0x40) { nic_RxEnd();
                                       return 21;    // not IPv4
                                     }
        //
        if (iphhdr.ipdest!=myIP)     { nic_RxEnd(); // IP destination is
                                       return 23;   //   not for me..
                                     }
        //
//**     Compute IPH header size and datagram size......................
        iph_hsize = (u16) ((iphhdr.hdr&0x0F)*4);   // save IP header size
        iph_dsize = mac_ntohs(iphhdr.dsize);       // save datagram size

//**     If relevant, read rest of IP options header ...................
        if (iph_hsize>20)                     // Must save somewhere
          { w=iphhdr.opt;                     // as they are needed for
            nic_RxDma ((u8*)&w, iph_hsize-20); // calculating checksum.
          }                                   // Can be dumped later!

//**     Check if IP Header checksum is OK..............................
        w= iph_ChkBlock((u8*)&iphhdr,iph_hsize);
        if (w != 0xFFFF)              { nic_RxEnd();
                                       return 25;   // Bad IP hdr checksum
                                     }              //   dump packet!

//**     Save source.IP.................................................
        tuIP=iphhdr.ipsrce;                        // we'll need this later

//**     Is it a UDP  datagram??........................................
        if (iphhdr.pcol==0x11)       return 40;     // handle elsewhere
        //
//**     Is it a TCP  segment???........................................
        if (iphhdr.pcol==0x06)       return 50;     // handle elsewhere
        //
//**     Is it else?? ..................................................
        if (iphhdr.pcol!=0x01)       { nic_RxEnd();
                                       return 29;   // unknown pcol, dump
                                     }
```

```
//**     Here if ICMP ............................................
         // If possible, read full ICMP payload into general RAM area.....
         // a better version would use malloc if available
         w=iph_dsize-iph_hsize;                      // ICMP payload size
         if (w>34)  { nic_RxEnd();
                        return 33;      // local ICMP buffer not big enough!
                   }
         nic_RxDma((u8*)ram, w);
         nic_RxEnd();                                // finish with RX
         //
         //* Is rx datagram a PING request??............................
         if (ram[0]==0x08)
         {  // Yes, assemble a PING reply and transmit
            nic_TxBeg();
            mac_FillHdr (IPHFRAME);    // send MAC header
            iph_FillHdr (w,0x01);      // send an IP (ICMP) header
            ram[0]=0x00;               // prepare ICMP payload data
            ram[2] +=8;                // bodge cheat checksum calc (demo)
            nic_TxDma((u8*)ram, w);    // send ICPM payload
            nic_TxEnd(3);              // Transmit now
            return 32;                 // OK ping reply
         }
         // Here if frame received was an unknown ICMP message
         return 39;
}
//=========================================================================
//=========================================================================


//*************************************************************************
//*************************************************************************
//**     Helper: called from other modules
//       - Calculates IP Checksum: Adds one u3 to an accrued checksum
//       - All numbers must be in host format
//
//       IN:     'i'             32 bit word to be added
//               'chksum'        stored checksum
//               return          accrued checksum
//*************************************************************************
u16     iph_ChkAddI  (u16 chksum, u32 i)
{       u16 n;
        n= chksum;
        n= iph_ChkAddW(n, (u16)(i>>16)   );
        n= iph_ChkAddW(n, (u16)(i&0xFFFF) );
        return n;
}
//=========================================================================
//=========================================================================
```

.

```
//******************************************************************
//******************************************************************
//**    Helper: called from other modules
//       - Calculates IP Checksum: Adds one u16 to an accrued checksum
//       - Could be improved if written in assembler (C has no 1's facility)
//       - Better be done in assembler as C has no 1's complement facilities
//       - All numbers must be in host format
//
//       IN:     'w'                 32 bit word to add
//               'chksum'            stored checksum
//               return              accrued checksum
//******************************************************************
u16     iph_ChkAddW  (u16 chksum, u16 w)
{       u16 n;
        n= chksum + w;
        if ( (n>chksum) || (n>w) ) return n;
        else                        return n+1;
}
//==================================================================
//==================================================================


//******************************************************************
//******************************************************************
//**    Helper: called from other modules
//       - Calculates IP Checksum: Adds one u8 to an accrued checksum
//       - All numbers must be in host format
//       - Input can be "even" or "odd" bytes
//
//       IN:     'b'                 Unsigned byte to add
//               'chksum'            Stored checksum
//               'odd'               0=byte is word_lsb.  1=byte is word_msb
//               return              accrued checksum
//******************************************************************
u16     iph_ChkAddB  (u16 chksum, u8 b, u8 odd)
{       u16 ub;
        ub=(u16)b;
        if(odd==0) return iph_ChkAddW(chksum, (ub&0xFF));
        else        return iph_ChkAddW(chksum, (ub*256 ));
}
//==================================================================
//==================================================================


//******************************************************************
//******************************************************************
//**    Helper: called from other modules
//       - Compute IP checksum of an array
//       - byte array can be odd or even
//       - Could be improved if written in assembler (C has no 1's facility)
//       - Result is in host format
//
```

```
//        IN:    'ptr'    Byte pointer to array
//               'nb'     nr of bytes in array (can be odd)
//        RET:            computed checksum
//*********************************************************************
u16     iph_ChkBlock (u8* ptr, u16 nb)
{       u32 csum; u16 w,nb2; u16* pw;
        csum=0;
        pw = (u16*)ptr;
        nb2 = nb / 2;
        for (w=0; w<nb2; w++) csum += pw[w];
        // deal with odd byte
        if (nb & 1)   csum +=*(u8*)pw;
        // end-around-carry addition
        while (( w = (u16)(csum>>16))!=0) csum = (csum&0xFFFF)+w;
        return (u16)csum;
}
//===================================================================
//===================================================================


//*********************************************************************
//*********************************************************************
//**     Helper: called from other modules
//        - Fills IP Header and moves to DMA area of Ethernet controller
//        - User must call nic_TxBeg() and mac_FillHdr() first
//        - IP header created has no options field
//        - IP header created has no fragments
//
//        IN:     'psize'  size of payload that follows (dgramsize - 20)
//                'pcol'   protocol byte:  0x01=ICMP 0x06=TCP 0x11=UDP
//
//        GLOBALS (which must be filled by user)
//                'tuIP'       Dest IP  address to use
//                'myIP'       My  IP   address to use
//                'tuHA[6]'    Dest MAC address to use
//                'myHA[6]'    My  MAC address to use
//*********************************************************************
u8      iph_FillHdr (u16 psize, u8 pcol )
{       struct S_IPHHDR iphhdr;

        iphhdr.hdr=     0x45;                      // no options
        iphhdr.tos=     0x00;
        iphhdr.dsize=   mac_htons(psize + 20);     // datagram size
        iphhdr.id=      mac_htons(iph_idnum++);    // autoincrement ID
        iphhdr.frag=    0x0040;                     // no fragments
        iphhdr.ttl=     128;
        iphhdr.pcol=    pcol;
        iphhdr.ipsrce=  myIP;
        iphhdr.ipdest=  tuIP;
        iphhdr.chk=     0;
        iphhdr.chk=     ~iph_ChkBlock((u8*)&iphhdr,20); // calc checksum
        //
```

```
        nic_TxDma((byte*)&iphhdr,20);  // send hdr to DMA buffer
        return 0;
}
//========================================================================
//========================================================================


//========================================================================
//========================================================================
#endif      // !defined (IPH-LIB_C)
```

udp-lib.c

```
//************************************************************************
//************************************************************************
//      udp-lib.c
//      - UDP DATAGRAM handler Demo
//      - Copyright 2002 eixltd.com
//
//************************************************************************
//************************************************************************
#if !defined      (UDP-LIB_C)      // allow3s file to be multiply included
#define           UDP-LIB_C

#include          "nic-lib.C"
#include          "mac-lib.C"
#include          "iph-lIb.C"

//************************************************************************
//
//   PROTOTYPE DECLARATIONS
//   ======================
//
//   udp_Init();      // Call once at beg of prog to init system
//
//   udp_Handler(u16* cs, u16* nb);
//                    // Handle UDP
//                       - see below for return codes
//                       - Call this on 40 return from iph_Handler()
//                       - recovers 'tuPT'
//                       - returns accrued checksum to date (minus payload)
//                       - returns size of payload data still to read
//                       - else returns FFFF if error
//
u8 udp_Tx(u8* pb, u8 nb);
//                    To transmit a UDP datagram (to toIP,toPT,toHA)
//
//   return code      Error code (odd), or status after an op (even):
//                    . 00  No data to process from Eth chip
//
//
```

289

```
u8  udp_User(u16 cs, u16 nb);
//                      // User Application (written by user)
//
//**********************************************************************

//**********************************************************************
//**     RAM areas
//
//**     UDP Header structure (8 bytes)...............................
struct  S_UDPHDR
{       u16    ptsrce;
        u16    ptdest;
        u16    usize;
        u16    ucheck;
};
//
//**********************************************************************
//**     Local RAM area................................................
u16     udp_chksum;                         // Local Stores checksum
u16     udp_myPt;                           // GLOBAL my port
u16     udp_tuPt;                           // GLOBAL
//
//**********************************************************************

//**********************************************************************
//**********************************************************************
//** Initialise
//    - Call once at start of user program
//    - Assumes 'myIP' and 'myHA' have been initialised
//    - Assumes PHY and ETH drivers have been initialised
//**********************************************************************
u8      udp_Init()
{
//**     Init local vars.............................................
        return 0;
}
//====================================================================
//====================================================================

//**********************************************************************
//**********************************************************************
//**     Main UDP Input Handler
//       - Handles UDP
//       - Call this on valid return from iph_Handler()
//
//       IN:         None
//       OUT:        cs    accrued checksum (header, but no data)
//                   nb    number of UDP payload bytes still in DMA
//       RET:        0     If processed OK
//**********************************************************************
```

```
u8          udp_Handler(u16* cs, u16* nb)
{           u16 usize,cks;
            struct S_UDPHDR udphdr;

//***       Datagram is UDP, so read UDP header (first 8 bytes)
            nic_RxDma((u8*)&udphdr,8);
            //
//**        Store source ports...............................
            udp_tuPt= udphdr.ptsrce;

//**        Do a few simple vaildity on the header & exit if bad...........
            if (udp_myPt != udphdr.ptdest) { nic_RxEnd(); // dest port is
                                         *nb=0;        //
                                         return 0;   // not for us, exit!
                                       }
            //
//**        Compute UDP payload data size ...............................
            usize=iph_dsize-iph_hsize-8;
//**        Calculate checksum (UDP header and Pseudoheader, no payload).....
            cks=iph_ChkBlock ((u8*)&udphdr,8);      // UDP header
            cks=iph_ChkAddI(cks, tuIP);             // add pseudoheader
            cks=iph_ChkAddI(cks, myIP);
            cks=iph_ChkAddW(cks, 0x1100);
            cks=iph_ChkAddW(cks, mac_ntohs(8 + usize));
//          checksum of data payload still needs to be added
            //

//**        End bits.....................................................
            *cs= cks;
            *nb= usize;
            return 0;
}
//=============================================================================
//=============================================================================

//*****************************************************************************
//*****************************************************************************
//**        Helper: called from other modules
//          - Call this to prepare and transmit an UDP Datagram
//
//          IN:      'pb'           Pointer to Payload Array to transmit
//                   'nb'           nr of bytes in payload, must be even
//
//          GLOBALS (which must be filled by user)
//                   'tuIP'         Dest  IP    address to use
//                   'myIP'         My    IP    address to use
//                   'tuHA[6]'      Dest  MAC   address to use
//                   'myHA[6]'      My    MAC   address to use
//                   'tuPt'         Dest  Port
//                   'myPt'         My    Port
//
//          RET:     Error or Process code, 0 if OK
//*****************************************************************************
```

```
u8         udp_Tx(u8* pb, u8 nb)
{          u8 b; u16 w1,w2,hsize;
           struct S_UDPHDR udphdr;

//**       Initvars.....................................................
           nic_RxEnd();                     // Finish RX, if not done already

//**       Assemble the UDP Header.......................................
           udphdr.ptsrce=              udp_myPt;
           udphdr.ptdest=              udp_tuPt;
           udphdr.usize =              mac_htons(8 + nb);
           udphdr.ucheck=              0x0000;
           // Compute chekcsum
           w1=iph_ChkBlock((u8*)&udphdr,8);        // chk of hdr
           w2=iph_ChkBlock((u8*)pb,nb);            // chk of data
           w1=iph_ChkAddW(w1,w2);
           // add chekcsum of pseudoheader
           w1=iph_ChkAddI(w1, tuIP);
           w1=iph_ChkAddI(w1, myIP);
           w1=iph_ChkAddW(w1, 0x1100);             // pcol
           w1=iph_ChkAddW(w1, mac_htons(8 + nb));  // udp size
           udphdr.ucheck= ~w1;                     // save it

//**       Assemble the Ethernet & IP Header, and send to DMA.............
           nic_TxBeg();
           mac_FillHdr(IPHFRAME);           // send MAC header
           iph_FillHdr(8 + nb, 0x11);       // send IP header (UDP pcol)
           nic_TxDma((u8*)&udphdr,8);        // send UDP header
           nic_TxDma((u8*)pb,     nb);       // send UDP payload
           return  nic_TxEnd(3);            // transmit now
}
//======================================================================
//======================================================================


//**********************************************************************
//**********************************************************************
//**     udp User call
//        - To be written by user
//        - This is called by udp_Handler()
//           when there is payload data to be handled
//        - User should read the remaining data from the DMA
//           and compute the checksum on the fly
//        - User could then send a reply using udp_Tx()
//        - This simple demo sends all UDP incoming bytes to the serial port
//           and replies with an 'OK' datagram, if all OK.
//
//        IN:     'nb'    Nr of payload bytes still in DMA
//                'cs'    accrued checksum so far (header checksums)
//
//
//        Ret     FF      if final checksum was in error
//                00      OK
//**********************************************************************
```

```
u8        udp_User(u16 cs, u16 nb)
{         u8 a,b,odd; u8 D[4];

//**      Read remaining data from DMA, computing checksum in the process...
          odd=0;
          for (b=0; b<nb; b++)
          { nic_RxDma((u8*)&a,1);
            cs=iph_ChkAddB(cs,a,odd);       // accumulates checksum
            odd=1-odd;
            // As an example we send rx bytes to serial port to prove arrival
            putchar(a);  // TEST
          }
//...............................................................................
//**      User application may now want to respond with another UDP datagram
          // Prepare a simple return message depending on checksum:
          if (cs!=0xFFFF) { D[0]='N'; D[1]='O'; D[2]='K'; D[3]=0; }  // bad
          else            { D[0]='O'; D[1]='K'; D[2]=0  ; D[3]=0; }  // good
          // Return the message as  another UDP datagram
          udp_Tx((u8*)D,4);
//...............................................................................
          return 0;
}
//=============================================================================
//=============================================================================


//=============================================================================
//=============================================================================
#endif       // !defined (UDP-LIB_C)
```

tcp-lib.c

```
//*****************************************************************************
//*****************************************************************************
//       tcp-lib.c
//       - TCP handler
//       - Copyright 2002 eixltd.com
//
//*****************************************************************************
//    PROTOTYPE DECLARATIONS
//    ======================
//
u8            tcp_Init    ();
//
u8            tcp_Handler ();
//
u8            tcp_User    (u16 cs, u16 nb);
//
u8            tcp_Tx      (u8 flag);
//
```

```
void            tcp_Timer   ();            // one second tick
//
u8              tcp_Putch   (u8 c, u8 tx);
//
//*********************************************************************
#if !defined    (TCPSUBS_C)
#define         TCPSUBS_C
#include "nic-lib.c"
#include "mac-lib.c"
#include "iph-lib.c"
//*********************************************************************

//*********************************************************************
//**    TCP Header structure definition .............................
struct  S_TCPHDR
{       u16     ptsrce;
        u16     ptdest;
        u32     seqno;
        u32     ackno;
        u8      hdr4;
        u8      flags;
        u16     window;
        u16     chk;
        u16     urgent;
        u8      opt[40];        // Options
};
//
//*********************************************************************


//*********************************************************************
//**    Global variables
u16     tcp_psize;              // TCP payload size

u16     tcp_rxmss;
u16     tcp_mywin;
u16     tcp_mymss;

u32     tcp_myseq;
u32     tcp_myack;
u8      tcp_state;              // state table
u8      tcp_touts;              // state timer
u8      tcp_toutp;              // tx pending timer

u16     tcp_myPt;               // my TCP port
u16     tcp_tuPt;

////     Local use: transmit buffer
#define TCPTX   7               // tx buffer nr of bytes-1 (7,15,31 etc)
u8      tcp_txdata[TCPTX+1];    // tx buffer
u8      tcp_txp,tcp_txp0,tcp_txp1,tcp_txp2; // pointers
u8      tcp_txn;                // nr of bytes to tx
```

```
//***********************************************************************
//***********************************************************************
//** Initialise TCP system
//***********************************************************************
u8      tcp_Init()
{
        tcp_state=      0;          // init state=CLOSED
        tcp_touts=      0;
        tcp_toutp=      0;
        tcp_myseq= 0x0100;          // some startup value
        tcp_myack= 0x0000;          // some startup value
        tcp_mywin=      576;        // 576 bytes
        tcp_mymss=      576;

        tcp_myPt=   0x1700;         //prov 23= telnet
        tcp_tuPt=       0;

        tcp_txn=        0;
        tcp_txp0=       0;
        tcp_txp1=       0;
        tcp_txp2=       0;

        return 0;
}
//=======================================================================
//=======================================================================

//***********************************************************************
//***********************************************************************
//** Handle TCP packet
//    - Called after iph_Handler()
//
//    - Return:    0       OK, no tcp_Send()
//                 2       OK, call tcp_Send()
//                 23      not my port
//***********************************************************************
u8      tcp_Handler()
{       u8 b,nb; u16 chkh, tcphsize; u1 tx; u32 dw,dw1;
        struct  S_TCPHDR tcphdr;

//*     Init vars..............................................
        tx=     0;

//*     Read TCP header (20 bytes w/o options)..................
        nic_RxDma((u8*)&tcphdr,20);
        //
//**     // Compute header size and other vars..................
        tcphsize= (u16)((tcphdr.hdr4/4)&0xFC);  // hdr + opts
        // compute TCP payload size.
        tcp_psize= iph_dsize - iph_hsize - tcphsize;

//**     if relevant, read rest of options header................
        if (tcphsize>20) nic_RxDma((u8*)&tcphdr.opt[0],tcphsize-20);
```

```
//**     if PORT not addressed for me, exit .............................
         if (tcphdr.ptdest!=tcp_myPt) { nic_RxEnd();
                                       return 23;
                                     }
//**     Save source port number.....................................
         tcp_tuPt= tcphdr.ptsrce;

//**     compute partial checksum (TCP full header minus payload)........
         chkh=iph_ChkBlock ((u8*)&tcphdr,tcphsize);   // full TCP header
         // add pseudoheader
         chkh=iph_ChkAddI(chkh, tuIP);
         chkh=iph_ChkAddI(chkh, myIP);
         chkh=iph_ChkAddW(chkh, 0x0600);                 // TCP pcol
         chkh=iph_ChkAddW(chkh, mac_htons(tcphsize+tcp_psize));

//**     Handle SYN segment received....................................
         if ((tcphdr.flags&0x02)!=0)
         { nic_RxEnd();                             // no more to read from DMA
           //// Ignore if connection already opened, bad checksum or data with SYN
            if ( (tcp_state!=0) || (tcp_psize!=0) || (chkh!=0xFFFF) )
               { return 0;
               }
           //
           //// Good SYN segment received, now get mss
            if (tcphdr.opt[0]==0x02)
               tcp_rxmss=tcphdr.opt[2]+(256*tcphdr.opt[3]);
           //
           /// next, get seq & ack
            tcp_myack=    mac_ntohl(tcphdr.seqno)+1;
            tcp_myseq=    0x0100;       // set our seq to a random number!
           //
           // goto SYN_RCVD state, and tx a SYN reply
            tcp_txp0=     0;
            tcp_txp1=     0;                       // reset tx buffer pointers
            tcp_txp2=     0;
            tcp_txn=      0;
            tcp_Tx(0x12);                          // send SYN
            tcp_state=    1;                       // set state to SYN_RCVD
            tcp_touts =  10;                       // set timer
            tcp_myseq++;                           // SYN = one character
            return 0;
         }
//..............................................................................

//**     Handle FIN segment.received....................................
         if ((tcphdr.flags&0x01)!=0)
         { nic_RxEnd();                            // no more to read from DMA
           tcp_state=0;                            // goto CLOSED state
           tcp_txn=0;
           tcp_Tx(0x10);                           // TX a ACK segment
           tcp_Tx(0x11);                           // TX a FIN segment
           return 0;
```

```
          }
//.........................................................................
//**      Handle RST segment.received...............................
          if ((tcphdr.flags&0x04)!=0)
          {  nic_RxEnd();                      // no more to read from DMA
             tcp_state=0;                       // goto CLOSED state
             return 0;
          }
//.........................................................................

//**      Handle Normal ACK segment...............................
          if ((tcphdr.flags&0x10)!=0)
          { /// if in SYN-RCVD state, just goto ESTABLISHED state
            //   Ideally, should check whether this segment contains data!
            if (tcp_state==1)
                { nic_RxEnd();                          // no more DMA to read
                  do a further check on ack number
                  if (mac_ntohl(tcphdr.seqno) == tcp_myack)
                        { tcp_touts=       0;          // reset timeout
                          tcp_state=       3;          // ESTABLISHED
                          return 0;
                        }
                  else    return 0;
                }
            //.........................................................
            //
            // Else, if NOT in the ESTABLISHED state, ignore.segment.........
              if (tcp_state!=3)
                  { nic_RxEnd();                         // no more DMA to read
                    return 0;
                  }
            //.........................................................

            // if data was sent previously, this may be an ack for it......
            if (tcp_txp0 != tcp_txp1)
                 { // get total nr of bytes sent not acked yet
                   if(tcp_txp1<tcp_txp0) nb=(tcp_txp1+TCPTX+1)-tcp_txp0;
                   else                  nb=tcp_txp1-tcp_txp0;
                   // check if pointer in range (PROV no wrap check!)
                   dw = mac_ntohl(tcphdr.ackno);
                   if ((dw >tcp_myseq) && (dw<=(tcp_myseq+(u32)nb)))
                          { // remote received our data ok!
                            tcp_toutp= 0;               // kill ack wait timer
                            dw1= dw-tcp_myseq;          // nr of bytes acked
                            tcp_myseq = dw;             // update our seq
                            tcp_txp0 = (tcp_txp0+((u8)dw1)) & TCPTX;
                            tcp_txn=   0;               // no more data to send
                            tx=        FALSE;
                          }
                   else if (dw  == tcp_myseq)
                          { // if hung on previous, resend
                            tcp_txp=   tcp_txp0;
```

```
                                tcp_txn=    nb;
                                tx=         TRUE;
                            }
                    else  { // if wrong seq, out of sync - resync
                                tcp_myseq= dw;              // !
                                tcp_txn=    0;
                                tx=         TRUE;
                            }
                }
            //.........................................................
            //
            // if incoming segment contains data........................
            if (tcp_psize>0)
                { // if data is expected
                    if (mac_ntohl(tcphdr.seqno) == tcp_myack)
                        { // OK accept. read data bytes
                            b=tcp_User(chkh, tcp_psize);
                            if (b!=0xFF) tcp_myack +=(u32)tcp_psize;
                            tx=TRUE;
                        }
                    else  { // wrong seq, send NAK
                            tx=TRUE;
                        }
                }
            //.........................................................
              //
            }
//...............................................................................
    nic_RxEnd();                                  // no more DMA to read
    if (tx) tcp_Putch(0,2);        // force a send
    return 0;
}
//=================================================================================
//=================================================================================

//*********************************************************************************
//*********************************************************************************
//**     tcp User call
//       - User written call to handle rx TCP stream
//
//       IN:   'nb'   Nr of bytes of payload still in DMA
//             'cs'   accrued checksum so far (header checksums)
//
//       Ret   FF     if cs error
//             00      CS OK and no data bytes to return
//             n>0     CS is OK, and n data bytes to return (in tcp_pdata)
//*********************************************************************************
u8      tcp_User (u16 cs, u16 nb)
{       u8 a,b,odd;
```

```
//**      Read bytes from DMA, accumulating checksum in the process.......
          odd=0;
          for (b=0; b<nb; b++)
              { nic_RxDma((u8*)&a,1);
                cs=iph_ChkAddB(cs,a,odd); // accumulated checksum
                odd=1-odd;
//////// now we got the user data, do something with it!
                putchar(a);                // simple echo to prove its arrived
              }
//.............................................................................
//**      DEMO: arrange for simple reply (depending on checksum received!)...
          if (cs!=0xFFFF) { tcp_Putch('N',0);
                            tcp_Putch('O',0);
                            tcp_Putch('K',0);
                            return 0xFF;
                          }
          // OK return
          tcp_Putch('O',0); tcp_Putch('K',0);
          return 0;
}
//========================================================================
//========================================================================

//*********************************************************************************
//*********************************************************************************
//**      tcp User call
//        - Send one character to trasmitter
//        - Adds char to circular tx buffer
//
//        IN:     'c'     Character to add to buffer
//                'tx'    0   add character to tx fifo
//                        1   add character and force a send
//                        2   force a send only
//
//        RET:    0       if OK
//                1       if buffer full, cannot add char to buffer
//*********************************************************************************
u8      tcp_Putch(u8 c, u8 tx)
{       u8 b;

//**      Add character to circular buffer.............................
          if (tx!=2)
          { b= (tcp_txp2+1) & TCPTX;
            if (b==tcp_txp0)  return 1;        // buffer full
            tcp_txdata[tcp_txp2]=c;
            tcp_txp2=b;
          }
//.............................................................................
```

```
//**     Set to transmit now..........................................
         if (tx>0)
         {  if (tcp_txp2<tcp_txp1) b=(tcp_txp2+TCPTX+1) - tcp_txp1;
            else                   b=tcp_txp2 - tcp_txp1;
            tcp_txn=b;
            tcp_txp=tcp_txp1;
            tcp_Tx(0x10);              // tx segment with our data
            tcp_txp1=tcp_txp2;
            tcp_toutp=  10;           // set timeout for waiting for ACK
         }
//............................................................
         return 0;
}
//=========================================================================
//=========================================================================


//*************************************************************************
//*************************************************************************
//** Helper Function: Transmit a TCP segment
//       - Used to send a segment.
//       - To send data to remote, use Tx_Send() instead
//
//    IN:     'flag'        0=  notn
//                         +1=  FIN
//                         +2=  SYN
//                         +4=  RST
//                        +10=  ACK
//
//    GLOBALS: must be filled before calling function
//            'tcp_txdata'  circular array with payload data (if used)
//            'tcp_txp'     circular pointer to start of data in array
//            'tcp_txn'     nr of bytes to tx in circ buffer
//            'tcp_myseq'   Seq nr to use
//            'tcp_myack'   ack number to use
//            'tcp_mymss'   MSS to use (only in SYN segments)
//            'tcp_mywin'   Window size to advertise
//            'myHA[6]'     my MAC address
//            'tuHA[6]'     dest MAC address
//            'myIP'        my IP address
//            'tuIP'        dest IP address
//            'tcp_myPt'    my port number
//            'tcp_tuPt'    dest port number
//*************************************************************************
u8       tcp_Tx (u8 flag)
{        u8 a,b,c,odd; u8* pd; u16 chk1,chk2,tcphsize;
         struct   S_TCPHDR tcphdr;

//**     Calc IPH/TCP header sizes with/without options..................
         if ((flag&2)!=0) tcphsize=28;    // if SYN segment, include a MSS
         else             tcphsize=20;  // else ,ord 20 byte size
//............................................................
```

```
//**      Init tcp header.............................................
          tcphdr.hdr4=     0x50;                      // updated later!
          tcphdr.chk=      0x0000;                    // updated later!
          tcphdr.ptsrce=   tcp_myPt;
          tcphdr.ptdest=   tcp_tuPt;
          //
          tcphdr.seqno=    mac_htonl(tcp_myseq);
          tcphdr.ackno=    mac_htonl(tcp_myack);
          tcphdr.urgent=   0x0000;
          tcphdr.flags=    0x0;
          if(tcp_txn>0)      tcphdr.flags=  0x08;     // PSH if data present
          if((flag&1)!=0)    tcphdr.flags|= 0x01;     // FIN
          if((flag&16)!=0)   tcphdr.flags|= 0x10;     // ACK
          if((flag&2)!=0){   tcphdr.hdr4=   0x70;     // SYN
                             tcphdr.flags|= 0x02;
                             tcphdr.opt[0]=0x02; tcphdr.opt[1]=0x04;   // MSS
                             tcphdr.opt[2]=0x05; tcphdr.opt[3]=0xB4;
                             tcphdr.opt[4]=0x01; tcphdr.opt[5]=0x01;
                             tcphdr.opt[6]=0x04; tcphdr.opt[7]=0x02;
                          }
          tcphdr.window=   mac_htons(tcp_mywin);      // window advertised
//...........................................................................
//
//**      Calculate TCP Checksum.......................................
          // calc checksum of circular data array
          chk1=0; odd=0;
          for (b=0; b<tcp_txn; b++)
              { c= (tcp_txp + b) & TCPTX;
                a=tcp_txdata[c];
                chk1=iph_ChkAddB(chk1,a,odd);         // data array csum
                odd=1-odd;
              }
          //
          chk2=iph_ChkBlock ((u8*)&tcphdr,tcphsize);  // TCP header csum
          chk1=iph_ChkAddW(chk1,chk2);
          chk1=iph_ChkAddI(chk1, tuIP);               // + pseudo-header
          chk1=iph_ChkAddI(chk1, myIP);
          chk1=iph_ChkAddW(chk1, 0x0600);
          chk1=iph_ChkAddW(chk1, mac_htons(tcphsize+tcp_txn));
          tcphdr.chk= ~chk1;                          // set value
//...........................................................................

//**      Assemble the Segment & send to DMA...........................
          nic_RxEnd();                                // end rx just in case.
          nic_TxBeg();
          mac_FillHdr(IPHFRAME);                      // send MAC header
          iph_FillHdr(tcphsize + tcp_txn, 0x06);      // send IP header
          nic_TxDma((u8*)&tcphdr,tcphsize);           // send TCP header
          if (tcp_txn>0)
              { for (b=0; b<tcp_txn; b++)             // send data
                    { c= (tcp_txp + b) & TCPTX;
```

```
                              a= tcp_txdata[c];
                              nic_TxDma((u8*)&a,1);
                      }
              }
        nic_TxEnd(3);                              // transmit now
        return 0;
}
//=========================================================================
//=========================================================================


//*************************************************************************
//*************************************************************************
//** TCP Timer
//   - Called from main program every second or so
//*************************************************************************
void    tcp_Timer()
{       u8 b;
//**     Handle timeout during SYN-RCVD.................................
        if (tcp_touts==0) return;
        tcp_touts--;
        if ( (tcp_touts==0) && (tcp_state==1))
        { tcp_state=0;          // if no ack rcvd during SYN-RCVD state
          tcp_txn=0;            //  after some time, kill the connection
          tcp_Tx(4);
          return;
        }
//.........................................................................

//**     Handle timeout during ack wait (after txting a segment).........
        if (tcp_toutp==0) return;
        tcp_toutp-;
        if ( (tcp_toutp==0) && (tcp_txp1!=tcp_txp0) )
        {   tcp_txp=tcp_txp0;
            if (tcp_txp2<tcp_txp0) b=(tcp_txp2+TCPTX+1) - tcp_txp0;
            else                   b=tcp_txp2 - tcp_txp0;
            tcp_txn=b;
            tcp_Tx(0x10);                  // IF no ack rcvd after sending our
                                                  data,
            tcp_txp1 = tcp_txp2;
            tcp_toutp = 0;                 // only one retry
            return;
        }
//.........................................................................
}
//=========================================================================
//=========================================================================

//=========================================================================
//=========================================================================
#endif      // !defined (TCPSUBS_C)
```

Bibliography

This bibliography provides additional resources that may be of some help to readers. The references are arranged by topic area.

Electronics Theory

1. Millman, J. and Taub, H. *Pulse Digital and Switching Waveforms*. New York: McGraw Hill, 1969. A good introduction on digital components, and digital communications.

Manufacturers Data Sheets

1. National Semiconductors. *National Interface Databook*, 1999 Edition. Includes many data sheets and application notes on hardware line drivers and line driving techniques.

2. RTL8019S Ethernet controller data sheet. Realtek Semiconductors Corp. Various datasheets on the RTL family of devices; www.realtek.com.tw.

3. National Semiconductors Corp. '*DP8390 Ethernet Network Interface Controller. An Introductory Guide*'. AN-475, May 1993. Data sheets and application notes on Ethernet controllers (RTL8019 compatible); www.national.com.

4. CS8900 Ethernet Controller. Cirrus Logic www.Data sheets and application notes on Ethernet controllers; www.cirrus.com.

5. LAN91C9111 10/100 Mbps Ethernet Controller Data Sheets. Standard Microsystems Corporation; www.smsc.com.

6. CH2124 Internet Appliance Modem. Cermetek Microelectronics. Datasheets and application notes on embedded modem/TCP stack device; www.cermetek.com.

7. Rabbit TCP/IP Modules; www.rabbitsemiconductor.com.

8. *Microchip Technical Library*, CD-ROM. Complete set of data sheets and application notes for PIC microcontrollers and other devices; www.microchip.com.

9. *PCM Compiler for the PIC*. Custom Computer Services; www.ccsinfo.com.

General Web Resources

1. Sites dedicated to microcontroller devices: www.microcontroller.com; www.embedded.com; www.eg3.com/embe/index/htm; www.embeddedinternetworking.com.

2. Magazines with special section on embedded systems and TCP/IP networking: www.circuitcellar.com; www.ednmag.com.

3. RFC (request for comments): www.faqs.org/rfcs.

4. Information data and application notes on 802.11b radio systems: www.intersil.com.

5. Sites dedicated to gate array microcontroller cores: www.opencores.org; www.altera.com; www.xilinx.com; www.actel.com; www.atmel.com; www.asics.ws.

6. Affordable TCP/IP stacks: www.cmx.com; www.wattcp.com; www.sics.se; www.ethernut.de; www.iready.org; www.orlin.com; www.livedevices.com; www.iosoft.co.uk; www.rabbitsemiconductor.com.

7. TCP/IP FAQ: this online newsletter contains a very useful monthly updated list of various resources (books, web sites, FAQS, newsgroups, and useful net techniques) intended to help any newcomer to learn about TCP/IP. The list is published monthly in various newsgroups such as comp.protocols. tcp-ip.ibmpc, and is also available as a web page at: www.private.org.il/tcpip_rl.htmlm, and also at www.faqs.org/faqs/internet/tcp-ip/resource-list/index.html.

Programming Techniques – TCP/IP

1. Mealy, G.H., A method for synthesizing sequential circuits, *The Bell System Technical Journal*, **34**, American Telephone and Telegraph Company, September 1955.

2. Moore, E.F., Gedanken-experiments on sequential machines, *Automata Studies, Annals of Mathematics Studies*, Number 34 (eds C.E. Shannon and J. McCarthy), Princeton, NJ: Princeton University Press, 1956.

3. Stevens, R. *TCP/IP Illustrated*, Vol. 1. Reading, MA: Addison Wesley, 1994.

4. Huitema, C. *IPV6 – The New Internet Protocol*. Upper Saddle River, NJ: Prentice Hall, 1997.

5. Lee, T. and Davies, J. *Microsoft Windows 2000 TCP/IP Protocols and Services, Technical Reference*. Microsoft Press, 2000.

6. Miller, P. *TCP/IP Explained*. Digital Press, 1997.

7. Heywood, D. *Networking with Microsoft TCP/IP*. New Riders Publishing, 1998.

Glossary

10BASE2A   Wired LAN standard, commonly known as Ethernet and defined in IEEE802.3b. This is designed to work over $50\,\Omega$ (RG58U) coaxial cable.

10BASE5   The original specification for the CSMA/CD network access using $50\,\Omega$ coaxial as the medium, commonly known as thick Ethernet. This is defined in 802.3.

10BASET   A standard for the use of twisted pair cables defined in 802.3i. Sometimes called twisted pair Ethernet or UTP.

802 Series   A set of standards developed by the IEEE. Several such standards now exist and further are planned. For example, 802.1, 802.3, 802.3, etc.

802.2   Specifies the logical link control (LLC), common to all 802-series LANs.

802.3   Specifies a CSMA control and physical layer specifications for wired LANs.

802.4   Specifies a token passing, bus access method and physical layer specifications for wired LANs.

802.5   Specifies a token passing, ring access method and physical layer specifications for wired LANs.

802.10   Specifies security and privacy access methods for both wired and wireless LANs.

802.11   Specifies medium access and physical Layer methods for wireless connectivity for LANs. The basic system operates at 1 and 2 Mbps.

802.11a   A variation of 802.11 using orthogonal frequency division multiplexing (OFDM) in the 5 GHz frequency band at up to 54 Mbps.

802.11b   A variation of 802.11 using direct sequence modulation (DSSS) for data rates up to 11 Mbps in the 2.4 GHz frequency band.

Access point   An interface between a wireless network and a wired network in a LAN.

ACK   Acronym for ACKnowledgment. This is a returned message indicating that data has arrived at a destination. ACK is assumed a 'positive' acknowledgment (see NAK for negative acknowledgment).

Acknowledged connectionless service   A datagram style service that includes error- and flow-control mechanisms.

Address   A method of uniquely identifying a node, a station or an individual in a network. Several types of addressing exist; depending on the hierarchical layer they stand.

Ad hoc   The name generally given to a wireless network composed only of stations and no central access point.

Analog cellular   A telephone system that uses radio cells using frequency modulation (FM) to carry voice signals.

ANSI   American National Standards Institution. A standards marking body in the United States.

Appliance   A generic name given to devices that run applications and have visual interfaces between the user and the equipment or network. Appliances may include personal computers, personal assistants; Internet enabled domestic and office equipment.

Application layer   Layer seven in the OSI reference model. See Chapter 3.

ARP   Address resolution protocol. A general purpose protocol designed to pair Internet (network) addresses to hardware (MAC) addresses. See Chapter 6 and RFC 826.

ARP cache   A table for each interface of static or dynamically resolved IP addresses and their corresponding MAC addresses.

ARQ   Automatic repeat request. A method of error correction in which the receiving node detects errors and uses a feedback path to the sender for requesting the retransmission of incorrect frames.

ASCII   American Standard Code for Information Interchange. A standard encoding scheme commonly used in the computer industry for encoding character text and numerals into seven (or eight) bit data bytes or octets.

Association   A service that enables the mapping of a wireless station to the LAN via an access point.

Authentication   A process by which a system (or person) can identify itself to other parties. IEEE 802.11 offers two forms of authentication: open system and shared key.

AWG   American Wire Gauge. The standard by which wiring cables are defined based on their diameter.

Backbone   A single cable segment used in a bus topology that connects all computers in a direct line between them.

Bandwidth   The occupancy (in Hertz) of a data stream. In other words, the proportion of the frequency spectrum taken by a modulated data signal.

Baseband   A method of transmitting data where only one signal may be present on the medium at any one time.

Baud   Term used to measure data rate speed that describes the number of state transitions that occur in 1 s.

Bluetooth   A specification published by the Bluetooth Special Interest Group (BSIG) for 1 Mbps data rates in the 2.4 GHz band at relatively short ranges. Bluetooth is not a LAN service; it is more of a personal area network.

BootP   Bootstrap protocol. A protocol that uses UDP and IP to allow network devices to load up start-up information, for example, initialization programs or data. See Chapter 8 and RFCs 951, 1497 and 1532.

Bridge   A store and forward device, used to channel traffic between two separate LANs.

Broadband   A transmission method where multiple signals may coexist on the medium at the same time.

Broadcast   A packet or frame destined to more than one user (in fact to all users).

BSI   British Standards Institute. The standards making body responsible for approving standards in the United Kingdom.

BSS   Basic service set. A set of 802.11 compliant stations that operate as a fully connected wireless LAN.

BSSID   Basic service set identification. A 6-byte address that distinguishes a particular access point from others. Also known as a network ID or network name.

CAM   Channel access method. The rules used to determine which computer can send data across the network, thereby preventing collisions.

Carrier current LAN   A local area network that makes uses of power lines for data transmission.

CAT3, CAT5   Category 1–5. The EIA/TIA designations for unshielded twisted pair cable as described in terms of quality categories. Also known as UTP cable.

CCA   Clear channel assessment. A function that determines the state of the wireless medium in an 802.11 network.

CCITT   International Telegraph and Telephone Consultative Committee.

CCK   Complementary code keying. A modulation technique used in 802.11b radios.

Checksum   A value that is calculated from the components of a packet, and usually transmitted with it. A receiving station can make use of this field to re-compute the checksum of the packet to ensure it has arrived intact.

Circuit switching   A communications method that requires a dedicated line be set up between the two stations for the duration of the session.

Client   A system that requires the services of another. The other station is usually called the server.

Collisions   A condition that occurs on shared medium networks when two stations attempt to send data at the same time.

Congestion   A situation that arises in a network when data arrives faster than it can be processed.

Connectionless   A data communications method that does not require stations to agree beforehand on how to conduct the transaction.

Connection-oriented   A channel where a protocol establishes a formal connection between the two parties before any data is exchanged.

Cooperative multitasking   A form of multitasking in which each individual process controls the length of time it maintains exclusive control of the CPU.

CRC   Cyclic redundancy check. A common method for computing checksum calculations. The CRC is a polynomial that is applied to a block of data using finite field linear arithmetic operations.

C-SLIP   Compressed SLIP. A simple compression scheme used to compress IP and TCP headers to a 3–5 byte header on a SLIP link.

CSMA/CA   Carrier sense multiple access with collision avoidance. A contention-based channel access method in which computers avoid collisions by broadcasting their intent to send data. Reference in 802.11.

CSMA/CD   Carrier sense multiple access with collision detect. A method for handling multiple stations wanting to use a shared medium. Computers avoid collisions by listening to the network before sending any data. Reference is 802.3.

Datagram   The basic unit for transmission in an IP environment. Another word for packets in a connectionless environment.

De-fragmentation   The process of reconstructing a larger IP datagram from a collection of smaller ones.

DHCP   Dynamic host configuration protocol. A protocol for providing computes with IP hosting configuration details. A DHCP server provides IP addresses and configuration details on demand to other users in a local network.

Disassociation   An IEEE 802.11 term that defines the process a station uses to notify that it is terminating an existing association.

DLL   Data link layer. Layer two in the OSI reference model. See Chapter 3.

DNS   Domain naming system. A protocol used for mapping host (human readable) names to IP addresses.

Domain   A group of nodes sharing a common purpose, for example, a LAN.

Domain name system   A set of services for holding, updating and resolving computer names and associated IP addresses.

DSSS   Direct sequence spread spectrum. A method of modulation that is created by the mixing of the data stream with a much higher frequency chip rate, usually a pseudorandom signal. The net effect is to produce a low-power spectrum signal which causes little interference to other standard carrier-based services.

EBCDIC   Extended Binary Coded Decimal Interchange Code. A standard method for encoding characters to numeric codes, developed by IBM.

EIA   Electrical Industries Association. A US standards marking body responsible for communication standards, notably RS-232.

EISA   Extended industry standard architecture. A 32-bit PC bus architecture, that is backwards compatible with the older 16-bit ISA bus architecture.

EMAIL   Electronic mail. The colloquial name used for the method of interchanging messages between users or computers using POP3 or SMTP protocols.

EMI   Electromagnetic interference.

Encapsulation   A method by which payload date is carried within another.

Encryption   A technique used to scramble or modify the contents of a data stream so that they are not easily recognizable by a third party and thus avoid eavesdropping.

ESS   Extended service set. In IEEE 802.11, a collection of basic service sets tied together via a distribution system.

Ethernet   The original medium access system (developed by Digital, Intel and Xerox) employing CSMA/CD. Ethernet defines a 10 Mbps baseband signaling system originally developed for coaxial cable. This has since been enhanced by the IEE and now uses multiple media type including twisted pairs and fibre optic cable. Ethernet II is used in TCP/IP networks, Ethernet 802 in Novell, IPX/SPX networks.

FCC   Federal Communications Commission. A US government body that regulates the use of the radio spectrum in the United States.

FCS   Frame check sequence: a field in the data link layer protocol (e.g. Ethernet) used to carry a checksum for the transmitted frame.

FDDI   Fibre distributed data interface. Developed by the ANSI as standard X3T9.5. This defines a 100 Mbps ring topology that was originally developed for use over optical fibre.

FEC   Forward error correction. A method of error control in which the receiving end is able to correct bits in error. This is done by the sending sequence containing many redundant bits of information from where the position of the bits in error can be deduced.

FHSS   Frequency hopping spread spectrum. A modulation system in which the data signal is modulated in turn by carriers of different frequencies. A pre-programmed hopping code defines the rate and sequence of frequencies to be used. The receiver uses an inverse algorithm to tune its front end to the right frequencies.

FINGER   A management protocol that allows one host machine to interrogate another network device to obtain information about valid or current users. See RFC 1288.

Firewall   A device that interfaces a LAN to the outside world, providing access security from external unauthorized users. This is done by blocking traffic containing invalid port numbers, etc.

Fragment   A part of an IP datagram. When a router forwards a packet, it must know the maximum data size the carrier can take. If this is less than the packet size, the router must break the packet into smaller pieces in an orderly fashion so that they can be transmitted over the carrier. Each smaller packet is called a fragment of the larger packet.

Fragmentation   The process by which IP datagrams are broken into smaller ones in order to adhere to constraints imposed by network physical size characteristics.

Frame   The unit of data transfer at the data link (or network access) layer.

FTP   File transfer protocol. A protocol that allows users in one machine to transfer files to and from another machine. See RFC 959.

Gateway   Another word for a router. A gateway may also be used to translate one protocol to another.

Gopher   A simple protocol that allows a client host to access hierarchical and file information on a server. See RFC 1436.

Hayes compatible   Modem standards based on the original Smart modem manufactured by Hayes.

HDLC   Higher data link control. A general purpose data link control protocol commonly in used over WAN data links.

Header   The portion of a packet or frame that contains control or addressing information. The other portion of the packet is usually called the payload.

Host   A device or computer that resides on a network and provides services to others.

HTML   Hypertext mark up language. A language used to create pages of information used in the World Wide Web.

HTTP   Hyper text transfer protocol. The protocol used to transfer world wide web pages. See Chapter 8 and RFC 1945.

HiperLAN   A network system developed by the European Telecommunications Standards Institute (ETSI) Broadband Radio Access Network (BRAN) organization. HiperLAN/1, operates in the 5 GHz radio band at up to 24 Mbps. HiperLAN/2 operates in the 5 GHz band at up to 54 Mbps.

IANA   Internet Assigned Numbers Authority. A central registry of all numbers associated with Internet protocols (port numbers, protocol IDs etc), see RFC 1700.

IBSS   Independent Basic Service Set Network. An IEEE 802.11 network that has no backbone infrastructure and that consists of stations only. See also ad hoc network.

ICMP   Internet control message protocol. A protocol that is part of IP and used to report errors or other system messages. See Chapter 7 and RFC 792.

IEEE   Institute of Electrical and Electronics Engineers. Responsible for the introduction and standardization of many network access methods. The most relevant for networking is 802.X. Many documents can be downloaded free of charge from the IEEE web site on http:www.ieee.org.

IETF   Internet Engineering Task Force. The body that defines the Internet protocol and oversees the development of the Internet and the evolution of TCP/IP. The standard developed by the IETF are published as RFCs.

IGMP   Internet group management protocol. An extension to the IP that allows host groups to be formed. This protocol allows routers capable of multicast forwarding to determine where host group members reside and forward messages to them. See RFC 1112.

Impedance   The resistance of a cable to the transmission of signals. Impedance is a function of the physical dimensions of the cable (but not its length). See Chapter 4.

Internet   The worldwide network to which many businesses and homes are connected to. The Internet is in reality, a collection of separate networks interconnected together. An internet (with a lower case 'i') is a collection of networks interconnected via routers and run primarily for private use.

Internet address   The unique address assigned to a device or user on a network. Several addresses can apply to the same device, an Internet IP address, a MAC address and a host name.

IP   Internet protocol. The network layer protocol of the Internet protocol suite. This is a connectionless, unreliable protocol that relies on upper layers to provide for reliance. See RFC 791, RFC 950, RFC 919, RFC 922.

IP address   A 32-bit number, normally expressed in dotted decimal notation, which is used to uniquely identify each host or user within the Internet.

ISA   Industry standard architecture. Originally an 8-bit PC bus architecture, ISA was expanded to 16 bits with the introduction of the IBM PC/AT in 1984.

ISDN   Integrated services digital network. A wide area technology that allows the transmission of voice, data, video and other information over a single cable. See Chapter 4.

ISM band   Industrial, scientific and medical radio band. Radio frequency bands allocated by government organizations for wireless LANs. The bands are also shared with other services, which may interfere with communications.

ISO   International Standards Organization. Responsible for the introduction of many standards for computer and communications.

ITU   International Telecommunications Union. Standards body that developed the V-series modem standards.

LAN   Local area network. A network that is designed to span a small geographical area, possibly within a building or office.

LAP   Link access procedure. An error correction protocol derived from the HDLC standards.

Layer   The functions or tasks that subdivide communications protocols.

Leased line   A dedicated telephone data circuit over which data may be sent. Leased lines are point to point wide area network components.

LED   Light emitting diode.

LLC   Logical link control. The upper sub-layer of the IEEE 802 model for the data link layer of the OSI reference model. Its purpose is to provide error free delivery and flow control as well as provide a standard interface to the network layer regardless of the physical technology employed in the link. See 802.2.

MAC   Media access control. The lower sub-layer of the data link layer. Used to provide medium access services in IEEE 802 LANs.

MAC address   The hardware encoded address of a device. Each physical device connected to a network such as Ethernet must have a fixed, uniquely allocated MAC address. MAC addresses are related to the hardware, IP addresses are related to the user.

Medium   A physical link that provides a basic building block to support the transmission of data.

MIME   An encoding method for transmitting data over character limited channels. See RFCs 1741 and 1767.

MRU   Maximum receive unit. The maximum amount of data that can be received by a device. This value is usually negotiated at the beginning of a session.

MSS   Maximum segment size. The maximum segment size advertised for an TCP segment.

MTU   Maximum transmission unit. The largest frame that can be transmitted as a packet in a frame based network (1526 bytes for Ethernet).

Multicast   The term used to describe a packet of frame destined to more than one destination.

Multihomed host   A host that has more than one connection to a network.

Multitasking   A mode of CPU operation where a computer processes more than one task at a time. This is usually done by time slicing.

NAK   Negative acknowledgment. An acknowledgment message sent in response to a bad or corrupted packet.

NCP   Network control protocol: A protocol for negotiating the data link characteristics of a point-to-point connection.

Network   A data communications system used to interface computer systems either locally or remote.

Network layer   Layer three of the OSI reference model. The network layer handles addressing and routing between LANs.

NIC   Network interface card. A network adapter inserted into a computer. Usually has a MAC address permanently wired into it.

NNTP   Network news transport protocol. A protocol used by computers for managing the articles posted on network newsgroups.

NTP   Network time protocol. A protocol used to time synchronize stations on a network. See RFCs 868 and 1305.

Octet   Another word for byte. That is, 8 bits of data.

OFDM   Orthogonal frequency division multiplexing. A modulation technique that divides a high speed serial information signal into multiple low-speed subsignals that the system transmits simultaneously at different frequencies in parallel. OFDM is the basis of the IEEE 802.11a standard.

OSA   Open system authentication. An authentication method used in IEEE 802.11. This is a two step process, first the station wanting to authenticate sends an authentication management frame containing the sending station's identity. The receiving station then sends back a frame stating whether it recognizes the identity of the sending station.

OSI   Open systems interconnection. A suite of protocols designed by the International Standards Organization.

OSI reference model   A seven-layer architecture model used to describe the way in which computers communicate.

Packet   The basic unit of data transmitted across a network. Other words related to packet are frame, datagram and segment.

Packet switching   General name given to a transmission method where packets may be sent between senders and destinations via different paths. Packets may arrive in any order.

Payload   The data part of a packet.

PDU   Packet data unit. A data unit associated with processing at a given layer in the OSI reference model.

Peer-to-peer   A type of network in which each computer can be a client of other computers, and act as servers as well.

Physical layer   Layer one of the OSI reference model. This details cables, adapters, connectors and hardware behaviour.

PING   Packet internet groper. A simple application used to test the reachability of a network. See Chapter 7 and RFC 792.

POP3   Post office protocol 3. A mail delivery protocol. See Chapter 8 and RFCs 1725 and 1734.

Port   Within the TCP/IP, used to describe a demultiplexing service channel.

POTS   Plain old telephone network, see PSTN.

PPP   Point-to-point protocol. A protocol used over serial links to allow the transmission of multiple higher level protocols. See Chapter 6 and RFCs 1332–1334, 1570, 1661, 1663 and 1717.

Pre-emptive-multitasking   A form of multitasking in which the OS retains control over the length of time a process can maintain exclusive use of the CPU. See Chapter 2.

Presentation layer   Layer six of the OSI reference model. See Chapter 3.

Propagation delay   Signal delay that is created by either a cable of considerable length, or by delays incurred in store and forward devices.

Protocol   A description of the rules and formats associated with the transfer of data.

PSTN   Public switched telephone network. The system provided by PTTs using dial up modems and standard telephones. See Chapter 4.

RARP   Reverse address resolution protocol. A protocol similar to ARP, but allowing the resolution of IP addresses where only MAC addresses are known. See RFC 903.

RFC   Request for comment. The vehicle by which Internet protocols and standards are published. This includes general information about standards, experiments, etc. All the RFCs are available at no charge through electronic mail or by using anonymous FTP across the Internet. The quickest way to obtain an RFC is by just entering its full number in an online search engine. See Chapter 3.

RFC 822   The standard header format used for mail and other text based IP protocols. See Chapter 8.

RIP   Routing information protocol. A distance vector based dynamic routing protocol. RIP bases its routing path on the distance or number of hops to the destination. RIP maintains optimum routing by sending out routing update messages if the network topology changes.

RJ-11   A four wire modular jack commonly used in telephone handset connections.

RJ-45   An eight-wire modular jack used for networking connections. This is also used in some PABX system to connect extension telephones.

Rlogin   A virtual terminal application similar to Telnet.

Router   A store-and-forward device used to pass data from one network to another.

SAP   Server access point. A point at which the services of an OSI layer are made available to the next.

SCTP   Stream control transmission Protocol. A message oriented offering acknowledged error-free non-duplicated transfer of datagrams. See Chapter 8.

SDLC   Synchronous data link control

Segment   The TCP unit of data transfer. Effectively, a TCP packet of data.

Server   A computer that provides shared resources to clients across a network.

Service primitive   A communications element for sending information between layers. In software terms, a function call or a message passing system. See Chapter 2.

SLIP   Serial line internet protocol. A simple protocol used to carry IP datagrams over serial lines.

SMTP   Simple mail transfer protocol. A TCP-based protocol used to transmit and receive electronic mail messages. See Chapter 8 and RFCs 821 and 822.

SNMP   Simple network management protocol. A protocol used to manage network devices. See RFC 1157.

SNTP   Simple network time protocol. See Chapter 8 and RFC 1769.

Socket   General name given to an IP network address and data access port number pairing.

Spread spectrum   A modulation technique that spreads a signal's power over a wide bandwidth. This can make the signal less susceptible to electrical noise and radio based interference.

STP   Shielded twisted pair, see CAT cable.

T1, T3   US standard communications facilities for carrying data at 1.544 and 44.746 Mbps, respectively.

TCP   Transport control protocol. The generic protocol used in the Internet for many applications. See Chapter 7 and RFC 793.

TCP/IP   The colloquial name given to the Internet protocol suite.

Telnet   A simple application protocol used for simple teletype (virtual terminal) communication between two computers. See Chapter 8 and RFCs 854 and 855.

TFTP   Trivial file transfer protocol. A UDP-based protocol used to transfer files between devices or hosts. See Chapter 8 and RFC 1350.

Thicknet   Another name for 10Base5 LAN systems.

Thinnet   Another name for 10Base2 LAN systems.

Token ring   A LAN system originally developed by IBM and standardized by IEEE 802.5.

Topology   A term used to describe the geography of a network.

Transport layer   Layer three in the OSI model. Provides mechanisms for the establishment, maintenance and orderly termination of virtual circuits. See Chapter 3.

TTL   Time to live. A field within the IP datagram that ensures the timely destruction of lost packets on a network.

Twisted pairs   Type of medium using twisted copper wires. The twisting prevents radiation and minimizes interference.

UDP   User datagram protocol. A connectionless transport protocol used with IP. See Chapter 7 and RFC 768.

Unacknowledged connectionless service   A datagram style service that does not involve any error control or flow control mechanisms.

USENET   Network news. The collection of discussion groups maintained on the Internet, see NNTP.

UTP   Unshielded twisted pair cables. See CAT cable.

V21   An ITU standard for asynchronous 0-300 bps full-duplex modems.

V34   An ITU standard for 28 800 bps modems.

WAN   Wide area network. A network created to span large geographical areas, usually over dedicated third-party owned lines called carriers.

WEP   Wired equipment privacy. An optional 802.11 function that offers frame transmission privacy similar to that of a wired network.

Wi-Fi   Wireless fidelity. A standard sponsored by the Wireless Ethernet Compatibility Alliance (WECA). Wi-Fi is actually a brand that signifies 802.11 interoperability with other Wi-Fi certified products.

Windows sockets   A series of application interfaces (APIs) that an application can call to transfer data with TCP/IP protocols.

Winsock   See Windows sockets.

WWW   World Wide Web. General name given to resources available worldwide over the Internet.

X21   An ITU standard for a circuit switched network.

X25   An ITU standard for an interface between a terminal and a packet switching network. This is a WAN technology based on virtual circuit based packet switching. X25 was designed in the 1970s and provides a reliable connection-oriented network interface layer.

Index